The Democratic political order in the United States defined the main themes, policies, and organized forms of national politics from the 1930s through the 1960s. David Plotke explores the dramatic changes in American politics that occurred during the 1930s and 1940s. In these decades an expanded federal government and a new labor movement emerged as Republican power waned. World War II and the Cold War reshaped the Democratic order without ending it. And national political debate about civil rights was opened.

The central dynamic of this era was the creation and maintenance of a distinctive new political order, built by progressive liberals in alliance with mass movements, notably labor. At its core was a powerful triangle formed by a national state, a leading party, and major interest groups and movements. Democratic and modernizing themes fused together in a progressive liberalism that advocated government action to achieve economic stability, protect social security, and expand political representation. In building the Democratic order the expansion of the national state played a crucial role – and the eventual decline of Democratic power was due in large part to its reliance on that state. Far from being nonideological, the Democratic order defined itself in sharp conflicts with forces on its right and left. Democratic progressive liberalism recast American political institutions and discourses in ways that went well beyond what was foreseen in the early 1930s, and in forms strong enough to endure long after Roosevelt's death.

BUILDING A DEMOCRATIC POLITICAL ORDER

Reshaping American Liberalism in the 1930s and 1940s

DAVID PLOTKE

New School for Social Research

CAMBRIDGE
UNIVERSITY PRESS

Published by the Press Syndicate of the University of Cambridge
The Pitt Building, Trumpington Street, Cambridge CB2 IRP
40 West 20th Street, New York, NY 10011-4211, USA
10 Stamford Road, Oakleigh, Melbourne 3166, Australia

First published 1996

Printed in the United States of America

Library of Congress Cataloging-in-Publication Data
Plotke, David.
Building a democratic political order : reshaping American
liberalism in the 1930s and 1940s / David Plotke.
p.   cm.
Includes index.
ISBN 0-521-42059-8 (hardcover)
1. Democratic Party (U.S.)   2. United States – Politics and
government – 1933–1953.   3. Liberalism – United States.   I. Title.
JK2316.P56   1996
320.973'09'043 – dc20   95–36206
CIP

A catalog record for this book is available from the British Library.

ISBN 0-521-42059-8 Hardback

Contents

v

Preface

I began working on this book when Ronald Reagan's second term was well underway. In debates about the meaning of his victories, many discerned an enduring Democratic majority underneath the sharp national shift to the right. If such a view now seems slightly ridiculous, it was reasonable at the time, and it reflected the long and deep influence of the Democratic political order in the United States.

I was critical of the political direction of the Reagan administrations and sought to understand why he could inflict stunning defeats on candidates whose positions were continuous with the main Democratic commitments of previous decades. That interest led me back to the 1930s, to the Great Depression, the New Deal, and the establishment of an expanded administrative and regulatory state. My project started as an inquiry into origins, and became a larger task of trying to understand the entire course of the Democratic regime. From the 1930s my interests continued forward, through the long phase of Democratic national domination that ended with spectacular crashes in the late 1960s and early 1970s. The present book is a result of that project, and includes a general argument about how political orders are built and decline. The other main part of my project, to be published separately, examines the turbulent final decade of the Democratic order.[1] Both books try to understand the main dynamic of American national politics in the half-century after 1932, and to clarify the central elements of post-Democratic politics through to the end of this century.

To understand the course of Democratic national power I had to change parts of my own views. Some changes concerned my political orientation, which was mainly formed in the New Left in the late 1960s, when Democratic leaders were more often antagonists than allies. My analytical commitments also changed. The Gramscian neo-Marxism I

---

1. David Plotke, *Democratic Breakup* (Cambridge University Press, forthcoming).

had adopted in the 1970s was inadequate to explain the origins and staying power of the Democratic order, however suggestive some of its concepts remain.

I had to give up the idea that an enduring Democratic majority (or one even further to the left) lay beneath the surface of American political life, covered up by Nixon's machinations and Reagan's charm. This idea might be described as a populist hope. Instead, I came to regard any such majority as at most a possibility, as something that would have to be built politically rather than a latent, quasinatural force. Actual Democratic majorities had been broken up in the decade after Goldwater's crushing defeat in 1964.

I also had to give up the idea that Democratic domination was the natural political condition of the United States in the late twentieth century. In the 1960s and 1970s, analysts of many perspectives had come to see a moderate reform party firmly committed to market institutions as best suited to the political and economic needs of an advanced market country like the United States (a virtual default option). This conception was doubly misleading – it minimized the conflict that existed between Democratic policies and business elites in the 1930s and 1940s, and grossly understated the weight of antistatist and socially conservative forces in American political life then and later. Instead of seeing reform liberalism as the naturally dominant force in American politics, I came to regard it as one major political choice. When reform liberalism does prevail, that condition has to be explained rather than presumed.

In looking at the course of the Democratic order I became increasingly aware of the limitations of the often naive critiques of claims about American exceptionalism that permeated the American left in the 1960s and 1970s. Proponents of these critiques too often thought they (we) had made decisive counterarguments against claims of an enduring liberal framework in American politics by revealing illiberal practices (as in slavery or industrial despotism) or showing that much dissensus about the practical meaning of liberalism could usually be found. This might be called the disharmony view of American politics. While the following chapters contain many criticisms of the American exceptionalism view (and of dominant tendencies in American liberalism), it remains valid to recognize the mainly liberal character of American national politics in the twentieth century.

Moreover, I had to reject the multiple forms of social and economic determinism that permeate not only neo-Marxism but many other perspectives in political science and sociology. A broad commitment to social and economic determinism cuts across many analytical and political divides to define the approach of those who regard political outcomes as due mainly to economic imperatives, class conflict, or competition among economic interest groups. Instead, political factors, including political argument, ought to be given a central role in explaining political outcomes.

These shifts in my views were partly a result of efforts to understand problems posed by the founding years of Democratic power in the 1930s. They were not easily accomplished, as to varying degrees I was committed to the positions I have noted. It was difficult to make political and theoretical shifts that were not total ruptures with my previous views. It may be easier to imagine starting with a clean slate than to try to integrate elements of a prior view within what seems to be a richer and more accurate perspective.

Yet together these changes meant making a real break with a story about the 1930s and 1940s that has been told many times. In this story, popular movements that were produced in response to the Great Depression force recalcitrant political elites to the left, where, in cooperation with reform-minded business elites, they devise programs that accede just enough to popular demands to integrate movement leaders and reduce disorder. Then, after World War II, economic and social needs for growth and order both domestically and internationally drive political elites farther to the right. The promise of a consistently left-reformist or even social democratic course that appeared at moments in the 1930s and early 1940s disappears into a postwar consensus built on commitments to growth, stable labor relations, and anti-Communism.

This story is so flawed that it is basically wrong. It is wrong to claim that social and economic causes were decisive for the main political outcomes in the 1930s and 1940s. In political terms, this story misunderstands the basic alignment of forces in those decades. It greatly overstates the weight of political currents to the left of the Democratic leadership and fails to grasp that the main alternatives to the course taken were almost always well to the right. Yet the preceding story flows easily and almost irresistibly from the positions I found inadequate: a left-populist view of the American electorate, a conception of reform liberalism as the normal form of national political rule, a naive emphasis on political and cultural diversity beneath the surface of American liberalism, and more or less sophisticated variants of social and economic determinism. None of these views is entirely wrong, but together they are very misleading. They focus too much on shifts to the left that did not happen and were never likely. They direct attention away from the democratic shifts that did occur, and from the conservative options that were strongly advanced and not easily defeated. In theoretical terms these positions and the story they generate make it hard even to think about political dynamics that are not readily reduced to the strategic pursuit of social and economic interests.

In trying to construct a positive account of the 1930s and 1940s, I found a further move important. A new "institutionalism" took shape in political science and sociology in the 1980s and early 1990s. This perspective was valuable in stressing the autonomy of political institutions and to some extent their causal importance. Yet proponents of this approach were not able to combine their account of institutions with a plausible view of how individuals act to sustain or change them. Because of this inability, advocates of a new institutionalism appeared in the end to be proposing a new formalism, in which actions are mainly given by the requirements of legal and constitutional forms.

For many decades political scientists have been claiming to find real political life apart from or underneath such forms, in political "behavior" or social and cultural forms or economic dynamics. The position at which I arrived resembles these familiar modes of unmasking insofar as I do not take institutions as given. But I do not try to find the "real" story of politics in extrapolitical factors. I stress the creative role of political actors in concentrating power across institutions when they build political orders. Typically, building a political order overflows and disrupts normal institutional routines, and cannot be explained as their result. Yet institutions remain important as a starting point and an object of conflict in my account. Thus in this book the main story still lies within the realm of national political institutions and discourses, rather than in a somehow stronger reality below or outside that realm.

The present book could not have been written by the author who began it. The changes of perspective I have described were difficult. They required political and theoretical rethinking, which is always a good thing in principle and a hard thing to do. This process complicates the pleasure of acknowledging the many personal and intellectual debts I have accumulated. I am sure that some who have greatly aided me will feel themselves not well repaid by arguments with which they will disagree. For the sake of brevity I group together a number of valued and admired colleagues, friends, and advisers: Fred Block, Michael Burawoy, Todd Gitlin, David Gordon, the late Carol Hatch, Victoria Hattam, Richard Healey, Ira Katznelson, Michael Kazin, William Kornhauser, David Matza, Michael Omi, Michael Rogin, James Scott, Ian Shapiro, Jim Shoch, Carmen Sirianni, Stephen Skowronek, Rogers Smith, Judith Stacey, Michael Walzer, and Ari Zolberg.

While writing this book I have had the opportunity to work at three excellent institutions: as a graduate student in sociology at the University of California at Berkeley, and then as a member of the faculties of Yale University and the Graduate Faculty of Political and Social Science of the New School for Social Research. Several institutions also provided financial and technical support: the Institute for Advanced Study; the Franklin D. Roosevelt Library in Hyde Park, New York; the Harry S. Truman Library in Independence, Missouri; and the Lyndon Baines Johnson Library in Austin, Texas. In each place I received valuable administrative and secretarial help – special thanks to Nancy Shealy at the New School, Lucille Allsen at the Institute for Advanced Study, and Pam O'Donnell at Yale. Thanks as well to research assistants at the New School and Yale, including Joseph Luders, Debra Morris, Melissa Nobles, Mark Redhead, and Scott Savaiano, whose creative work was invaluable in designing tables and figures.

Cambridge University Press has been a continual source of editorial wisdom and support. Alex Holzman provided valuable advice at several crucial points. Thanks also to his predecessor, Emily Loose. Carolyn Viola-John's editing made the text more readable and helped clarify my arguments. The comments of several Cambridge reviewers provided extensive and valuable guidance.

Elaine Zimmerman, my wife, has been a primary source of political insight and personal support. The insights have come partly from her own political experiences. For years she has tried to devise and implement democratic and workable public policies – as a community organizer, legislative analyst, public educator, and now as director of a state commission on policies affecting children. I have benefited greatly from her daily reports on what has been a difficult front of political conflict in the 1980s and 1990s. She has provided me with an inspiring model of how to combine a strong attachment to democratic principles with a deep commitment to responsible political action. If she has benefited half as much as I have from our conversations about public policy and politics I will be proud of it. While I completed this project she has rightly urged that I write the books I intended to write, engaging the historical material as deeply as possible while staying connected to political arguments late in the twentieth century.

Introduction: The Democratic order as a political project

The Democratic order in the United States defined the main themes, policies, and organized forms of national politics from the 1930s through the 1960s. Contemporary American politics remains deeply influenced by the accomplishments of the Democratic order and by its limits. Key features of that regime remain the focus of fierce political debate. Thus conflicts about the appropriate role of the state in social welfare provision and economic regulation intensified in the mid-1990s, while stringently antistatist positions gained a growing public role.

This book is about the creation and renewal of the Democratic political order in the 1930s and 1940s.[1] By political order I mean a durable mode of organizing and exercising political power at the national level, with distinct institutions, policies, and discourses.[2] The Democratic political order in the 1930s defined new relations among the Democratic Party, the national state, and political interest groups and social movements, notably the labor movement. It fused democratic and modernizing themes in a progressive liberalism that advocated government action to achieve economic stability, enhance social security, and expand political representation. Its eventual decline several decades later was largely the unintended result of reliance on the state for political support. This

1. A related book, David Plotke, *Democratic Breakup* (Cambridge University Press, forthcoming), analyzes the successes and dramatic demise of the Democratic order in the 1960s.
2. I often use the term discourse to refer to the thematic content of political views and to the practical side of those themes, as they appear in party programs, speeches by presidents and other leaders, judicial decisions, legislative acts, and guidelines for state agencies. A discourse is a set of claims (descriptive and prescriptive) connected through reference to shared meanings and symbols; all politics has a discursive dimension. A political discourse depicts how social relations are and should be organized. I prefer "discourse" to "ideology," to avoid long debates about whether ideology should be counterposed to true knowledge. I prefer discourse to idea as a way to signal the practical side of political arguments, and their imbeddedness in institutions and policies.

dynamic eroded nonstate Democratic forces and made it difficult to respond politically to deep social and economic change.

The Democratic order as a political project

My account of the construction and renewal of the Democratic regime in the 1930s and 1940s makes several arguments about political development in the United States. These concern the importance of the concept of political order (or regime); the centrality of political action in building the Democratic order; and the distinctive character of that order's progressive liberalism. Here I provide an overview of these arguments and locate my perspective with respect to other views.

Understanding American political development requires giving a central place to the processes through which political orders are formed and sustained. Political orders frame the conflicts and achievements of routine politics. In analyzing the Democratic order I distinguish between normal political times and times of crisis, uncertainty, and transition. This does not equate normal times with the absence of conflict; stability always has to be attained. Yet there are phases when a solid framework defines the issues contested – and others when political conflict focuses on defining such a framework. To identify periods, in these terms, is to designate a characteristic political terrain on which actors declare and pursue their aims. Claims about a political period are claims about durable basic features of politics and the likely distribution of outcomes in important conflicts. Thus periods are constituted by the development of political orders.

It is not conventional to apply the concept of regime to American political development. American social scientists often use "regime" to name configurations of power in other countries, as in regimes with a single dominant figure – the Castro regime, the Pinochet regime – or a lasting form of rule, such as the Soviet regime.

The connotations of "regime" most often stigmatize a government as undemocratic; we in the United States control our government, while less fortunate nations are burdened with regimes. Yet many who are reluctant to apply any concept of regime to the United States acknowledge a post-World War II regime in Italy (Christian Democracy) or Japan, or perhaps in Thatcher's Britain. Do differences between the latter countries and the United States warrant two different vocabularies, one concerned with regime formation and change, the other with the dynamics of routine political competition?

American government is not so diffuse and episodic – or so transparently democratic – that we can dispense with efforts to define coherent ensembles of power relations. Efforts to periodize political development might be futile if a fluid process of self-determination always made political choices open and allowed sharp changes in overall direction to occur easily and often. But this image is not true to political life in the United States, which has been marked by durable forms of power that were hard to construct and did not fade quietly away.

Resistance to using a regime concept to examine modern American politics also stems from viewing American institutions and their power as distinctively separated, even fragmented and dispersed. There is no denying the complexity of American political institutions. A constitutional and legal framework that defines and distinguishes federal institutions is not a mask but a real political force. Nonetheless, in the twentieth century, political power operates effectively at the national level. To make sense of the organization of national power requires concepts beyond the conventional and official names of American political institutions (parties, Congress, courts, executive).

The story of building the Democratic order is significantly a story of national political integration, which was augmented and given new thematic and institutional forms through Democratic efforts. Politics in the modern United States has been increasingly state-centered, executive-centered, and president-centered. The Democratic order made a powerful contribution to this process. While Congress and the courts were and are important in national political life, they are not equivalent to the presidency in their capacities or in public perceptions of their significance, notwithstanding moments when a relatively strong Congress confronts a weak president, such as that following the Republican electoral victories in 1994.

National political power can be organized in a relatively coherent and purposeful way by those who build and sustain a political order. If political orders tend to be president-centered, they also cut across and reconnect institutions.[3] The Democratic order was constituted by a tri-

---

3. However named, the state- or executive- or president-centered character of modern American politics is rarely denied by contemporary political scientists. Yet significant work often proceeds without taking this reality much into account. One example is the discussion of a frequent pattern of the 1980s and 1990s in which the president is of a different party than the majority in one or both houses of Congress. Much of this discussion seems to presume a rough equality of importance between Congress and the presidency, so that "divided party control" of national government makes sense as a way to name the problem. But this dubious premise is not much examined. See Morris P. Fiorina, *Divided Government* (New York: Macmillan Publishing Company, 1992).

Table Intro.1. *How political outcomes are shaped*

		Source of causal influence	
		Political	*Economic*
Form of causal influence	*Action*	Political action (the present work)	Rational choice
	Institutions	Neo-Weberian institutionalism	Neo-Marxist political economy

angle of relations among the national state, a leading party, and major nonparty interest groups and movements. The features of this triangle are a central topic of subsequent chapters.

A related theme of this book stresses political action in building and sustaining the Democratic order. This theme is developed with regard to key events in the 1930s and 1940s, notably the passage of the Wagner Act in 1935 and Truman's surprising election in 1948. It is also a theoretical claim, at the intersection of two long debates in the social sciences. Analysts differ about the relative weight they accord to political and economic forces in causing important political results. They also differ about whether such forces should be conceived mainly in structural (institutional) terms, or in terms of agents' actions. This book argues for the casual importance of political action.

The main theoretical choices are presented in Table Intro. 1. All these perspectives have long and accomplished histories. Explaining politics as the result of economic action has had several phases of wide popularity. A recent version, called a new political economy by some proponents, is mainly an applied neoclassical economics.[4] The most influential combination of economic and institutional emphases in explaining politics has been Marxism, whose proponents have produced valuable studies of twentieth-century American political development.[5] Institutional-

4. Among the most insightful practitioners of this approach is Douglass North, whose work along with that of like-minded colleagues is represented in James E. Alt and Kenneth A. Shepsle, eds., *Perspectives on Positive Political Economy* (Cambridge University Press, 1990).
5. See, for example, Martin J. Sklar, *The Corporate Reconstruction of American Capitalism, 1890–1916: The Market, the Law, and Politics* (Cambridge University Press, 1988).

political approaches have achieved major results in analyzing twentieth-century American politics, mainly regarding the national state and social policies.[6]

My argument emphasizes the causal role of political forces and political action. First, I show how political projects help define the meaning of social and economic processes, rather than being only subject to their exogenous effects. Second, I outline political dynamics that can yield strong (and often unintended) outcomes, in which political themes (or ideas, or discourses) matter a great deal in shaping agents' choices and defining the practical meaning of self-interest. On the basis of this argument I stress the distinctive character of the reformist progressive liberalism of the Democratic order. I underline its break both with Republican themes and policies from the 1920s and with prior Democratic conceptions. And I emphasize the deep differences between Democratic liberalism and political currents on the left that gained significant strength in the 1930s and 1940s – Popular Front Communism, radical populism, and social democracy. To understand the main political battles requires distinguishing progressive liberal from social democratic views, in terms of both substantive aims and strategic approaches.

While the argument of this book owes a considerable debt to Marxian modes of analysis, it is post-Marxist. I intend this term in both a normative and analytical sense. Normatively the Marxist tradition does not provide a very useful standpoint from which to evaluate Democratic practices, which can readily be criticized in other terms as well. Nor does it much raise the level of historical understanding or contemporary political argument to criticize progressive liberals who were self-conscious about their perspective for failing to recognize the virtues of alleged socialist (or even social democratic) alternatives. Analytically, my account places considerable weight on economic and social factors in shaping political outcomes, but usually as secondary elements, or as factors that gained their full meaning through political interpretation. This approach cannot readily be developed in Marxist terms. On that terrain, a polarization of analytical choices is strongly encouraged when any significant economic influence is taken to reveal the subtle workings

---

6. See Stephen Skowronek, *Building a New American State: The Expansion of National Administrative Capacities, 1877–1920* (Cambridge University Press, 1982), as well as the studies of social policy in Margaret Weir, Ann Shola Orloff, and Theda Skocpol, eds., *The Politics of Social Policy in the United States* (Princeton, N.J.: Princeton University Press, 1988). Skocpol's reluctance to allow factors other than the shape of political institutions to qualify as major causal forces is qualified in her later book on American social policy, *Protecting Soldiers and Mothers: The Political Origins of Social Policy in the United States* (Cambridge, Mass.: Harvard University Press, 1992).

of an ultimately determining economic mechanism. I aim to give the economy and class relations their due within a political framework.

Analyzing the Democratic order

This book is about building and renewing a dominant political force. The first two chapters provide a framework for this analysis. Chapter 1 assesses approaches to change in terms of whether American political development should be regarded as containing one, two, or many distinct periods. The perspective developed in the 1950s and 1960s by Louis Hartz and others, which draws on Tocqueville and stresses "American exceptionalism," considers all of American politics as one period unified by enduring political commitments. Though this view retains power it has trouble explaining political change or how stable political forms are sustained. A second view of American political development locates a basic division in the early twentieth century. Before that time politics revolved around elites, courts, and parties; demands for order and integration generated by social and economic change encouraged the emergence of a modern politics of large institutions. This view pays far too little attention to conflicts about distribution, cultural legitimacy, and principles of decision making.

Chapter 1 also considers the political realignment approach, which posits several periods framed by dramatic electoral shifts at roughly forty-year intervals in the nineteenth and twentieth centuries. The political realignment perspective rightly insists that there have been more than two major periods in American political development. Yet political realignment studies do not adequately explain why or when realignments occur, and debates about the concept have often declined into narrow fights about precisely what aspects of which elections count as realigning. My focus on building an American regime returns to broad questions about political change that the realignment perspective initially addressed.

The limits of the best accounts of large-scale change in American politics direct attention to their theoretical premises. Chapter 2's account of regime dynamics considers politics as an active, creative process of organizing and directing social relations. I focus on how the choices made by individuals seeking to support a regime generate long-term political costs, via statism and the results of socioeconomic modernization. I then sketch the development of the Democratic order in terms of two processes: the growing role of the Democratic state with respect to nonstate Democratic institutions and activities, and socioeconomic changes encouraged by Democratic policies. Both dynamics were rooted in reasonable choices by Democratic leaders and activists about how to sustain a regime to which they were politically committed. In the 1930s and 1940s these choices helped sustain the Democratic order; eventually they reduced the capacity of Democratic forces to support the regime and made it vulnerable.

Democratic ascent and endurance

Chapters 3 through 10 examine key moments in the history of the Democratic order in the 1930s and 1940s, focusing on electoral and legislative episodes that raise basic questions. Chapters 3 through 6 explain the construction of the Democratic order amid political turmoil, especially in 1935–7 – why was the Democratic order built at all, and against what alternatives? I start from the crisis of Republican domination in the late 1920s and early 1930s. I trace the emergence of new dominant political forces via the 1936 presidential election and the passage and implementation of the Wagner Act. The latter measure – and by extension the Democratic order – was a political project of progressive liberals, who, in alliance with new mass political forces, constructed a regime centered on an expanded state, a renovated party, and vigorous popular movements.

Chapters 7 through 10 assess the conflicts of 1947–9, centering on the 1948 election and the fights over the Taft-Hartley Act. An extension and renewal of the Democratic order occurred, despite widespread expectations that Democratic power would rapidly decline after the end of the Depression and the death of Franklin Roosevelt. The persistence of the Democratic order derived from the enduring political capacities of the Democratic triangle built in the previous decade. Progressive liberals in and around the state organized a defense of the regime against postwar adversaries. Important political changes after World War II – the anti-Communist campaign, Taft-Hartley, and the emphasis on growth in economic policy – are best understood as shifts within an enduring political framework.

Where in this story is the Democratic Party? In my account the Democratic Party is always present but rarely if ever at the center. This partly reflects difficulties in fixing the party as an object of inquiry, owing to its diversity, complex ties to other institutions, and relative weakness as a national organization.[7] Conventionally the Democratic label refers to

---

7. To focus on the Democratic Party per se might seem plausible – but the inadequacy of this conception is suggested by the great difficulty of finding even basic information about the structure and practices of national (or other) Democratic organizations. This is partly due to poor or nonexistent record-keeping. There was no permanent national

party identification and to a weak party structure. Thus "Democratic Party" points to mass loyalties or to a specific but modest political agent. Yet it makes sense to retain the Democratic label to designate a political order whose initial leaders often downplayed their partisan identity. And as the Democratic order's capacities emerged in practices that cut across conventional boundaries, it makes sense to say that a strong Democratic order was supported by a weak Democratic Party.[8]

The international dimension

In the United States in the 1930s and 1940s, political outcomes were shaped primarily by domestic dynamics, with international factors playing a secondary role. Yet the international dimension of the Democratic order requires attention because that regime shaped the entry of the United States into international politics on a larger scale and in a more sustained manner than had ever been the case. The Democratic order built a new and radically expanded international role for the United States from the mid-1930s to the end of the following decade. The leaders of the Democratic order drew on and elaborated prior internationalist currents in American politics in preparing the way for American entry into World War II. The war was fought in an alliance with the Soviet Union; its aims were defined as the unconditional surrender of the opposing states and the destruction of their fascist regimes. Major

---

Democratic office until the 1920s. Since then records have been kept casually, often leaving offices with the individuals involved. Relatively recent works about party structure and activities in the United States include: Cornelius Cotter, et al., *Party Organizations in American Politics* (New York: Praeger, 1984); Leon Epstein, *Political Parties in the American Mold* (Madison: University of Wisconsin Press, 1986); David Mayhew, *Placing Parties in American Politics* (Princeton, N.J.: Princeton University Press, 1986); and Byron Shafer, *Quiet Revolution: The Struggle for the Democratic Party and the Shaping of Post-Reform Politics* (New York: Russell Sage, 1983).

8. In research for this book I used data from a variety of sources. The records of the national Democratic Party are mainly at the presidential libraries. I used records at the Franklin D. Roosevelt Library for the 1935–7 period and at the Harry S. Truman Library for 1947–9. Relevant materials are sometimes filed under "Democratic Party" or "Democratic National Committee," at other times included in the papers of presidents and their aides. I examined materials relevant for the elections and legislative contests on which I focused, and for national Democratic Party affairs in general. Where material was filed by state, I emphasized California, Georgia, Illinois, Iowa, Michigan, and New York, due to their political importance and their social and ideological diversity. The public record – congressional debates, presidential speeches and other statements by regime leaders, press conferences, and public papers – is a crucial source, along with memoirs and interviews at the presidential libraries.

economic changes resulted in a new international economic order centered on the United States.

The dynamic of building and sustaining a leading international role for the United States resembled domestic political processes. There was an initial break with previous economic and political practices and the emergence of new internationalist discourses. The expansion of American international activity meant taking on more complex and extensive commitments, in political, economic, and military relations. Inability to curtail an expansionist logic eventually made growing commitments very hard to manage; the dangers of overexpansion were realized in the 1960s, notably in the Vietnam war.

In claiming that the Democratic order reshaped the world role of the United States I reject the idea that any American regime would necessarily have acted the same way. The international policies of the United States were selected by domestic political dynamics from among a range of feasible alternatives. Domestic politics significantly influenced all major aspects of American foreign policies. After World War II the Cold War was a central reality in relations between domestic and foreign policies in the United States. I will engage debates about the origins and meaning of that conflict, but with caution. It is difficult to analyze relations between American and international politics during the early Cold War at a time when the interlocked endings of the Cold War and the Soviet Union are so recent. A widespread account of the postwar international role of the United States claims that the combined effects of the Vietnam debacle, declining American international strength, and growing Soviet military power brought a brief "American century" to an end. Much of that story has been undermined by events of the late 1980s and early 1990s, and arguments are underway on how these historic changes should influence our view of events in the 1940s.

The pertinence of the Democratic order

From the end of the Democratic order to the early 1990s few major political figures called for overturning the accomplishments of its first two decades. Even Ronald Reagan invoked Franklin Roosevelt as an honored symbol of a determination to use presidential power to achieve urgent national aims.

While the Democratic order has long been shattered, returning to its first two decades raises questions of continuing political importance. Some of these questions refer to specific Democratic policies, as in social welfare provision or labor relations. Others concern broad themes, such as the appropriate relation between state action and markets. Major questions also refer to the political processes through which the Democratic order was built. Contemporary political actors can return to the early Democratic order to see how a durable regime was built. Creative political actors, potentially capable of forging a political order, do not duplicate prior regime-building efforts but learn from them how to begin amid different and surprising conditions.

1

When does politics change?

Is there any gain in dividing American political development into phases? If so, how should lines be drawn? Does the resulting framework illuminate political conflicts in the 1930s and 1940s?

American political development has occurred in a series of distinct political orders. The Democratic order defined one major period, marked by a greatly increased role for the federal government in economic regulation and social provision, and by a substantial growth of presidential power. There was a wide expansion of opportunities for political and social action among groups who were politically marginal or excluded from the preceding regimes, from labor in the 1930s to the civil rights movement three decades later.

The Democratic order was liberal in its commitments to individual rights and to representative political institutions. But its liberalism, full of progressive and democratic themes, differed considerably from the main discourses of the preceding political order. "Progressive" meant modernizing reforms, with national coordination of programmatic and administrative efforts. "Democratic" meant broadening the range of groups and individuals actively engaged with politics, and extending basic forms of social and economic security. Combining progressive and democratic themes within a liberal framework was powerful and dynamic.

The preceding claims about the Democratic order rely on concepts of political order and period. These concepts are means of analyzing how national politics changes over time. American politics has developed in distinct phases: variance across these phases concerns the forms of the state, the shape of party politics and nonparty political agents (movements and interest groups), and the character of political discourses. Political orders are durable modes of organizing and linking major national political institutions and discourses. Political practices and discourses are central in creating and sustaining political orders, which in turn constitute distinct periods. To define periods in this way is to claim that key features of political life structure political processes and outcomes (as against the claim, for example, that political periods are defined by phases of economic development). Claims about the main features of a period provide a basis for explaining the main elements of politics within it, through specifying the context political actors face when making choices and illuminating the commitments that shape their choices.

In this and the following chapter my account of American political orders refers to the entire course of the Democratic order, not only to its construction and early course. It is necessary to provide a full analytical framework to be able to use it to examine the turbulent events of the 1930s and the next decade's surprising maintenance of Democratic power. I first assess major views of American political development that might explain the dramatic events of the 1930s and 1960s as well as the relative stability of the intervening years. One account considers that American politics since the inception of the republic contains only one period. Another distinguishes two long periods, with a transition at the beginning of the twentieth century. Political realignment accounts demarcate a number of periods, separated by bursts of political change. All these conceptions tend to understate the scope of change in American politics and the causal importance of politics.

No periods?

Theories of American exceptionalism, organizational accounts of American political history, and analyses of party realignment try to explain American political development over time. The broad historical concerns of these theories distinguish them from much contemporary research on mass political behavior, and from the main concerns of recent efforts to apply economic theories to politics. Most voting studies, for example, consider the electorate to be composed of voters whose behavior depends on a mixture of relatively stable party affiliations and (perceptions of) economic interests. The aim is to explain electoral outcomes in terms of variance around a normal vote. The focus is on short-term changes, rather than on the political and social frameworks in which partisan and economic identities are located.[1]

---

1. While seeing voters as partisan loyalists differs from seeing them as economic calculators, the distance between these views can be reduced by treating party identification as a device for saving on information costs. The effects of political stability on theories of electoral change mark Angus Campbell et al., *The American Voter* (Chicago, Ill.: University of Chicago Press, 1960), which stressed the durable partisan basis of voting.

For many students of voting and political participation, this short-term focus is less a theoretical choice than a result of a conventional division of labor in the social sciences. For others, such as proponents of theories of politics based on neoclassical economics, such a focus is strategic. The choice of limited empirical cases aims to highlight theoretical issues in explaining politics in terms of rational (economic) action.

Does a basically economic logic of political action operate across societies and over time with enough force and precision to be the primary explanation of most outcomes?[2] Regarding American political development, to conceive politics as the articulation of permanent forms of economic action suggests that only one period has existed – and we are in it. Since political actors everywhere are in the grip of the same logic, we might just as well say that there really are no periods. Politics everywhere is considered as interest-seeking behavior, similar in form to economic action. In this view analytical progress occurs by clarifying a deep logic of political action: We study congressional subcommittees because they are analytically interesting, not because of claims about their role in shaping political outcomes. This approach has no interest in periodization because little or nothing basic is believed to have changed regarding the core features of political action. History is illustrative, offering cases to test hypotheses about economic-maximizing action in political settings.[3]

This mode of theorizing depends on strong and implausible views about the general primacy of rational/economic action in social life, so that political action is essentially invariant from classical Greece to contemporary Mexico.[4] Yet the response should not be radical historicism. If the thin general features of political action across all periods and societies cannot ground the sort of universal science of politics to which some analysts aspire, significant theoretical claims are feasible regarding more limited but large sets of societies, such as feudal societies or state socialist societies. Political explanation often requires concepts mainly applicable to specific types of social formations.

2. Group theories of politics also tried to identify universal bases and logics of group formation and interaction. See David B. Truman, *The Governmental Process: Political Interests and Public Opinion,* 2nd ed. (New York: Alfred A. Knopf, 1971) [1st ed., 1951].

3. Most rational choice work in political economy still shows relatively little interest in specifying the historical and institutional settings to which theories can best be applied. For a good example, see William H. Riker, *Liberalism Against Populism* (Prospect Heights, Ill.: Waveland Press, 1983).

4. See James E. Alt and Kenneth A. Shepsle, "Editors' Introduction," and Peter Ordeshook, "The Emerging Discipline of Political Economy," in Alt and Shepsle, eds., *Perspectives on Positive Political Economy* (Cambridge University Press, 1990), 1–30.

One period – American exceptionalism
and American liberalism

There is a ready way to combine skepticism about the theoretical significance of periods with attention to American political development. One can argue that American political development is so continuous that periodization is irrelevant. Thus accounts of American exceptionalism contend that everything of basic political importance in the United States has been here from the start. This country has had only one regime, and its political history has expressed liberal commitments present from the outset.

The point of accounts of American exceptionalism (whether or not the term is used) is to stress distinctive features of American politics, so that the single period of American political history looks different from politics elsewhere.[5] Thus what stands out about the 1930s in the United States is less the severity of political conflict compared with prior decades but the restraint and moderation of the main actors compared with political forces in that decade in Europe. The American exceptionalism argument defines the United States as a distinctive case, even compared with other British settler colonies.

Does the American exceptionalism view provide adequate grounds for considering American political development to have had only one period? The basic answer is no, but its arguments retain considerable power. In the 1950s and 1960s accounts of American exceptionalism linked key features of the political history of the nineteenth and twentieth centuries to the earliest periods of colonization and nation-building. Major statements were Hartz's *The Liberal Tradition in America,* Richard Hofstadter's *The Age of Reform* and *The American Political Tradition,* and Seymour Martin Lipset's *Political Man* and *The First New Nation.*[6]

For Hartz, political change in the United States mainly restates conti-

---

5. One might say that rational choice approaches do best in examining politics in the society depicted in American exceptionalism. This historicizing move would be rejected by most proponents of rational choice theories.

6. Louis Hartz, *The Liberal Tradition in America* (New York: Harcourt, Brace, Jovanovich, 1955); Richard Hofstadter, *The Age of Reform* (New York: Random House, 1955), and *The American Political Tradition* (New York: Alfred A. Knopf, 1948); Seymour Martin Lipset, *The First New Nation: The United States in Historical and Comparative Perspective* (Garden City, N.Y.: Doubleday, 1967), and *Political Man: The Social Bases of Politics* (Baltimore, Md.: Johns Hopkins University Press, 1981). "American exceptionalism" was first used in Marxist polemics to disparage accounts that contrasted the patterns of American political life with those predicted by orthodox Marxist analysis in order to question the latter's relevance.

nuities. The society that Americans created had no feudal past. No feudal heritage meant no serious illiberal feudal or aristocratic political tendencies – thus the feeble efforts of the slaveowners to justify their regime disappeared quickly after the Civil War. Equality has been basic:

> One of the central characteristics of a nonfeudal society is that it lacks a genuine revolutionary tradition, the tradition which in Europe has been linked with the Puritan and French revolutions: that it is "born equal," as Tocqueville said.[7]

The course of American development was inscribed in its origins and has seemed natural. Freedom was identified with independence and property; equality was equality of opportunity; class was unacknowledged. A composite political image emerged in the eighteenth and nineteenth centuries to represent the experience and aspirations of small entrepreneurs, craftsmen, and farmers. This "American democrat" dominated the political landscape, combining "in his own small propertied liberal personality the ancient feudalism and the incipient socialism of Europe."[8]

Without an old regime, without a language of class, without a palpable, institutionalized class system, socialist and other radical ideas could not take root as major political forces in the United States – notably early in the twentieth century. The political weakness of American Marxism in these years testifies to the durability of the liberal tradition, especially as the social context once so propitious for economic autonomy had changed significantly.[9] The New Deal was a triumphant reassertion of American themes; Franklin Roosevelt remained an energetic and optimistic liberal when liberalism in Europe was on the defensive.[10]

Richard Hofstadter also stressed the extent of political and cultural unity in the United States:

> Above and beyond temporary and local conflicts there has been a common ground, a unity of cultural and political tradition, upon which American civilization has stood. That culture has been intensely nationalistic and for the most part isolationist; it has been fiercely individualistic and capitalistic.[11]

---

7. Hartz, *Liberal Tradition*, 5.   8. Hartz, *Liberal Tradition*, 116.
9. Hartz's position must be qualified if one focuses on intellectual life in the United States, where Marxism was a significant force at several points. On early twentieth-century radicalism see Paul Buhle, *Marxism in the USA* (London: Verso, 1987); Christopher Lasch, *The New Radicalism in America, 1889–1963: The Intellectual as a Social Type* (New York: Vintage, 1967).
10. Hartz, *Liberal Tradition*, 59–65.
11. Hofstadter, *American Political Tradition*, x.

Hofstadter argued that the popular American left has mainly accepted capitalism while fighting special privileges and alleged conspiracies. Sometimes the result of this was a paranoid populism, which Hofstadter saw as the unhappy fate of a left formed in a stable, narrow, and moralistic political culture.[12] Yet the idealistic and moralistic themes of American liberalism were sublimated into the mature pragmatic reformism of the New Deal.[13] Lipset linked Hartz and Hofstadter's themes to modernization and political development theory.[14] The United States was privileged by its modern political culture, liberal political institutions, and early start on a relatively smooth course of economic development. In *The First New Nation* Lipset stressed the values of equality and achievement: "The dynamic interaction of these two predominant values has been a constant element in determining American institutions and behavior."[15] Whether values or economic capacities were deemed primary, American development was viewed as guaranteed from the outset.

Much of the American exceptionalism perspective has survived endless critiques because it rightly argues that political life has been relatively stable and predominantly liberal in the United States. The most obvious problem – the Civil War – was handled badly by Hartz and most who followed his interpretation. The durability of the American slave regime, whose demise required a long, bloody war, qualifies claims about inherent political stability. And defenders of that regime produced a substantial body of nonliberal political and social thought.[16] Nonetheless, before and after the Civil War, American political change has been mainly constitutional and legal. And American politics has been mainly liberal, committed to a view of individuals as bearers of rights that are not constituted by prior governmental acts. It has been liberal in stressing the limited role of government, and in insisting that government ought to be responsive to and representative of the citizenry. The main currents in American liberalism have regarded market relations not only as legitimate, but as a source of many benefits for sustaining a liberal polity. Given these enduring commitments, there is room for argument

---

12. Hofstadter, *Age of Reform*, 20–1.   13. Hofstadter, *Age of Reform*, 308–19.

14. "Perhaps the most common generalization linking political systems to other aspects of society has been that democracy is related to the state of economic development. The more well-to-do a nation the greater the chances that it will sustain democracy." Lipset, *Political Man*, 31.

15. Lipset, *First New Nation*, 101.

16. Eugene Genovese analyzes the antiliberal thought of major antebellum Southern intellectuals in *The Slaveholders' Dilemma: Freedom and Progress in Southern Conservative Thought, 1820–1860* (Columbia: University of South Carolina Press, 1992).

about their practical meaning and relation to other themes. But the frequent presence of other thematic elements is consistent with a predominant liberalism.

There have been many critiques of the Tocqueville-Hartz view of American politics. One critique asserts that other currents have existed alongside liberalism as major autonomous and durable traditions. A second critique highlights the persistence of illiberal forms of authority in the United States, either in local politics or outside the official political sphere. A third type of critique claims that dominant liberal themes were given such varied meanings by different political and social groups as to render analytically dubious any claim of an overarching liberal framework. In all three cases, those who deny the primacy of liberalism in American politics typically fail to go beyond American exceptionalism.

What about the claim of separate traditions? To take a major case, in the last two decades an impressive literature has stressed the importance of republican themes in American politics, and has at the least established their presence in the colonial and revolutionary periods.[17] Yet no one has demonstrated that distinctly nonliberal republican themes were coequal to those of a liberalism concerned with political rights and economic opportunities. Nor has it been shown that after the late eighteenth century, republican themes of virtue, public interest, and civic integrity formed an autonomous discourse able to compete with liberalism for predominance in American political life. Claims that a coherent republicanism has been an enduring reality in American politics are more persuasive if recast as claims about republican motifs within a liberal framework.

Those who posit a strong republican tradition try to show that its conceptions were influential in many settings, such as urban politics and labor activity in the 1820s and 1830s. Thus Sean Wilentz has argued for the presence of an artisanal republicanism in the 1820s in New York. Yet his account shows that with the exception of a small number of radical democrats and utopian socialists, most of these New York republicans resembled the less narrow-minded among pro-Jackson Democrats

---

17. Key works include: J. G. A. Pocock, *The Machiavellian Moment: Florentine Political Thought and the Atlantic Republican Tradition* (Princeton, N.J.: Princeton University Press, 1975); Bernard Bailyn, *The Ideological Origins of the American Revolution* (Cambridge, Mass.: Harvard University Press, 1967); and Gordon Wood, *The Creation of the American Republic* (New York: W. W. Norton, 1969). On the fate of republican themes in the early American republic see Joyce Appleby, *Capitalism and a New Social Order: The Republican Vision of the 1790s* (New York: New York University Press, 1984).

(whose victories in the late 1820s opened the way for local working-class politics).

When all the pertinent qualifications are taken into account – the special nature of New York, the fragility of radical currents outside Jacksonian democracy – the blows struck against Hartz's account of American artisans and mechanics as petit bourgeois democrats are much weaker than Wilentz intends. His reliance on a truncated notion of liberalism to establish the weight of republican themes is clear when he describes the speeches at public affairs put on by craftsmen in the early nineteenth century: "Most striking were the ways in which the speakers invoked the key concepts of eighteenth-century American republicanism – independence, virtue, equality, citizenship and commonwealth (or community)." As this list suggests, Wilentz shows at most that republican themes persisted amid liberal commitments to independence, equality, and citizenship, not that such themes were fully autonomous and certainly not that republican themes predominated.[18]

Political conflicts at the time of the Civil War also exhibit republican themes – on all sides, from the defense of white supremacy in the South to Lincoln's calls to save the union. Yet these themes did not define a distinct nonliberal conception, with the notable exception of some Southern proponents of the slave system. In the North we are dealing with republican liberals.[19] Republican themes have since recurred, from the Populist movement of the late nineteenth century to the nativist campaigns of the 1920s, the anti-Communism of the 1950s, and the civil rights movement of the 1960s. They appear as elements in conflicts among mainly liberal alternatives, and are often expressed strongly in statements of opposition to the national regime.[20]

18. Sean Wilentz, *Chants Democratic: New York City and the Rise of the American Working Class, 1788–1850* (New York: Oxford University Press, 1984), 92–4, 145, 212–14. Hartz downplays thematic conflicts in the Jacksonian period when he criticizes progressive accounts of the people's march toward democracy, including Arthur Schlesinger, Jr.'s influential *The Age of Jackson* (Boston: Little, Brown and Company, 1945).

19. John Diggins downplays the republican dimension of Lincoln's thought in *The Lost Soul of American Politics: Virtue, Self-Interest, and the Foundations of Liberalism* (New York: Basic Books, 1984). For Diggins, Christianity was a key influence on Lincoln's liberalism: "Machiavelli's distinction between republican virtue and moral virtue was meant to purge from statecraft precisely the values and concepts that Melville and Lincoln wanted to restore to politics. It was not only knowledge of 'sin' and 'evil' that America needed but understanding of goodness, kindness, magnanimity – qualities Machiavelli believed too private and subjective to contribute to the public good" (332).

20. On liberalism and republicanism in early American politics, see Robert Shalhope, "Republicanism and Early American History," *William and Mary Quarterly* 39 (April 1982): 344–58; John Patrick Diggins, "Comrades and Citizens: New Mythologies in

Acknowledging the presence of republican themes means qualifying rather than rejecting a Hartzian view of American politics. American liberalism has been flexible enough to incorporate republican themes – in national, communal, and religious terms – without the latter becoming primary or appearing as a full alternative political discourse.[21] Republican elements have been significant in state and local resistance to legal and political changes associated with the civil rights movement from the 1950s on, as with opposition to school desegregation. They have been mobilized on behalf of protectionist economic strategies, as in the oil crisis of the 1970s. They appeared in the movement against the war in Vietnam in the 1960s and 1970s.[22] It is wrong to see republican themes as a coherent popular alternative to elitist and modernizing liberal positions. While localist republican motifs have sometimes had a democratic meaning, such motifs have also converged with racist and nativist themes against democratic national projects.[23]

To claim a powerful republican tradition distinct from (even coequal with) liberalism in the United States is a misguided assessment of the main themes of American politics. Such claims often depict liberal political thought as radically and exclusively individualistic from Locke on. Given this portrait, any expression of concern for the public good in political argument seems to show the strength of republican themes, rather than to indicate the complexity of the liberal tradition.[24] More-

---

American Historiography," *American Historical Review* (June 1985): 614–38; and Joyce Appleby, *Liberalism and Republicanism in the Historical Imagination* (Cambridge, Mass.: Harvard University Press, 1992). On later movements in which republican elements have been significant, see John Higham, *Strangers in the Land: Patterns of American Nativism, 1860–1925* (New Brunswick, N.J.: Rutgers University Press, 1955); Daniel Bell, ed., *The Radical Right: The New American Right* (Garden City, N.J.: Doubleday, 1964); and David Garrow, *Bearing the Cross: Martin Luther King, Jr. and the Southern Christian Leadership Conference* (New York: W. Morrow, 1986).

21. There are forms of republican theory and politics for which an accommodation with liberal positions would be impossible or very difficult, such as the slaveowners' republicanism analyzed by Genovese in *The Slaveholders' Dilemma*, or the communist republicanism of Antonio Gramsci in Italy in the 1920s.

22. An influential argument for renewing and expanding republican themes in American politics was made by Robert Bellah et al., *Habits of the Heart: Individualism and Commitment in American Life* (Berkeley: University of California Press, 1985).

23. On republican resistance to school desegregation, see Ronald Formisano, *Boston Against Busing: Race, Class and Ethnicity in the 1960s and 1970s* (Chapel Hill: University of North Carolina Press, 1991). Republican themes have also appeared in efforts to enact "English only" language requirements.

24. Further recent discussions of relations between liberalism and republicanism in American politics include David F. Ericson, *The Shaping of American Liberalism – The Debates Over Ratification, Nullification, and Slavery* (Chicago, Ill.: University of Chicago Press, 1993); Daniel T. Rodgers, "Republicanism: The Career of a Concept,"

over, those who emphasize republicanism have misread liberals as expressing only enthusiasm for commerce and industry. But the basically positive liberal view of the market has often been accompanied by an awareness of the social and cultural costs of market relations, even when liberals too easily conclude that the costs are worth paying.

The arguments about a republican tradition exemplify problems with efforts to deny the primacy of liberalism in American politics. Liberalism has formed the defining matrix. Nonliberal perspectives have taken political shape mainly as criticisms of a prevalent liberalism, rather than as efforts to replace it with an integral alternative. If liberalism itself is amorphous in Hartzian accounts, its main American forms can be summarized positively as endorsing representative government; placing limits on government power; strongly affirming individual political liberties; and recognizing the legitimacy and value of extensive market relations.

Nonliberal political views are willing to trump these principles with others when faced with difficult choices. Thus republican conceptions propose to constrain political liberties and market relations in favor of measures aimed at sustaining a political community organized around shared notions of virtue. Nationalist conceptions modify liberal principles in favor of national unity and strength. Southern paternalist and racialist doctrines limited representation severely and constrained market relations to accommodate slavery. Socialist political proposals rejected the liberal view of the market and favored expansive government power to shape economic and social life.

Claims about liberal predominance in the United States refer first and primarily to national political institutions and practices and to closely linked discourses. It does not contradict these claims to show that nonliberal or antiliberal practices prevailed in other settings – in slavery, or many families, or in shops and factories. The idea that liberal concepts are properly applied not only to politics but within family and industrial life would have struck most eighteenth- and nineteenth-century liberals as clearly wrong and perhaps a bit strange. They believed that political liberties and self-government were ways to organize and limit a national regime. They were often divided about the proper range of application

Journal of American History, January 1992, 11–38; and Jennifer Nedelsky, *Private Property and the Limits of American Constitutionalism – The Madisonian Framework and Its Legacy* (Chicago, Ill.: University of Chicago Press, 1990). Ericson considers republicanism and what he calls pluralism as variants of liberalism in the late eighteenth and nineteenth centuries, and emphasizes their common features. Nedelsky's neo-Hartzian interpretation of American constitutionalism focuses on the central role of property.

of these principles, but few would have urged applying liberal principles anywhere in society that political processes could be found, such as in the economy.

The idea that a liberal political sphere can readily coexist with illiberal social practices was central for the Marxist critique of liberalism and of "bourgeois democracy." But this copresence was taken to show the hypocrisy of political liberalism, not to deny its existence. Criticizing accounts of liberal dominance and American exceptionalism, Karen Orren provocatively emphasizes the despotic elements in American labor relations in the nineteenth and early twentieth centuries. Yet she seems not to take much account of the separation between politics and other spheres that was central to liberal understandings of society:

> To the same extent that, for example, nineteenth century commercial relations were ruled by voluntary – that is to say, liberal – principles, and nineteenth century labor relations by prescriptive – feudal – ones, and these rules were sanctioned and administered by the state, then nineteenth century government was at once liberal and feudal. . . .[25]

By this logic, American government was also patriarchal (family law), democratic (New England towns), quasi-anarchist (frontier areas), and racial (slavery) – and there was probably no liberal government in this country or elsewhere until after World War II. Even though the liberal claim of separation was never fully true, polities should be defined first through their rules and practices about decision making, forms of participation, and membership. Thus it is possible – and historically frequent from the eighteenth century on to the present – to find liberal polities in societies with many illiberal institutions.

A third critique of claims of liberal dominance asserts not only that there have been many and diverse liberal formulations, partly owing to citizens' different social experiences. The claim is that this multiplication of liberal positions is so great as to undermine any general claims about the content of liberalism. If this argument were true, and no important shared meanings were entailed in the general use of liberal concepts, it is hard to see why those concepts would persist. If no meaning is expressed and no advantage is gained by using liberal concepts, why are they not quickly replaced by clearer and sharper statements of conflicting positions? Most contending political groups in the United States have made and still today make their political proposals in liberal terms. They almost always claim to be sincere – even if they are sometimes not sincere, claims to adhere to liberal principles constrain those who make

---

25. Karen Orren, *Belated Feudalism: Labor, the Law, and Liberal Development in the United States* (Cambridge University Press, 1991), 14.

them. It is reasonable to insist that there are many possible interpretations of liberal principles, but this flexibility is not the same thing as
indeterminacy.

Neither the correct claim that illiberal and undemocratic practices
have existed widely in American history nor the wrong claim that liberal
concepts can mean anything warrants discarding the idea of a basically
liberal framework in American politics. But both claims raise important
questions. These have to do with relations between democracy and
liberalism and with the range of meanings that liberal terms can convey.

Nonliberal views have emerged in American culture, and there have
been significant local political experiences in which nonliberal forces
played a role. Yet while many political views have appeared in American
intellectual and public life, nonliberal conceptions have failed to establish themselves as durable political realities. Liberal conceptions predominate, and other doctrines adapt to liberalism. In the twentieth century,
no nonliberal major party emerged in the United States, defining "major" as a party able to win over 10 percent of the presidential vote in
several consecutive elections. As with Tocqueville, the Hartzian point is
comparative: think of the range of political views among major parties
in Germany from unification through World War I, or in Britain from
World War II through the mid-1950s, or in Italy from World War II to
the mid-1980s.

Liberalism and democracy

Claims of American exceptionalism readily withstand attempts to depict
liberalism as only one among several American political traditions. Liberalism has defined the framework in which political projects have had
to present themselves. Where the latter have explicitly rejected core
liberal principles, the result has been national political failure.[26]

---

26. For a valuable effort to show that liberalism has been only one among several
    traditions, see Rogers M. Smith, "Beyond Tocqueville, Myrdal, and Hartz: The Multi-
    ple Traditions in America," *American Political Science Review* 87, no. 3 (September
    1993): 549–66. Smith argues that American political culture has been characterized
    by the copresence of liberal, republican, and "Americanist" (often nativist) themes,
    and underlines the role of exclusivist themes in American intellectual and political life.
    But the effectiveness of his challenge to Hartzian views is limited by two problems.
    First, he does not distinguish sufficiently between liberal and democratic themes,
    which leads him to identify any nondemocratic element as also illiberal (republican or
    nativist). He then cites such elements as evidence of the nondomination of liberalism.
    In several instances the ideas in question, such as excluding women from suffrage,
    were believed by many political actors to be compatible with liberalism, although
    contemporary democratic liberals would not agree. In other words, liberalism was not

A stronger challenge to Hartzian accounts asserts that they downplay tensions between liberal and democratic themes in American politics, conceiving liberalism as more naturally and easily democratic than has been the case. In Hartz's statements and others that rely on Hartz or Tocqueville, American liberalism is considered as intrinsically and irresistibly democratic. It is more accurate to depict American liberalism as open to democratic interpretations. The latter were usually contested, often in bitter conflicts. By democratic political themes I mean arguments for expanding the part of the population entitled to participate in choosing the government and for expanding the means by which citizens can directly influence their government. Many democratic themes also propose that government regulation of the market can be legitimate.

Relations between liberal and democratic themes have been far more difficult than most Hartzian accounts suggest. The universalistic cast of American liberalism has provided a durable basis for launching democratic projects, but no guarantee of their success. Democratic results have often required confrontations with dominant forms of liberalism, as in expanding the suffrage in the early nineteenth century, in the fight against slavery, in efforts to gain the vote for women, and in attempts to establish trade unions as legitimate political actors in the first half of the twentieth century.

In such instances resistance to democratization came partly from authentically liberal political and intellectual currents. Liberal critics of democratization charged that one or another group was not suited for the responsibilities of citizenship, or that a proposed institutional change would endanger individual rights. If it seems natural to say "liberal democratic," that term would have struck many American liberals as dubious well into this country's history.

Liberal doctrine had ample space for interpretations that were not wholly democratic. The notion of government as representative left open questions about who was competent to join in selecting the government and how the selection process should work. Political liberties were likewise understood to reside primarily in qualified citizens, and liberals were rarely united in comprehensive opposition to all limits on free expression. Liberal conceptions of limited government might readily be mobilized against efforts to regulate market relations by democratic

as democratic as he suggests. Second, the term "political culture" causes confusion because Smith does not make much of a distinction between organized national politics and intellectual life concerned with politics. Nonliberal currents have had and continue to have much more weight in the latter sphere than in the world of political parties, elections, and movements, where nonliberal political forces have rarely been major actors after the Civil War.

means. Along with this doctrinal openness, the moderate temper of American liberalism encouraged patience toward existing inequalities and restrained enthusiasm for democratic claims that reducing inequality was urgent. American liberals have been sensitive to the claims of strong proponents of community, order, and individual economic choice. The encounter between liberal and democratic themes has often been contentious, as it was in the two decades on which this book focuses.

Thus if liberalism has framed American political development, the Hartzian view cannot simply be adopted. In addition to downplaying tensions between liberal and democratic themes, this view conflates the origins and persistence of political and cultural forms. Moreover, Hartzian accounts too often rely on dubious aspects of modernization theory and on simplistic conceptions of political language. When they posit one American regime whose development is continuous and unproblematic, they cannot account for change in general. Nor can such accounts consider the course of the Democratic order in particular without trivializing the stakes of its founding and decline. If the American exceptionalism view means that no matter what the issues or forms of conflict, an enduring liberal constitution proves no real change has occurred, its analytical merit is dissipated. Such a view pays little attention to how cultural and political forms are sustained, and considers history as a seamless repetition of original conditions and commitments.

Major conflicts occurred and substantial political themes on the margins of liberalism emerged in the formative period of the Democratic order, and again near its end. To say these battles mark no departure from a history of narrow but fierce struggles within liberalism would diminish the democratic importance of conflicts about labor relations and social welfare provision in the 1930s and about racial politics three decades later. The point is not to chastise Hartz or Hofstadter for not predicting specific events in the 1960s and 1970s.[27] But their accounts strongly indicated a degree of stability that was not sustained.[28]

27. In *Political Man,* Lipset wrote: "The characteristic pattern of stable Western democracies in the mid-twentieth century is that they are in a 'post-politics' phase – that is, there is relatively little difference between the democratic left and right, the socialists are moderates, and the conservatives accept the welfare state" (82). Hartz claimed that the limits of American politics yield intolerance and ineptness in coping with a modern world full of political forces outside the boundaries of what American liberalism deems acceptable. Hartz, *Liberal Tradition,* 284–309.

28. The main works suggested a long period of Democratic domination, perhaps interrupted occasionally by centrist Republicanism. This is explicit in Lipset, *The First New Nation,* 315.

The role of modernization theory

American exceptionalism converged with theories of modernization that viewed the United States as the model endpoint of political development.[29] Early and thorough modernization meant a commitment to universalistic, rational, and individualistic values; these values helped make it possible to generate and sustain economic growth. Following Tocqueville, Hartz insisted that Americans were born modern as well as equal. This allowed the United States to escape the trauma of social revolution against an entrenched traditional order. What Hartz called a vast petite bourgeoisie is an optimal agent of modernization: a broad modern middle class, without ascriptive particularism, ambivalence about modern skills, or messianic ambitions.[30]

To depict American modernization as always unproblematic made the postwar political stability that framed both modernization theory and the main accounts of American exceptionalism seem permanent. The error was not to claim that an early modernization occurred, but to imagine that this accomplishment fixed in place a single regime. An early and thorough modernization created durable strong pressures that shape choices about institutional and cultural forms. But these pressures do not eliminate alternatives. The potential remains for deep conflict about which modern institutions and discourses should be developed.

A further influence of modernization theory on accounts of American exceptionalism was to discourage viewing politics as a causal force. In explaining political development, one strand of modernization theory emphasized economic development, another cited social conditions, while a third stressed the cultural and psychological prerequisites of modern political behavior.[31] Rather than providing a deeper explanation of what Hartz and Hofstadter analyzed, modernization theory accentuated their tendency to dissolve politics into other processes.

29. Lipset considered American politics as the exemplary achievement of a global development process in *Political Man*, 42, 340.
30. Hofstadter took more notice of resistance to modernization, as in his critical account of the popular radicalism of the late nineteenth and early twentieth centuries, but his view of the New Deal as the triumph of mature reformism saw modernization as securely achieved. As Hartz and Hofstadter ratified modernization theory, their accounts also influenced political development theorists. On these relations, see Robert Packenham, *Liberal America and the Third World: Political Development Ideas in Foreign Aid and Social Science* (Princeton, N.J.: Princeton University Press, 1973), 19–20, 318–19.
31. The first emphasis predominates in Lipset's *Political Man*, which links modernization theory with determinist Marxism. *The First New Nation* combined the second and third approaches.

Political language and political practices

Accounts of American exceptionalism overstate the degree to which liberal political terms convey common and coherent meanings. This view misses the substantial political change that can occur through a creative reworking of conventional terms or through incorporating elements of other political discourses.

For Hartz especially, language is complicated mainly when liberals misunderstand their own beliefs and wrap them in radical or republican rhetoric. Thus Roosevelt's occasional radicalism in the New Deal was really an emphatic liberal reformism, which seems radical only in the absence of a major left outside liberal boundaries. Whatever the rhetorical inflections, American meanings are liberal: government should be representative and limited, constrained by respect for individual rights. It should secure conditions for individuals to pursue their own interests. In this conception the agreement on premises that defines American politics also defines the conditions of consequential political speech. Correspondence among terms, meanings, and practices is fixed and consensual.[32]

Presuming a continuous and consensual identity between terms and meanings discourages inquiry into conflicts about the meaning of central terms. Repeated conflicts of this sort have occurred regarding the concept of liberty in American politics, in pre-Civil War debates about slavery and property, arguments about the political and economic role of large corporations at the turn of the century, and conflicts in the 1930s over expanded social welfare provision and government protection for trade unions. At times conventional relations between terms and meanings are ruptured and familiar terms gain new meanings. In the 1820s and 1830s, for example, democratic initiatives often relied on redefining constitutional commitments to government "by the people."[33]

---

32. I do not want to assert that meanings are arbitrary or fixed wholly through processes of domination. Strong continuities of meaning preclude a radical indeterminacy thesis – what sort of indeterminacy is so predictable? Responding to this problem, claims of indeterminacy are often reformulated to shift attention to the strategies of those agents who allegedly manipulate meanings to gain their objectives. But conceiving hegemony as pure domination raises further problems: How could an elite capable of insightful strategic maneuvers constitute itself, define ends, and devise effective means of realizing them if meaning were arbitrary with respect to language? How could such organization be sustained instead of collapsing from failures to communicate?

33. Daniel T. Rodgers, *Contested Truths: Keywords in American Politics Since Independence* (New York: Basic Books, 1987), 80–100.

Liberal boundaries do not require uniform acceptance of a particular interpretation of liberal political practices.[34]

Considering liberal terms always to mean the same thing allows effective description of phases of political stability, though even then the meaning of basic terms in the American political vocabulary is not uniform across groups. In conflictual phases such as the 1930s, when old political forces are in turmoil and new ones are built, the view of political language usually employed by accounts of American exceptionalism is much less adequate. It fails to grasp how political conflict occurs partly through reshaping conventional terms to produce new meanings. The flexibility of liberal political language allows an interplay with democratic themes.[35] Thus while accounts of working-class and popular politics in the nineteenth and early twentieth centuries do not show that an autonomous republicanism was a coherent alternative, popular political efforts did articulate republican and democratic themes within liberal discourses and thereby reshaped those discourses.

American exceptionalism knows one story, about the basic role of liberalism in framing American politics, and tells it well. Concerning the Democratic order (or others), American exceptionalism can say far more about the outer boundaries of legitimate national politics than about how that order was built (or why it did not last forever). Characterizing American political development as the unfolding of a single regime fails to recognize that major political changes have taken place.

What about restating the American exceptionalism perspective by taking American history as the story of a strikingly resilient "hegemony," insisting that consensus is formed as an asymmetrical result of political and ideological conflict? This approach most often only renames, with "hegemony" replacing "political values" as the expressive

---

34. Both an instrumental conception of political language and a view of the latter as wholly constitutive of political agents presume an unproblematic unity between signifier and signified. This makes it difficult even to recognize the crucial points when conventional signifiers are linked to new (signified) elements to yield new meanings. On the instrumental and constitutive dimensions of language, see Gareth Stedman Jones, "Introduction," in his *Languages of Class: Studies in English Working Class History, 1832–1982* (Cambridge University Press, 1983), 1–24; and Charles Taylor, "Theories of Meaning," in his *Human Agency and Language: Philosophical Papers,* Vol. 1 (Cambridge University Press, 1985), 248–92.

35. This flexibility also permits longstanding and serious conflicts to occur within a liberal framework. For a provocative argument about such conflicts in the nineteenth century, between liberals who sought to reform and improve people and liberals who took preferences mainly as given, see J. David Greenstone, *The Lincoln Persuasion: Remaking American Liberalism* (Princeton, N.J.: Princeton University Press, 1993).

core of political development. It tends to absorb difficult and conflictual experiences, such as those of the 1930s, into a seamless flow of American history, now cast as a history of domination. Clearly some major conflicts have confirmed ongoing forms of domination; yet others have destabilized them and extended democratic practices to a greater extent than is captured in notions of a perpetual hegemony.

Organizational change and political history

A number of political historians and political scientists divide American political development into two periods. One period extends from the beginning of the nineteenth century roughly to the end of that century, the other from around World War I to the present. The transition between the two periods is located variously from 1890 to 1918, or even as an extended phase including most of those years.[36] This periodization centers on

> organization building, both public and private, and the creation of new and elaborate networks of formal, hierarchical structures of authority that gradually came to dominate our economy, polity, and culture.[37]

The transition yielded the large corporation and the modern bureaucratic state, the institutional core of modern American history.

Before this great divide, politics was dominated by parties, local elites, and courts. Popular commitments were largely regional and ethnocultural. Political life was colorful, passionate, and participatory if not necessarily democratic. At the turn of the century new national elites and organizations arose in business, the professions, and government. Economic enterprises grew and large corporations were formed. National state regulation and bureaucracy expanded. Professions were established and grew more powerful. Large organized groups and associations of experts who claimed technical competence became increasingly

36. Works crucial in developing this perspective include Samuel Hays, *The Response to Industrialism, 1885–1914* (Chicago, Ill.: University of Chicago Press, 1957); and Robert Wiebe, *The Search for Order, 1877–1920* (New York: Hill and Wang, 1967). Also see Richard L. McCormick, *The Party Period and Public Policy: American Politics from the Age of Jackson to the Progressive Era* (New York: Oxford University Press, 1976), 220–7.

37. Louis Galambos, "Technology, Political Economy, and Professionalization: Central Themes of the Organizational Synthesis," *Business History Review* 57 (Winter 1983): 471.

important political actors. Since the transition, politics has mainly been about coping with further institutional differentiation.[38]

This perspective usefully calls attention to major political and economic changes in the late nineteenth and early twentieth centuries. But its claims to constitute an adequate theoretical framework regarding American political development are untenable. Almost all efforts to periodize American politics find an important break around the turn of the century. Does that agreement stamp these decades as the decisive phase of change in the last two centuries? Were these organizational changes more important for the American polity than the Civil War? Even if many political changes of the 1930s were rooted in earlier Progressive proposals, wasn't the scope of political and legal change in the 1930s at least comparable to that around World War I?

One sign that too much is being claimed for these organizational changes lies in the character of the transition itself. There were many disputes about the shape of economic, political, and social institutions, such as those concerning party organizations, antitrust policies, and labor relations.[39] Yet the Hartzian point has merit: From 1890 to World War I, modernization was in comparative terms neither traumatic nor convulsive. Extended, large-scale disruption was infrequent partly because large parts of the population were already committed to rapid economic and social development.[40] No violent destruction of a landed gentry or uprooting of a resistant peasantry was necessary; no politically serious antimodernizing current lasted among the middle classes.

Conflicts over the shifts on which proponents of an organizational synthesis focus were relatively manageable.[41] One index of this is the

38. Hofstadter's account of twentieth-century reform focused on status conflicts and the maturation of progressive impulses, and set out many of the themes developed by Hays, Wiebe, and the social scientists influenced by their work, in *The Age of Reform*.

39. On antitrust policies in the early twentieth century, see Martin J. Sklar, *The Corporate Reconstruction of American Capitalism, 1890–1916: The Market, the Law, and Politics* (Cambridge University Press, 1988).

40. There is a tendency for historians to exaggerate the depth of conflict in the spheres they examine – as with labor or populist movements in the late nineteenth century – especially when they sympathize politically with forces that were defeated. Because struggles were dramatic and difficult, great exaggeration is not required to portray some protest efforts as convulsive struggles over basic issues. Nonetheless, it is wrong to generalize from fierce local or even regional battles to claim that a radical, general opposition to the dominant lines of economic and social change was a major political force in the United States.

41. On populism see Lawrence Goodwyn, *Democratic Promise: The Populist Moment in America* (Cambridge University Press, 1987); on labor in the first two decades of the

extent of political repression linked closely to modernization. Although there was considerable political repression in the late nineteenth and early twentieth centuries, notably regarding labor radicalism and trade unions, this repression was not centralized, permanent, or routinely extended into the political sphere. Moreover, the most extensive and brutal political repression was inflicted on the black population in the South, and this was not done on behalf of any modernizing project. Dissenting political forces were not usually prevented from assembling, publicizing their aims, and competing for office. By this standard, the experience of the United States until World War I was not highly repressive, compared with numerous countries where radical political currents were more harshly treated.[42]

All did not go happily in the transition to corporate capitalism, a bureaucratic state, and professional associations. There was much protest by workers and farmers, and widespread cultural criticism. Yet conflict took place with no basic threat to the constitutional system. Much of the United States was already modern regarding the role of the market, experience with urban centers, awareness of events outside of local communities, and commitment to representative politics. Thus a cultural and political framework existed in which a dramatic growth in organizational scale and complexity could be assimilated. (That political and organizational shifts were accompanied by steadily rising incomes helped allay conflict and increase support for modernizing changes.)

How can these decades be deemed the site of the single key shift in American history? One might claim that this phase was decisive because organizational growth and differentiation are the central processes of modern social life. Yet modernity is not defined simply by the presence

century, see David Montgomery *The Fall of the House of Labor: the Workplace, the State, and American Labor Activism, 1865–1925* (Cambridge University Press, 1987); on political ideas, see James Kloppenberg, *Uncertain Victory: Social Democracy and Progressivism in European and American Thought, 1870–1920* (New York: Oxford University Press, 1986).

42. For an effort to show that political repression in the United States was extensive and politically important, see Robert Goldstein, *Political Repression in America: From 1870 to the Present* (Cambridge, Mass.: Schenkman Publishing Company, 1978). On post-Civil War repression in the South see C. Vann Woodward, *Strange Career of Jim Crow* (New York: Oxford University Press, 1966); and W. E. B. DuBois, *Black Reconstruction in America, 1860–1880* (New York: Atheneum, 1985). On the political and economic views of American workers in these decades, see Michael Kazin, *Barons of Labor: The San Francisco Building Trades and Union Power in the Progressive Era* (Urbana, Illinois: University of Illinois Press, 1987); and David Montgomery, *Workers' Control in America: Studies in the History of Work, Technology, and Labor Struggles* (Cambridge University Press, 1980).

of large bureaucratic organizations. It entails attitudes and practices that can and often do arise prior to them.[43] Once basic forms of modernity have arisen, it should not be conceived as a uniform course that stringently determines institutional and cultural forms. Political choices remain to be made. For organizations to become larger, more formal, and more complex does not dictate specific socioeconomic and political forms to nearly the extent this organizational perspective claims.

In political life, modernization required an increase of state administrative capacities, and some dimunition of parochial and corrupt modes of party control of local politics. But these needs could have been met in a variety of more or less democratic and pluralistic ways. Progressive social reforms and piecemeal administrative changes were selected politically from among possible responses to the challenges of ongoing modernization.[44]

In economic life, modernization required larger enterprises and new modes of distribution and labor relations. But it is difficult to derive the specific forms of American corporations from these needs. The gap is clear in Alfred Chandler's influential work on changes in business organization. He argues that the "modern multiunit business enterprise replaced small traditional enterprise when administrative coordination permitted greater productivity, lower costs, and higher profits than coordination by market mechanisms." This argument drives his account of the late nineteenth and early twentieth centuries:

> The modern industrial enterprise – the archetype of today's giant corporation – resulted from the integration of the processes of mass production with those of mass distribution within a single business firm. . . . Almost nonexistent at the end of the 1870s, these integrated enterprises came to dominate many of the nation's most vital industries within less than three decades.[45]

Profit opportunities stemming from administrative coordination are not sufficient to explain the forms of economic modernization and reorganization analyzed by Chandler. Efforts to achieve profits could take several forms. Administrative coordination was also encouraged by economic and political factors that were not identical to an effort to maximize

---

43. Thus in Weber's work on bureaucracy and modernization Benjamin Franklin illustrates the emergence of a modern rational-capitalist spirit in the eighteenth century, well before large-scale capitalist enterprises or extensive bureaucratic modes of organization. Max Weber, *The Protestant Ethic and the Spirit of Capitalism* (New York: Scribners, 1976), 47–65.

44. Herbert Croly, *Progressive Democracy* (New York: The Macmillan Company, 1914).

45. Alfred D. Chandler, Jr., *The Visible Hand: The Managerial Revolution in American Business* (Cambridge, Mass.: Harvard University Press, 1977), 6, 285.

profits, such as a desire for institutional security in uncertain environments.[46]

When this underdetermination of political and economic results is pointed out to proponents of an organizational account, their main response is to cite efficiency as an evolutionary force, whether the subject is corporate modes of business organization or governmental regulation of economic interaction.[47] Proponents of this organizational view depict organizational change as an efficient response to environmental pressures. Yet for explanatory purposes there is a big difference between asserting that organizational growth and differentiation were relatively efficient responses to new challenges and claiming that the particular forms these processes took were selected because they were the most efficient. Other options were usually compatible with modernizing imperatives, and political factors helped in choosing among them.

Thus, regarding economic reorganization, Chandler's work and its successors can be charged with stretching efficiency arguments to include choices made mainly on behalf of economic elites' narrower interests in power and security. Several sympathetic accounts of late nineteenth-century populism have raised the question of whether other modes of modern agriculture were possible. Harry Braverman's critique of Taylorism provoked debate over the role of technical and social exigencies in reshaping work relations in the first decades of the twentieth century. And Christopher Lasch vigorously questioned the identification of new professional groups with progress in knowledge. If none of these critiques made a positive case in a fully convincing way, taken together they indicate that varied institutional choices were compatible with modernizing tendencies. Yet most of the organizational synthesis literature seems to assume that changes were selected as the most efficient responses to new challenges.[48] This conclusion might be right in particular

46. Neil Fligstein criticizes Chandler's work along these lines in *The Transformation of Corporate Control* (Cambridge, Mass.: Harvard University Press, 1990).

47. Berkhofer proposes that historians adopt an evolutionist perspective on organizational development: "When we consider the structural differentiation and integration over time in an organization, we begin to move toward the central idea of social evolution. The development of increasing complexity through the growing functional specialization and newly emerging levels of authority constitutes the fundamental idea of organizational evolution." He also claims that the organizational approach allows an analytical focus on the choices of elites in shaping institutional development. For this argument not to contradict his theoretical position, it is necessary to posit strong evolutionary pressures toward efficiency that constrain elite actions. Robert F. Berkhofer, Jr., "The Organizational Interpretation of American History: A New Synthesis," *Prospects – An Annual of American Cultural Studies* 4 (1979): 614.

48. Charles Perrow, "Markets, Hierarchies, and Hegemony: A Critique of Chandler and Williamson" in Andrew Van de Ven and William Joyce, eds., *Perspectives on*

cases but is unwarranted as a premise or general claim. Proponents of an organizational perspective have relied on the most deterministic formulations in long debates about how much diversity is possible in a modern institutional and cultural framework.[49]

In the organizational view political change is mainly determined by social and economic pressures. Except for economists who trace everything to administrative coordination driven by profit-seeking, proponents of this view do not make clear the causal sequence.[50] Key passages list demographic, technical, and socioeconomic factors without sorting them out:

> ... [t]he crucial synthetic principle is provided by the fundamental transitions that began to take place in America's economy, geopolity, and demography around the end of the nineteenth century. Then a fast-growing "extensive" economy gave way to a slower-growing "intensive" system. Population growth slowed. The nation's frontiers stabilized. These conditions created a need for new institutions that would provide Americans with a greater measure of security and with the kinds of ongoing technical and organizational innovations essential to our economic success over the long run. The result was America's organizational revolution.[51]

Galambos does not say how organizational change is related to demographic, geographical, technical, and economic forces. Explanations of political change need to indicate how these relations work.

Organization Design and Behavior (New York: Wiley Interscience, 1981); Harry Braverman, *Labor and Monopoly Capital* (New York: Monthly Review Press, 1974); Magali Sarfatti Larson, *The Rise of Professionalism – A Sociological Analysis* (Berkeley: University of California Press, 1977); and Christopher Lasch, *Haven in a Heartless World: The Family Besieged* (New York: Basic Books, 1977).

49. Parsons conceived the result of social evolution in these terms: "Fundamental to the structure of modern societies are, taken together: bureaucratic organization of collective goal-attainment, money and market systems, generalized universalistic legal systems, and the democratic association with elective leadership and mediated membership support for policy orientations.... [W]e may think of them as together constituting the main outline of the structural foundations of modern society." He stressed the force of pressures toward convergence across modern societies. Talcott Parsons, *On Institutions and Social Evolution: Selected Writings* (Chicago, Ill.: University of Chicago Press, 1982), 326.

50. The term "organizational synthesis," adopted by proponents of this view is somewhat unfair to those engaged in organizational studies in sociology and related disciplines, who are often more aware of the limits of a formal organizational account in explaining outcomes than those whose views are now under discussion. See Sharon Zukin and Paul DiMaggio, eds., *Structures of Capital* (Cambridge University Press, 1990); and Walter W. Powell and Paul DiMaggio, eds., *The New Institutionalism in Organizational Analysis* (Chicago, Ill.: University of Chicago Press, 1990).

51. Louis Galambos, "Technology, Political Economy, and Professionalization: Central Themes of the Organizational Synthesis," *Business History Review* 57 (Winter 1983): 493.

The initial studies in this vein, such as those by Robert Wiebe and Samuel Hays, focused on the late nineteenth and early twentieth centuries. Efforts to develop this perspective have mainly examined further features of the same years. The organizational perspective is a plausible account of overall political development only at that time, when many key political issues explicitly concerned how to manage organizational growth and differentiation. Even then, other major issues arose: conflicts about the legal position and distributive share of labor; battles over political inclusion, as regarding immigrants and women; cultural conflicts, as with temperance; and racial conflicts, from the establishment of legal segregation in the South to urban confrontations in the North.

Later conflicts in the twentieth century about income distribution, government regulation, power and status among professional groups, relations among regions, the regulation of market activity, and race relations have had a significant organizational dimension. But that aspect does not typically predominate, and is linked with substantive political and social choices. If modernization requires large and differentiated organizations, it does not require the American social welfare system rather than that of Sweden. Modernity does not dictate American forms of corporate organization as opposed to Japanese or German modes, nor does it determine American forms of labor relations rather than those of France or Canada.[52] In twentieth-century America, organizations are large, bureaucratic, and relatively centralized; issues are frequently national in scope; and large interest groups, including those of professionals, are major players in policy disputes. Yet these realities only partly define political conflicts. Proponents of an organizational view claim to have explained the core features of American politics before and after a crucial transition. Instead, they have provided an insightful though formalistic account of important changes in the late nineteenth and early twentieth centuries.

52. In one effort to bring the organizational perspective toward the present, case studies of national government institutions show that no single course has been dictated by organizational pressures. Carolyn Weaver argues that the "bureaucracy" played a crucial role in the postwar evolution of social service programs, while Heywood Fleisig argues that politicians are the decisive force in fiscal and (with qualifications) monetary policies. Although there is an important organizational dimension in all policy areas, no uniform process of organizational development makes institutions take the same shape. Nor does power move uniformly toward the bureaucratic managers of government agencies. Carolyn L. Weaver, "The Social Security Bureaucracy in Triumph and in Crisis"; and Heywood Fleisig, "Bureaucracy and the Political Process: The Monetary and Fiscal Balance," in Louis Galambos, ed., *The New American State: Bureaucracies and Policies since World War II* (Baltimore, Md.: The Johns Hopkins University Press, 1987), 54–84, 109–36.

Political realignment

The concept of political realignment frames a body of work that has been relatively successful in dividing politics in the United States into distinctive periods. Yet there are problems with the realignment approach that preclude adopting it to explain the Democratic experience, even regarding the changes of the late 1920s and early 1930s that provide it with a strong case. Accounts of realignment do not persuasively explain why it happens, or how realignments are linked to phases between them – in this case, how the dramatic changes of the mid-1930s were connected with the politics of the next decade.[53]

V. O. Key initiated the contemporary use of "realignment":

> Even the most fleeting inspection of American elections suggests the existence of a category of elections in which voters are . . . unusually deeply concerned, in which the extent of electoral involvement is relatively quite high, and in which the decisive results of the voting reveal a sharp alteration of the preexisting cleavage within the electorate.[54]

He identified the elections of 1896 and 1928 as realigning elections.[55] Developing Key's arguments, Walter Dean Burnham tried to define realignment:

> . . . eras of critical realignment are marked by short, sharp reorganizations of the mass coalitional bases of the major parties which occur at periodic intervals on the national level; are often preceded by major third-party revolts which reveal the incapacity of "politics as usual" to integrate, much less aggregate, emergent political demands; are closely associated with abnormal stress in the socioeconomic system; are marked by ideological polarizations and issue-distances between the major parties which are exception-

---

53. Burnham locates realignment within the stability provided by enduring constitutional and discursive forms: "If parties seeking to organize the lower strata of American society along collectivist lines have been so evanescent, if the two major components of the system have so feebly performed the educative and policy-making functions, the reason for this must lie not only in our dispersive political institutions but more fundamentally within the American political culture itself. Of all theses regarding that culture, the one which has the greatest explanatory power is the theory of the liberal tradition in America which has been developed by Louis Hartz . . ." Burnham, "American Politics in the 1970s; Beyond Party?" in William N. Chambers and Walter Dean Burnham, eds., *The American Party Systems*, 2d ed. (New York: Oxford University Press, 1975), 281.

54. V. O. Key, "A Theory of Critical Elections," *Journal of Politics* 17 (February 1955): 3–4.

55. In 1959, Key added an account of cumulative changes in the electorate, which he termed secular realignment, in "Secular Realignment and the Party System," *Journal of Politics* 21 (1959): 198–210.

ally large by normal standards; and have durable consequences as constituent acts which determine the outer boundaries of policy in general. . . .[56]

Burnham linked realignment to the weakness of American political parties: Dramatic eruptions of constituency demands force recalcitrant parties to take up new issues.[57] He used the realignment concept to ask questions about political discontinuity:

> Such a theory must inevitably emphasize the elements of stress and abrupt transformation in our political life at the expense of the consensual, gradualist perspectives which have until recently dominated the scholar's vision of American political processes and behavior.[58]

The realignment view usefully designates broad electoral changes in American politics.[59]

Realignment does occur. Critical treatments have shown electoral change to be more complex than most statements of the concept suggest – in its timing and duration, in the composition of electoral blocs, and in relations between national and other voting. Yet if depicting realignment as a single stunning moment of change with all voters moving together is simplistic, it is more simplistic to say that electoral change is endlessly varied.[60]

56. Walter Dean Burnham, *Critical Elections and the Mainsprings of American Politics* (New York: W. W. Norton, 1970), 10. Trilling and Campbell propose: "A realignment is a durable and significant redistribution of party support. A critical realignment is a realignment in which the bulk of the redistribution takes place within reasonably defined time limits." Bruce A. Campbell and Richard J. Trilling, "Toward a Theory of Realignment: An Introduction," in Campbell and Trilling, eds., *Realignment in American Politics: Toward a Theory* (Austin: University of Texas Press, 1980), 29–30.

57. In a related account, James Sundquist emphasizes divisive issues: "1. A realignment is precipitated by the rise of a new political issue. . . . 2. To bring about a realignment, the new issue must be one that cuts across the existing line of party cleavage. . . ." James L. Sundquist, *Dynamics of the Party System* (Washington, D.C.: Brookings Institution, 1973), 304.

58. Burnham, *Critical Elections*, 3–4.

59. For a forceful restatement of the realignment view, see Walter Dean Burnham, "Critical Realignment: Dead or Alive?", in Byron E. Shafer, ed., *The End of Realignment? Interpreting American Electoral Eras* (Madison: University of Wisconsin Press, 1991), 101–39.

60. Allan Lichtman persuasively rejects the idea that 1928 alone was a critical election in the sense Key intended. yet even if there were never an election in American history with precisely those attributes, the concept of realignment would survive as a way to call attention to the shape of changes in voting behavior, partisan identification, and other electoral phenomena. See Allan Lichtman, "Critical Election Theory and the Reality of American Presidential Politics, 1916–1940," *American Historical Review* 81 (1976): 317–48.

While the realignment view usefully summarizes electoral shifts at the outset of the Democratic order, it does not explain that regime's formation.[61] Moreover, the realignment view takes too little interest in the content of the regimes it demarcates. If regimes are not defined, there is not likely to be much agreement about what distinguishes them or what counts as realignment. When analysts measure realignment by changes in party identification, voting rates, and election results, they often confuse these measures with the changes that realignment is supposed to mark.

Explaining realignment

Realignment accounts do not adequately explain the patterns they identify, and focus too narrowly on parties and elections. Realignment is often attributed to stimuli that overload the party system, without explaining why some stimuli and not others are disruptive.[62] For Sundquist, realignment can follow when an issue disrupts existing cleavages. But why can some threatening issues be mediated and not others?[63] Burnham more plausibly links realignment to the weakness of parties, whose limits as governing and policy-making organizations encourage mass entry into the political process when unmet constituent demands accumulate.[64] Thus critical elections reconnect citizens to the party system. But when does a party system yield to realignment rather than renew itself? Burnham also suggests that realignment equilibrates a modernizing socioeconomic sphere with slowly adjusting political institutions. But this relocates the problem: When is modernization politically destabilizing, and when can it be managed without realignment?

At crucial points the realignment view ascribes political change and development to extrapolitical forces and downplays the causal role of

---

61. And it has not fared well regarding political developments after the mid-1960s, as realignment views have been used to claim almost everything: that a Republican realignment occurred, that restructuring the party system would strengthen the Democratic–New Deal coalition, or that the two parties have deteriorated so far that neither can initiate realignment. Walter Dean Burnham, *The Current Crisis in American Politics* (New York: Oxford University Press, 1982), 269.
62. Bruce A. Campbell, "Realignment, Party Decomposition, and Issue Voting," in Campbell and Trilling, eds., *Realignment in American Politics*, 82–109.
63. Similarly, Sinclair's study of changes in the policy agenda during the New Deal depicts policy shifts as responses to social or economic stimuli. Barbara Deckard Sinclair, "Party Realignment and the Transformation of the Political Agenda: The House of Representatives," *American Political Science Review* 71 (September 1977): 940–53.
64. Burnham, "American Politics in the 1970s," 278.

political conflict.[65] Thus Burnham's work after *Critical Elections* portrays realignment as directly the result of socioeconomic change – the Depression yields the New Deal. Ladd and Hadley also designate political phenomena as causally secondary.[66] Why should political variables be given so little weight in accounting for political change? Perhaps the reason is that if one defines realignment as a sharp general electoral shift, and seeks to explain it with reference to political variables based on conventional categories (mass partisanship and parties), political explanations do not look promising. Most realignment accounts propose this sequence: Partisan change leads to voting shifts, which lead to new electoral outcomes – the core of realignment – and then to policy shifts. Here it is not clear what causes partisan change. What if political parties are proposed as the prior cause of partisan change and thus of realignment? The weakness and fragmentation of American parties make it hard to conceive them as the primary authors of such changes. If attributing causal force to political factors means focusing on party efforts, the limitations of those parties make cultural or socioeconomic explanations appealing.[67]

Trying to explain political change via the realignment concept encounters another difficult issue about American parties: To what extent should they be conceived as (unitary) agents concerned with gaining office? Parties vary in both their agency and their goals. Some parties are unified for global political purposes toward which electoral victory is only one means; others are coherent and disciplined organizations concerned solely with electoral victory. American parties are not highly unified; sometimes it is difficult even to impute agency to them. Yet their main elements are committed to winning elections. This combination of features makes it hard even to locate American parties in the conventional debates about parties. These debates counterpose a notion of parties as unitary rational actors aiming to win elections (as in the work of Anthony Downs or Joseph Schlesinger) with a view of parties as

65. Thus Sundquist treats political factors as expressing the socioeconomic changes that cause realignment, and Campbell and Trilling subordinate parties to socioeconomic stimuli. Sundquist, *Dynamics of the Party System,* 29; Campbell and Trilling, eds., *Realignment in American Politics: Toward a Theory,* 9.

66. "[P]arties, elections, and voting are all seen, in a fundamental sense, as dependent variables. They exist as parts of the political system which is, precisely, a subunit of the larger social system. As such, they are much more acted upon than acting upon." Everett Carll Ladd with Charles D. Hadley, *Transformations of the American Party System: Political Coalitions from the New Deal to the 1970s* (New York: W. W. Norton, 1975), 22.

67. "The functions which the parties perform and the forms which they assume will be determined by the emergent needs of the broader social and political system, and not by the parties themselves." Burnham, "American Politics in the 1970s," 307.

complex organizations concerned primarily to maintain their positions (as in the work of Angelo Panebianco).[68]

American parties at the national level are often not coherent enough to be plausible agents of a Downsian theory.[69] When they are relatively coherent, they may not be powerful enough for their strategies to be crucial for political development. Nor is it common for American parties to be organizationally and ideologically developed enough to be at the center of an account of national politics focused on organizational maintenance. Thus a study of political change in the United States cannot be a party study per se, even if it is reasonable to name political orders by their leading party. In the Democratic order the Democratic Party was an agent, but it was often divided enough to make its agency problematic. Most Democrats tried to win most elections, but that aim meant different and sometimes conflicting strategic and thematic choices, rather than defining a common approach.

Given the problems entailed in defining parties as leading agents, party-based accounts of realignment are apt to flounder analytically. The result is often to search for determining nonpolitical variables. But this move is not required, because parties are not the only political agents capable of taking political initiatives that have major political (and social) effects. Political orders are built by political blocs that include party forces, movements and interest groups, and state-based organizations and political currents. There are many agents, even if they do not fit easily into conventional categories. Given this conception, political change does not need to be construed as a moment of electoral realignment. Instead, we can focus on the processes of building a political order and on how political orders structure politics between realignment phases.[70]

68. Anthony Downs, *An Economic Theory of Democracy* (New York: Harper & Row, 1957); Joseph Schlesinger, *Political Parties and the Winning of Office* (Ann Arbor: University of Michigan Press, 1991); Angelo Panebianco, *Political Parties: Organization and Power* (Cambridge University Press, 1988).

69. Schlesinger follows Downs in defining a party as "a team seeking to control the governing apparatus by gaining office in a duly constituted election." To anticipate the argument of later chapters, in the 1930s and 1940s the dominant "team" seeking to win national elections was a Democratic bloc that cut across institutions rather than the Democratic Party per se. Downs, *An Economic Theory of Democracy*, quoted in Schlesinger, *Political Parties and the Winning of Office*, 6.

70. Several accounts of realignment propose to give politics a significant causal role and examine the regimes between realignments. Clubb, Flanigan, and Zingale argue that a purely electoral analysis fails to grasp the broad changes that initially made the realignment concept attractive: changes in policy, styles of governmental leadership, and party ideology. Thomas Ferguson argues that the realignment approach is undermined by simplistic assumptions of voter sovereignty – focusing only on electoral data

Realignments and long economic cycles

Despite the criticisms leveled at the concept of realignment, the term and the main periodization remain valuable. In this scheme the key elections are 1828, 1860, 1896, and 1932, which delimit these periods: 1789–1820 (with 1820–8 as a sort of interregnum); 1828–60; 1860–93; 1894–1932; and 1932–?.

Burnham's account of the 1980 election and the Reagan administrations relies on a socioeconomic explanation of realignment. He stresses the erosion of America's international position and the decline of corporate profits in the United States after 1968. Clearly these events matter politically; yet Burnham and advocates of similar views have been vague about how this socioeconomic determination operates. Why do major social and economic events cause realignment only on some occasions?[71] One way to affirm a socioeconomic determination of realignment processes is to link such processes to long-term economic cycles. Burnham's claim that political realignment adapts slowly changing political institutions to rapidly developing socioeconomic relations points toward economic shifts as a source of political dynamics. Can political cycles be derived in this way? David Gordon, Richard Edwards, and Michael Reich define economic "long swings" as "... alternating periods (of approximately twenty-five years) in the world economy of vigorous and sustained economic activity, followed by equally sustained periods of stagnation."[72] Long swings include an "A" phase of expansion and a "B" phase of stagnation:

misses the large extent to which electoral patterns result from other processes. Yet these works do not provide the political analyses they propose. While Clubb and his coauthors argue for a shift in focus, their work mainly treats voting behavior. Ferguson focuses on alleged elite coalitions based on the immediate interests of industrial sectors; he opts for socioeconomic determinism to account for broad political changes. See Jerome M. Clubb, William H. Flanigan, and Nancy H. Zingale, *Partisan Realignment: Voters, Parties, and Government in American History* (New York: Sage, 1980), 16, 115, 267; Thomas Ferguson, "Party Realignment and American Industrial Structure: The Investment Theory of Political Parties in Historical Structure," in Paul Zarembka, ed., *Research in Political Economy* 6 (1983): 19–25; and "From Normalcy to New Deal: Industrial Structure, Party Competition, and American Public Policy in the Great Depression," *International Organization* 38 (Winter 1984): 41–94.

71. Burnham's earlier arguments about the modest and declining capacities of American parties suggested a political logic. As he has taken more account of economic and social factors, the causal role of political elements has diminished in ways that are theoretically problematic. Burnham, *Current Crisis,* 271.

72. David Gordon, Richard Edwards, and Michael Reich, *Segmented Work, Divided Workers: The Historical Transformation of Labor in the United States* (Cambridge University Press, 1982), 8.

IA   1790 to 1820
IB   1820 to mid-1840s
IIA   Mid-1840s to ca. 1873
IIB   Ca. 1873 to late 1890s
IIIA   Late 1890s to World War I
IIIB   World War I to World War II
IVA   World War II to early 1970s
IVB   Early 1970s to present.[73]

If political shifts occurred directly as a function of these deep economic changes, they would be most likely to occur soon after the onset of an "A" phase of expansion. Realignments would reward the organizers of economic expansion and sustain favorable conditions. But the conventional dates for realignments and the preceding periodization of long swings reveal no such pattern. In 1828, the country was well into a "B" phase of stagnation. In 1860 an "A" phase was nearing its end. In 1896 a realignment and a new "A" phase occurred at roughly the same time. In 1932 the country was deep in the midst of a gruesome "B" phase. And in 1968, which marks the beginning of a Republican regime, a new "B" phase was at hand. Thus while there is a loose fit between moments of economic and political change (three cases out of five), only in 1896 did a realignment occur at the same moment or very soon after the onset of an "A" phase of expansion. This lack of fit makes it very difficult to claim that economic long swings cause political realignments.

If it is not feasible to derive political realignments directly from economic shifts, how might political and economic changes be connected? Gordon, Edwards, and Reich use a concept of "social structure of accumulation," defined as "the specific institutional environment within which the capitalist accumulation process is organized."[74] A social structure of accumulation provides a framework for economic expansion. When capital accumulation reaches the limits of that framework, stagnation begins. Strains arise within the social structure of accumulation, encouraging experimentation. Spurred by the pressure of class struggle, some of the resulting innovations are assembled to establish a new social structure of accumulation that facilitates new growth. Self-correcting mechanisms do not avoid crises and yield smooth development because institutional factors give a cyclical form to innovation and investment.[75]

73. Gordon et al., *Segmented Work, Divided Workers*, 12.
74. Gordon et al., *Segmented Work, Divided Workers*, 9.
75. ". . . social structures of accumulation will exhibit considerable inertia, and coalitions aiming to change those institutions will emerge only slowly. As a result, capital accumulation within a given social structure of accumulation is likely to encounter

Gordon, Edwards, and Reich depict social structures of accumulation as arising almost entirely from social adaptation to economic needs.[76] Yet if they are right in their view that several economic choices are typically feasible, it is illogical to portray causality as so exclusively economic. Selection among feasible economic choices must arise from the interplay of economic and political tendencies. Long economic cycles cannot strictly determine the realignment sequence if cycles are already shaped by political elements, some of which presumably have to do with the institutions and discourses undergoing change.

Could phases between realignment be considered as social structures of accumulation? The different timing of the long swing and realignment sequences does not recommend this strategy for the twentieth century. And there is a deeper problem in treating realignment purely as a means of creating a new social structure of accumulation. Even if the causal arrow ran entirely from economic to political variables in shaping economic growth, there is more to politics than organizing and regulating the economy. The political dynamics that converge in a national regime – from cultural conflicts to distributive issues to foreign policy questions – cannot be grouped as a single functional response to economic pressures. The realignment and long swing patterns are neither identical nor linked in an obvious way. Yet it is valuable to think of a social structure of accumulation as an institutional ensemble that mediates between political and economic orders. The stress on institutional sources of economic stagnation can help to incorporate political elements in explaining economic development.

In sum, the concept of political realignment designates major changes in American political life. I will use the term and accept the claim that a major political break occurred in 1928–36. This starting point raises

diminishing returns to continuing capital investment, and this deceleration is likely to intensify until substantial adjustments in the social structure of accumulation can be made." Gordon et al., *Segmented Work, Divided Workers,* 36. For further discussion of economic long swings and their relation to social structures of accumulation, see David M. Gordon, "Inside and Outside the Long Swing: The Endogeneity/Exogeneity Debate and the Social Structures of Accumulation Approach," *Review* 14, no. 2 (Spring 1991): 263–312. I have benefited from David Gordon's comments on an earlier version of this chapter and from conversations with him about the relations between economic and political change.

76. A related neo-Marxist current proposes a significantly more economistic view than that of Gordon, Edwards, and Reich, depicting social and political development wholly as a function of the emergence and decline of regimes of accumulation. See Michel Aglietta, *A Theory of Capitalist Regulation: The US Experience* (London: New Left Books, 1979).

questions about why realignment occurred and about the shape of the new regime.[77]

Many cycles and no periods?

Accounts of American exceptionalism and organizational change help specify the discursive and institutional materials with which the Democratic order was built. Political realignment accounts provide a good map of American electoral history. Yet while interesting efforts have been made to link these theories, no existing approach to periodizing American political development is adequate for analyzing the Democratic order.[78]

Reasonable doubt about the value of periodization might have arisen over the last sections of this chapter. In viewing the big picture offered by accounts of realignment, for example, there are many problems with an image of change in which partisan, policy, and electoral shifts are abrupt, thorough, and simultaneous. Moreover, periodization schemes tend to propose reductive accounts of political development. Some American exceptionalism views reduce politics to cultural and political values. And most variants of Marxism offer a periodization in which politics reflects socioeconomic processes. Efforts at periodization are

---

77. A "regime" formulation has been made by an analyst who emphasizes the role of political power in modernization. Huntington distinguishes between party realignment (similar to critical realignment) and political realignment. He terms the latter a "fundamental restructuring of the relations between the principal social forces in society and the principal institutions in the political system. It involves changes in the powers, functions, and constituencies of governmental institutions, usually including but certainly not limited to political parties." Thus political realignments generate new regimes. Samuel Huntington, *American Politics – The Promise of Disharmony* (Cambridge, Mass.: Harvard University Press, 1981), 122.

78. Huntington, in *American Politics,* argues that American national identity is uniquely political and homogeneous. Political values are strongly democratic, and institutions necessarily fall short of these ideals. This gap makes American politics susceptible to outbursts of "creedal passion," when reforms aim to bring "political institutions and practices more into accord with liberal-democratic values and principles" (112). Huntington argues that analysts puzzled by the absence of realignment in the 1960s and 1970s looked for party realignment when they should have been looking for a broader political realignment. Their mistake is encouraged by the distinctive autonomy of American political institutions from social forces, which permits the periodic reconstitution of parties and other political institutions in response to changing social forces – without the institutions being transformed. Although this argument provides a basis for recognizing distinct regimes, political change again dissolves into a recurring cycle organized around unchanging value elements.

always marred when periods are considered as pure and uniform expressions of core elements.

Such issues make it reasonable to be reticent about periodization. Do they warrant rejecting it? If one makes that move in order to assess what happened at a particular time in a society, the result is apt to be the opposite of what was intended. Explaining what occurred will likely entail the direct application of a very general theory, calling on propositions about the nature of markets, group formation, or human needs to explain what has been richly described. Periodization – of institutions and forms of action – is necessary to specify the application of general theories and to construct coherent local theories (e.g., of family dynamics in advanced market countries).

Wary of pure description, those who reject simplistic periodizations of entire societies sometimes aim to multiply periodizations, treating all major institutions and processes in terms of their allegedly distinct logics. These are specified regarding the presidency, or modes of judicial action, or relations between party and nonparty forms of political mobilization. The premise is that each logic is distinct and complex. The task is to render as many such logics understandable as possible. As against approaches for which a period expresses an essence that defines all of political life, such a conception is appealing.[79] Yet in selecting a process or institution for historical analysis the number of candidates – institutions, practices, discourses – is almost endless. Few would propose that efforts to periodize all of them are equally important and necessary. If everything is not possible, why periodize the presidency or the party system rather than state legislatures, the coast guard, or water management systems? Unless choices about what to analyze are treated as matters of taste, they need to be grounded in judgments about the importance for overall political development of what is being studied.

Once claims about the significance of particular processes and institutions are made, to argue that something matters for political development implies that the latter has an overall shape and course. One might respond: I may not understand every aspect of political development in a given nation, but I am sure the phenomena in question (e.g., party systems or presidencies) deserve attention. But to know this requires at least a rough conception of the relation between these phenomena and others.

---

79. Martin J. Sklar proposes a sophisticated essentialist view when he periodizes American history in terms of stages of capitalism, in "Periodization and Historiography: Studying American Political Development in the Progressive Era, 1890–1916," *Studies in American Political Development* 5 (Fall 1991): 173–213.

Thus choosing to examine one major political institution or practice over time implies a conception of how the polity is organized. This is clear if one thinks about presenting the findings of any such study. Imagine that research on y has been completed (for example, the evolution of judicial decision making); it shows that y exhibits a distinct dynamic y_1. How do we explain y_1? How do we know if it is endogenously determined, rather than expressing the influence of x or z (presidential elections, or shifts in public opinion) through their own dynamics x_1 and z_1? A claim that one knows y_1 to be sufficiently autonomous and powerful to be causally significant for y implies an account of relations among diverse political institutions and practices.

Institutions and discourses are not so tightly integrated that their times are identical.[80] Yet it is possible to specify relations among their paths without taking any process as the essence of the entire complex. The result designates a period as a durable configuration of institutions and discourses that frames choices by political agents.

It might be argued that the logical possibility of periodization is no guarantee of its practicability. Perhaps the limits of what is feasible are reached by selecting major institutions and discourses, presuming their independence, and analyzing their course. This case for modesty is skeptical about overall periodization, while admitting that relations among institutions and discourses might be mapped at some point. Proponents of this view doubt that any such periodization is in sight and consider that the dangers of excessively reductive procedures make it more fruitful to consider diverse institutional trajectories as autonomous. Such resistance to periodization aspires to get some things right rather than blurring everything in grand and vague categories. Yet a persuasive account of the course of a single major institution – a judicial system or a legislature or a network of interest groups – requires a conception of its relation to other institutions and their dynamics, and implies the possibility of periodizing the polity of which it is part.

The unity achieved in constituting a period is never complete or uncontested, as periods do not express essences. Yet unity is nonetheless produced, through sustained and creative political efforts. In the 1930s, dynamic and successful efforts to build a new political order occurred in the United States. This outcome cannot be explained by the main approaches to periodizing American politics. Rational choice and Ameri-

---

80. Nancy Cott's study of feminist political and intellectual currents after World War I makes clear that phases of gender relations cannot be demarcated in precisely the same years as changes in the national political order. Nancy F. Cott, *The Grounding of Modern Feminism* (New Haven, Conn.: Yale University Press, 1987).

can exceptionalism theories find no good grounds for marking a major political break in that decade. The "organizational synthesis" defines the main political shift in American history as occurring two decades earlier. Realignment accounts are more accurate but do not adequately explain why change occurred or what resulted from it. The next chapter proposes a framework for understanding the deep political shifts through which the Democratic order emerged.

2

Creating political orders: the logic of the Democratic experience

This chapter outlines the development of the Democratic order. Analyzing the construction of a new political order in the United States in the 1930s and its endurance through the next decade requires an overall conception of how political orders are built and sustained, and why they decline. Absent such a conception, it is hard to explain the relation between the origins of the Democratic order and the end of the preceding Republican regime. And it is hard to account for the persistence of Democratic power after Roosevelt's death. Thus the argument in this chapter concerns the whole period of Democratic domination, from the 1930s through the 1960s. And it is based on a general account of political orders. Regimes, or political orders, are central in shaping political life in advanced market societies.[1] Serious conflict arises over many issues, from cultural differences to economic choices to questions about how to organize political institutions. This conflict leads to major changes that are usually combined in a new regime. The new regime defines a normal political spectrum and routine modes of competition.

In building a political order, a major mobilization of party, movement, and other forces reshapes the state and the normal terms of political argument and conflict. Yet efforts to sustain the political order yield a reliance on the state that eventually undermines the regime. This weakening occurs because the state in advanced market societies cannot

---

1. A reticence to recognize regimes in American political development is often linked to the view that political change takes place mainly as an alternation in power between moderate nonideological parties that compete to occupy the political center. Proponents of such views often hold that the success of these parties depends mainly on their capacity to deliver positive economic results – thus barring economic disaster we should expect change to appear in modest shifts around a center defined largely in terms of economic performance. For such views the most influential work remains Anthony Downs, *An Economic Theory of Democracy* (New York: Harper & Row, 1957).

fully replace nonstate forms of political support. It cannot directly create new parties, labor or professional associations, or communal groups, though it can sometimes encourage such efforts. Alongside this dynamic, a political order usually encourages economic development that first strengthens it. Over time, however, the resulting social and economic changes erode the political order's initial bases of support, through reordering industries, cities, and regions.

This view of political orders frames my account of the Democratic order, which dominated political life for four decades in the United States. It was established in the 1930s through creative leadership by progressive liberals (including such figures as Senator Robert Wagner, Harold Ickes, Felix Frankfurter, and Franklin Roosevelt) in conjunction with emergent political forces in the Democratic Party, the unions, and other organizations and movements. The state was responsible for extensive economic regulation and expanded social welfare provision. The new political order encouraged political action and interest group organization by previously excluded groups.

Political reliance on a growing Democratic state produced major Democratic victories in the 1930s and 1940s – and eventually led to great vulnerability. Postwar social and economic policies eroded the initial social bases of Democratic support. Government policies aided major industrial and occupational changes and large population shifts. The coal–steel–auto complex – a source of union support and economic growth crucial to Democratic support – began to decline.

Reliance on the state for the political support needed to sustain the political order (statism) and the resulting political logic of postindustrial change were primarily responsible for ending the Democratic order in the late 1960s and early 1970s. In the last decade of the Democratic order its leaders made poor strategic choices about matters directly related to the core dynamics of the political order and about other major issues of the day. The worst was made of several very difficult situations, most dramatically with the Vietnam debacle.

The course of the Democratic order raises questions about links between domestic politics and international political and economic relations.[2] In general, domestic dynamics are primary in shaping domestic outcomes and policies, while international relations have an auxiliary

---

2. I considered dropping the term "Democratic order" because it suggests a greater role for the Democratic Party than was the case. But the term is worth keeping. It retains an association with party-centered accounts of American politics while pointing beyond them – there was not only the Democratic Party, but a Democratic state and closely linked Democratic organizations. "Democratic order" also draws attention to questions about whether themes and practices are democratic.

role. Domestic political dynamics also play a significant role in shaping foreign policies and intrastate relations. The Democratic order's internationalism, framed in progressive liberal terms, played a major role in expanding American international power and activities. International developments from the late 1930s into the early 1960s mainly had the effect of strengthening the regime, crucially through the outcome of World War II and the postwar shape of the international political economy. Yet a dynamic of overcommitment arose from Democratic international policies and led to grave problems in the 1960s.

In my account political institutions and discourses are causally important for both political and socioeconomic outcomes. It would misrepresent things badly to imagine that everyone but old-fashioned Marxists takes politics seriously as a causal force. Many influential theories view politics as having little causal weight for either political or socioeconomic processes, and attribute political results mainly to economic or social psychological factors. Thus theories of politics based on neoclassical economics depict political outcomes as the result of economic action, with political institutions playing a subsidiary role.[3]

There are several theoretical sources for asserting the causal importance of politics. Antonio Gramsci's writings are one referent.[4] He analyzed the political convulsions that shook Europe from World War I and the Russian Revolution to the rise of fascism in Italy and elsewhere. In this setting he conceived politics as having a creative and transformative character. Gramsci's main insights are condensed in the concepts of hegemony and historical bloc.[5] "Hegemony" designates a process of

3. Taking political institutions into account is a recent move in economic theories of politics. A central problem for such efforts is to explain why inefficient political institutions would survive competitive pressures. If the answer is that inefficient institutions will not survive for long, political institutions have only a mediating role in the expression of economic tendencies. If there are powerful independent reasons for this survival, the notion of a mainly economic theory of politics becomes problematic.

4. Why not start before Gramsci, with the Marxist tradition in general? Key Marxist claims about politics are unacceptable, while most of what is valuable in that tradition remains in Gramsci. Marx stressed the role of politics in social transformation, and linked politics to class and economic forces in a powerful master argument. Yet his main accounts of politics reduce the political scene to the representation of class forces, which in turn are mainly determined by socioeconomic relations.

5. Gramsci depicts hegemony as a political effort: "to gain the upper hand, to propagate itself throughout society – bringing about not only a unison of economic and political aims, but also intellectual and moral unity, posing all the questions around which the struggle rages not on a corporate but on a 'universal' plane, and thus creating the hegemony of a fundamental social group over a series of subordinate groups." He argues that the "Modern Prince" (a communist party) is: "the proclaimer and organizer of an intellectual and moral reform, which also means creating the terrain for a

political leadership in shaping social relations; thus one can periodize social formations on the basis of successive forms of hegemony. Perhaps the best known use of this concept in studies of American politics is Eugene Genovese's work on the antebellum South.[6] "Historical bloc" denotes a fusion of political and socioeconomic elements in a process that aggregates and transforms them. The result is a new and dynamic political force, represented dramatically by the Italian Resistance during World War II or in a less turbulent form by the construction of ruling social democratic forces in several Northern European countries in the 1940s and 1950s.[7]

The rich concepts of hegemony and historical bloc treat politics as causally powerful. Yet Gramsci leaves key analytical and normative problems unresolved. For example, the concept of hegemony includes a notion of consent, as against views of political leadership as pure domination. Sometimes Gramsci depicts this consent as relatively active and reasoned, by contrast with most Marxist theories of ideology or Foucauldian theories of discourse. But the nature of the consent that accompanies force in the process of hegemony is never really clear. Here as elsewhere Gramsci's writings offer valuable theoretical proposals rather than an adequate framework for exploring relations between politics and other social processes.[8]

subsequent development of the national-popular collective will towards the realisation of a superior, total form of modern civilisation." Antonio Gramsci, *Selections from the Prison Notebooks of Antonio Gramsci*, Quintin Hoare and Geoffrey Nowell Smith, eds. and trans. (New York: International Publishers, 1971): 182, 132–33.

6. Eugene Genovese, *The World the Slaveowners Made* (New York: Pantheon Books, 1969); and *Roll, Jordan, Roll* (New York: Pantheon Books, 1974).

7. On Scandinavian social democracy and social democracy in general, see Walter Korpi, *The Democratic Class Struggle* (London/Boston: Routledge and Kegan Paul, 1983); John Stephens, *The Transition From Capitalism to Socialism* (Highlands, N.J.: Humanities Press, 1980); and Gosta Esping-Andersen, *Politics Against Markets: The Social Democratic Road to Power* (Princeton, N.J.: Princeton University Press, 1985).

8. Gramsci's analyses contain both reductionist and nonreductionist elements, and show at most a partial awareness of the authoritarian elements of Leninism. Gramsci, *Prison Notebooks*, 365–6. A number of other accounts of politics make contributions where Gramsci's revised Marxism is inadequate. Jurgen Habermas has for several decades criticized the Marxist reduction of interaction to labor while proposing a concept of communicative interaction as uncoerced dialogue oriented toward understanding. See Jurgen Habermas, *Theory and Practice* (Boston: Beacon Press, 1973); *Legitimation Crisis* (Boston: Beacon Press, 1975); *Communication and the Evolution of Society* (Boston: Beacon Press, 1979); "A Reply to My Critics," in *Habermas: Critical Debates*, John B. Thompson and David Held, eds. (Cambridge, Mass.: MIT Press, 1982): 219–83; and *The Theory of Communicative Action*, Vol. 1 (Boston: Beacon Press, 1987). Earlier, Talcott Parsons distinguished between politics as an analytical element of all social settings, and political institutions as sites where politics predominates. He argued

Politics in advanced market societies

The following claims about politics refer to advanced market or advanced capitalist social formations, not nonmarket societies or all capitalist societies.[9] In economic terms, "capitalist" means production for the market based on wage labor and private ownership of major resources. "Advanced" designates high levels of productivity, complex technologies, and large economic units. The empirical contrast is between the countries of Western Europe, North America, and Japan on the one hand, and on the other, the few remaining state socialist countries as well as less developed market societies in Asia, Africa, and elsewhere.

Politically, "advanced" denotes a state capable of broad intervention in socioeconomic relations. It signifies operative citizenship rights for the great majority of the adult population. Socially, "advanced" means institutional differentiation and diversity. Culturally, it means widespread individualism and a broad commitment to rational action. These elements combine, in relations of mutual determination, to provide a concept of advanced market society.

What is politics? Politics is the directive, guiding element of a social formation. Politics appears in institutional and discursive forms, irreducible to any single location (party, state, or ideology).

Power is the capacity to articulate and realize goals, including efforts made against direct opposition. Thus political power is the capacity to achieve goals in organizing and directing social relations. In this sense

in favor of a non-zero sum conception of political power, a view suggested but not elaborated in Gramsci's work. See "On the Concept of Political Power," in Talcott Parsons, *Politics and Social Structure* (New York: Free Press, 1969), 371–96.

9. There are good but not decisive reasons for avoiding the term "capitalist" altogether. The term is problematic for those who believe the social forms of post-World War II OECD countries are the only ones compatible with advanced modernity. It also troubles those who wish to build market societies on the ruins of state socialism in Eastern Europe and the Soviet Union, but who are not eager to recreate some of the characteristic problems of Western capitalism. A third objection might be that my claims are not easily evaluated regarding an advanced society that contains extensive markets but is not capitalist. The first two objections to the term "capitalism" have more political than analytical force. The third refers to a society that so far is nonexistent. If there were such a society, the arguments made here would apply to it because of the likely separation of state from society, limits on state action, and good prospects of political opposition. A fourth objection, probably the most compelling, is that "capitalist" includes so many forms of economic organization as to have little specificity. Yet the term retains enough analytical meaning about property and labor relations to make it useful, though I will mainly use "advanced market" to designate OECD-type social formations.

we can consider that the Conservative Party in Britain was politically powerful in the 1980s, or that American business created a powerful political force in that and the preceding decade, without conceiving this power as total domination or as primarily coercive.[10]

Political goals are partly constituted through the dialogues and strategic interaction of politics. They are not fixed interests given by structural positions. Such positions can only provide a starting point for politics. Thus the extent to which political forces articulate class themes and seek to represent class forces varies among advanced market societies. There is in principle nothing surprising about the fact that class has often played a more prominent and explicit role in politics in Italy than the United States or that regional questions figure more prominently as political matters in Britain than Sweden or Japan. Significant political forces can be constructed with respect to numerous social relations, such as gender, race, region, or economic sector.

Politics includes coercion and consent – political power is both power "over" and power "to." The relation between coercion and consent varies within limits: A permanent authoritarian organization of politics is unworkable, as it violates cultural norms, provokes fierce political opposition, and yields deep economic problems. Even brief efforts at authoritarian control of political and economic affairs meet sharp and usually effective resistance. Yet without a possible resort to coercion, many social and political antagonisms might be impossible to manage. For much of the twentieth century this would have been true of labor relations in the United States, as well as of relations among racial groups.

Where is politics located? Politics is everywhere – and concentrated distinctively in a state and political system.

Politics is diffused throughout advanced market societies. There is no exclusive center of politics, and it is correct to speak of a politics of primarily nonpolitical institutions. Thus we can discuss a politics of the family, regarding how authority should be organized between genders and generations, how resources should be shared, and how competing claims on family members' time and energies should be adjudicated. Or we can analyze a politics of production, regarding how authority and control over resources are combined as tasks are allocated, rewards distributed, and conflicts within firms mediated.[11]

Yet politics is concentrated in a network of institutions and discourses

10. On the British experience, see Andrew Gamble, *The Free Economy and the Strong State: The Politics of Thatcherism* (Durham, N.C.: Duke University Press, 1988); and Joel Krieger, *Reagan, Thatcher, and the Politics of Decline* (Cambridge, England: Polity Press, 1986).

11. On the politics of contemporary family life see Susan Moller Okin, *Justice, Gender, and the Family* (New York: Basic Books, 1989); and Judith Stacey, *Brave New*

Table 2.1. *The comparative concentration and centralization of politics*

	Low concentration of politics	High concentration of politics
Low centralization of politics	Advanced market countries	LDC #1[a]
High centralization of politics	LDC #2[b]	State socialism

[a]LDC #1 refers to less developed countries where a decentralized state concentrates political power -- an unusual circumstance.
[b]LDC #2 refers to countries where a centralized state is unable to incorporate many crucial political processes, as in less developed countries with bureaucratic states and powerful oligarchies outside their reach.

in which it is the central activity. This concentration is recognized in conventional ways of talking about politics. Even those who claim to oppose its politicization speak of a politics of the family or education, while talking about a politics of parties, interest groups, or the state seems redundant. The political system always includes the state as the locus of political power – and it includes other institutions and activities where the latter are mainly concerned with organizing and directing social relations.

In comparative terms, politics in advanced market societies is relatively dispersed. Political processes – dialogues and decisions about how to organize social relations – are diffused through several levels of the political system and into economic and social institutions (see Tables 2.1 and 2.2). The concentration and centralization of politics vary among advanced market societies regarding the extent to which political power operates through political institutions and the degree to which political power is condensed at the top of national polities.

With respect to centralization, in all advanced market societies the national state controls the use of military force in interstate relations. Yet there is always some decentralization among political units, its extent varying widely. Much contemporary debate concerns the extent to which politics is and should be concentrated in political institutions.

Families: Stories of Domestic Upheaval in Late Twentieth Century America (New York: Basic Books, 1990). On the politics of production, see Charles Sabel, *Work and Politics: The Division of Labor in Industry* (Cambridge University Press, 1982); and Michael Burawoy, *The Politics of Production* (London: Verso, 1985).

Table 2.2. *The concentration and centralization of politics in advanced market countries*

	Low concentration of politics	High concentration of politics
Low centralization of politics	United States	Italy
High centralization of politics	Japan	France

At one boundary, no state in advanced market societies can directly and fully incorporate the politics of the economy (or the family, or other institutions). Many significant decisions about the organization and direction of social relations occur outside the political system. Yet no state parcels out control over legitimate violence in a routine way. In fact, any significant dispersal of legal authority – derived from the political legitimacy of the regime – is carefully supervised. And despite the blurred boundaries between the political system and other institutions (e.g., in public enterprises, regulatory practices, universities), no advanced market society is close to a situation where political power is evenly distributed across institutions.

These are wide boundaries, and advanced market societies are placed differently within them. There are pressures both for and against the concentration of politics. Barriers to a full inclusion of economic units and the market in the political system derive largely from objections to the inefficiencies expected to result if the state takes over economic activities. These objections concern the absence of market constraints on grossly inefficient choices and the costs entailed when the state tries to administer the complex political processes already present in the economy, such as those among groups of employees in firms or among firms in regions and sectors. Strong fears also exist that any form of state expansion, even when the immediate results are mainly positive, will spur the growth of inefficient modes of state control. Yet market disorganization, demands for regulation, and international pressures all encourage state interventions that move political decisions into the political system.[12]

Political pressures affecting the concentration of politics also exist.

12. Market disorganization spurs participants to seek governmental aid to achieve stability. Market failures spur citizens to seek government aid in coping with externali-

Deep liberal commitments, often imbedded in constitutional provisions, pose major obstacles to political concentration. Yet efforts by political actors to achieve policy objectives can encourage political concentration in many areas, from foreign policy to social welfare provision.[13] There is no single equilibrium where all advanced market societies come to rest amid these pressures. The distinction between political centralization and concentration is important for actual political forces, who may favor a centralization of power at the top of national institutions while preferring a dispersal of political power at that level toward labor, professional, and business associations.[14]

What is the relationship between politics and other social practices? Politics helps determine central features of the other main elements of advanced market societies – political processes are independent variables. Politics also helps to produce political and socioeconomic outcomes. The effects of politics range from regulating existing relationships to creative intervention that establishes new institutions such as public corporations. While the government cannot dictate winners in every economic competition, nor simply mandate an overall course of economic development, it can bestow important advantages on enterprises and regions. It can use its tax, spending, and other policies to influence the forms and location of investment. To take an example from another area, government action helps to define particular family forms as more or less attractive and feasible.[15]

These points imply further claims. First, political change occurs as an

ties. And firms, labor organizations, and local governments seek state protection from international competition or help in taking advantage of international opportunities.

13. Foreign policy is an evident case of concentration – as well as centralization – given the concept of sovereignty and the immediacy of issues about the control of legitimate violence. Regarding social welfare provision, proponents of its expansion and advocates of cutting it back in the United States both advocate using government power to achieve their objectives. See David Ellwood, *Poor Support: Poverty in the American Family* (New York: Basic Books, 1988); and Charles Murray, *Losing Ground – American Social Policy 1950–1980* (New York: Basic Books, 1984).

14. One can define several normative positions by how they combine preferences on these dimensions of organizing politics. To take the boundary cases: A simultaneous preference for extreme decentralization and extreme dispersal of political power is expressed by most variants of anarchism. A strong corporatist view proposes to combine a high degree of centralization with considerable dispersal of political power to national associations not formally part of the state. A local republicanism advocates the reverse, to concentrate power in political institutions while decentralizing the latter. And various forms of Jacobin politics propose both to centralize and concentrate political power.

15. On the political dimension of economic organization see Fred Block, *Postindustrial Possibilities: A Critique of Economic Discourse* (Berkeley: University of California Press, 1990).

endogenous dynamic. Political efforts can generate new elements not reducible to extrapolitical sources, as when conflict among party factions leads to changes in party forms.

Second, as politics is about how to organize social relations, it must be discursive as well as institutional. Because political actors have substantive aims which motivate their actions, discourses about the nation, or race, or equality can have causal power regarding individual choices and then political outcomes. Consequently, political change is unlikely to be explained well by models that neglect the causal role of discursive elements or treat them in purely strategic terms.

Third, politics creates political subjects. If political relations have an internal dynamic, that dynamic can reshape political forces as they ally and conflict. Thus new forces can be built through politics; they are not determined by the shape of class or other social or economic relations.[16] Major political efforts usually entail a definition of aims and commitments, not just their announcement in a new setting. For example, in the United States the Progressive movement in the early twentieth century and the civil rights movement in the 1960s and 1970s drew on and interpreted important social experiences. Through political engagement previous aims were modified or even rejected and new aims were defined. In the emergence of political orders, political forces may change their initial views substantially, partly through dialogue and negotiation with other elements of the new bloc.

In sum, politics is the directive, organizing element of a society. It is creative and transformative in coordinating social and economic relationships and stimulating new patterns. Politics plays a central role in defining distinct periods of social development.

Is this view of politics too voluntaristic? Does it imply, for example, that any political force can be constructed at any time? My claim is not that anything is always possible, but that building political forces entails a substantially political causality. Limits are posed by the orientations and capacities of political forces, as well as by social and economic

---

16. The term "representation" is often used in ways that understate the transformative side of the appearance of political forces. It implies that a group already formed in a social or economic location (in industry or ethnic relations) then appears in politics. This is clearest in fiduciary notions of representation, which can be translated easily into the contemporary language of principal–agent relations. Yet entering the political scene will often cause the preferences of principals to undergo significant changes. On representation and deliberation, see Hannah Pitkin, *The Concept of Representation* (Berkeley: University of California Press, 1967); and Joshua Cohen, "Deliberation and Democratic Legitimacy," in Alan Hamlin and Philip Pettit, eds., *The Good Polity: Normative Analysis of the State* (London: Basil Blackwell, 1989), 17–34.

relations. Thus it is possible to show that in Canada there is no chance of building a significant neofascist or communist political force in the 1990s; or that making a major liberal force into a social democratic movement is improbable in the United States in this decade.

The main concept I use to develop the preceding arguments is political order. A political order is a durable national mode of organizing and directing social relations in advanced market societies. It designates continuities in the scope and forms of the state and of party politics, the shape of nonparty political agents, and the character of political discourses. Relations among these elements vary across political orders, especially regarding the role of parties and nonparty political forces. Political orders vary in their stability, durability, and capacities, and these qualities do not always go together.[17] Thus one can claim that the postwar Christian Democratic regime in Italy was durable and the Conservative political order in Britain has been powerful without claiming they were similarly distinguished in terms of other attributes. The Conservative regime is unlikely to last nearly as long as the Italian regime, which was durable yet often unstable.

Political orders can be destroyed and replaced within more enduring institutional and discursive frameworks. Thus the new political order in the United States in the 1930s did not replace the constitutional system. Nor did the Thatcherite regime rupture the British political system.

Must a political order always exist? Political orders are usually present in advanced capitalist societies, but there are phases of stagnation and instability when no regime seems to exist. Such moments do not immediately result in utter social disorder because enduring institutional and cultural forms can survive the decay of particular regimes. But the rewards to those who establish a new regime and the mounting costs of instability spur efforts to form a new political order.

The concept of political order aims to incorporate and restate two concepts that it resembles: regime and hegemony. "Regime" denotes patterned ways of organizing and defining political commitments, political norms, decision-making procedures, and modes of intervention into socioeconomic relations. It draws attention to durable ways of linking major institutions and discourses, and highlights the political conflicts entailed in creating those links. Yet there are problems with the conventional uses of "regime," which often connotes political rigidity and an

---

17. A full comparative account of political orders would relate these attributes to institutional and discursive configurations, yielding such claims as: The greater the role of nonparty political forces in a political order, the less likely it is for that order to be stable.

authoritarian domination of social life. The term has also been used loosely to designate any configuration of power (an educational regime, a labor regime, and so forth). I will use "regime" much less than political order.[18]

Gramsci's "hegemony" can be used to convey a sense of political dynamism that "regime" often does not express. It also underlines the complex interweaving of consent and coercion that occurs in political orders in liberal polities. "Hegemony" can point to the creative and transformative dimension of politics; I will sometimes use that term to designate the construction and maintenance of a political order.[19]

In advanced market societies political processes are linked together in political orders.[20] This integration is never total or completely stable. First, no political order exhausts politics in a society, as there remain significant political processes in mainly nonpolitical institutions. Second, nothing guarantees that the times of diverse fields of social relations (of gender, region, or religion) be precisely synchronized, even if a national regime can establish outer limits of variance. Third, no political order can prevent disruptive opposition forces from making claims. Both inter-

18. The concept of regime has enjoyed a revival in studies of international relations and international political economy, where it provides a conceptual point of reference for analysts who resist conceiving international relations entirely in terms of economic metaphors. Krasner defines a regime as "principles, norms, rules, and decision-making procedures around which actor expectations converge in a given issue area." Krasner says that regimes arise from self-interest, political power, diffuse norms and principles, custom, and knowledge; this list suggests that in his field the concept is burdened excessively with tasks normally undertaken by a range of sociological and political theories of institutions and discourses. Stephen Krasner, "Regimes and the Limits of Realism: Regimes as Autonomous Variables," *International Organization* 36 (1982): 497–510; reprinted in Krasner, ed., *International Regimes* (Ithaca: Cornell University Press, 1983).

19. Ernesto Laclau and Chantal Mouffe provide a provocative discussion of the concept of hegemony in *Hegemony and Socialist Strategy* (New York: Verso, 1985).

20. Political and social integration is often attributed to nonpolitical sources, either economic action or values. Yet economic action does not generate sufficient cooperation to yield stability and values do not interpret and enforce themselves. For others, no durable political and social integration occurs; some claim even the appearance of "society" is illusory. To reject the concept of integration depends on boldly overstating several valid points: Advanced market societies are complex and heterogeneous, and political and social conflict is permanent and open. Seamless and perfect social integration never occurs. Yet if social formations were not significantly integrated, and societies did not really exist, it would be unnecessary and perhaps incomprehensible to say so. For an influential attempt to derive social order from individual economic action, see Robert Axelrod, *The Evolution of Cooperation* (New York: Basic Books, 1984). For a sophisticated discussion of the alleged impossibility of society, see Ernesto Laclau, *New Reflections on the Revolution of Our Time* (New York: Verso, 1990).

nal conflicts and changing environments ensure new challenges. These factors do not prevent political orders from enduring, often for decades. But such regimes are projects that always need to undergo change, and never attain total control of their polities.

The dynamic of political orders

The concept of political order aims to periodize political development and specify relations among political processes. To formulate a model of political change focused on that concept I have adapted and reformulated elements of several approaches.[21] The following model of the rise and decline of political orders contains four phases.

Phase one: Building a political order

In the first phase, a political order is in a crisis that makes its maintenance problematic (as with the Labor political order in Britain in the 1970s). To create a new political order requires a political leadership with the programmatic and ideological ability to address the problems that confounded the old order, as well as popular opposition to that regime.

An insurgent political leadership attacks the old order and mobilizes support for new initiatives. This process usually reshapes the prospective leadership of a new regime. Gaining support for a new course also entails the emergence of new collective political identities and orientations. At the founding moment, high levels of political mobilization accompany the creation of new political identities – such as that of a Christian Democratic worker, a progressive Democratic professional, or a Republican evangelical.

The new order emerges both in thematic commitments and distinctive relations among the state, a leading political party (or parties), and interest groups and social movements. Varied political agents – parties, interest groups, civic and professional associations, social movements,

---

21. From Burnham and Key, I take the idea that major shifts in American politics occur in phases of realignment. I reinterpret the concept of social structure of accumulation proposed by Gordon and his coauthors to signify institutions and practices that mediate between political and economic orders. I transpose elements of Mancur Olson's argument about the negative effects of interest group activity from an economic to a political terrain. Olson argues that in extended periods of political stability and freedom of association, self-interested individuals generate institutions that limit innovation and impede growth. Mancur Olson, *The Rise and Decline of Nations* (New Haven, Conn.: Yale University Press, 1982), 74, 84, 107.

and state agencies – perform the activities that build and sustain the new order.

Providing political support has four main elements. Support must be *recruited;* individuals and groups must be persuaded to support and even identify with the political order, creating political attachments. Supporters must be *organized* to make their preferences politically relevant – the party is the classical instrument. For organization to be effective, those who support the political order must be *mobilized* to take salient actions, from voting to making financial contributions and attending public events.[22] And those who support the political order must be *educated* about the political situation and persuaded to help support it. There is a continual need to reinterpret the basic commitments of the regime in the light of new internal and external challenges.

In this first phase, a party (or parties) and movements are active in all aspects of providing political support, especially in organizing and mobilizing. Vigorous and extensive political efforts occur, from electoral campaigns to demonstrations and strikes. The state helps secure conditions in which party and movement forces can engage in such activities, whether they be efforts to gain civil rights, establish unions, or oppose busing to integrate schools. Political support is recruited and educated as regime leaders advocate and implement new programs and policies. Much practical persuasion goes on in delivering services and benefits.

Yet there are already limits to what the state can do in organizing and mobilizing political support. Major cultural and political barriers rule out state-run mass political or social organizations, like those in fascist, authoritarian corporatist, or state socialist regimes with their state parties, youth organizations, women's organizations, and communal associations. States in advanced market societies can confer major benefits by recognizing nonstate political groups, but they cannot simply create effective groups, much less compel participation.[23] In this phase constraints on state action do not pose basic problems for the political

22. Organization and mobilization can occur simultaneously, but that is not necessarily the case. For example, mass political parties or trade unions may enroll large memberships, yet be unable to mobilize this membership effectively even for voting. Alternatively, a party or political movement may have few means of durably organizing its supporters but be able to mobilize them powerfully at selected moments, provided the aims are relatively clear. Thus populist movements can mobilize substantial forces with little organization.

23. The distinction between aiding nonstate political forms and literally creating them was sometimes blurred in the discussion of corporatism in the 1970s and 1980s. The result was to overstate what the state could do, by considering instances of state support for interest groups and associations as constitutive acts. Philippe Schmitter and Gerhard Lehmbruch, *Patterns of Corporatist Policy-Making* (London/Beverly Hills: Sage Publications, 1982).

order. A vital party and movements organize and mobilize support. This action is required partly to defeat two likely adversaries: loyalists of the old order, and opponents of that order who also reject the developing regime.[24]

If attempts to found a political order occur in the stagnation phase of an economic long swing, the emergence of the new order requires preventing further deterioration and proposing a credible plan of economic renewal. Relations between the political order and socioeconomic processes can then become a major source of political support. The regime is credited with encouraging an overall economic improvement – and there is also the powerful attraction of specific measures that encourage adherence by those who receive government pensions, or price subsidies, or jobs in state-sponsored industries. Gaining political support in these ways can yield impressive results – yet the separation between state and economy precludes direct state action to seize and redistribute resources. (In contrast, consider the hold on parts of the Mexican population created by the ruling party's redistribution of land, or the ability of state socialist regimes to create clients by allocating managerial positions.)

Phase two: Consolidation and maintenance

In the second phase, new state–party–movement relationships are sustained, amidst lower levels of mobilization and a greater political role for the state. Basic institutional and discursive continuities link phases one and two. Yet the high levels of mobilization of phase one decline, as cultural complexity and institutional differentiation impede party and movement efforts to mobilize. Many who were active in building the political order prefer alternatives to continual intensive political mobilization, which they find in work and professional projects, family life, or religion. Moreover, political mobilization is costly (in time and re-

---

24. As loyalists of the old order are apt to retain positions of strength in the state administration, courts, and legislative bodies, further conflicts arise over reforming state activities. The stickiness of elements of the old political order is due both to institutional differentiation and liberal discourses. The new political order encompasses a wide array of agencies, whose employees (appointed by the prior regime) have local and technical knowledge that often precludes dismissing them. And there are often procedural safeguards against acts of purely political exclusion. Ironically, this stickiness tends to enhance the prospects that a new regime will be formed when an old one is far into its decline. The reason is that partisans of the old order who are still in legislatures and administrative positions do not believe that even a wrenching political defeat must result in the total destruction of their careers (or in broad political repression). If those active in the old political order feared that its demise would mean their political death they might do everything possible to continue, making regime change more turbulent and difficult.

sources) and sometimes risky for individuals. And the successes attained in establishing the political order may make continued energetic political action seem less attractive (i.e., groups have trouble sustaining commitment from individuals who achieve much of what they initially aimed to achieve).

Party and movement forces continue, retaining some of their dynamism from the previous phase. If the political order appears to be in jeopardy, major episodes of renewal can occur, as in the United States in 1947–9. The state is now more active in recruiting and educating new political forces while parties and movements are less active in mobilizing and organizing. The state can partly compensate for this decline through its indirect contributions to mobilizing and organizing. Thus when government policies create new homeowners or increase pensions, the recipients may be responsive to organizing and mobilizing efforts that the state itself cannot make.

The state's growing role in the activities that maintain the new order is rooted in the strategies of political actors who act in accord with proregime commitments. These actors' choices both express substantive aims and lead toward increasing reliance on the state. The state is an obvious and acceptable place to turn for further support to advance their projects and defend their positions. This turn toward the state is encouraged by public statements and appeals from elected and appointed officials, the distribution of services and contracts, popular identification with successful policies, and the diffuse but substantial benefits of the state's legitimacy. Proregime actors have recent experiences of the wisdom of this course, as the state's aid probably helped to secure their political standing.

Relying on the state also seems less costly and risky than the alternatives. Large, intense party and movement efforts are hard to sustain for long periods or to renew quickly. The costs of obtaining political resources from the state seem smaller than those required by major new mobilization and recruitment efforts. The latter demand extensive resources, and they are dangerous: Too vigorous a mobilization can destabilize prior agreements and spur a counterattack, while insufficient mobilization weakens the position of those leading it. For example, a local leader of the regime party who faces an electoral challenge might try to meet it by rebuilding a strong organization. Or he or she could seek to publicize the virtues of the national administration, while encouraging that administration (and its nearest local representatives) to distribute benefits for electoral purposes and to speak directly to the citizenry on behalf of the political order. If there were no constraints on time and resources, doing both would be desirable. In reality most local leaders will choose to rely on the state.

To take another example: A local union leadership faces a recalcitrant company that repeatedly violates labor laws. The choices are to rebuild a militant union local capable of waging energetic battles in the workplace, or to ask a sympathetic local government to pressure the company to comply with the law. While some workplace pressure may be necessary, the case for relying on the state is again compelling, given the dangers of open and uncontrolled confrontation with the company.

As these examples indicate, choices in favor of relying on the state not only make strategic sense: They are attractive because the state is identified with the policies of the new political order. The driving force is political actors' efforts to gain their political objectives.

In this phase the political order's relations with socioeconomic processes are a source of strength, so long as the regime provides economic stability. If stability leads to real growth, so much the better. The political order gains recruits from those who perceive conditions to have improved, and from those who anticipate further improvement. Those who helped found the political order are rewarded by policies that deliver benefits via tax policies, service provision, and investment. The political order is constrained by the need to sustain business confidence. Here the separation of state and economy strongly discourages measures that might be briefly popular but would jeopardize investment, such as expropriations and large-scale transfers of productive resources.

Phase three: Maintenance and emergent statism

Amid the relative stability of phases two and three, many phenomena appear for which analyses of political action as strategic economic action are pertinent. In these normal times, political and ideological parameters seem fixed, and actors pursue their already-defined interests within them.

The key feature in distinguishing the third phase from the second is that reliance on the state has now proceeded so far as to become a central element of the political order. Reasonable political choices by supporters and leaders of the regime aimed at sustaining its institutions and principles have augmented the role of the state greatly in relation to other components of the political order. The result is a net decline in the potential political support available to the political order, especially in organization and mobilization.[25]

<hr />

25. I benefit from Offe and Wiesenthal's revision of Mancur Olson's view of collective action. See Claus Offe and Helmut Wiesenthal, "Two Logics of Collective Action: Theoretical Notes on Social Class and Organizational Form," *Political Power and Social Theory* 1 (1980): 76, 79. This essay also appears in Claus Offe, *Disorganized Capitalism: Contemporary Transformations of Work and Politics* (Cambridge, Mass.: MIT Press, 1985): 170–220.

This statist evolution does not preclude major successes, as the state remains powerful and popular, but it does limit the political order's capacities for renewal. Though the main features of the political order persist, decisions to rely on the state's resources and capacities yield a decline in the organizing and mobilizing capacities of the party and "old" movements. Cultural and political barriers block explicit state efforts to replace these capacities. As before, the state cannot compel membership in proregime parties or associations, and has even less prospect of constituting effective new state-sponsored groups. Reliance on the state now also poses barriers to entry for potential new political forces. Entering a national regime requires extensive resources. Moreover, new forces may find little space open to them in a political order whose leading positions are firmly occupied.

In this setting, there are major obstacles to overcoming the problems produced by relying on the state. To redistribute positions of power requires one of two unlikely conditions: a general willingness to sacrifice by many elements in the dominant bloc or a proregime leadership with enough foresight and power to impose compromise. For the first alternative, major groups in the political order must be willing to share their positions. "Old" party elites must turn over some of their power and positions to insurgents. Previously dominant ethnic or racial groups must do the same with respect to new groups when the latter affirm their commitment to the principles of the political order. And entrenched unions or business associations must embrace new partners and relinquish part of their influence over government policies, hoping to preserve the core of their positions over the long term. Few examples of such generous farsightedness come to mind. If the political order seems able to continue, most in positions of power will prefer to retain their positions rather than sacrifice part of them to strengthen the regime.

The second road to renewal features a leadership group in the political order with the foresight and power to force the incorporation of new political forces. Yet it is rare for a coherent and autonomous leadership to arise that is not greatly constrained by organizational and ideological ties to the same groups – in the leading party, state administration, or key associations – who would be required to give up positions to new entrants. Leading groups in a political order are also apt to reinterpret original commitments in ways that discourage innovation. Key principles may be taken to mean respect for the claims of a particular political group, with a major ethnic, religious, or occupational dimension. Equity, for example, may be understood as dutiful attention to the social and political claims of established ethnic groups. Requests for special consideration by newer ethnic groups may then seem illegitimate to the leaders of a political order, even as they seem reasonable for prospective entrants who hear the regime's general statements as an invitation to press their claims.

The permanence of political competition means that leadership in a political order does not confer unilateral power to allocate positions within it among contending groups. Leadership groups need to sustain and renew their support, not issue commands and proclamations. Simply to reallocate positions to new groups risks provoking the departure of partners and allies, with no guarantee that concessions to these new groups will sustain their adherence.

One way out of this tangle is the political equivalent of printing money: to expand the state further, so new groups can be incorporated without redistributing existing positions. Thus new government agencies can be opened to delay or soften collisions between old and prospective adherents of the political order. If important positions are created and new groups gain a significant portion of them, blockage at the top can be mitigated for a period by this approach. Then conflict over positions and access to decision making is apt to reappear, with elements of new groups now inside the regime and able to press their claims even more strongly. This course increases the political order's reliance on the state, because state resources are essential in starting major new projects (as in urban affairs, or economic and social regulation, or aiding regional development).

In this third phase another tension emerges: The economic achievements of the political order have reduced the prospects of political support, even if social change and economic growth still enhance immediate political prospects. Economic development in phases two and three usually erodes social groups that helped provide the basis for political forces central to the new political order. Economic development redistributes the population, disrupting communities that supported the political order. Growth changes the occupational and sectoral shape of the workforce, reducing the weight of groups initially allied with the political order. These processes have been widespread in OECD countries since World War II, as economic development has weakened the positions of farmers, small business owners, miners, industrial workers, and other groups important in various political orders.

When economic achievements undermine the political order, the state–economy separation and the dynamic of business confidence limit strategies of renovation. There are immense barriers to seizing resources to gain immediate political support (e.g., confiscating a major corporation and awarding it to friends of the regime, or taking over private housing to offer it to prospective supporters). Every political order faces a question: To what extent should its economic and social policies be clientelistic, as against efforts to enhance overall development? The political costs of pure clientelism can be large when it appears to come at the expense of a broader advance. Yet a less clientelistic policy requires hard decisions that hurt favored groups and entail political risks, as in farm, labor market, tax, and trade policies.

In phase three the political order persists amid growing tensions. One possible course is renewal through a new phase of party- and movement-based mobilization. So long as reliance on the state seems feasible, this risky course is unlikely. New political mobilization is more apt to originate when political forces taking shape outside the political order seek to enter and perhaps to reshape it. Such forces often find daunting barriers to entering the regime, which reduces the chance that incorporation will occur in a dynamic and positive way. Given this likely blockage and the other problems noted above, the tensions of phase three usually lead to the deterioration of the political order.

Phase four: Decay and decline

In phase four the political order is greatly weakened. Its persistence is in question, and normal political routines are disrupted. The long-term result of reasonable efforts to sustain the political order has been the atrophy of nonstate modes of political support. Yet the political order's leadership (in state and party institutions and allied interest groups) can still limit access by new forces.

New movements and interest groups mobilize, partly in response to social and economic change. Their legitimacy can usually be defended in terms of the norms of the political order. Yet there is no repetition of phase one, when emergent movements could gain positions and shape the main themes of a new regime. New forces are simultaneously encouraged to seek access to the political order and blocked. Factional conflict is likely inside the political order between those committed to its present forms and those more concerned with incorporating new groups.

At such a juncture, efforts by elites in the political order to reach over this blockage to renew the regime through a mobilization of current and prospective supporters do not often occur and rarely succeed. As in previous phases, the regime's leaders cannot directly substitute the state for parties and movements, even when the executive has great powers of persuasion and administrative capacities have grown. Further, several power centers now exist in the political order and compete for its leadership. No single force can simply impose its choices.

A coalition among powerful groups aimed at renewal by reaching over the web of groups and institutions at the top of the political order is also unlikely. The main problem is not free riding by prospective partners, such as party factions. Rather, possible coalition members will be deeply ambivalent about the substance of any renewal and the means of attaining it. Prospective coalition members may reject the new themes that appear. They may fear (with good reason) the disruption that attends factional conflict. Especially if such conflict involves a wide mobilization, it may lead to electoral defeat (partly because disruption reduces the flow of benefits to constituencies). Thus, sections of a national regime's leadership might want to force local party organizations to incorporate new groups but fear that doing so would damage local government and harm the political order's candidates.

Long-term shifts in political and economic relationships are now apt to have strongly negative effects. Social and economic change has dispersed and reduced the social forces from which the political order initially drew its main support. Political blockage limits the incorporation of new socioeconomic groups. For example, the trouble that Democrats in the United States or Labor in Britain had in gaining political support from new social layers between the industrial working class and the professional middle classes in the 1960s and 1970s intensified the problems of each political order. By now it is little comfort that such problems stem largely from prior policy achievements, as in sustaining employment growth, expanding exports through trade policies, or encouraging regional development. If economic stagnation marks this fourth phase, conflicts increase among groups linked to the political order, and economic disarray reduces any chance of recruiting new support.[26]

Together these political and economic processes put the regime in a precarious situation. There are four possible outcomes. The political order might be renewed, as envisioned by Robert Kennedy in the United States in 1968. A new political order might promptly replace it, as seems to have occurred in the shift from Labor to Conservative predominance in Britain. In a third case, no new political order emerges for a sustained period, and the resulting instability is contained by basic political institutions and discourses. Finally, the end of a political order might yield the collapse of basic constitutional institutions and political discourses. This

---

26. Thus economic downturns influence political orders in different ways depending not only on their severity but on the phase of the political order in which they occur. There is a boundary to this variance: After the formation of a political order sustained depression conditions will always be destructive. And no regime looks forward to economic hard times. But because economic shifts are mediated in politics by judgments of their significance, uniform negative effects should not be expected.

dire outcome has often been predicted for Italy in recent decades, but so far it has not occurred, even after the demise of the Christian Democratic Party.

Renewal and total collapse are the least likely outcomes. Renewal is blocked by the problems discussed above and most likely by the growth of opposition forces. Total collapse is prevented by the strength of political and economic commitments "beneath" particular political orders in advanced market societies. When a political order falls apart it does not automatically mean general political collapse, despite turbulence and even a degree of violence. If the end of a political order in a society seriously threatens such a collapse, this prospect indicates a lack of separation between the forms of a regime and any underlying institutional and discursive framework. This lack of separation in turn implies that commitments to a constitutional framework are not deeply held, and may reflect only ties to a particular regime.

When a political order has entered the fourth phase (of decay and decline), the probable outcomes are a rapid establishment of a new order or stagnation followed by the creation of a new regime. For either result an opposing political force must weld disparate groups into a new bloc. Potential support for an alternative may exist in elements of the conventional opposition to the political order, as with Goldwater Republicans in the 1960s and French Socialists and Communists in the 1970s. Prior supporters of the political order who split off from it may provide another resource for a new bloc, as with elements of George Wallace's northern support in the 1960s or disaffected Labor supporters in Britain in the 1970s. And support for a new regime may come from emerging social groups who have not yet attained a clear political identity (or identities), as with new middle-class groupings in many advanced market countries in the 1970s and 1980s.

Whether oppositional political forces can put a new political order in place depends both on their capacities and on how the political order declines.[27] The prospect is that a new order will be created (instead of protracted stagnation or collapse). The driving force is competition among political forces with different conceptions of how social relations should be reorganized. From among these projects, a new bloc will likely emerge. Durable blocs – such as the broad French left in the 1970s, or Thatcherism in Britain – are united by substantive commitments, not

27. For example, if a relatively strong traditional opposition remains, in rigid and uncreative forms, it may block the emergence of a viable new opposition to the political order. The prospects of rapidly forming a new order are enhanced when the prior order's decline is clear enough to pose the question of alternatives, but slow enough to allow the construction and development of new forces.

only by the promise of immediate material gains. An emerging bloc can engage in efforts to build a wider coalition. Here debate about political aims can lead to relatively sturdy agreements, rather than endless circulation among alternatives.[28]

Phase four resembles phase one: Sharp ideological battles erupt, as do conflicts over forming and maintaining collective political identities. The political spectrum splits apart, as opposed to the normal experience of stable alignments in phases two and three. Previously extreme positions can become part of the center of a redefined political spectrum, as with conservative regimes in Britain and the United States in the 1970s and 1980s.

The autonomy of politics

Core elements of advanced market societies provide conditions for a relatively orderly change of regimes, mainly by limiting or ruling out many of the strategies available to the leaders of a political order who might be tempted to try to dictate its persistence. Though regime transition is not easy, neither is it typically violent nor in continual danger of yielding an authoritarian outcome (as was often true of the transitions away from and back toward more pluralistic institutions in Latin America in the 1970s and 1980s, for example).

The separation of politics from economic and other social institutions is key in enabling regime change to occur without sustained and violent political convulsions. This separation precludes many authoritarian measures, such as state efforts to support the political order by creating and controlling political and social organizations. The autonomy of politics also fosters a dynamic of business confidence that prevents leading forces from simply seizing economic resources and directing them toward politically desired ends.

Barriers to state political action also limit the use of populist appeals in restoring a political order late in phase three and in phase four. Such appeals, which address "the people" as an agent counterposed to malign power, can help to tear groups and individuals away from the old order and formulate themes for a new regime. Yet late in the course of a

---

28. If political actors were purely economic-actors-in-politics, and their relations were exclusively strategic, the prospects of bloc formation would be greatly diminished. Clearly there is a strategic dimension to this process: For members of the new bloc (and allies) the prospective political order is more promising than disorder or any plausible alternative regime. But normative and strategic elements are interwoven in these judgments. For the main economic account of political coalitions, see William Riker, *The Theory of Political Coalitions* (New Haven: Yale University Press, 1962).

political order, populist appeals are usually not able to stimulate durable new nonstate forms of mobilization and organization on behalf of the regime.

Finally, the autonomy of politics encourages opposition. Political and social complexity and decentralization provide many opportunities for critics of the regime to assemble and campaign. And constitutional safeguards at least partly protect opposition. In advanced market societies the possibility of using political power to break up opposition and forcibly prevent its renewal is usually not open. (Repressive efforts that do not approach silencing all opposition, such as repressing small political groups in Italy and West Germany in response to terrorism in recent decades, require elaborate justification.)

In this model the analytical starting point is the permanent reality of conflicts over control of the state and over the definition of political identities. These conflicts occur in two modes. In the first, the construction of a political order is at stake. This means a contest to establish relatively durable power relations and political identities. This regime politics frames a second mode of conflict, a routine politics where issues are narrower and stakes more limited. The dynamic that links normal politics and regime politics is the effort of supporters of the regime to achieve their goals. In doing so they may amplify tendencies (statism and socioeconomic change) that over time weaken the institutions and practices they seek to maintain.

A note on crises as conflicts

I have presented this model without emphasizing a concept of crisis. That concept is too often used as though crises were virtual agents whose requirements explain other developments.[29] Here "crisis" refers to conflicts that jeopardize mechanisms of social reproduction; they always contain discursive elements.[30] Crises have two dimensions. One includes recognized indices of serious problems – declining investment, growing unemployment, or dramatic shifts in electoral support. The other is the process through which major actors come to regard the maintenance of prior relations as uncertain. Thus beliefs about the possibility of change accompany economic or political dysfunctions. Conflicts

29. The Marxist tradition links the concepts of crisis and period so that economic crises drive history from one period to the next, in dramatic functional adaptations. See G. A. Cohen, *Karl Marx's Theory of History: A Defence* (Princeton, N.J.: Princeton University Press, 1978), 278–96.

30. There is no nondiscursive level of social reality where "objective" problems appear as full crises. On this issue, see Jurgen Habermas, *Legitimation Crisis*, 3.

then arise concerning how to reorganize normative and institutional features of the area in question.

Crises can be distinguished according to their severity. A first type involves a routine disequilibrium – an election, or a phase of a business cycle – when existing relations are only temporarily disturbed. A second type jeopardizes an enduring form, such as a political regime or a particular organization of the market. A third type of crisis threatens basic relations, such as a market in large-scale property or a constitutional system. General social crises arise out of multiple crises of the second and third types. In American politics, shifts between political orders mainly involve crises of the second type, with the exception of the Civil War.

The course of the Democratic order

The preceding account of political orders provides a framework for examining the Democratic order. Most of this book analyzes the formation and maintenance of that regime in the 1930s and 1940s. While my account mainly concerns phases one and two of the model, all four phases are relevant. The characteristic processes of phase four were significant in the demise of the Republican order that dominated American politics in the 1920s. And the dynamics established early in the Democratic order, from which it drew great strength, would eventually make it vulnerable. The following claims about the Democratic order take the chronology of the realignment argument as a starting point.

1. The Democratic order originated in the 1930s through an active political process of building new institutions and discourses (phase one). There were serious economic, social, and political crises in the United States; building the Democratic order entailed their resolution. The initial leadership for the political order came from sections of a previously existing political force. Yet the new order required a political construction of new political subjects, beyond mobilizing existing forces. The political order was defined by new relations among the state, the dominant party, and social and political movements, as well as new relations between political and socioeconomic processes.
2. Major institutional and discursive continuities marked the four decades of the Democratic political order. These continuities registered the capacities of the party, state, and movements to recruit, organize, mobilize, and educate political support for the Democratic order (phases two and three).
3. Political tensions emerged within the political order, and sustaining its dynamism proved difficult. The Democratic order was founded not only through energetic new mobilizations and a transformation of the Democratic Party but through an expanding state. Over time, the party and other Democratic forces increasingly relied on the resources of the national state, tending to

merge into it, while the new state was identified with the party. This reduced the capacity of Democratic political forces to organize and mobilize. In the face of an emergent party—state apparatus, the space available at the top for further new political forces was limited, yet the political order continued to stimulate their formation (phase three).

4. Major problems for the Democratic political order developed in relation to socioeconomic processes. Growth reshaped socioeconomic relations in ways that strained the Democratic order by weakening social groups important to it and eroding Democratic political networks. Growth also yielded new socioeconomic groups which were not sources of Democratic support – partly because of obstacles posed by the Democratic order's reliance on the state (phase three).

5. The Democratic order ended (in the late 1960s and early 1970s) owing to political failure to cope with statism and socioeconomic change. These tendencies arose from Democratic efforts to sustain the political order and spur growth – over time they eroded support for the Democratic order, weakened its political capacities, and opened it to attack. In the resulting conflicts the Democratic order was destroyed. The appearance of new political forces did not doom the Democratic political order, but failure to integrate them was very damaging. The ensuing dynamic polarized opponents of the new political groups against the Democratic order. This new opposition, in conjunction with elements of the conventional opposition, defeated the leading forces of the Democratic order (phase four).

Although no single case could show such a model to be correct, the Democratic order is important enough to be analytically significant. This book focuses on two crucial moments of political definition and conflict: 1935–7 saw the formation of the Democratic order, and 1947–9 saw its definite consolidation. A related work analyzes the last years of the Democratic order – in 1963–5 it flourished amid serious problems, and then splintered apart in 1968–72.

The Democratic order and international politics

In the course of the Democratic order there was a significant interaction between domestic and international factors. To explain the international dimension of the Democratic order requires addressing two issues: Were domestic or international elements more important in shaping the political order? Were domestic or international elements more important in defining the international position of the United States? The development of the Democratic order was caused mainly by domestic dynamics. Thus the emergence of the Democratic order was not determined by the deep international depression of the 1930s – the comparative record shows that other responses could have occurred.[31] World War II did not create a new order, but consolidated a regime. The postwar growth of American power did not destroy the Democratic order, but amplified internationalist and anticommunist tendencies present from its inception.

When the aim is to explain the construction and development of a national regime, there is a basic asymmetry in the relation between domestic and international factors. Domestic factors shape domestic political outcomes and are their main direct causes. Here international factors are a secondary causal factor. They influence the choice of domestic outcomes by placing boundaries (usually wide ones) around a feasible set of domestic policies; within that set international factors can make some choices appear more attractive than others. A number of domestic policies are commonly possible – it is rare that a major domestic policy is wholly determined by the international setting.[32]

At the international level, causal relations are not reversed. Instead, domestic factors play a significant role in selecting a nation's international policies – a larger role than international relations play in determining domestic outcomes.[33] In an international system without a central authority, few important explanatory claims can be made that abstract entirely from the political and economic features of the member states. At a minimum, analytically relevant distinctions among states concern whether their domestic regimes are pluralistic or closed, and whether their economic prospects are ascending or declining.[34]

31. The claim is not that any government in any country could have selected any policy in response to the Depression. But governments in most countries had real choices about how to proceed. The choices they made cannot be wholly explained by the fact of international depression or by the location of states in the international system. On divergent international responses to the Great Depression, see Peter Gourevitch, *Politics in Hard Times – Comparative Responses to International Economic Crises* (Ithaca, N.Y.: Cornell University Press, 1986).

32. The best case for a strong determination of domestic factors by international factors is made in work that focuses on economic policies and on relatively small countries. Yet the relevant economic policies, while important, constitute only part of the political concerns of a modern state. On small states in the world economy, see Peter J. Katzenstein, *Small States in World Markets: Industrial Policy in Europe* (Ithaca, N.Y.: Cornell University Press, 1985).

33. On the relationship between the state and nonstate social and political forces in shaping international policies, see G. John Ikenberry et al., eds., *The State and American Foreign Economic Policy* (Ithaca, N.Y.: Cornell University Press, 1988).

34. I am taking a position in vigorous theoretical debates about international relations. The predominant position has been a self-defined "realism" that proceeds on the basis of three premises: States are the key actors in international relations; states seek

In the 1930s and 1940s domestic forces played a major role in forming the international policies and position of the United States. The Democratic order organized an expansive presence in world politics. The process of doing so was transformative, and deeply changed the predominant understanding of the appropriate scale of American international involvement. Democratic policies were committed to open economies, strongly opposed to Communist and pro-Communist regimes, and encouraged liberal polities. Debate concerned how to weigh these commitments. Thus early in the Cold War it was often argued that anti-Communism should always trump the other goals where conflicts arose among them.

Democratic policy – progressive liberal internationalism – contained a political dynamic similar to that which shaped the domestic course of the Democratic order. The first phase of the Democratic order was marked by growing internationalist tendencies among its leadership. These tendencies were linked to core progressive liberal commitments, which reformulated Wilsonian internationalism with greater sensitivity to the constraints of the domestic and international setting.

These internationalist tendencies were translated into practical choices, crucially moving in the late 1930s toward a full confrontation with the fascist powers. In alliance with the Soviet Union, the Democratic order led a global coalition against fascist regimes aiming at their unconditional surrender. During and after the war the Democratic order encouraged and helped sustain a dramatic expansion of American power. The result of this new international role for the United States was to benefit the regime. Democratic political efforts enhanced first the security and then the dominant international position of the United States, and thereby improved the domestic standing of the Democratic order. The expanded international economic role of the United States

power; and they act rationally. This formulation mirrors other efforts to extend the analytical framework of microeconomics to political and social phenomena, from political parties to families. As there is no corner of social life to which rational action is wholly foreign, there is no knock-down argument that could show this realism to be entirely wrong. To establish the strong claims made by proponents of this view, however, arguments about power and state interests would have to be developed in a far more convincing way than has been done. It is not much of a defense to say that states will generally prefer more rather than less power. This claim is probably true but not very interesting if there are significant tradeoffs among wealth, security, and autonomy. For the contemporary realist view of international relations, see Kenneth N. Waltz, *Theory of International Politics* (Reading, Mass.: Addison-Wesley, 1979). For a partial critique see Robert Keohane, "Theory of World Politics: Structural Realism and Beyond," in Keohane, ed., *Neorealism and its Critics* (New York: Columbia University Press, 1986), 158–203.

contributed to postwar growth, which in turn strengthened the political order.

Successful American international efforts led toward their further expansion. This tendency was encouraged by a political dynamic within the United States in which broad commitments were further extended. If the United States intervened in country or region x or y, on grounds of principle or on grounds of an urgent need to contain the power of the Soviet Union, why did such reasons not apply with equal force to most other settings?

Expansion also grew from interest group pressures. Groups who benefited from Democratic international successes wanted to sustain the flow of benefits, while additional groups sought to participate in this apparently happy cycle. Thus policies aimed at increasing overseas sales of U.S. agricultural products might achieve that objective; encourage the beneficiaries to strive to retain or increase what they gained; and encourage groups in other industries to formulate and pursue similar aims. Pressures from outside the United States also encouraged expansion. Commitments were cumulative – once an obligation was assumed, it was likely to remain in effect. The result was an international cognate of the domestic statism I outlined above, in which regimes allied with the United States would be likely to rely on American resources and political strength.

Within the United States international political success created expectations of more achievement. As some international efforts were costly and almost all required justification, there was an inflationary tendency in arguments on behalf of intervention. Given a global conflict with the Soviet Union, the combination of that conflict with what might be called threat inflation led to defining a growing number of commitments as vital. This process went beyond the 1940s into the remaining decades of the Democratic order.

While the Democratic political order was strengthened by its international commitments, the latter had substantial economic and political costs. Three changes shifted the balance. First, the perceived benefits of international commitments in preserving national security declined in the 1960s. This was partly a result of prior successes in the policy of containing the Soviet Union and partly because an expansive definition of American interests led to interventions in areas that the public refused to regard as crucial, such as Southeast Asia. Second, expansion meant that the overall cost of American commitments rose, while efforts at further expansion (at the margin of existing commitments) could be especially costly. Third, the domestic course of the Democratic order meant that the political resources available to its leadership were limited.

Given these shifts, the chances increased that international commitments would become more expensive than Democratic leaders could afford.[35]

The tension between limited political resources and expanding international commitments encouraged major misjudgments about where and when American intervention was feasible. The potential for trouble was dramatically realized by Democratic leaders' miscalculations in Southeast Asia. They greatly underestimated the political, military, and financial costs of achieving what they defined as vital American objectives in defending the regimes of Vietnam, Laos, and Cambodia. And they overestimated the availability of domestic political resources to pay those costs. Vietnam detonated a volatile situation and the ensuing conflicts helped to destroy the Democratic regime.

In this book, my account of the Democratic order in its first two decades emphasizes political elements as causal forces in domestic and international relations. Creative political initiatives built the Democratic order in the 1930s and changed America's international role. In the 1940s Democratic political capacities defined a basic continuity between the Roosevelt and Truman administrations. Political life was dominated by a triangle among a Democratic state, party, and nonparty political forces (political movements and interest groups). Continuity resulted from fierce conflicts as leaders of the Democratic order redefined the boundaries of reasonable political argument and defeated adversaries within and outside them.

35. I have benefited from the arguments of Jack Snyder and Paul Kennedy. Kennedy argues that economic power leads its bearers toward military activity, to protect and enhance their position in a competitive and unstable international setting. Eventually military efforts exceed what can be sustained by the nation undertaking them – because of inherently uneven economic development and because military preparations may have negative economic consequences. Then decline ensues. Snyder discerns a dynamic of overexpansion in the policies of great powers. He attributes it primarily to the formation of coalitions among powerful interests who combine to take control of the state and use it to pursue their aims. They produce policies that would not result from a farsighted view of the general interests of the state and nation in question. Paul Kennedy, *The Rise and Fall of the Great Powers – Economic Change and Military Conflict from 1500 to 2000* (New York: Vintage, 1987); Jack Snyder, *Myths of Empire: Domestic Politics and International Ambition* (Ithaca, N.Y.: Cornell University Press, 1991).

3

Democratic opportunities in the crises of the 1930s

In 1932 the issue was the restoration of American democracy: and the American people were in a mood to win. They did win. In 1936 the issue is the preservation of their victory. Again they are in a mood to win. Again they will win.

– Franklin Roosevelt, 1936[1]

In the 1930s progressive liberals in the Roosevelt administration and Congress allied with new mass political forces to build the Democratic order. They led the way in forming a Democratic political bloc whose elements cut across conventional institutional boundaries and whose themes reshaped American liberalism. The new order entailed an expanding state, a renovated Democratic Party, and new movements and interest groups, most notably the labor movement. It was committed to modernization, efficiency, and moderately egalitarian social and economic reform.[2]

The events and outcomes of the decade are still the subject of lively debates, which are often linked to contemporary political positions. For some, the 1930s (and 1940s) show a healthy politics of interest-aggregating parties. Others argue that a special chance was lost to develop a more aggressively reformist liberalism, perhaps a mass social democratic force.[3] Arguments persist about the labor movement and

---

1. Franklin D. Roosevelt, Campaign Address at Madison Square Garden, October 31, 1936, in *Public Papers and Addresses of Franklin D. Roosevelt*, vol. 5, *The People Approve – 1936*, compiled by Samuel I. Rosenman (New York: Random House, 1938), 566.
2. The term also refers to the Progressive movement of the early twentieth century; I capitalize it when designating that movement in particular, but not when I refer to the broad current of political and social opinion that movement helped to shape.
3. For versions of this argument, see James MacGregor Burns, *Roosevelt: The Lion and the Fox* (New York: Harcourt, Brace, and World, 1956); Michael Davis, *Prisoners of*

the decade's radical political movements, as well as about New Deal agricultural policies and racial practices.[4]

Chapters 3 to 6 treat the formation of the Democratic order. This brief chapter begins with a narrative sketch of the 1930s and then examines the decade's crises – their political dimension was crucial in opening the possibility of a new order. Chapter 4 analyzes the passage of the Wagner Act in 1935 and assesses its consequences. Chapter 5 analyzes the other elements of the Democratic triangle, the Democratic Party and new political and social movements, as they aided a Democratic triumph in 1936 that confirmed popular support of New Deal programs.[5] Chapter 6 analyzes Democratic discourses in the 1930s.

The main events

The 1930s began with the nation reeling from a deep depression. Wages fell and unemployment rose steadily, reaching astonishing proportions

   the American Dream (London: Verso, 1986); Theda Skocpol, "Legacies of New Deal Liberalism," *Dissent* (Winter 1983): 33–44; and Steven Fraser and Gary Gerstle, *The Rise and Decline of the New Deal Order, 1930–1980* (Princeton, N.J.: Princeton University Press, 1989).

4. On the labor movement, see Irving Bernstein, *The Lean Years: A History of the American Worker, 1920–1933* (Boston: Houghton Mifflin, 1960) and *Turbulent Years* (Boston: Houghton Mifflin, 1970); and David Brody, *Workers in Industrial America: Essays on the 20th Century Struggle* (New York: Oxford University Press, 1980), 120–72. Alan Brinkley's *Voices of Protest: Huey Long, Father Coughlin, and the Great Depression* (New York: Alfred A. Knopf, 1982) offers a sympathetic view of 1930s populism. For treatments of the Communist experience, from sympathetic to severely critical, see Alexander Richmond, *A Long View from the Left: Memoirs of an American Revolutionary* (Boston: Houghton Mifflin, 1973); Mark Naison, *Communists in Harlem During the Depression* (Urbana: University of Illinois Press, 1983); Maurice Isserman, *Which Side Were You On? The American Communist Party During the Second World War* (Middletown, Conn.: Wesleyan University Press, 1982); Harvey Klehr, *The Heyday of American Communism: The Depression Decade* (New York: Basic Books, 1984); and Irving Howe and Lewis Coser, *The American Communist Party: A Critical History* (Boston: Beacon Press, 1957). On race relations, see Doug McAdam, *Political Process and the Development of Black Insurgency, 1930–70* (Chicago: University of Chicago Press, 1982); Harvard Sitkoff, *A New Deal for Blacks: The Emergence of Civil Rights as a National Issue* (New York: Oxford University Press, 1978); and Nancy J. Weiss, *Farewell to the Party of Lincoln* (Princeton: Princeton University Press, 1983).

5. Valuable overall treatments of the decade include: William E. Leuchtenburg, *Franklin D. Roosevelt and the New Deal, 1932–1940* (New York: Harper and Row, 1963); Arthur M. Schlesinger, Jr., *The Age of Roosevelt* (3 vols.) (Boston: Houghton Mifflin, 1957–60); Burns, *Roosevelt: The Lion and the Fox;* and Kenneth S. Davis, *FDR, The New Deal Years, 1933–37* (New York: Random House, 1986).

in 1931 and 1932.[6] This catastrophe was beyond the grasp of the Hoover administration and helped to end a period of Republican domination.[7]

Although the old order was rejected in 1932, the Democratic platform combined progressive proposals with vague and even conservative formulations:

> We advocate an immediate and drastic reduction of governmental expenditures by abolishing useless commissions and offices, consolidating departments and bureaus, and eliminating extravagance to accomplish a saving of not less than twenty-five per cent in the cost of the Federal Government.[8]

Franklin Roosevelt used his electoral mandate to pass ambitious measures that, despite what planning advocates hoped, did not yield rapid economic recovery. The crucial measure, the National Industrial Recovery Act, was eventually ruled unconstitutional, but before its legal demise the measure proved unsatisfactory in generating economic recovery or political and social cooperation.[9] Perhaps the depression would have gone even deeper without the NIRA; but that was not a strong argument in support of full-scale planning. By the mid-1930s the administration's emphasis had shifted toward economic regulation aimed at spurring

6. On the Depression see Bernstein, *The Lean Years;* Robert S. McElvaine, *The Great Depression: America, 1929–1941* (New York: Times Books, 1984); and John Kenneth Galbraith, *The Great Crash, 1929* (Boston: Houghton Mifflin, 1972).

7. Accounts of the Republican system appear in the major works on Populism and Progressivism and in James Sundquist, *Dynamics of the Party System: Alignment and Realignment of Political Parties in the United States* (Washington, D.C.: The Brookings Institution, rev. ed., 1983); Walter Dean Burnham, "The System of 1896: An Analysis," in Paul Kleppner et al., *The Evolution of American Electoral Systems* (Westport, Conn.: Greenwood Press, 1981), 147–202; and Walter Dean Burnham, *Critical Elections and the Mainsprings of American Politics* (New York: W. W. Norton, 1971).

8. "Democratic Platform for 1932," in Donald Bruce Johnson, ed., *National Party Platforms,* vol. 1, 1840–1956 (Urbana: University of Illinois Press, 1978), 331.

9. With the NRA, economic elites did not always oppose state involvement when they perceived it as a means of stabilizing markets and assisting their own organization. When state intervention appeared to favor labor, business opposition grew. Thus business attitudes toward the NRA were ambivalent, as that measure provided more encouragement to labor than is suggested by accounts in which the new regulatory apparatus was simply captured by large businesses. On the National Recovery Administration see Donald R. Brand, *Corporatism and the Rule of Law: A Study of the National Recovery Administration* (Ithaca, N.Y.: Cornell University Press, 1988). Legal conflicts over the NIRA are treated in Peter Irons, *The New Deal Lawyers* (Princeton: Princeton University Press, 1982): 17–107. Also see Ellis W. Hawley, *The New Deal and the Problem of Monopoly: A Study in Economic Ambivalence* (Princeton, N.J.: Princeton University Press, 1966), 53–71, 270–80; and Bernard Bellush, *The Failure of the NRA* (New York: W. W. Norton, 1975).

expansion, along with social reform. New standards were set for labor relations and social insurance in the Wagner Act and Social Security Act.[10]

Though little growth occurred soon after 1932, the economic plunge stopped. Signs of recovery appeared by mid-decade. Unemployment declined from 25 percent in 1933 to 14 percent in 1937, and the gross national product rose as the economy moved toward pre-Depression levels.[11] Disastrous economic conditions improved to become merely dreadful, while insurgent political forces mobilized amid polarization between the administration and economic elites.[12] In 1936, Roosevelt ran on his record of halting economic decline, responding to the social chaos of the Depression, and supporting attempts to organize new political and social forces.

Roosevelt's first campaign capitalized on anti-Hoover sentiment and was sometimes vague about the positive course proposed.[13] The 1936 election was a referendum on a Democratic course whose direction was now clear. Secretary of Interior Harold Ickes wrote Roosevelt in 1935 about the upcoming election:

> The immediate future of the Progressive movement is at stake. If you should fail of reelection, the Progressive movement as we have understood it, the aim of which has been to bring about a reasonable economic and social reconstruction of the country in the interest of the average man without a violent swing to the left, will, in my judgment, have gone down into a tragic grave.[14]

Roosevelt's victory in 1936 affirmed his policies and compelled acknowledgment of their popular support.[15] There was even a temporary

---

10. Leuchtenburg, *Roosevelt and the New Deal*, 63–94.

11. Bureau of the Census, *Historical Statistics of the United States – Colonial Times to 1970*, D1-10, "Labor Force and Its Components: 1900 to 1947"; F31, "Average Annual Growth Rates of Gross National Product: 1909 to 1970"; F32-46, "Gross National Product: 1929 to 1970" (Washington, D.C.: Government Printing Office, 1975), 126, 226–8.

12. The classic account of popular mobilization, stressing the opposition of business elites to the New Deal, is Arthur Schlesinger's *The Politics of Upheaval*, vol. 3 of *The Age of Roosevelt*.

13. Leuchtenburg, *Roosevelt and the New Deal*, 10–12; also see Kenneth Davis, *FDR: The New York Years, 1928–1932* (New York: Random House, 1979), 355–75.

14. Letter, Harold Ickes to Roosevelt, September 7, 1935, President's Secretary's File 74 (Folder – Harold Ickes 1934–6), Franklin D. Roosevelt Library.

15. Studies of the popular vote for president and Congress as well as of congressional voting all identify major shifts. See Barbara Sinclair, *Congressional Realignment, 1925–1978* (Austin: University of Texas Press, 1982), 18–36.

reversal of the long-term decline in voting rates.[16] The changes initiated in 1934–6 were then consolidated.[17] By the end of the decade the new Democrats were a majority party identified with the New Deal and Roosevelt.[18]

The middle of the decade was a high point of popular mobilization, from strikes to populist movements. And the New Deal measures that the Democratic Party later proudly claimed as its main accomplishments were passed. The crucial years were 1935–7, when deep policy shifts, wide popular mobilization, and massive electoral changes converged. This starting point is compatible with accounts of political realignment that posit intervals of 35–40 years between realignments. If periods between political realignments are taken to include nine presidential elections, then counting Democratic victories in each set while taking successive elections as a midpoint yields this result: with 1936 or 1940 as the midpoint of a set of nine elections, there were 5 Democratic victories; with 1944, 6; with 1948, 7; with 1952, 6; and with 1956 or 1960, 5 victories. This suggests a midpoint of 1948 in a period of Democratic presidential domination starting in 1932. The 1932 election broke apart the Republican regime and opened the possibility of a new order.

In the mid-1930s conservatives in both parties were on the defensive. By the late 1930s they could only block measures to expand and reorganize the New Deal, not present a plausible alternative.[19] Thus when they defeated Roosevelt's plan to reorganize the Supreme Court and frustrated his effort to reform the Democratic Party in 1938, the result was only to limit the Democratic order rather than to create any immediate prospects of overturning it.[20]

The 1930s were dominated by economic disaster, political volatility,

---

16. Walter Dean Burnham, "The 1980 Earthquake: Realignment, Reaction, or What?" in Thomas Ferguson and Joel Rogers, ed., *The Hidden Election: Politics and Economics in the 1980 Presidential Campaign* (New York: Pantheon, 1981), 101.

17. See Samuel Lubell, *The Future of American Politics*, third edition (New York: Harper & Row, 1965), 43–46; and James Sundquist, *Dynamics of the Party System*, 199.

18. Despite the continued strength of Democratic conservatism, the contrast with the narrowness and sectionalism of the pre-Depression Democratic Party is clear. See David Burner, *The Politics of Provincialism: The Democratic Party in Transition, 1918–1932* (New York: Alfred A. Knopf, 1968).

19. George H. Mayer, *The Republican Party, 1854–1964* (New York: Oxford University Press, 1964), 378–427; James T. Patterson, *Congressional Conservatism and the New Deal: The Growth of the Conservative Coalition in Congress, 1933–1939* (Lexington: University of Kentucky Press, 1967).

20. On these setbacks see Burns, *Roosevelt: The Lion and the Fox*, 291–315, 358–80; and Richard Polenberg, "The Decline of the New Deal, 1937–1940," in John Brae-

and social protest. Domestic turbulence occurred in an ominous international setting, beginning with the vividly international character of the Depression and extending through the rise of aggressive fascist movements and the violent involution of the Soviet regime. The severe crises of the 1930s were linked to the prior Republican political order, which had been in place for more than three decades. The Republican order directed the transition to an economy and society increasingly composed of large bureaucratic organizations, while enhancing the position of business elites. Employers used many strategies, from violence to welfare capitalism, to reduce workers' collective strength and limit unions.[21] In this political order a conservative, probusiness Republican Party had a broad social base, including not only much of the middle classes and business elites, but also farmers and many workers. It benefited from a strong ethnic and religious identification as Anglo-American and Protestant.[22]

In this Republican period the state underwent significant expansion and a degree of rationalization.[23] The state's reshaping was encouraged by the antiparty spirit of the Progressive movement, by government mobilization and planning during World War I, and by the challenges posed by economic growth and cultural and organizational change.[24] The Republican state was out of reach for many popular constituencies. Southern Jim Crow rules disenfranchised blacks. The foundation of the post-1890s Republican order as a modernizing, national effort meant hostility to Western and Southern populism.[25] The nativism of Southern

man, Robert H. Bremner, and David Brody, eds., *The New Deal – The National Level* (Columbus: Ohio State University Press, 1975), 246–66.

21. Bernstein's *Lean Years* offers a graphic account of employers' rout of the unions by the end of the 1920s. Also see David Montgomery, *The Fall of the House of Labor: The Workplace, the State, and American Labor Activism, 1865–1925* (Cambridge University Press, 1987); and David Brody, *Steelworkers in America: The Nonunion Era* (New York: Harper & Row, 1969), 231–78.

22. Mayer, *The Republican Party;* Schlesinger, *The Crisis of the Old Order, 1919–1933,* vol. 1 of *The Age of Roosevelt;* and Robert H. Ziegler, *Republicans and Labor, 1919–1929* (Lexington: University of Kentucky Press, 1969).

23. See Stephen Skowronek, *Building a New American State: The Expansion of National Administrative Capacities, 1877–1920* (Cambridge University Press, 1982).

24. See James Gilbert, *Designing the Industrial State: The Intellectual Pursuit of Collectivism in America, 1890–1940* (Chicago, Ill.: Quadrangle Books, 1972); and Gabriel Kolko, *The Triumph of Conservatism* (New York: Free Press, 1963).

25. The link between the defeat of Populism and the consolidation of the "system of 1896" helps explain the modest extent of mass mobilization associated with that political order and the sectional weaknesses of the Democratic Party within it. For a sympathetic account of Populism see Lawrence Goodwyn, *Democratic Promise: The Populist Moment in America* (New York: Oxford University Press, 1976).

and Western Democrats along with the probusiness stance of Republicans made it hard for urban working-class and lower middle-class groups to find a place in either party.

A spiraling economic crisis

The Republican order entered into a deep crisis in the early 1930s: Gross national product fell by almost 10 percent per year from 1929 through 1933.[26] The economic breakdown was triggered by failures in financial markets, but, in the context of major structural economic changes, financial and market failures were detonators rather than basic causes of the collapse.[27] Important new industries were emerging while sustained productivity growth in new and old sectors meant potential output was expanding more rapidly than effective demand. Productivity increases totaled roughly 50 percent between 1910 and 1930 (and continued into the Depression).[28] The growth of productivity beyond market and social capacities led to an imbalance between the volume of production and

26. Bureau of the Census, *Historical Statistics*, F31, "Average Annual Growth Rates of Gross National Product: 1909 to 1970," 226–7.

27. For a valuable account of the Depression that emphasizes tensions between prior economic and social relations and emergent forms of mass production, see Michael A. Bernstein, *The Great Depression: Delayed Recovery and Economic Change in America, 1929–1939* (Cambridge University Press, 1987). For a useful survey of views of the origins of the Great Depression, see Gerard Dumenil, Mark Glick, and Jose Rangel, "Theories of the Great Depression: Why Did Profitability Matter?" *Review of Radical Political Economics* 19, no. 2 (1987): 16–42. The authors maintain that profit problems played a central role, as against monopoly, underconsumption, or monetary problems, but they do not show a clear causal link between profit levels in the late 1920s and severe economic instability.

28. Bureau of the Census, *Historical Statistics*, W1-11, "Indexes of National Productivity: 1889 to 1970." Without the Depression, would productivity increases have permitted employers to gain acquiescence in welfare capitalism through increasing wages? Brandes argues that while the system managed to work through the 1920s, workers were not happy with the package of conditions and benefits supplied. Horowitz makes a similar argument in her study of labor in the 1930s. Cohen's work on industrial workers in Chicago in the 1920s and 1930s provides a slightly more favorable account of what welfare capitalism provided workers, and indicates that this system won a certain degree of loyalty from employees in firms that took seriously their claims to provide social security. In her view welfare capitalism was overwhelmed by the Depression, when employers were unable and unwilling to keep their prior promises. See Stuart D. Brandes, *American Welfare Capitalism – 1880–1940* (Chicago, Ill.: University of Chicago Press, 1976), 136–48; Ruth Horowitz, *Political Ideologies of Organized Labor: The New Deal Era* (New Brunswick, N.J.: Transaction, 1978); and Lizabeth Cohen, *Making a New Deal: Industrial Workers in Chicago 1919–1939* (Cambridge University Press, 1990), 174–238.

demand, despite rising wages. Employment problems were also potentially severe because even large increases in demand would produce only
modest new employment.[29] In the 1930s the concept of underconsumption was used both to note insufficient effective demand and to designate
a range of structural economic problems that many attributed to deep
tendencies toward stagnation in American capitalism.[30] Whether the
terms used are those of the underconsumption and stagnation arguments
of the 1930s, or of recent accounts of structural adjustment, economic
problems in that decade were tightly linked to broad social questions.

The economic crisis arose through struggles on the economic terrain
formed by developments of the 1920s and the crash. The crisis put in
question the economic model that had developed from the turn of the
century through the 1920s. This model, encouraged by the Republican
order, combined concentrated market structures, coercive forms of organizing labor, and sustained increases in productivity. It failed to provide means for structural economic adjustment and intensified tendencies toward underconsumption. The main forms of growth weakened
the relative role of craft positions in industry, and increased mass production positions. By the early 1930s many industries had been reorganized on the model of the automobile assembly line. A new working
class in mass production industries was a potential basis for aggressive
economic and political action that might challenge an authoritarian
factory regime.

Economic disasters became a full economic crisis when groups took
shape on the terrain of the collapse, not only protesting but also aiming
to alter the relations that produced it. The years from 1929 to 1933
saw striking expressions of popular discontent, along with unpersuasive

29. The socioeconomic dynamics of rising productivity within a capitalist context were
    termed "disaccumulation" by Sklar; Block and Hirschhorn linked Sklar's analysis to
    theories of post-industrial society. Both accounts locate emergent disaccumulation
    tendencies in the 1920s and view the Depression as a disaccumulation crisis. Martin
    J. Sklar, "On the Proletarian Revolution and the End of Political-Economic Society,"
    Radical America (May–June 1969); Fred Block and Larry Hirschhorn, "New Produc-
    tive Forces and the Contradictions of Contemporary Capitalism: A Post-Industrial
    Perspective," *Theory and Society* 7 (1979): 363–95.

30. It is wrong to equate stagnationist and Keynesian conceptions, as the latter turned on
    the possibility of stimulating major expansion. But both rejected the idea that unim-
    peded markets would return an advanced economy to a path of steady growth in a
    brief period. The stagnationist perspective is discussed in Michael A. Bernstein, "Why
    the Great Depression Was Great: Toward a New Understanding of the Interwar
    Economic Crisis in the United States," in Fraser and Gerstle, eds., *The Rise and Fall
    of the New Deal Order*, 32–54; and G. E. McLaughlin and R. J. Watkins, "The
    Problem of Industrial Growth in a Mature Economy", *American Economic Review*
    29 (March 1939) supplement: 1–14.

statements of confidence from business elites.[31] The discontent of the early 1930s was less organized and less politically focused than that of the mid-decade, but it was passionate and contained radical currents. And this discontent seemed capable of growing much larger were Depression conditions to worsen or to continue without significant improvement.

Economic failures appeared as broken social mechanisms rather than problems of absolute scarcity, especially given the recent prosperity. The crisis took shape as fierce battles over the form of a new economic order. Conflicts between workers and employers exploded in firms and communities. Widespread rural discontent included efforts to organize agricultural workers.[32] The limits of prior government policies were contested everywhere.

The Republican order had helped create the conditions for an economic crisis of which it would be the victim. This crisis opened the way for political-economic strategies aimed first at moving back from complete collapse, then at renewing economic growth. Economic breakdown was causally important; the massively painful realities of the Depression weakened the Republican order, and its severity helped move the range of possible political solutions to the left. Yet the new political order was not a necessary response to economic breakdown or changing socioeconomic relations. Many other domestic courses were proposed, and the diverse international responses to the Depression show that economic collapse did not dictate any single political direction.

Political and social crises

Social and political changes underway in the Republican order enhanced the possibility that its problems would become full-scale crises. By the

31. Popular discontent is chronicled in the accounts of Schlesinger and Leuchtenburg previously cited, and in Paul Taylor, *On the Ground in the Thirties* (Salt Lake City, Utah: Peregrine Smith Books, 1983). For a view of the movements of the early 1930s as large and powerful see Frances Piven and Richard Cloward, *Poor People's Movements: Why They Succeed, How They Fail* (New York: Vintage, 1979), 41–95.

32. On rural unrest and the politics of agriculture, see: Jerold S. Auerbach, *Labor and Liberty: The La Follette Committee and the New Deal* (Indianapolis, Ind.: Bobbs-Merrill, 1966), 177–196; Donald H. Grubbs, *Cry from the Cotton: The Southern Tenant Farmers' Union* (Chapel Hill: University of North Carolina Press, 1971); Theodore Saloutos, *The American Farmer and the New Deal* (Ames: Iowa State University Press, 1982); Kenneth Finegold, "The Political Origins of New Deal Agricultural Policy," *Politics and Society* 11, no. 1 (1982); and Cletus Daniel, *Bitter Harvest, a History of California Farmworkers, 1870–1941* (Ithaca, N.Y.: Cornell University Press, 1981).

early 1930s the vast immigration of the late nineteenth and early twentieth centuries was far enough in the distance to allow the entry of first- and second-generation Americans into new cultural and social relations. The Republican order had relied on the economic subordination of these immigrants while encouraging their social assimilation. Politically, where these groups were not wholly excluded they were contained by urban machines (often Democratic). The importance of ethnicity in organizing the social lives of lower middle-class and working-class whites was in decline. Ethnic identities were now less important either as obstacles to economic organization or as badges of political identification. Antagonisms between blacks and whites in the mass production industries were also less sharp than they had been in the years immediately after World War I.[33] By the end of the 1920s the former immigrant masses and their children were much more able to intervene in politics.

Deep social and technical changes spread rapidly after the turn of the century, including urbanization, improved transportation, and growing use of electronic media of communication. These modernizing processes were integral to the Republican vision of national economic and social development. Yet Republican successes created a new more nationally integrated socioeconomic field that deemphasized the regional differences which had been vital in building the regime. Republicans could less easily claim to be the only truly national political force. The way had been cleared for the emergence of new political forces able to go beyond sectional and narrowly ethnic limits in their programs and appeals.[34]

Republican success as a modernizing force amplified the social meaning of the economic crisis. Americans correctly perceived a vast gulf between expanding social and technical capacities and the chaos of the Depression. The destruction of the 1930s was thus not merely an economic nightmare, but a savage and frightening rupture with norms of social progress and control.

There was a distinct and severe political crisis in the early 1930s. The Republican-dominated party system was in deep trouble; some assert that political realignment was bound to happen without the Depression.

---

33. See Samuel Lubell, *The Future of American Politics* (Garden City, N.Y.: Doubleday, 2nd ed., rev., 1956) 29–30; Lizabeth Cohen, *Making a New Deal*, 324–5; and Peter Friedlander, *The Emergence of a UAW Local, 1936–39: A Study in Class and Culture* (Pittsburgh, Penn.: University of Pittsburgh Press, 1975).

34. The relative decline of sectional cleavages in the politics of the 1930s is clear even in the analysis of Richard Bensel, whose general argument stresses the centrality of sectionalism in all phases of American politics. Richard Franklin Bensel, *Sectionalism and American Political Development, 1880–1980* (Madison: University of Wisconsin Press, 1984), 148.

Evidence for this claim appears in the movement of urban and working-class voters toward the Democrats in 1928, though not enough to warrant such a strong statement.[35] The Republican order had initially counterposed a national, modernizing program to a warring collection of regional and sectoral Democratic interests. The dominant forces of the Republican order were weak by the early 1930s, though the opposition of a sectional and quarrelsome Democratic Party could not replace them. The Republican order had trouble incorporating new groups, notably the growing urban and working-class electorate. This limited the political resources available to elites and provided targets of opportunity for prospective opponents.[36] Party weaknesses became party crises through the efforts of "mislocated" or excluded constituencies to define and represent their interests in political struggles from the 1920s into the 1930s.

The party crisis intersected a crisis of the state in the early 1930s, one that put in question the state's ability to maintain social order: "Society seemed to be disintegrating, a disjointedness caught in the fragmented "Newsreel" of Dos Passos' *U.S.A.*, in the theater scene in Nathanael West's *A Cool Million*, in the final anguished writing of Hart Crane, who took his life in 1932."[37] Chaos and fear took shape as a political crisis through struggles to compel state activity. The Hoover administration met these struggles with force, as in the attack on the Bonus Army in summer 1932, or with seeming indifference to widespread growing hardship.[38] Even in 1932, Republicans affirmed Hoover's leadership:

> True to American traditions and principles of government, the administration has regarded the relief problem as one of state and local responsibility.

35. The claim that realignment would have happened anyway is made in Schlesinger, *Crisis of the Old Order*. The movement of urban and working class voters is traced in Kristi Andersen, *The Creation of a Democratic Majority, 1928–1936* (Chicago, Ill.: University of Chicago Press, 1979), 28–38; and Burner, *The Politics of Provincialism*, 216–43. Andersen and Burner do not make as strong a claim as Schlesinger about what would have happened without economic crises.

36. The existence of such opportunities follows from data on low voting rates in the 1920s and accounts of Democratic organization and politics. See Andersen, *The Creation of a Democratic Majority*, 48; Burner, *The Politics of Provincialism*; and Davis, *FDR: The New York Years*.

37. Leuchtenburg, *Roosevelt and the New Deal*, 28–9.

38. Revisionist treatments of the Hoover administration claim he showed more concern for social integration and more interest in state intervention than pro-New Deal accounts have allowed. Such accounts downplay or omit evidence of how modest and unimpressive Hoover's practical efforts were in the crucial first years of the Depression. For an interesting account see Peri E. Arnold, "Ambivalent Leviathan: Herbert Hoover and the Positive State," in J. David Greenstone, ed., *Public Values and Private Power in American Politics* (Chicago, Ill.: University of Chicago Press, 1984), 109–36.

The work of local agencies, public and private, has been coordinated and enlarged on a nation-wide scale under the leadership of the President. . . . There has been magnificent response and action to relieve distress by citizens, organizations, and agencies, public and private, throughout the country.[39]

While there were taut limits to the action Hoover would take, opposing political forces gained the strength to challenge them. Democratic elites recognized a political opportunity, given Hoover's failures and the electoral shifts of the late 1920s. Popular protest – consumer and tenant protests, organizations of the unemployed, bitter strikes – underlined the potential of an anti-Republican politics. The resulting crisis of the state registered the inability of the administration to cope with mounting economic and social devastation. The disorder was a central concern early in Roosevelt's first administration.[40]

The ominous crises in the United States in the early 1930s were linked to the main features of the Republican order, which appeared politically incapable as well as highly responsible for grotesque social and economic failures. Republican responses to political critiques of their policies were unconvincing. In this harsh setting the normal times of the Republican order in the 1920s disappeared, and were replaced by a political phase of fierce clashes over basic matters.

The international setting

In the first years of the Democratic order the international setting was grim. A wrenching international economic crisis lasted from the early 1930s through the decade. Political turmoil in Europe combined the historic concerns of its main states for achieving security with modern ideologies of social revolution and cultural redemption. On balance international crises had positive effects on the Democratic order, because they opened space for the political experimentation through which the new order was built. Democratic leaders in 1936 did not claim to be able to solve the international problems then apparent – international questions did not even play a major role in the campaign of 1936. It would misread the sequence to consider the Democratic order as a determined response to international problems.

The global economic collapse widened the room for maneuver open to Democratic reformers, by reducing the force of external pressures

39. "Republican Platform of 1932," in Johnson, *National Party Platforms*, 341; also see Leuchtenburg, *Roosevelt and the New Deal*, 14–15.
40. Burns, *Roosevelt*, 161–208.

on the United States. This made it easier for the Roosevelt administration to pursue demand-oriented policies that might otherwise have been deemed irresponsible in terms of their likely effects on the international position of the American economy. As no major European country was prospering in these years, opponents of domestic political and economic reform could not cite any actual counterexample to rule out reform efforts.[41]

Isolation was what many Americans preferred. World War I and the perceived failures of Wilson's postwar diplomacy deepened historic suspicions of involvement in European controversies. Ironically, American disengagement from European politics early in the decade made a further contribution to building a progressive liberal order because tensions between isolationist and internationalist elements among progressive liberals were not forced to the surface. Had external events moved that conflict to the center of political debate, forming a new order would have been far more difficult. Had international events become central more rapidly, or had the progressive liberal leadership strongly pressed an internationalist position, severe strains would have resulted. Progressive Republicans who were isolationist or represented states where that view predominated would have been hardpressed to remain allied with the administration. The same might well have been true with moderate Democrats from the South. And Democratic internationalism would have further inflamed the Republican opposition and provided a target for countermobilization.

In guiding American policies, Roosevelt and the Democratic leadership from the early 1930s to the end of that decade generally chose what they regarded as the most feasible internationalist option. They opposed an isolationist course and preferred to expand American engagement.[42] But there was no bold declaration of internationalist aims. Especially in international economic matters, the administration was willing to compromise with nationalist and protectionist forces.[43] With much qual-

41. In the main accounts of American politics in the first two thirds of the decade, international relations are secondary or marginal. On American foreign policy see Lloyd Gardner, *Economic Aspects of New Deal Diplomacy* (Boston: Beacon Press, 1964); Joan Hoff Wilson, *American Business and Foreign Policy, 1920–1933* (Lexington: University Press of Kentucky, 1967); and Robert Dallek, *Franklin D. Roosevelt and American Foreign Policy 1932–1945* (New York: Oxford University Press, 1979).

42. For an overview of the Democratic foreign policy trajectory, see Leuchtenburg, *Roosevelt and the New Deal*, 190–230.

43. Block depicts Roosevelt's policies in these terms: "Roosvelt and Morgenthau essentially stumbled onto a sound Keynesian foreign economic policy. Throughout this period, Keynes argued that the only way toward international recovery was for nations to pursue expansionary domestic economic policies while defending them-

ification and hesitation, American economic policies took a more internationalist course.[44] Democratic policies responded to dire conditions on the basis of longstanding progressive liberal commitments, and through the 1930s and into the next decade enacted the view that economic recovery required expanded international economic activity. Those in favor of economic internationalism argued that the intensity and length of the Depression was linked with protectionist practices.

The Democratic political trajectory had a strongly internationalist character that led toward unprecedented commitments. An internationalist course was always Roosevelt's inclination, although early in the 1930s he did not advertise this preference. The internationalist orientation of the Democratic order had several sources: in Progressive and Wilsonian hopes for a fairer and better-ordered world; in calculations that American security would be enhanced by international involvement, given the danger and instability of the international political scene; and in the belief that an open international political environment would facilitate economic openness, which in turn would enhance American recovery. Yet Democratic internationalism was not a defining public issue through the mid-1930s. Had political debate centered on whether to expand American international commitments, Democratic victory would have been uncertain even amid the debacle of the Hoover administration.

In sum, Roosevelt sought internationalist options while trying to avoid full-scale confrontations with the powerful forces of isolationism. The Democratic order emerged in the last decade when isolation was a barely plausible account of the American condition or of a feasible American policy.

selves from the deflationary impact of the world economy." Block goes on to note that as the decade progressed Keynes and like-minded analysts moved increasingly toward internationalist economic conceptions. Fred L. Block, *The Origins of International Economic Disorder: A Study of United States International Monetary Policy from World War II to the Present* (Berkeley: University of California Press, 1977), 26.

44. On the movement toward economic internationalism also see Jeffrey Frieden, "Sectoral Conflict and U.S. Foreign Economic Policy, 1914–1940," and Stephen Haggard, "The Institutional Foundations of Hegemony: Explaining the Reciprocal Trade Agreements Act of 1934," both in G. John Ikenberry, David A. Lake, and Michael Mastanduno, eds., *The State and American Foreign Economic Policy* (Ithaca, N.Y.: Cornell University Press, 1988), 59–90, 91–119. Haggard explains this shift in terms of state decisions. Frieden emphasizes economic interest groups, arguing that internationalism is a function of sectoral overseas investment. His evidence falls far short of his claims. He does not show that the economic sectors he posits were real economic entities, nor does he show an extensive involvement in politics of the sort he claims. Neither type of analysis has much room for considering the logic of political argument in the Democratic order about the relation between national and international recovery, a logic that drew Democratic leaders toward more internationalist positions.

Crises and opportunities

In the 1930s political and economic crises were deep and forceful. These crises did not emerge in a mechanical fashion as an objective breakdown – instead, they were defined by political conflicts in the context of dramatic failures of prior economic and political arrangements. In other words, political conflicts turned deep economic and political problems into full-blown crises.

There was no automatic determination of crisis outcomes. The new political order was not required by the Depression, as other responses were possible. Instead, the Democratic order was built through creative responses to the multiple crises of the 1930s. Democratic policies prevented the economic situation from deteriorating further after the early 1930s. The new political order helped reform labor relations and greatly reduced the extent to which industrial conflicts created wide social disorder. The construction of new political forces overcame the rigidity and exclusiveness of Republican political practices.

The next chapter develops these themes in examining the passage of the National Labor Relations Act. This measure remains important for its role in redefining labor relations. And its passage reveals the centrality of a new Democratic bloc and progressive liberalism in the decade's key political shifts. In its importance the Wagner Act has few serious competitors in the 1930s, most notably the Social Security Act. Popular mobilization in support of the Social Security Act was narrower, less explosive, and more reliant on lobbying and electoral activities. Business was much less unified in its view of the Social Security Act than in its opposition to the National Labor Relations Act. With the former one can make a serious argument that sections of business helped initiate the reform process. With the NLRA it is hard to get such an argument off the ground empirically.[45] But these claims run ahead of my argument, which now turns to the great battles about labor relations of the mid-1930s.

45. On the Social Security Act, see Edward Berkowitz and Kim McQuaid, *Creating the Welfare State – The Political Economy of Twentieth Century Reform* (New York: Praeger, 1980), 113, 165–7; Jerry R. Cates, *Insuring Inequality: Administrative Leadership in Social Security, 1935–54* (Ann Arbor: University of Michigan Press, 1983); G. William Domhoff, "Corporate-Liberal Theory and the Social Security Act: A Chapter in the Sociology of Knowledge," *Politics and Society* 15, no. 3 (1986–7): 297–330; Jill Quadagno, "Welfare Capitalism and the Social Security Act of 1935," *American Sociological Review* (1984): 632–47; Jill Quadagno, *The Transformation of Old Age Security: Class and Politics in the American Welfare State* (Chicago, Ill.: University of Chicago Press, 1988), 99–111; and Theda Skocpol and John Ikenberry, "The Political Formation of the American Welfare State in Historical and Comparative Perspective," in *Comparative Social Research*, vol. 5, *The Welfare State, 1883–1983*, ed. Richard F. Tomasson (Greenwich, Conn.: JAI Press, 1983), 87–148.

4

Passing the Wagner Act and building a new Democratic state

In 1934, I went to work for TVA as a secretary in the filing department. They didn't mind that I was blacklisted. TVA was very liberal and pro-union at that time, and they had an office workers' union – the American Federation of Office Employees, which I joined – so they were used to dealing with unions. All the time I worked for TVA, I stayed active in the labor movement as a delegate to the Central Labor Council and a volunteer organizer through their general organization committee.

On Labor Day of 1936 we put on the biggest and longest parade this part of the country had ever seen. We marched down Gay Street (our main street) to the tune of five high school bands. Every local union, under the banner of the AFL, had a big float. . . . We had a beauty queen, a wrestling match, and free barbecue – all the hoopla that goes with a celebration.

– Lucille Thornburgh, a union activist in Tennessee[1]

Who passed the Wagner Act?

The Wagner Act (National Labor Relations Act, or NLRA) passed in 1935 amid economic and political crises. Its passage was due primarily to the efforts of progressive liberals inside and outside the government, allied with a mass labor movement. The measure played a key positive role in forming durable new industrial unions.

Who passed the Wagner Act? – progressive liberals and the labor movement. What caused the Wagner Act to pass? – the political efforts of both forces. These two answers are so similar because I emphasize the causal role of political variables in political outcomes. In identifying who passed a bill, asking "what happened?" is apt to yield an answer featuring politicians. But there is a distinction between defining the agents

---

1. Thornburgh's oral history is in Eliot Wigginton, ed., *Refuse to Stand Silently By – An Oral History of Grass Roots Social Activism in America, 1921–64* (New York: Doubleday, 1992), 126–7.

most directly responsible for a political event, and identifying the causal sequence that best explains it.

The first aim – saying who passed the Wagner Act – is not as easily reached as it may seem. Acts are passed by legislators, whose votes are recorded. But it may require a careful search to find the most responsible individuals and groups, given partisan and ideological conflicts and credit-claiming. Identifying responsible agents is not the same as providing a causal account, unless one presumes that intentions and causes are always identical. The presumption in political science and political sociology is often close to the opposite, that legislative acts should be explained in terms of nonpolitical variables (demographic, economic, or social) or the requirements of political institutions. The actions of the immediately responsible agents are regarded as caused by forces mostly beyond their control (and perhaps their understanding). Thus numerous accounts of the Wagner Act attribute it mainly to economic pressures (related to the Depression) or movements (labor) or the alleged needs of business elites with whom progressive liberals were in contact.

Progressive liberals caused the passage of the NLRA in two crucial ways. They forged that measure out of many possible responses to a dire situation. And they helped form a political bloc with the strength to bring about its passage and implementation. Progressive liberals were certainly not the only causal force, but they were far from being agents whose actions merely registered forces originating elsewhere.

The Wagner Act drew on decades of state and local policy experience and articulated progressive conceptions of a cooperative, efficient social order. The requirement that a measure withstand stringent judicial review and the experience of prior New Deal legislation influenced the formulation of the NLRA. The National Industrial Recovery Act (NIRA, passed in 1933) and its labor policy were major reference points, positively in their assertion of union rights and negatively in the shortcomings of Section 7(a):

> Every code of fair competition, agreement, and license approved, pre-scribed, or issued under this title shall contain the following conditions: (1) That employees shall have the right to organize and bargain collectively through representatives of their own choosing, and shall be free from the interference, restraint, or coercion of employers of labor, or their agents, in the designation of such representatives or in self-organization or in other concerted activities for the purpose of collective bargaining or other mutual aid or protection; (2) that no employee and no one seeking employment shall be required as a condition of employment to join any company union or to refrain from joining, organizing, or assisting a labor organization of his own choosing; and (3) that employers shall comply with the maximum

hours of labor, minimum rates of pay, and other conditions of employment, approved or prescribed by the President.[2]

The NIRA's lack of enforcement provisions blocked efforts to use Section 7(a) to force employers to recognize unions.[3] When the Supreme Court overturned the NIRA in May 1935, the vacuum in labor legislation provided a context in which advocates of prolabor reform could gain support.

The Wagner Act affirmed workers' right to form unions and bargain with employers:

> It is hereby declared to be the policy of the United States to eliminate the causes of certain substantial obstructions to the free flow of commerce and to mitigate and eliminate those obstructions when they have occurred by encouraging the practice and procedure of collective bargaining and by protecting the exercise by workers of full freedom of association, self-organization, and designation of representatives of their own choosing, for the purpose of negotiating the terms and conditions of their employment or other mutual aid or protection.[4]

The Act stated that none of its sections should be construed as interfering with the right to strike.[5] A new and more powerful labor board was authorized to conduct representation elections and to investigate employers' efforts to avoid recognizing or dealing with unions. Through the National Labor Relations Board and the courts, the Wagner Act could compel employer recognition of unions.

The Wagner Act strongly asserted a right to organize, prohibited unfair labor practices by management, and provided significant means of enforcement. It broke sharply with prior formulations that equated labor's right to organize with management's right to block unions. The NLRA reformulated regulatory themes present on the left of progressive liberal policy circles for several decades. It did so in ways that strongly encouraged building unions – thus in terms of actual national policies the Wagner Act was sharply discontinuous with prior practices.[6]

---

2. National Industrial Recovery Act, H.R. 5755, June 16, 1933, *Public Laws of the U.S.A.* – passed by the Seventy-Third Congress, 1933–34 (Washington, D.C.: Government Printing Office, 1934), 195–200.
3. Complaints about the inability of the labor relations machinery to secure compliance and to protect efforts to achieve unions began in 1933 and persisted. These problems were reported to Roosevelt many times. Letter, William Connery to Roosevelt, 11/26/33, Folder 1933–4, Official File 407 (Labor), FDR Library.
4. National Labor Relations Act, S1958 July 5, 1935, *Public Laws of the U.S.A.* – passed by the Seventy-Fourth Congress, 1935–6 (Washington, D.C.: Government Printing Office, 1936), 449–50.
5. National Labor Relations Act, 457.
6. See Irving Bernstein, *New Deal Collective Bargaining Policy* (Berkeley: University of California Press, 1950); Joseph P. Goldberg, "The Law and Practice of Collective

Debating the Wagner Act

Arguments about the Wagner Act deserve more attention than they usually get in accounts of its passage. Debates were loud and vigorous before and after 1935, regarding authority in enterprises, the relative power of competing social groups, and the macroeconomic consequences of unions.[7] In normal politics, such debate might be only a conventional statement of settled aims and understandings. But in the fluid, conflictual moment when the NLRA was passed, groups and their aims were not rigidly fixed. The debates helped shape the bill and its consequences.

Passing the Wagner Act was in no way routine or predictable. The attacks on the Wagner Act were weak partly because they were rigid and formulaic, making their proponents appear unable to grasp the seriousness of the crises underway. Critics stressed that unions protected by the NLRA would unfairly restrict the rights of owners and managers and destroy legitimate company unions. New and prospective unions were depicted as insensitive and narrowly self-interested groups whose striving for power would lead to coercion even against their own members.[8] State assistance of unionization would yield arbitrary and inefficient closed shops. Further, the NLRA was an unnecessary and destructive intrusion into basically private matters. Employers claimed it was

Bargaining," in Joseph P. Goldberg, ed., *Federal Policies and Worker Status Since the Thirties* (Madison: University of Wisconsin/Industrial Relations Research Association, 1976), 13–19; and J. Joseph Huthmacher, *Senator Robert F. Wagner and the Rise of Urban Liberalism* (New York: Atheneum, 1948), 103–45.

7. In 1934 there was extensive testimony on an earlier version of the Wagner Act before the Senate Labor Committee. The following summary relies on the records of those hearings, as well as other congressional records in 1934–5. Debates in Congress, the executive, and the press are discussed at length in Bernstein, *New Deal Collective Bargaining Policy;* Daniel Albert Sipe, "A Moment of the State: The Enactment of the National Labor Relations Act, 1935" (Ph.D. dissertation, University of Pennsylvania, 1981); Ruth Horowitz, *Political Ideologies of Organized Labor: The New Deal Era* (New Brunswick, N.J.: Transaction, 1978); Peter Irons, *The New Deal Lawyers* (Princeton, N.J.: Princeton University Press, 1982); and Christopher Tomlins, *The State and the Unions: Labor Relations, Law, and the Organized Labor Movement in America, 1880–1960* (Cambridge University Press, 1985).

8. Christopher Tomlins's valuable account of labor law in the 1920s and 1930s is sympathetic to the AFL's voluntarist conception of unions as autonomous, private organizations engaged in supplying labor. While his account of the adaptation of voluntarism to organizational pressures for individualism (and against republican themes) early in the twentieth century is provocative, his account of later decades tends to lose sight of the overall political and ideological context. Thus, Tomlins pays little attention to the great vulnerability of a voluntarist conception of unions as private entities supplying labor to a conservative/populist critique of them as privileged interests. Tomlins, *State and Unions*, 103–60.

unconstitutional, and awaited a favorable judicial outcome.[9] Amid grave crises and great hardship, such arguments appeared as rhetorical professions of a faith whose public appeal was rapidly declining.

The hostility of many critics of the NLRA to genuinely independent unions hampered the construction of a blocking coalition that might have been made with forces in the American Federation of Labor (AFL) anxious about the statist potential of the NLRA. The conventional voluntarism, which once might have provided grounds for adamant opposition to many aspects of the NLRA, was losing influence among union supporters. The AFL moved toward a stance of accepting the NLRA, hoping that it would provide a public framework for private bargaining. This adaptation was pushed along by pressures from within the middle and lower ranks of the organization. (Later, when the National Labor Relations Board [NLRB] appeared to favor the Congress of Industrial Organizations [CIO], the AFL was compelled to fight on a new discursive terrain that presumed extensive state intervention in labor relations.) Conventional AFL notions of unions as private organizations contracting to supply labor could not easily be applied to the new mass industrial settings in ways that were plausible and attractive. In these settings a large and growing semiskilled production force was present in and dependent on the factory. Workers were already in production, not contracting with employers to engage in discrete projects that happened to be located in owners' facilities.

The arguments for the Wagner Act much more directly addressed the nation's crises. Advocates claimed the measure would temper cyclical downturns by remedying economic problems that resulted in insufficient demand. Their view appeared in the text of the NLRA:

> The inequality of bargaining power between employees who do not possess full freedom of association or actual liberty of contract, and employers who are organized in the corporate or other forms of ownership association substantially burdens and affects the flow of commerce, and tends to aggravate recurrent business depressions, by depressing wage rates and the purchasing power of wage earners in industry and by preventing the stabilization of competitive wage rates and working conditions within and between industries.[10]

As the NLRA would permit workers to gain a larger share of national income, it would stabilize and then expand demand. Doubtless Senator Robert Wagner (of New York) and others knew this argument might

9. Bernstein, *New Deal Collective Bargaining Policy*, 106–110; Irons, *New Deal Lawyers*, 247.

10. National Labor Relations Act, 449.

make the act more appealing to some of those uneasy about unions per se. They also knew that a commercial defense improved the NLRA's prospects of surviving judicial review. Yet this positive view of the act's economic meaning was no ploy, as underconsumption analyses of the crash and Depression were influential among policy makers and economists.[11]

A second theme was orderly social development. Wagner and others argued that disorganized and arbitrary labor relations were destructive – the underconsumption argument was intertwined with notions of the desirable economic and social consequences of industrial order.[12] The Wagner Act would stabilize industrial relations, whose irrationalities were dangerous. This argument emerged from a combination of working-class pressure and progressive concern for stable administration and economic recovery. Without mass strikes and related action, "order" would not have required labor law reform. The scale and public effects of labor conflict precluded conceiving labor relations in purely private terms; unions were agents representing workers in a setting that was a proper object of public concern.

A third claim was that the Wagner Act would establish greater fairness among competing social groups. The lack of unions was an obstacle to a free play of interests; state intervention would allow fairer contests and better outcomes. Fairness could be conceived in organizational terms, as balancing employers' power, or in terms of the needs of the downtrodden for respect.[13] Labor groups rarely made the fairness argument in class terms; the emphasis was on the right of groups of individuals to seek political and economic benefits.

Among these pro-NLRA themes, arguments for economic improvement and social order were stressed by economists and other profession-

11. Michael Bernstein, "Why the Great Depression Was Great: Toward a New Understanding of the Interwar Economic Crisis in the United States," in Steve Fraser and Gary Gerstle, eds., *The Rise and Fall of the New Deal Order, 1930–1980* (Princeton, N.J.: Princeton University Press, 1989); Walter S. Salant, "The Spread of Keynesian Doctrines and Practices in the United States," in Peter A. Hall, ed., *The Political Power of Economic Ideas* (Princeton, N.J.: Princeton University Press, 1989), 27–51.

12. Letter, H. A. Millis to Roosevelt, June 21, 1935, Folder NLRB July–October 1935, Official File 716 (National Labor Relations Board), FDR Library. See also Bernstein, *New Deal Collective Bargaining Policy*, 112; and R. W. Fleming, "The Significance of the Wagner Act," in Milton Derber and Edwin Young, eds., *Labor and the New Deal* (Madison: University of Wisconsin Press, 1957), 129.

13. Ellis W. Hawley, *The New Deal and the Problem of Monopoly: A Study in Economic Ambivalence* (Princeton, N.J.: Princeton University Press, 1966), 195, 276; and James MacGregor Burns, *Roosevelt: The Lion and the Fox* (New York, Harcourt, Brace, and World, 1956), 218–19.

als who supported the measure. The NLRA's prolabor supporters emphasized fairness.[14] When Roosevelt addressed labor relations, his view of fairness meant a duty to spare the poor and oppressed from degradation. He also expressed a willingness to support popular efforts of many types to build organizations that would encourage more dignified and effective participation in American political and social life. Despite its paternalism Roosevelt's view was compatible with the CIO's emphasis on unions as representative agents. This convergence could lead to a conception of unions as helping management to sustain order and govern workers. Yet the voluntarist alternative to a union discourse on the importance of public representation was feeble – it could only affirm the right of individual workers to collaborate in negotiating the terms of their employment. Representation was a powerful concept partly because it provided a bridge between claims about how unions would improve labor relations and broad commitments to democracy that extended far beyond the labor movement and its closest allies. Appeals to a right of representation expanded the audience for arguments on behalf of independent unions.[15]

Newer labor voices and the NLRA's progressive liberal proponents sometimes made a fourth argument after 1935, claiming the NLRA would encourage "industrial democracy" as a complement to political democracy.[16] Industrial democracy was mostly posed as a negative demand, to end humiliating forms of workplace domination. For most who used the term, industrial democracy meant organized representation of workers by active and powerful industrial unions, with bargained agreements. Industrial democracy was a major term for many CIO leaders. It meant unionization and cooperative industrial relations, not comanagement (much less employee ownership). Fraser emphasizes the managerial side of the views of Hillman and the early CIO:

> [The CIO] had a strategy, national industrial unionism; a social perspective, functional integration within an interdependent economy of complex, large-scale bureaucratic organizations; and a political economy, planned, expanded production and state sanctioned redistribution of income in the interests of security and consumption.[17]

---

14. In 1935 Roosevelt was deluged with such arguments from labor and prounion forces; they appear in Official File 407 (Labor), FDR Library.
15. Tomlins downplays this dimension of the political conflict about unions. Tomlins, *State and Unions*, 239, 243.
16. Horowitz, *Political Ideologies of Organized Labor*, 175–7; Huthmacher, *Robert F. Wagner*, 192.
17. Steven Fraser, *Labor Will Rule: Sidney Hillman and the Rise of American Labor* (New York: The Free Press, 1991), 332.

Here Fraser understates the democratic meaning of CIO views in the labor relations context of the 1930s. Yet he rightly indicates the limited character of what industrial democracy meant for most of its proponents. It was conceived as providing workers with a voice, regular forms of interest articulation, and procedural safeguards. While parts of the labor movement and some of its supporters envisioned more participatory forms of industrial relations, such aims were not put clearly in positive terms. Industrial democracy generally did not mean the extensive democratization of ownership and control proposed by some advocates of workplace reform in the 1970s and 1980s.

Labor's arguments for the NLRA were not well developed in the prepassage debates. The unions had trouble articulating a public position beyond demanding recognition. This stance relied on the progressive defense of unions as legitimate interest organizations essential for order and fair competition in a complex society. Strong independent unions would balance rights and obligations between employers and workers. Yet unions gave little account of the actual arrangements that might take shape to express the new balance.[18]

It was not easy to find concepts with which to think about the industrial order that might arise from the Wagner Act. Progressive liberal discourse was not developed or specific in this area. Although there had been considerable debate about policies among progressive liberals, there was little practical experience of the industrial relations proposed by the Wagner Act.

Yet there were few feasible alternatives to progressive liberal themes. The Wagner Act was not defended on grounds that it would redistribute political and social power toward the working class. Class terms were marginal to the discourses of existing unions and only a little more prominent among emergent union forces. That the unions rarely made claims in class terms is clear in histories of labor in the decade, including accounts sympathetic to working-class radicalism.[19]

Would any available language of class have enhanced the clarity and power of workers' claims? The Communist Party's internal language – working-class power leading toward the dictatorship of the proletariat – had no prospect of being widely accepted, and the alternative it pro-

---

18. Horowitz, *Political Ideologies of Organized Labor*, 127–30; Tomlins, *State and Unions*, 149.
19. See Frances Piven and Richard Cloward, *Poor People's Movements: Why They Succeed and How They Fail* (New York: Vintage, 1979); Staughton Lynd and Alice Lynd, *Rank and File: Personal Histories by Working Class Organizers* (Boston: Beacon Press, 1973); and Stanley Vittoz, *New Deal Labor Policy and the American Industrial Economy* (Chapel Hill: University of North Carolina Press, 1987), 164–6.

posed was deeply unattractive. The language of the non-Communist socialist left was abstract and rhetorical; its maximalist inclinations also meant political impracticality in the mid-1930s.[20]

Political and social forces drawn from subordinate classes waged battles for rights and group interests in progressive liberal and pluralist discourses far more than they made their case in class terms. This was a reasonable choice – when it was even considered as a choice – because the available class discourses did not provide plausible remedies for the weaknesses of progressive liberal conceptions of fairness among competing interests. Thus the NLRA was debated in terms of its economic contribution, the proper role of the state, the rights of unorganized groups to compete for power, and the limits of employers' property rights.[21] Unions were advocated as representative institutions in a new industrial order: They would favor social stability, economic growth, and democratic norms.

The preceding sketch of debates about the Wagner Act is already enough to undermine several interpretations. It discourages viewing that measure as primarily a business initiative – explicitly probusiness arguments almost always opposed the Wagner Act. Unions were attacked as self-interested groups apt to violate property rights, yield economic ruin and social chaos, and thrive on intrusive state action. The arguments labor made for the NLRA do not support a strong claim that unions caused its passage, as these arguments were neither original nor distinctively powerful.

Advocacy of labor law reform was most powerful when it combined

---

20. The contrast between Popular Front concepts of popular democracy and an internal language dominated by the conventions of Marxism-Leninism is noted by most analysts of the Communist experience in the United States in the 1930s, and by a number of participants in that experience. In addition to works cited earlier on American Communism, see Dorothy Healey and Maurice Isserman, *Dorothy Healey Remembers a Life in the American Communist Party* (New York: Oxford University Press, 1990); Steve Nelson, James R. Barrett, and Rob Ruck, *Steve Nelson, American Radical* (Pittsburgh: University of Pittsburgh Press, 1981); and James Weinstein, *Ambiguous Legacy: The Left in American Politics* (New York: New Viewpoints, 1975). There was less distance between the public and internal discourses of the Socialist Party, but a public avowal of socialist objectives was not an effective means of gaining popular support.

21. Karl Klare rightly stresses the extent to which the Wagner Act restricted employers' range of action in operating businesses, in their view infringing on prior rights. He devotes insufficient attention to the language in which limiting employers' activities was justified, with its emphases on efficiency, order, and fairness. Thus he is tempted to overstate the measure's radicalism; it is possible to advocate limiting property rights without regarding that as a step toward transforming them. Karl Klare, "Judicial Deradicalization of the Wagner Act and the Origins of Modern Legal Consciousness," *Minnesota Law Review* 62, no. 3 (March 1978): 277–90.

progressive themes of order, efficiency, and fairness with a strong democratic impulse. The pro-NLRA case rejected authoritarian labor practices and claimed that unions would improve the economic and political position of workers. In the 1930s this position had a radical content both regarding relations between workers and employers and concerning the role of the government.[22]

Why the NLRA passed: the alignment of forces

The votes for the NLRA were overwhelming in the House and Senate in June 1935. Roosevelt signed the measure early in July.[23] This sweeping approval is misleading, as many who would have preferred a different bill or no bill at all did not oppose it when passage seemed certain. In 1934 a similar measure had failed, receiving little support from the administration. Roosevelt did not strongly urge changes in labor law that year, and was aware of the strong opposition to the first version of the Wagner Act.[24]

The charged context in which the NLRA passed was certainly important to that outcome. The previous year, 1934, saw widespread strikes and demonstrations, sometimes as part of dramatic citywide political movements.[25] In 1935 such strikes declined, yet overall strike activity persisted at a high level. The turbulence of 1934 strongly ex-

---

22. That the NLRA was not framed as a way to produce more radical shifts (such as "workers' control") is no surprise if one listens to its protagonists and their opponents. Even militant workers in the labor movement were generally not calling for "workers' control," much less socialism. In several neo-Marxist accounts there is a striking absence where one might expect discussion of what workers said they wanted. Thus the notion of a blocked radical upsurge, which is central for these accounts, is not sustained by reference to actual frustrated radicals. Instead it relies on a notion of what was "objectively" possible, presuming that economic and political radicalism are the natural and appropriate forms of political consciousness for the working class in capitalist societies. See Michael Davis, *Prisoners of the American Dream* (London: Verso, 1986); Piven and Cloward, *Poor People's Movements*, 96–180; and Michael Goldfield, "Worker Insurgency, Radical Organization, and New Deal Labor Legislation," *American Political Science Review* 83 no. 4 (December 1989): 1257–82.

23. The final vote in the Senate was 63 to 12; efforts to modify the prounion emphasis of the bill in the House were voted down. The House then approved the bill without a record vote. Harry A. Millis and Emily Clark Brown, *From the Wagner Act to Taft-Hartley: A Study of National Labor Policy and Labor Relations* (Chicago: University of Chicago Press, 1950), 28.

24. Memo, "President's Conference with Senators," April 14, 1934, Folder "U.S. Senate 1933–36," *President's Secretary's File* 188, FDR Library. See also Bernstein, *New Deal Collective Bargaining Policy*, 63–70; and Sipe, "Moment of the State," 147–9.

25. Bernstein tracks the major upsurges of 1934–5 in *Turbulent Years* (Boston: Houghton Mifflin, 1970). Dramatic press accounts are collected in Melvyn Dubofsky, ed., *American Labor since the New Deal* (Chicago: Quadrangle Books, 1971).

pressed working-class and popular discontent.[26] A sweeping Democratic victory in the 1934 midterm elections expanded congressional reform forces and widened their field of maneuver. Polarization grew between the national administration and business elites, while populist movements burgeoned.[27]

In this dramatic setting major political actors were aligned in a way that seems not to predict the result. Political interest groups representing business opposed the NLRA. In 1935 business antagonism to the Roosevelt administration was mounting on many fronts.[28] With regard to the NLRA, the great majority of business leaders preferred that the law not pass and favored company unions or none.[29] Attempts have been made to demonstrate that business played a major role in shaping the New Deal in the mid-1930s. But these efforts have found only very limited business support for the main projects of the Roosevelt administration. A small number of business leaders were involved in negotiations about several New Deal measures. Thomas Ferguson has sought to show that business groups were crucial, but without much success. His positive evidence boils down to the fact that Gerald Swope and several other liberal corporate leaders met with Wagner and favored labor law reform. Even if much more contact between progressive liberals and business could be found than seems to have occurred, it would not demonstrate that business forces played a strong causal role. To prove that claim would require showing that such involvement was a distinct initiative undertaken by a reasonably broad section of business elites. Otherwise it is more reasonable to conclude that a small group of liberal business leaders responded positively to and assisted progressive efforts to cope with emerging political and economic crises.[30]

26. In 1934, 1,856 strikes resulted in 19.6 million days of absence from work; in 1935, 2,014 strikes resulted in 15.5 million days of absence. Bureau of the Census, *Historical Statistics of the United States – Colonial Times to 1970*, D970-985, "Work Stoppages, Workers Involved, Man-Days Idle, Major Issues, and Average Duration: 1881–1970" (Washington: Government Printing Office, 1975), 179.

27. Arthur M. Schlesinger, Jr., *The Politics of Upheaval* (Boston: Houghton Mifflin, 1960), 242–54.

28. Although analysts differ on the depth of business opposition, it was clearly the predominant stance in 1935, especially in the spring and summer of that year. In addition to Schlesinger's account in *Politics of Upheaval*, 270–320, see Hawley, *New Deal and Monopoly*, 154–5.

29. Business opposition to the measure is depicted in Bernstein, *Turbulent Years*, 336–51; and Vittoz, *New Deal Labor Policy*, 149–53.

30. One can avoid these problems simply by presuming that whenever one sees business participation in a project, the general power of business warrants treating the outcome as due to business efforts. Ferguson might not be happy with resting his case on this premise, but given his weak evidence, doing so would be necessary to make it persuasive. See Thomas Ferguson, "From Normalcy to New Deal: Industrial Structure, Party

Efforts to establish the predominant power of business have often tried to find an economic cleavage among firms that could be linked to support for the New Deal. For example, it has been argued that business groups and allied politicians who wanted to accelerate development in the South and West played a key role in shaping Democratic choices.[31] Several sectoral candidates have been proposed as key sources of business support: capital-intensive firms; firms producing goods for mass consumption; and firms with large interests in international trade and investment. These claims do not outline a single coherent group but designate overlapping sets of firms that together would make up a large part of the national business elite. The basic image underlying such arguments is that large modern firms were open to the New Deal insofar as it promised to produce a smoother and less conflictual form of corporate capitalism. Perhaps they should have been. But there has been no moment of sharper antagonism between a national administration and business in the United States in the twentieth century than in the mid-1930s.[32]

Most accounts of the New Deal in terms of economic interest groups

Competition, and American Public Policy in the Great Depression," *International Organization* (Winter 1984): 88.

31. Jordan A. Schwarz, *The New Dealers: Power Politics in the Age of Roosevelt* (New York: Alfred A. Knopf, 1993), provides interesting portraits of political and economic figures of the 1930s. His account of the New Deal as a regional development project for the less industrially advanced parts of the country shows some of the empirical defects of conceiving the New Deal as defined by large internationally oriented firms or by mass-production firms. But he does not make his positive case persuasively, partly because he relies on a similar conception of politics as conflict among economic interest groups. He simply defines these groups in regional terms.

32. In a study of the political economy of the New Deal, Colin Gordon characterizes business support for the Wagner Act in this way: "Some labor-intensive industries and firms hoped the act would give teeth to the NRA's policies, which had placed the onus of organization on a weak labor movement and done little to coerce chiselers. Some mass-production firms hoped the act might encourage industrial rather than craft unionism, arguing that the former made it possible to regulate labor costs across an industry with little managerial sacrifice. And some consumer-goods firms and retailers, again pointing to the failure of the NRA, continued to hope that the act might revitalize or redistribute mass-purchasing power." This implies broad business support for the Wagner Act. Gordon, like others who make such claims, does not indicate the number, size, or activities of these allegedly pro-NLRA firms. Nor does he show which of the many possible economic logics he cites was predominant in defining positive business views of unionization. Lacking evidence of the first point or clarity on the second, he immediately qualifies his claim and says that business had serious reservations about the NLRA. His argument, more judicious and careful than most of its type, illustrates the limits of efforts to explain the Wagner Act through theories in which the political domination of business groups is presumed. Colin Gordon, *New Deals: Business, Labor, and Politics in America, 1920–1935* (Cambridge University Press, 1994), 215.

downplay the extent of political antagonism between business and the administration in the mid-1930s, even disparaging public expressions of severe hostility as unserious. This misunderstanding of the political situation flows from their analytical position: If politics amounts to the pursuit of economic interests through the state, other sorts of political arguments will appear superfluous or as a mask for interest-seeking. Steven Fraser's account of labor politics in the 1930s and 1940s illustrates the problems of trying to explain large national political trends on the basis of alleged sectoral economic interests. Evidence for direct business leadership in defining the NLRA is not compelling, which leads him to qualify his claims about the role of business:

> [A]t the height of the "Second New Deal," the newly empowered "Keynesian" elite enjoyed at best limited support among the great mass of entrepreneurs and practically no support among older industrial groups. Rather, the Keynesian instinct was given coherence and political form by men and women who stood outside the marketplace: industrial engineers, social scientists and economists, foundation administrators, "scientific" social workers, lawyers, "Progressive" legislators, and even, on occasion, a labor leader like Hillman.[33]

Progressive liberals were usually not entrepreneurs, but the idea that they were "outside" the marketplace is either wrong (industrial engineers, lawyers, labor leaders) or confusing (social workers, social scientists). Fraser has trouble locating them in the class or economic interest group terms on which he relies to explain political action. He wants to explain political outcomes as the result of efforts by powerful economic groups to attain their interests. When a result occurs that is clearly contrary to what his approach would suggest – as when a highly mobilized and unified business community is defeated on what it regards as a major issue – he has no analytical answer, and is left with vague descriptions of the agents who were responsible. What is missing is any notion of a political sphere with its own dynamics and forms so that its outcomes cannot be considered purely as a function of the social and economic power of the groups to which political actors appear to be linked.

Most of the Republican Party had nothing good to say about the NLRA. Closely tied to business elites who opposed it – or representing rural districts suspicious of unions – Republicans made their opposition clear before and after the NLRA's passage. Even muted formulations, as in the 1936 Republican platform, had a critical edge given business

33. Fraser, *Labor Will Rule*, 266.

claims about outside interference in labor relations by national unions: "We pledge ourselves to: Protect the right of labor to organize and to bargain collectively through representatives of its own choosing without interference from any source."[34] By the mid-1930s progressive Republicans provided important support for the New Deal, but they certainly did not represent the leadership of the Republican Party.

Republican and business opposition is no surprise. Yet there was little enthusiasm for a prolabor measure from the organized Democratic Party. Its 1932 platform made no reference to passing such a measure, or even to unions.[35] Nor was labor law a central Democratic issue in the 1934 campaign, although the militant labor upsurge of that year influenced the campaign debate.[36] The Democratic forces represented by James Farley, head of the Democratic National Committee, as well as more conservative Democrats in the Cabinet, did not view the Wagner Act as a priority, and offered at most qualified support.

There was at first no more than lukewarm support from President Roosevelt.[37] Disinterested in the 1934 bill, he was not very supportive early in 1935. When the Supreme Court's nullification of the NIRA (May 27, 1935) created a void in labor relations, his interest grew.[38] Roosevelt's eventual support was crucial (guaranteeing the measure would not be vetoed, and signaling his allies about the appropriate stance), but he did not take the initiative.

Labor's political representatives supported the Wagner Act. The AFL lobbied for it in 1935, though its leaders remained cautious about state

34. "Republican Platform of 1936," in Donald Bruce Johnson, ed., *National Party Platforms*, vol. 1, 1840–1956 (Urbana: University of Illinois Press, 1978), 367.
35. Johnson, *National Party Platforms*, 331–2.
36. Roosevelt was aware of the year's labor conflict and received many warnings of its severity, such as Memo, Isador Lubin (Bureau of Labor Statistics) to Roosevelt, n.d., Official File 407B (Strikes), FDR Library. He also received many letters complaining about disorder and urging action against strikes, as in Folder 1934, Folder 1935, OF 407B (Strikes), FDR Library.
37. See Fleming, "Significance of the Wagner Act," 128; and Frances Perkins, *The Roosevelt I Knew* (New York: Harper & Row, 1964), 239.
38. Participants in the pre-NLRA labor boards criticized the lack of mechanisms for securing compliance with decisions; compliance with decisions that required employers to make concessions occurred at most one-third of the time, probably less. Letter, J. W. R. Maguire to Roosevelt, 5/9/35, and Memo, Hopkins to Roosevelt, 2/12/35, both in Folder Labor 1935, OF 407 (Labor), FDR Library. Roosevelt's low level of interest is indicated by the lack of attention given to the NLRA in his main statements and speeches in 1935. See *The Public Papers and Addresses of Franklin D. Roosevelt*, vol. 4, *The Court Disapproves – 1935*, compiled by Samuel I. Rosenman (New York: Random House, 1938); and William E. Leuchtenburg, *Franklin D. Roosevelt and the New Deal, 1932–1940* (New York: Harper & Row, 1963), 145.

intervention.[39] When the forces that would soon become the CIO entered the debates, they strongly supported the NLRA. Yet the industrial unions were only taking shape in 1934–5 and could not play a major direct political role.

The Communist Party criticized the NLRA, as it did many New Deal measures in 1934 and 1935. Its rejection of the act was cast alternately in ultramilitant and quasi-voluntarist terms, linked by hostility to the administration and the New Deal.[40] The Communist Party did not try to pass the Wagner Act; its efforts at mobilizing the industrial working class indirectly increased pressure for it. Populist currents were uncertain about the potential power of the unions. Though these forces tended to favor labor law reform (especially when their leaders were trying to outflank Roosevelt from the left), passing the Wagner Act was not their priority.[41]

How can one explain the NLRA if the support of Roosevelt, the unions, and the Democratic Party was qualified by lack of enthusiasm or power? My answer is that in formulating and passing the Wagner Act, the leading agent was a progressive liberal political leadership. This political force took shape across several institutions, crucially the national state; but it was not the state per se, nor the party in general. Democratic progressive liberals formulated the bill and carried it through the administration and Congress. Their arguments and actions were the primary cause of the NLRA – as well as of the political course of which it was a crucial component.

Beyond the efforts of progressive liberals, the weakness of political forces who would normally have stopped it encouraged the NLRA's passage. The Republican Party lost badly in 1932 and 1934. Its grip on the national state had ended; its position in Congress was reduced to an unprecedented extent. The political representatives of business shared the burden of Republican defeats. The crucial power of business elites to withhold investment was limited by the grave economic difficulties, for which business was widely blamed. It was risky for business groups to threaten to disrupt an already devastated economy.[42]

39. Horowitz, *Political Ideologies of Organized Labor*, 110–27, 131.
40. See Bert Cochran, *Labor and Communism: The Conflict That Shaped American Unions* (Princeton, N.J.: Princeton University Press, 1977), 78; and Bernstein, *New Deal Collective Bargaining Policy*, 108–9. Sympathetic accounts of the role of the Communist Party in the labor movement pay little or no attention to its opposition to the NLRA. A good example of this delicacy is Roger Keeran's *The Communist Party and the Auto Workers* (Bloomington: Indiana University Press, 1980), 121–47.
41. Alan Brinkley, *Voices of Protest: Huey Long, Father Coughlin, and the Great Depression* (New York: Alfred A. Knopf, 1982), 246–8.
42. Fred Block argues that economic crises offer opportunities for reform coalitions between state managers and subordinate social groups; they expand the power and

The pre-NLRA New Deal state was weakened both by its evident incapacity to manage labor relations and by divisions (even in the cabinet) over labor legislation.[43] This disorder hindered forces in the state who preferred a less strongly prolabor measure. Opposition from voluntarist tendencies in organized labor also waned. The hardships suffered by the AFL's members compelled a more positive attitude toward state intervention – so did the competitive pressure from a growing industrial unionism.[44]

Labor insurgency

The economic crisis and labor movement were causally important – it is hard to imagine the Wagner Act without either. The economic crisis shaped the context in which the measure was proposed and passed. Yet it did not determine that the NLRA be enacted. The labor movement deeply influenced the political context, via its mobilization in workplaces and cities. Popular pressure was expressed in the strikes of 1934 and 1935 and other modes of protest. This pressure threatened public order and industrial stability at a point when simply settling disputes on employers' terms was politically unacceptable. Popular pressure was also an electoral threat, which materialized in 1934.[45]

The labor insurgency encouraged political mobilization against the Republicans and business interest groups. It enhanced the position of prolabor forces in the emergent Democratic coalition, who now could more credibly argue that only strong measures would restore stability. Without widespread and sustained labor unrest, a measure as strongly prolabor as the Wagner Act would probably not have succeeded. Yet the strikes were not enough, nor did they yield a movement that could itself pass the NLRA.

The unions in 1935 were not strong enough to achieve the Wagner Act. They included only a modest proportion of the labor force and could not play the leading legislative role. Labor did not write the

freedom of maneuver of state managers and reduce business elites' ability to prevent reform. Fred Block, "The Ruling Class Does Not Rule: Notes on the Marxist Theory of the State," in Fred Block, *Revising State Theory: Essays in Politics and Postindustrialism* (Philadelphia: Temple University Press, 1987), 51–68.

43. Many examples of state incapacity are reported to Roosevelt in OF 716 (NLRB); a good collection of them appears in Hermann Kebrunk, "Report to the National Labor Relations Board," 2/26/36, OF 716 (NLRB), FDR Library.

44. The persistence of AFL voluntarism is a major theme both in Tomlins, *State and Unions,* and in Horowitz, *Political Ideologies of Organized Labor,* 73, 121.

45. It was not hard to notice that many of the major strikes of 1934 occurred after the earlier version of the NLRA was withdrawn by its sponsors because of lack of support. Leuchtenburg, *Roosevelt and the New Deal,* 114–17.

legislation, nor were all their proposals accepted by the main authors, Robert Wagner and his aide, Leon Keyserling.[46] Working-class pressure was mediated through other channels, as when administration officials made reports calling for action:

> When I was in Detroit in December [1934] automobile manufacturers told me frankly that section 7a was a mistake and they did not intend to live up to it. This statement was made at a meeting of the Regional Labor Board and representatives of employees heard it. The sentiment aroused by this attitude is largely responsible for the growth of union membership in Detroit in recent months, and the cases were brought to the National Labor Board primarily to get the Government to inform the automobile industry that it could not pursue such a lawless course. The employees were confident that the National Labor Board and the Administration would make a decision that section 7a can not be violated by the automobile companies or any one else. They have been disappointed in that, and the attempt to compromise and conciliate without making a clear cut decision on the charges of law violation is, I think, a very serious mistake in policy, that will forfeit confidence of working people in the Administration.[47]

Despite the significance of working-class action, that upsurge did not dictate the enactment of Wagner's bill or a similar measure. Given the political weakness of labor, several responses to the strikes and demonstrations might have been made, most of them much less helpful to the development of the labor movement.

The central role of progressive liberals

The passage of the Wagner Act was primarily due to the determined efforts of progressive liberals, who developed the measure and guided it through Congress. Senator Robert Wagner was the leader and a representative figure. He advocated the NLRA knowing that many in Congress shared his views.[48]

Explanations of the Wagner Act are summarized in Table 4.1. Viewing the Wagner Act as political reform provides the best explanation of the measure's passage and meaning. The number and diversity of forces relevant to the NLRA make it important to consider causality as a relation whose form and intensity varies. Table 4.1 downplays a causal relation that is rarely part of useful accounts of these events – full

---

46. Huthmacher describes the preparation of the bill in *Robert F. Wagner*, 187–97.
47. Letter, William M. Leiserson to Frances Perkins, April 11, 1934, OF 407B (Strikes), FDR Library.
48. Murray Edelman, "New Deal Sensitivity to Labor Interests," in Derber and Young, eds., *Labor and the New Deal*, 186–8.

Table 4.1. *Paths to the Wagner Act*

Wagner Act	Economic crisis	Labor movement	Liberal capital	Political reformers
As capitalist reform	3	2	3	1
As working class conquest	3	3	1	1
As pluralist compromise	2	2	2	1
As political reform	2	3	1	3
As economic crisis adjustment	4	1	1	1

1 -- reflects (transmits causal pressures originating elsewhere)
2 -- selects (exerts causal influence)
3 -- shapes (exerts strong causal influences)
4 -- determines (sufficient cause)

determination, where a single variable sufficiently influences the outcomes of interest to produce all the variation in question. I use "selects" to mean that an agent or process influences an outcome mainly within terms set by another, analytically prior variable. For example one might claim – incorrectly – that liberal Democrats selected the Wagner Act, but the range of their choices was fixed by economic crisis problems. I use "shapes" to designate a stronger causal claim. To say that factor *a* shapes outcome *b* means that *a* "chooses" *b* within limits set by features of *a* as well as by exogenous factors.

To ascribe the main causal role to progressive liberals calls for an account of the form and shape of this group. It emerged by linking individuals and small groups from several places at the top of American politics. The links were made and strengthened through political discussion and argument among prospective participants and through shared experiences of conflict with other forces. The resulting networks then expanded as new progressive liberal institutions were developed.[49] Because it cut across conventional institutions and was not organized explicitly as such, there is no membership list to which one can point.

---

49. In referring to new progressive liberal institutions I mean to designate new agencies of the federal state, new agencies of state and local governments, and new or renovated professional and academic associations. Progressive liberals had positive conceptions of what they were doing. But their aims were clarified and often expanded through the process of building these forms, because of the extensive dialogue among adherents of the new order, as well as what they learned from their initial efforts.

Figure 4.1. *The shape of leadership in the Democratic order*

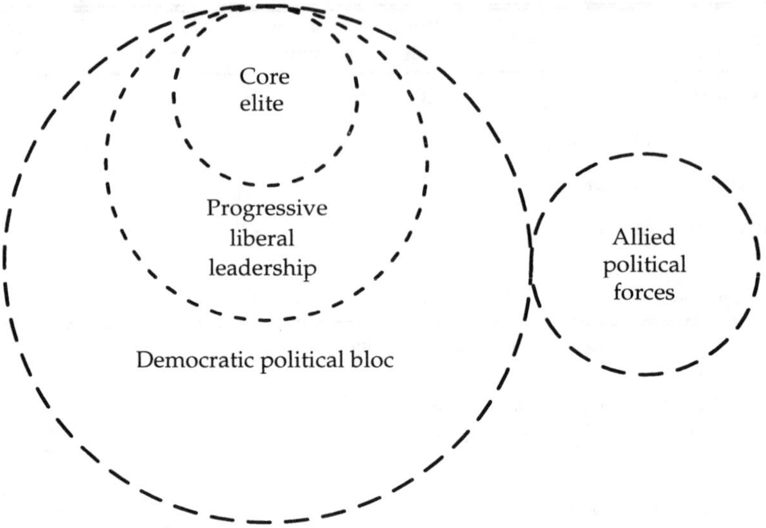

Yet this political force had a definite shape, even amid the political and institutional fluidity of the mid-1930s.

At the heart of Democratic progressive liberalism was a group of two to three hundred people, designated as the core elite in Figure 4.1. This group included advisers to Roosevelt and cabinet members such as Harry Hopkins, Harold Ickes, Frances Perkins, Donald Richberg, Rexford Tugwell, Adolf Berle, and Samuel Rosenman. With them were leading Democratic elected officials, such as Senator Wagner, and a small number of Republican or independent progressives such as Robert La Follette, Jr. There were prominent legal figures (notably Felix Frankfurter) and academics and policy specialists in university or government positions, such as Alvin Hansen, Mariner Eccles, Harry Millis, Wesley Mitchell, and Leon Keyserling.

A larger group of progressive liberals numbered several thousand people. It included secondary advisers to Roosevelt, less prominent progressive liberals in Congress and their advisers, and major officials in the new agencies of the decade, from the NIRA to the relief agencies, the NLRA, and the Social Security Administration. This group included a significant portion of the Democratic membership of the House and Senate, and numerous state and local elected officials and party officials.

It also contained hundreds of influential academics and professionals in law, social work, and other fields.[50]

When I refer to the progressive liberal leadership of the Democratic order – as in Figure 4.1 – I am referring both to the core elite and to this larger group. The distinction between these groups was based on formal office, practical decision-making power about the main questions that faced those trying to build a new order, and political and intellectual influence in defining overall Democratic aims. The boundaries between the core elite and other sections of the progressive liberal leadership were fluid and porous. During their careers, many people crossed this boundary in both directions. But the path from the broad leadership group to the core elite was not a routine result of ascending the ranks of new agencies or gaining seniority in Congress. A position within a significant institution was a requirement for sustained participation in the progressive liberal leadership. Yet within that framework, political judgment and skills mattered as much as institutional rank in selecting members of the core elite.

The progressive liberal leadership is almost invisible if one takes an inventory of political forces solely based on conventional institutional boundaries. Such an inventory finds dissent and conflict almost everywhere. The places where progressive liberals were clearly in charge were significant – they included some of the new agencies of the decade – but obviously did not include Congress or the federal judiciary. If the search for political leadership is confined to conventional categories, the disappointing results encourage a focus on Roosevelt's personal leadership or a small group of his key advisors.

Broadening a notion of Democratic leadership to Roosevelt's entire administration does not capture the distinctive shape of the new leading group. Progressive liberal strength in the administration was central in building the Democratic order. But the progressive liberal leadership was so effective partly because it extended outside the administration to cut across a number of institutional lines and draw together political forces from a wide range of settings. (And more than a few people within the administration did not share the views of progressive liberals.)

50. Among these professionals, lawyers have received the most extensive treatment, doubtless because of their role in national policy making. Similar stories could be told about other fields in which many younger professionals were engaged with the New Deal. See James Gilbert, *Designing the Industrial State: The Intellectual Pursuit of Collectivism in America, 1890–1940* (Chicago, Ill.: Quadrangle Books, 1972); and William W. Bremer, *Depression Winters: New York Social Workers and the New Deal* (Philadelphia: Temple University Press, 1984).

The progressive leadership of the Democratic order was self-conscious about reshaping national policies and institutions.[51] It exercised leadership partly through the political links it created and sustained. Its ties went downward into national administrative agencies, and into state and local government and professional associations. It built close ties with parts of the organized Democratic Party. And its connections reached horizontally toward nonparty political movements, especially the labor movement. Many labor leaders and organizers were in substantial agreement with the perspectives of leading progressive liberals. A significant number of the labor movement's leaders were in practice part of the progressive liberal leadership, though few were part of the core elite group in an ongoing way. The uncertain location of the top labor leadership was a source of friction when leaders like Lewis or Hillman came to think not only that they should be included in the progressive liberal leadership, which was feasible, but that they should be major figures within the core elite. Such hopes were not realized.

By following downward and outward the links forged by Democratic leaders we can trace the contours of a dynamic progressive liberal (or Democratic) political bloc. It included parts of the Democratic Party, unions, interest groups, professional associations, and other forces, extending outward to the most politically aware and active pro-New Deal voters. This political bloc was sufficiently coherent to allow the progressive liberal leadership to make broader alliances with other forces who were willing to cooperate with progressive liberal initiatives in some areas. Given the formation of a strong Democratic bloc, alliances could be made with diverse groups, such as Southern Democrats in Congress, or Democratic leaders of urban machines in the North, or moderately progressive Republican officials in the West, or nonpartisan leaders of civic and professional associations. Progressive liberals could be both flexible and principled; they were able to define an overall course for which there was strong support in the Democratic bloc while pursuing alliances to gain electoral and legislative victories.[52] The distinction

---

51. Memoirs – in sufficient numbers to check on self-serving claims – are a good source of information about the networks at the top of the new political order and participants' understandings of those networks. Leading progressive liberals were highly aware of the nature of their project. See, among many accounts, Perkins, *The Roosevelt I Knew;* Harold Ickes, *The Secret Diary of Harold Ickes – The First Thousand Days, 1933–1936* (New York: Simon and Schuster, 1953); Samuel Rosenman, *Working with Roosevelt* (New York: Harper & Brothers, 1952); and Rexford Tugwell, *The Brains Trust* (New York: Viking, 1968).

52. The distinction between a political bloc and its allies allows a distinction between principled and unprincipled alliances. For a political bloc, a principled alliance is not one that is purely supportive of basic commitments; in that case the ally might as well

between the Democratic bloc and its alliances separated genuine and active supporters of the New Deal from equivocal supporters or nonsupporters open to cooperation on particular measures. This line cut across political institutions, including the organized party, again underlining the irreducibility of the actual leading political forces to conventional categories such as the "Democratic Party," or "Congressional Democrats," or "the administration."

In sum, when I refer to forces that built and led the Democratic order, I mean first to designate the core elite and the progressive liberal leadership. When I refer to the Democratic political bloc as a whole, I am also including the most engaged constituencies of the political order and the many activists who helped construct and defend it in a wide range of political and social settings.

What held all these elements together? It was certainly not party discipline. Nor could Roosevelt command unity. The Democratic bloc was held together in the first instance by political commitments. A distinctive progressive liberal position was developed and articulated by the core elite and the progressive liberal leadership, and it gained substantial agreement from the diverse elements of the Democratic bloc. This position had a number of features that distinguished it basically from the positions of the Hoover administration, conservative Democrats in the 1930s, and the socialist and communist left.[53] Here I will discuss progressive liberalism as it took shape in the new Democratic leadership – in Chapter 6 I will pursue how this progressive liberalism appeared as a new common sense in American society as a whole. The formulations are very similar, as there was no secrecy about Democratic aims.

be incorporated into the political bloc. A principled alliance results from judgments about anticipated consequences, when the conclusion is that the alliance on balance enhances the prospects of realizing basic political commitments. An unprincipled alliance takes place when sections of a political bloc make deals that put their narrow interests above the constitutive political aims of the bloc, or when the negative results of an alliance are simply ignored or denied. Thus, alliances with Democratic machine leaders or moderately progressive Republicans can clearly be defended as reasonable judgments about how to attain progressive liberal aims. Alliances with conservative Democrats in the South present a much tougher case, given their negative effects on race and labor relations. The latter alliances were marginally justified in the 1930s because of great uncertainty about what was needed to put the Democratic order in place.

53. On continuities between earlier forms of Progressivism and the New Deal, see Donald R. Brand, *Corporatism and the Rule of Law: A Study of the National Recovery Administration* (Ithaca, N.Y.: Cornell University Press, 1988). On economic currents among progressive liberals, see Hawley, *New Deal and Monopoly.* On progressive liberal views of the state, see Alan Brinkley, "The New Deal and the Idea of the State," in Fraser and Gerstle, eds., *The Rise and Fall of the New Deal Order,* 85–121.

First, progressive liberals regarded social life as a field of potentially cooperative interaction among groups with legitimate needs. As it was thought that such interaction could nourish social order, progressive liberals did not oppose efforts at organization by groups whose efforts had previously been hindered or blocked. The Progressive movement was ambivalent and paternalistic toward labor.[54] Democratic progressive liberalism in the 1930s was more sympathetic to labor and more deeply critical of the political and economic leadership of business elites.

In the 1930s progressive liberals came to view labor as an ally in a process of democratic reform and reorganization. Progressives who previously had been ambivalent about labor issues were influenced to shift their positions by positive state and local experiences, disillusionment with the strands of progressivism represented in the Hoover administration, and disappointment with business leadership in the early 1930s. Major shifts had to occur before most sections of American progressive liberalism had a clearly positive stance toward labor.

In constructing a new regime there was room for disagreement between advocates of political and social competition among diverse groups, and a much smaller number who favored a more formal integration of larger groups and associations at the national level. Such debate, dominated by the first position, was located in a new political space defined by the exclusion of several alternatives: a purely market-based conception of social life, a localist commitment to communal groups, and a full-scale state-directed corporatism. This cooperative image of society presumed diversity and conflict and proposed to temper it through government regulation and the calming effects of social and economic improvement.

Second, progressive liberals thought the state should intervene strongly and widely in society. This view sharply distinguished progressive liberals from those who opposed an expanded role for the national state on grounds it would distort the market or disrupt local practices. Within the new progressive liberal framework there were arguments, such as between those in favor of a formalist conception of how state policies should be defined and administered and influential advocates of what they claimed would be more flexible and efficient discretionary

---

54. Claims about the convergence of American progressivism with European social democracy in the first two decades of the century are not convincing in the area of labor relations. In Europe even the most conservative tendencies within social democracy were in cooperation with organized working-class political and social movements who presented themselves as leading agents of overall reform. There is a considerable practical difference between viewing the labor movement as a leading force in a broad project of democratic reform – a social democratic view – and regarding it as desirable that political and social citizenship be extended more fully to the working class.

practices. The latter approach predominated partly because when it was employed, the result was not arbitrariness or unprincipled bargaining.[55] In the new agencies of the mid-1930s, progressive liberal administrators used their authority to implement their principles in politically charged situations. They often did so to the disadvantage of previously dominant groups and opened more space for democratic control of government activities than had previously existed.

This view of the state was linked with a national, modernizing orientation. Debate about reorganizing government activities presumed the rejection of earlier forms of Democratic localism and of most antimodernizing views. Bruce Ackerman rightly emphasizes the nationalizing dimension of the new political order: "New Deal democracy marked another great leap along the arc of nationalistic self-definition initiated by the American Revolution ... Henceforth, the federal government would operate as a truly national government, speaking for the People on all matters that sufficiently attracted the interest of lawmakers in Washington, D.C."[56] Progressive liberal leaders agreed on a positive state role – state regulation was regarded as a permanent reality rather than an emergency measure.

Third, progressive liberals favored redistributive policies. Never anticapitalist, Democratic progressive liberalism was serious about employing the state to enact reforms aimed at a fairer and more stable social order.[57] Debate about how energetic such policies should be oc-

---

55. Theodore Lowi's influential account of the New Deal mistakes an important tension within the new order – the relation between codification and discretionary authority – for the main story of the state's expansive redefinition. Lowi claims that lack of formalization leads to unprincipled interest-group bargaining. This view is not supported by the decade's developments. Even the quasi-corporatist forms of the NRA were capable of producing more principled and democratic results than Lowi allows. His argument relies for its polemical force on a contrast with an imaginary liberal state that cleanly separates lawmaking and administration and protects both from interest-group corruption. No such state existed in the United States before the Democratic order. Lowi's argument might be recast by claiming that initially democratic results are undermined over time by interest-group conflict in which new elites come to exert control. Philip Selznick's classic study of the TVA might be cited to support this restatement of Lowi's critique of discretionary authority, but it would provide no support for his formalist alternative. See Theodore Lowi, *The End of Liberalism* (New York: W. W. Norton, 1979); and Philip Selznick, *TVA and the Grass Roots: A Study in the Sociology of Formal Organization* (Berkeley: University of California Press, 1949).

56. Bruce Ackerman, *We the People – Foundations*, vol. 1 (Cambridge, Mass.: Harvard University Press, 1991), 105.

57. In the early 1930s even those who contemplated a very wide extension of planning did not conceive their egalitarian and centralizing projects as anticapitalist. See Bernard Sternsher, *Rexford Tugwell and the New Deal* (New Brunswick, N.J.: Rutgers University Press, 1964); and Tugwell, *Brains Trust*.

curred in a space defined by recognition of an urgent need to aid the most disadvantaged and by the view that extreme social and economic hardship and inequality were socially and politically destructive.[58] This reform impulse helped inspire much of the social and labor legislation of the decade. It was not radical egalitarianism, and its proponents were not interested in state appropriation and redistribution of productive resources.

In addition to its defining political commitments, the leading progressive liberal group had partisan and social features that were significant for its development. The progressive liberalism of the 1930s was mainly Democratic (Republican progressives from the West and upper Midwest offered important support for the New Deal). It had roots in the Progressive movement that before World War I spanned both parties. Late in the Republican order, Democratic progressivism was influential in a number of state and local administrations and in academic and intellectual life. Roosevelt was linked with this tendency in the 1920s as he aimed to reorient the national Democratic Party.[59]

In social terms progressive liberals were usually middle class, rather than farmers, owners of large businesses, or industrial workers. They were most often professionals – lawyers, academics, social workers, members of the new planning professions.[60] None of these social strata were wholly progressive, or entirely Democratic; thus one cannot depict progressive liberalism as the necessary political expression of professional middle strata. Instead, this perspective was a plausible articulation of themes relevant to the experiences of these professionals.

Large numbers of professionals directed part of their work toward progressive liberal goals, whether or not they entered government service. At the outset of the New Deal few progressive liberals were em-

---

58. A commitment to alleviating extreme hardship had strong roots in several decades of reform liberalism, including the experience of a number of leading progressive liberals, such as Frances Perkins, in social work. James T. Kloppenberg emphasizes the reformist side of Progressivism in *Uncertain Victory: Social Democracy and Progressivism in European and American Social Thought* (New York: Oxford University Press, 1986), 349–84.

59. David Burner stresses Roosevelt's party reform role in the 1920s in *The Politics of Provincialism: The Democratic Party in Transition, 1918–1932* (New York: Alfred A. Knopf, 1968), 142–57. See also Sean J. Savage, *Roosevelt – The Party Leader, 1932–1945* (Lexington: The University Press of Kentucky, 1991); and Kenneth S. Davis, *FDR – The Beckoning of Destiny, 1882–1928* (New York: Putnam, 1972).

60. Huthmacher, *Robert F. Wagner*, 118–30; Irons, *New Deal Lawyers*, 3–10; and Marion Clawson, *New Deal Planning – The National Resources Planning Board* (Baltimore, Md.: Johns Hopkins University Press, 1981).

ployed by the federal government.[61] By the mid-1930s the ranks of progressive liberalism were a major source of those hired to direct and staff new state agencies. Thus the early National Labor Relations Board benefited from a large inflow of progressive liberal lawyers and administrators who could run it effectively.[62] These activist intellectuals often had considerable prior experience in professional life, as well as in policy making and politics at state and local levels. They had relatively few obligations to national party structures or to the interest groups of capital or labor.

In the mid-to-late 1920s it is possible to identify many potential elements of a new progressive liberalism. But they are just that – forces and ideas scattered across the political landscape. In the 1930s progressive liberals worked with the raw materials provided by prior Progressive and democratic commitments and created something new. A leading group of several thousand people was at the center of a new political bloc able to exercise national power. That group helped to build even wider alliances, including forces – parts of the AFL, Democrats from the South, urban political machines – who were very far from endorsing every progressive liberal commitment.

Other views of the NLRA

The claim that the passage of the Wagner Act was caused primarily by progressive liberal reform efforts applies to the Democratic order as a whole. The people who passed the Wagner Act and administered the new labor relations framework were an important component of the emerging Democratic bloc that led the construction of the new political order. Progressive liberals wanted to pass a measure which they expected would benefit labor and promote overall political and social stability and development. From the progressive liberal leadership group, those especially concerned with labor relations included people such as Senator Wagner himself and his aide Leon Keyserling; economists, lawyers,

---

61. See Huthmacher, *Robert F. Wagner*, 103–15; Kenneth Davis, *FDR – The New York Years, 1928–1932* (New York: Random House, 1979), 269; and Jerold S. Auerbach, "Lawyers and Social Change in the Depression Decade," in John Braeman, Robert H. Brenner, and David Brody, eds., *The New Deal – The National Level* (Columbus: Ohio State University Press, 1975), vol. 1, 132–69. Auerbach argues that the anti-Semitism of elite private legal circles helped make public service an attractive choice for Jewish lawyers.

62. In addition to the works by Millis, Huthmacher, and Irons cited earlier, see James Gross, *The Making of the National Labor Relations Board – A Study in Economics, Politics, and the Law*, vol. 1, 1933–7 (Albany: State University of New York Press, 1974), 130–56.

and administrators such as Francis Biddle, Harry Millis, William Leiserson, Edwin Smith, Philip Levy, and J. Warren Madden; and Frances Perkins in Roosevelt's cabinet.

The NLRA was a progressive liberal measure that aimed at achieving stable cooperation among responsible organizations in labor relations. It was a work of radical reform inspired by strong political commitments. The Wagner Act articulated progressive liberal approaches to economic stabilization, government regulation, and distributive equity. The NLRA was a major component of a broad and articulate political project. It was also pragmatic – a context-sensitive interpretation of basic principles.

Many views of the genesis of the Wagner Act are reluctant even to consider the possibility that political forces were causally primary. Where political actors figure in a causal story, it is by mediating powerful forces that arise elsewhere, such as class conflict, liberal ideas, or organizational development. One such reading of the Wagner Act claims it was the work of farsighted capitalist elites. But there is not enough evidence of business support for the NLRA to show that business elites caused the reform to occur.[63] And the strength and vehemence of business opposition, with the exception of a handful of leaders of large firms who were well to the left of the business community as a whole, warns against this interpretation.

There is much more truth in attributing the act to working-class efforts. Yet this claim overstates the direct causal role of the 1934 strikes and labor's political capacities. A plausible argument that working-class efforts were primarily responsible for the NLRA should show that those who passed the measure – writing it, arguing and voting for it – directly represented the labor movement. This was not the case. While Wagner and other progressive liberals were allied with labor, they did not regard themselves primarily as labor's agents. Few major figures on the political scene in 1934–5 were viewed as labor's representatives, though there were many prolabor progressives whom the labor movement regarded as valuable allies.

A more modest claim would be that working-class pressure from outside the political system created a context in which the Wagner bill had to be passed. Thus political actors could be regarded as responding

63. Not surprisingly, an account of the New Deal that centers on business self-organization and the state's cooperation with business projects contains no discussion of the Wagner Act. Gabriel Kolko, *Main Currents in Modern American History* (New York: Harper & Row, 1976), 100–56.

to demands they could not refuse. This approach relies on the idea that labor action severely narrowed the set of feasible labor law measures, perhaps to one. In fact, a number of political possibilities existed, virtually all of them less prolabor than the NLRA.[64] Working class pressure was intense and persistent enough to mean that something had to be done. But what? The response might have been extended repression, expanded company unions, support for AFL unions and their initiatives in mass production industries, a minimal NLRA and limited recognition of industrial unions, – or a measure that strongly encouraged broad industrial unions and also facilitated the expansion of older union forms. Progressive liberals were politically creative in defining and implementing the last alternative, and they were supported by newly mobilized labor forces.

Michael Goldfield attributes the Wagner Act mainly to working-class pressure. Yet his actual positive claims are not so bold: "The most reasonable hypothesis to account for the passage of the NLRA is that labor militancy, catapulted into national prominence by the 1934 strikes and the political response to this movement, paved the way for the passage of the act." "Paving the way" is in fact a modest claim. To strengthen it Goldfield argues that working-class radicalism and militancy precluded repression. Indeed, full-scale repression was not likely in 1934–5. But political factors were crucial in shaping this reality; it was not imposed from outside politics by the primordial force of a mounting working-class mobilization. That very mobilization was encouraged by national political shifts. And for both substantive and strategic reasons the Democratic leadership did not want to oversee a brutal repression.

Goldfield rightly argues that working-class pressure was a significant causal element in passing the NLRA. But he does not seriously consider the range of regulatory measures that might have been passed given the levels of working-class and popular mobilization that existed. Thus

---

64. In 1935 substantial forces in the administration sought to modify the prounion force of the NLRA. Suggested changes were offered to Senator Wagner by Attorney General Cummings, summarizing a White House conference of May 24 on the bill. A letter from Secretary of Commerce Roper argued for including clauses to protect employees from "union intimidation," implying a defense of their right to join company unions. Other administration figures supported the bill, including Frances Perkins, who opposed "mutuality" provisions that would have weakened its prolabor thrust. Memo, Homer Cummings to Roosevelt, 5/28/35; Letter, Harold Stephens to Robert Wagner, 5/27/35; Memo, Daniel Roper to Roosevelt, 6/20/35; Letter, Frances Perkins to Mr. McIntyre, 6/18/35 (all in Folder Labor 1935, OF 407 (Labor), FDR Library).

citing the growing strength of labor's action does not justify the strong causal claims about the NLRA that he wants to make.[65]

Another social explanation of the Wagner Act considers it middle-class reform. This claim captures the social origins of many progressive liberals, but has little analytical merit. It is more accurate to see these reformers' social features as indicating the separation of the political sphere from socioeconomic classes, because the political capacities of this grouping far exceeded the social weight of "its" class. While progressive liberalism can be linked to the experience of many sections of the middle classes, that experience could be interpreted in different terms and make other choices attractive, from "left" Hooverism (in the 1920s) and staunch probusiness opposition to the New Deal to Popular Front Communism. Rather than expressing the interests of a single class, progressive liberalism articulated an overall political conception of how American society should be (more fairly) organized and (more actively) regulated.

Can the NLRA be explained as the result of state elites' efforts to expand and rationalize the state? Progressive liberalism had a rationalizing thrust, and the NLRA expanded the state. Yet the Wagner Act was not mainly a self-serving initiative by state managers seeking to increase their power.[66] It was a political initiative by forces in and outside the state, which had the effect of reshaping and extending state forms and practices.

By "state" I mean an institution that coordinates the organization and direction of social relations in a social formation. This definition attributes a capacity for agency to states, not as imaginary individuals, but as complex organizations with structures through which decisions about

---

65. Michael Goldfield, "Worker Insurgency," 1273. See also his exchange with Theda Skocpol and Kenneth Finegold, "Explaining New Deal Labor Policy," *American Political Science Review* 84 (1990): 1297–1315.

66. Block explains state actions in terms of interest seeking by state managers in "The Ruling Class Does Not Rule." A similar conception appears in most of the articles on American politics and social policy by Theda Skocpol and various coauthors, such as "Political Response to Capitalist Crisis: Neo-Marxist Theories of the State and the Case of the New Deal," *Politics and Society* 10, no. 2 (1980): 155–201; and Margaret Weir, Ann Shola Orloff, and Theda Skocpol, eds., *The Politics of Social Policy in the United States* (Princeton, N.J.: Princeton University Press, 1988). Given state managers as maximizers, the outcomes of policy conflicts are explained largely in terms of their varying ability to realize state-building aims. This variance derives from the fact that state managers' resources and the obstacles they face differ across policy areas. This conception emphasizes a rationalistic view of who state managers are and why they act rather than examining the political framework in which they act and their substantive aims. More recently Skocpol has qualified this state-centered rationalism to give somewhat more weight to political factors.

how to act can be taken. States coordinate political processes, but do not monopolize them. Given this conception, if the American state is meant to include the national bureaucracy, presidency, army, and Congress, it cannot be assigned responsibility for the NLRA. Many key actors in passing it were mainly outside this state, in universities, labor unions, party organizations, and professional associations. And divisions over the NLRA cut through it. What about using a broad definition of the state – to include party leaders and professional and labor groups linked to the government? Leaving aside the analytical problems with this definition, it opens the way to conceiving the NLRA as an order-seeking measure because it captures more of the progressive liberals who were involved. But this broader state was also divided about the NLRA. And it should be stressed that the "state" in both senses was being zsconstructed as a new Democratic state, rather than acting as a coherent and well-defined agent with clear interests.

Thus caution is required in attributing a major causal role to the state in 1934 and 1935. While state elites had an interest in order, several forms of order were possible. One needs to explain the outcome in labor relations with reference to the political dynamic through which a particular form of order was selected.[67] In 1935–7 a progressive liberal state was being shaped by political conflicts in and around it. In labor relations it is a mistake to posit the state as already a coherent actor with clear notions of what forms of order were to be achieved. Events were driven by political forces with substantive reasons for wanting to create new modes of state activity. Progressive liberals wanted to reorder and stabilize labor relations, and their aims overlapped those of a burgeoning new labor movement.

Reshaping labor relations and building a new state

Passing the Wagner Act did not guarantee implementation. The harsh conflicts required to implement it in ways supportive of new unions underline the extraordinary character of this political moment. In normal times, we expect legislation that has passed to be implemented – with grumbling by losers, and efforts by everyone to shape its practical interpretation. In crisis times, when legislative victories can be a major step toward building a new regime, some will flatly reject the new measure and openly refuse to comply.

67. For further discussion of whether political reformers should be conceived of mainly as state elites or as progressive liberals, see David Plotke, "The Wagner Act, Again: Politics and Labor, 1935–37," *Studies in American Political Development* 3 (1989): 105–56.

The Wagner Act was subjected to such a challenge in the mid-1930s. The NLRA's encouragement of unions was resisted by employers in large enterprises and small companies. They continued many of the practices in which they had engaged before the Wagner Act, from firing prounion employees to company-sponsored violence against strikers. They often refused to deal with unions with strong employee support. Major Senate hearings held by the LaFollette Committee focused on employers' resistance to the new law. The proceedings were politically important in implementing the Wagner Act, as they built support for that measure in response to the publicity given to employers' illegal and violent actions.[68]

Employers' refusal to recognize the NLRA set the terms for bitter conflicts after its passage. Strikes increased in 1936 from an already high level, and then doubled in 1937 to 4,740. In 1935–7 the proportion of strikes over union recognition was much higher than in 1929–33. These strikes aimed at establishing unions to bargain effectively with employers and to reform a factory regime now considered intolerable.[69] Although advocates had urged the NLRA as a way to provide industrial stability, that was not the immediate result – mainly because employers did not cooperate. Even employers who made flexible public statements often fought unions in their own firms, still hoping to avoid unionization. The NLRB was deluged with cases in which employers refused to bargain and discriminated against employees with union affiliations.[70]

Employers' resistance was partly based on their view of recent labor relations. They had ample evidence of their strength and the weakness and conservatism of the AFL and much of the working class. Antiunion efforts had worked in the decade before the Depression, when welfare capitalism and brutal antiunionism undermined the union strength achieved by the end of World War I. Business resistance was also based on reasonable political judgments. The Supreme Court had ruled against several major New Deal measures, and the Wagner Act seemed open to

68. See Jerold S. Auerbach, *Labor and Liberty: The La Follette Committee and the New Deal* (Indianapolis, Ind.: Bobbs-Merrill, 1966).
69. In 1937 there were almost twice as many strikes mainly about union recognition as there were about wages and hours. Working conditions – the pace of work, the abusive power of foremen, the lack of seniority protection – were at least as powerful as wage issues in the labor upsurge of 1935–7. Bureau of the Census, "Work Stoppages"; David Montgomery, *Workers' Control in America: Studies in the History of Work, Technology, and Labor Struggles* (Cambridge University Press, 1980), 140–9.
70. This is clear in reports sent to Roosevelt from the NLRB, such as: Letter and Memo, J. Warren Madden to Roosevelt, January 28, 1936, Folder NLRB 1936, OF 716 (NLRB), FDR Library. This resistance is discussed in Millis and Brown, *From the Wagner Act to Taft-Hartley.*

similar objections. The restraint-of-commerce objections to the NIRA might well have been upheld against it.[71] Why comply with a law soon to be overturned? Political support for the Wagner Act might subside; for most of the century, after all, popular support for trade unions had been modest. Conservative forces attacked the Wagner Act and Roosevelt fiercely, judging that the New Deal labor program could be defeated.[72]

Employers' actions made passing the NLRA insufficient to create a new industrial order. Working class mobilization, including the 1937 sit-down strikes, was crucial. Yet the act was not simply enforced "from below." The sit-down strikes, the most dramatic instance of working-class militancy, were primarily an effort to secure recognition of unions. Thus they were highly concentrated even in the late 1930s, rather than becoming a common tactic over a sustained period. Eighty-two percent of all sit-down strikes that took place from 1936 through 1939 occurred in 1937. These actions declined from 477 in 1937 to 52 the next year and only 6 in 1939.[73]

Workers could often strike for long enough to halt a firm's activities. In a few cases they could extend that process across industries, and in even fewer they could strike across factories in major cities. In industrial and urban conflicts where labor organization and militancy exceeded its normal forms, what came next? All signs are that many employers were inclined to engage in further resistance and were dissuaded from doing so mainly when political agents – courts, local governments, and the federal government – intervened to push for settlements in which unions

71. A Supreme Court ruling against the NLRA was expected by Republican and Democratic conservatives, and this expectation was widely publicized in the work of the Liberty League. The likely reason for overruling the measure would have been that the NLRA was an unwarranted federal intrusion into private contracts. Liberty League, "Report on the Constitutionality of the National Labor Relations Act" (Washington, D.C.: American Liberty League, 1935).

72. Many attacks featured the Wagner Act and the labor upsurge as key examples of what had gone wrong. Leuchtenburg, *Roosevelt and the New Deal*, 177–9; Schlesinger, *Politics of Upheaval*, 515–47; and James T. Patterson, *Congressional Conservatism and the New Deal: The Growth of the Conservative Coalition in Congress, 1933–1939* (Lexington: University of Kentucky Press, 1967), 71–5. See also James Holt, "The New Deal and the American Anti-Statist Tradition," in Braeman et al., *The New Deal*, vol. 1, 27–49.

73. Figures are from *Monthly Labor Review* 1939: 1130; 1940: 1105, cited in P. K. Edwards, *Strikes in the United States, 1881–1974* (Oxford: Basil Blackwell, 1981). Roosevelt received much criticism for the administration's refusal to force workers to abandon their sit-down in the automobile strike. Folder Auto Workers' Strike, 1937, OF407B (Strikes), FDR Library. On the sit-down strikes, see Cochran, *Labor and Communism*, 114–22.

were recognized. Unions could not be durably established "from below" without political enforcement by the emerging Democratic order.

Progressive liberal officials and their advisers made decisions limiting the use of violence against strikers and their supporters; less dramatically, other progressive liberal officials made decisions about how to pursue the process of judicial review. Democratic political efforts helped to produce the surprising Supreme Court decision in *NLRB v. Jones & Laughlin Steel Corp.* in 1937, which redefined the context for battles over the NLRA. Now union efforts were legally protected and state violence was not routinely available against unionizing efforts. Employer noncompliance persisted, but more as local combat than as a strategy to block unions altogether.[74] Had the Supreme Court rejected the NLRA, building industrial unions would have been much slower and more difficult, and in some sectors might not have happened.

The passage and implementation of the Wagner Act was a crucial and exemplary political project led by progressive liberals and supported by the labor movement (Table 4.1). The measure promised federal support for labor's efforts – it stimulated a dramatic increase in the labor movement's capacity to form and sustain unions.

The NLRA's course illustrates crucial features of how the Democratic order arose, notably regarding the state. It is hardly news to say that the state grew: The point is that its growth was a political project. State expansion did not mainly result from self-aggrandizement by existing state forces (which were uncertain about the Wagner Act). In the fight to pass and implement the NLRA, an emerging progressive liberal leadership allied with new mass forces to produce a major state intervention. The implementation of this reformist effort was guided by a progressive federal agency closely tied to the most active new parts of the labor movement. The employees of the NLRB encouraged unionization and were supported by progressive liberals in Congress and the Roosevelt administration.[75] Those who advocated the NLRA and those who led and staffed the agency opened a new front of state action. The number

---

74. The role of the Supreme Court decision is emphasized by those involved in the NLRB's work, such as J. Warren Madden, "Birth of the Board," in Louis G. Silverberg, ed., *The Wagner Act: After Ten Years* (Washington, D.C.: Bureau of National Affairs, 1945), 34–42.

75. The performance of the early NLRB was competent enough to limit the number of NLRB decisions overturned by the courts. The lawyers and administrators who built the NLRB thus limited the effectiveness of criticism from the act's intransigent political opponents. Howard Smith, a conservative Democrat from Virginia, headed a House committee that investigated and aimed to undermine the early NLRB, much of whose initial leadership was forced out in the late 1930s and early 1940s. In explaining the change of leadership, analysts variously emphasize conservative and AFL opposition to the NLRB's course, administrative failures by the NLRB staff, and

Table 4.2. *The growth of federal activities and expenditures in the 1930s*

	Department Expenditures (thousands)			Recovery relief and expenditures (millions)
Year	Agriculture	Interior	Labor	
1933	250,981	74,580	13,678	1,277
1934	58,363	45,922	10,832	4,002
1935	62,037	55,211	13,012	3,657
1936	76,749	79,970	15,254	3,291
1937	101,266	92,115	15,836	2,846
1938	112,774	98,878	18,102	2,238
1939	126,492	118,524	18,845	3,105

Source: Statistical Abstract of the United States, 1938; Statistical Abstract of the United States, 1939; Statistical Abstract of the United States, 1940 (Washington D.C.: U.S. Department of Commerce and Bureau of the Census, 1939, 1940, 1941).

of positions created was modest – in its first year the NLRB had roughly 180 employees.[76] Despite limited resources, the NLRB entered numerous industrial conflicts, widened the scope of state regulation, and enhanced prospects of future growth.

Progressive liberals who aimed to achieve ordered fairness in labor relations saw prounion government action as necessary to protect and legitimate unions. Here the process of passing and implementing the NLRA was exemplary. It illustrates the political accomplishments that resolved the crisis of the state opened by the Republican failure to address the social devastation and political disorder of the Depression. Government responsibilities and activities grew dramatically. From 1932 to 1937 federal civilian employment grew from roughly 600,000 to 900,000, while federal expenditures for items other than military spending, veterans' benefits, and interest increased by over 100 percent. Federal expenditures for relief efforts increased sharply; department expenditures also grew (see Table 4.2). Federal, state, and local expendi-

political arrogance and insensitivity (stemming in part from maladroit and sectarian behavior by procommunist NLRB staffers). For a sympathetic account of NLRB performance, see Millis and Brown, *From the Wagner Act to Taft-Hartley*, 235–43. On the Smith Committee and the right's attack on the NLRB, see James Gross, *The Reshaping of the National Labor Relations Board – National Labor Policy in Transition 1937–1947* (Albany: State University of New York Press, 1981), 3, 209–32. Tomlins strongly criticizes the early NLRB leadership in *State and Unions*, 196–213.

76. Tomlins stresses the NLRA's role in expanding the state in *State and Unions*, 146, 150–60, 185, 221. On the shape of the NLRB, see the first *Annual Report of the National Labor Relations Board*, submitted January 4, 1937, for the fiscal year ending

tures on public welfare more than doubled between 1932 and 1936, from 445 to 997 million dollars.[77]

As agencies proliferated to direct reform projects, state efforts helped prevent further social and economic deterioration. Republican attacks on the New Deal's alleged drift toward state domination rang hollow owing to Hoover's memorable ineffectiveness and insensitivity. Progressive liberal efforts were variously effective. Sometimes, as in agriculture, the main beneficiaries were narrow groups who used the new agencies to secure privileged positions.[78] In public works and relief efforts, inter-agency and personal competition were messy and led to inefficiency; yet new social welfare policies helped alleviate the worst hardships and began to establish new standards. The success of progressive liberal initiatives depended on the quality of their programs, the strength of opposition, the extent to which previous policies had created relevant government capacities, and the availability of competent managers.

The Wagner Act was a central 1930s success story from the standpoint of progressive liberal reform. Battles about how workplaces would be organized and how labor would be represented in firms and the political system helped produce a new leading political force and an expanding state. The NLRA's passage required a vigorous progressive liberal leadership and active mass efforts. Both elements were usually essential for major reforms. The Social Security Act resulted from a similar dynamic, though with a much more positive role for business elites. A series of movements, from protests about rents and unemployment early in the decade to the Townsend movement several years later,

June 30, 1936, along with Letter, J. Warren Madden to Roosevelt, January 4, 1937, plus "Appendix 1 – Names, Salaries, and Duties of All Employees and Officers in the Employ or under the Supervision of the Board," Official File 716 (NLRB), FDR Library. The Office of Management and Budget illustrates the modest scale of the main agencies; until the mid-1930s that office had less than fifty employees. See Larry Berman, *The Office of Management and Budget and the Presidency, 1921–1979* (Princeton, N.J.: Princeton University Press, 1979), 8–11.

77. Bureau of the Census, *Historical Statistics of the United States – Colonial Times to 1970* (Washington: Government Printing Office, 1975), 1102, 1115, 1121. Y308-317, "Paid Civilian Employment of the Federal Government: 1816 to 1970"; Y466-471, "Outlays of the Federal Government by Major Function: 1900 to 1939"; Y533-566, "Federal, State, and Local Government Expenditures, by Function: 1902 to 1970."

78. See Christiana Campbell, *The Farm Bureau and the New Deal: A Study of the Making of National Farm Policy* (Champaign-Urbana: University of Illinois Press, 1962); Edwin G. Nourse, Joseph S. David, and John D. Black, *Three Years of the Agricultural Adjustment Administration* (Washington, D.C.: Brookings Institution, 1937); and Richard Kirkendall, *Social Scientists and Farm Politics in the Age of Roosevelt* (Columbia: University of Missouri Press, 1966).

urged that social provision be expanded. And progressive liberal elites strongly favored a broad extension of social protection.[79] Where progressive liberals found a project compelling but could establish no links to popular mobilization (or where the latter was insubstantial), the results were mixed or unimpressive, as in administrative reform efforts later in the decade or attempts to impose progressive liberal discipline in the Democratic Party. Where popular pressure mounted but progressive liberal leaders had little positive involvement – as with agricultural workers in California or Southern tenant farmers – success was out of reach, and it was difficult to turn such mobilizations into durable political forces.[80]

79. On the Townsend movement see Brinkley, *Voices of Protest*, 222–6.
80. On administrative reform, see Richard Polenberg, *Reorganizing Roosevelt's Government – The Controversy over Executive Reorganization* (Cambridge, Mass.: Harvard University Press, 1966). On party reform attempts, see Sean Savage, *Roosevelt*, 129–58. On efforts to organize farm workers and sharecroppers, see Cletus Daniel, *Bitter Harvest: A History of California Farmworkers, 1870–1941* (Berkeley: University of California Press, 1982); and Jerold Auerbach, *Labor and Liberty*, 177–96.

5

Party and movements in the Democratic upsurge, 1935–7

> Your apparent unwillingness to advise the Nation [of] your attitude toward the high handed, brutal and lawless display of power exhibited by labor union leaders as expressed in the prevailing epidemic of "sit downs" leaves many of us bewildered and apprehensive. Your silence can only be construed as politically inspired and as unmindful of the evil effects of such lawlessness upon the entire population.
>
> – R. D. Small to Roosevelt, 4/8/37[1]

When a political order has been dismantled and attempts to build a new order are underway, politics is surprising and volatile. Fluid political forces gain definition in sharp conflicts where the stakes are large and the rules uncertain. Political leadership means defining a new framework for routine politics. Such a phase occurred in the 1930s when a progressive liberal bloc built a new Democratic order. Prior Democratic forces were expanded and reshaped while new forces emerged.[2] The Democratic order cut across and included important parts of the state, the Democratic Party, and new political forces. This chapter examines the party and movements in the Democratic triangle in 1935–7, focusing on the 1936 campaign.

Changing the Democratic Party

The Democratic Party had to change in the 1930s to make a significant contribution to creating a new political order. Roosevelt's victories were

1. Letter, R. D. Small to Roosevelt, Folder 1937, January–May, Official File 407-B (Strikes), Franklin D. Roosevelt Library.
2. I distinguish between the social presence of individuals as industrial workers, blacks, farmers, etc., and organized political forces. A decade before, there were industrial workers, but no CIO; there were black people, but little black politics around the Democratic Party.

perceived as Democratic triumphs. Yet the Democratic Party was not the leading agent in those efforts; it was not powerful or coherent enough to create the New Deal. Parts of it flourished in a political bloc that cut across institutions – in this bloc the Roosevelt administration and new state agencies exercised more political leadership than the Democratic Party.[3]

In the 1920s the Democratic Party lost three national campaigns badly, and tore itself apart several times. Outside the South few states were reliably Democratic.[4] The party did not even have a permanent national office until 1928, and in 1932 it was neither well funded nor well coordinated.[5] On one side of the party stood forces from the South and West that contained reform and populist elements, as well as racist, nativist, and antilabor currents.[6] On the other side of the party were urban groups: a modest number of big city organizations (some with links to the AFL), progressive currents of opinion linked to the urban middle classes, and small sections of business, including some financial and banking groups in the North.[7] Al Smith's presidential candidacy in

---

3. For some progressive liberals in and around the administration, the subordination of the party was a desirable result likely to be encouraged by further administrative reform. See Sidney M. Milkis, "The New Deal, Administrative Reform, and the Transcendance of Politics," *Administration and Society*, 18, no. 4 (February 1987): 433–72; and Sidney M. Mitkis, *The President and the Parties: The Transformation of the American Party System Since the New Deal* (New York: Oxford University Press, 1993).

4. Paul David, *Party Strength in the United States, 1872–1970* (Charlottesville: University of Virginia Press, 1972), 36–7.

5. On the 1920s, see Davis, *FDR – The New York Years, 1928–1932* (New York: Random House, 1979), 36–7; and Burner, *The Politics of Provincialism: The Democratic Party in Transition, 1918–1932* (New York: Alfred A. Knopf, 1968), 142–57, 197–200. On the 1932 campaign, see Leuchtenburg, *Franklin D. Roosevelt and the New Deal, 1932–1940* (New York: Harper & Row, 1963), 7–17. Democratic campaign work for 1932 is collected in Folders, "Labor, Press Clippings"; "Polls"; and "Press Releases," all 1932–3, Papers of the National Committee of the Democratic Party, FDR Library.

6. See Arthur M. Schlesinger, Jr.'s account of the Democratic Party before the 1930s in *The Crisis of the Old Order* (Boston: Houghton Mifflin, 1957). Also see Richard Hofstadter's treatment of William Jennings Bryan in *The American Political Tradition* (New York: Alfred A. Knopf, 1948), 183–202.

7. After the 1932 campaign, major debts to wealthy individuals included $10,000 or more to Astor, Raskob, Kennedy, and Vanderbilt. "Statement of Deficit," 13 May 1933, Folder Democratic National Committee President's Secretary's File 143, FDR Library. Elite support for the Democratic Party in the late 1920s and early 1930s is treated in Thomas Ferguson, "From Normalcy to New Deal: Industrial Structure, Party Competition, and American Public Policy in the Great Depression," *International Organization* (Winter 1984): 70–7.

Table 5.1. *Presidential elections in three political orders*

Year	Average Democratic popular vote (%)	Average Democratic electoral college vote (%)
1896-1928 (9 elections)	40.8	37.4
1932-1964 (9 elections)	52.5	65.3
1968-1988 (6 elections)	42.9	14.0

Source: Congressional Quarterly's Guide to U.S. Elections, 2nd ed. (Washington, D.C.: Congressional Quarterly, Inc., 1985). Congressional Quarterly, Congress and the Nation 1989-1992 (Washington, D.C.: Government Printing Office, 1993).

Table 5.2. *Democratic strength in the House of Representatives, 1896-1990*

Year	Democratic seats (%)	No. of Congresses with House over 50% Democratic	No. of Congresses with House over 60% Democratic
1896-1930	45.3	3 (of 18)	1
1932-1966	59.7	16 (of 18)	9
1968-1990	60.2	12 (of 12)	5

Source: Congressional Quarterly's Guide to U.S. Elections, 2nd ed. (Washington, D.C.: Congressional Quarterly, Inc., 1985). Congressional Quarterly, Congress and the Nation 1989-1992 (Washington, D.C.: Government Printing Office, 1993).

1928 signaled the possibility of incorporating urban and working-class voters, though his approach was sectional and defensive.[8] Smith's defeat spared Democrats responsibility for the Great Depression. Starting from this weakness the Democratic Party achieved massive electoral successes that would extend decades into the future; these are summarized in Tables 5.1 and 5.2.

As Hoover failed, new Democratic possibilities took shape. Yet the repeated national failures of the party had weakened its previous leaders. Into this void came Franklin Roosevelt and an assortment of Democratic

8. Irving Bernstein, *The Lean Years: A History of the American Worker, 1920–1933* (Boston: Houghton Mifflin, 1960), 75–80; Burner, *Politics of Provincialism*, 179–216; "Democratic Platform for 1928," in Donald Bruce Johnson, ed., *National Party Platforms*, vol. 1, 1840–1956 (Urbana: University of Illinois Press, 1978), 270–8.

forces, including progressive liberals. With the defeat of Populism and the decline of the Socialist Party, by World War I progressive liberalism occupied much of the wide space to the left of center in the United States.[9] Liberal, social democratic, and nationalist themes might all appear in a progressive text or speech without the author being much troubled by tensions among them. After World War I progressive views retained influence in state and local Democratic parties and in academic and professional circles. They were also prominent in Robert LaFollette's presidential campaign in 1924.

Roosevelt entered the national scene as a modernizing, reformist progressive. His 1932 campaign retained sectional ties with the South and West, mobilized urban groups, and claimed to offer responsible leadership amid crisis.[10] The political crises of the old order – in party terms, a weakened Republican Party and a fragmented Democratic coalition – offered the possibility of a decisive rejection of Republican governance. Roosevelt attacked Hoover and the Republicans and sought to polarize the nation against them, when he might have taken a less confrontational direction toward electoral success.

After the anti-Republican landslide of 1932, Roosevelt received a majority from a wide array of groups and regions in 1936. The South remained a Democratic stronghold while the gap between Democratic voting there and elsewhere declined.[11] Racial alignments changed as 70 percent of blacks voted Democratic in the 1936 presidential contest.[12] Middle-class voters supported Democratic candidates – a majority of college-educated voters chose Roosevelt. Democratic support among the working class and poor grew sharply.

---

9. Democratic Progressivism once shared much with Republican Progressivism, as shifting party alignments before World War I suggest. Democratic Progressives advocated modestly egalitarian social reform and were more open to labor than were Republicans. In local settings the labor movement was often connected to the Democratic Party. Where Socialists were strong, they competed with Democrats for voters. See Richard Hofstadter, *The Age of Reform* (New York: Random House, 1955), 248–52; and Michael Kazin, *Barons of Labor: The San Francisco Building Trades and Union Power in the Progressive Era* (Chicago: University of Illinois Press, 1987).

10. On Roosevelt's nomination and the campaign, see James MacGregor Burns, *Roosevelt: The Lion and the Fox* (New York: Harcourt, Brace, and World, 1956), 130–45.

11. Everett Carll Ladd with Charles D. Hadley, *Transformations of the American Party System: Political Coalitions from the New Deal to the 1970s* (New York: W. W. Norton, 1975), 43.

12. Ladd and Hadley, *Transformations of the American Party System*, 60; see also Nancy J. Weiss, *Farewell to the Party of Lincoln* (Princeton, N.J.: Princeton University Press, 1983).

The Democrats failed to approach majority support mainly among business groups and closely allied professional elites.[13] Although some business forces did not share the all-out hostility of the most vocal sectors of the business community, business support for Roosevelt was limited and genuine enthusiasm was absent. Given the size and diversity of the American capitalist class, it would be surprising if no support at all could be found in its ranks for a candidate from a patrician family who insisted he meant to save capitalism. Yet the unity of business against the administration in 1936 is striking.[14] When modest business support appeared it was late in the campaign and registered dissatisfaction with the Republican candidate Landon as well as a judgment that Roosevelt was likely to win.

In 1932 and 1936, Democratic support increased among both working-class and middle-class voters. Especially in 1936, electoral results show little class polarization between the working and middle classes, as working-class and overall electoral support increased together. Democratic discourses were expansive in linking democratic,

13. The distinction between middle-class groupings and business elites is muddied in electoral studies that rely on survey materials which use a tripartite division of social groups (lower, middle, upper). In these years it is particularly misleading to combine upper middle-class strata – from which many people supported Roosevelt – with capitalist elites. The latter contained a much smaller number of people; combining them with small business owners, professors, and accountants gives the impression of even wider support for Roosevelt than existed. The animosity of capitalist elites to Roosevelt was widely reported in accounts of the campaign. In addition to the materials cited earlier, the records of the Democratic National Committee indicate unsuccessful efforts to change the situation. Folders May 1–30, 1936, and June 1–30, 1936, Official File 300 (Democratic National Committee), FDR Library.

14. The classic account of business opposition to Roosevelt is Arthur M. Schlesinger, Jr.'s *The Politics of Upheaval* (Boston: Houghton Mifflin, 1960), which is supported by Burns, *Roosevelt*, 264–88; and William E. Leuchtenburg, *Franklin D. Roosevelt and the New Deal, 1932–1940* (New York: Harper & Row, 1963), 183–96. Thomas Ferguson's argument predicts that sectors favoring free trade and reliant on capital-intensive production would favor Roosevelt. But his detailed account suggests that only a handful of individuals from such sectors did so, and when they did, it was often a last-minute switch away from Landon. Landon's likely demise might have had something to do with this! What Ferguson does capture is a pattern typical of most of the Democratic order: Elite business support for Democratic presidential candidates was provided by a handful of prominent individuals, while Republican business support occurred through more institutional means. This pattern was identified by Alexander Heard in *The Costs of Democracy* (Chapel Hill: University of North Carolina Press, 1960). Lack of support from previously Democratic businessmen was widely reported in letters to Farley. For example, see Letter, Charles Deuel to James Farley, 9/3/36, Folder California #1, Correspondence of James Farley, Papers of the National Committee of the Democratic Party, FDR Library. Ferguson's argument is in "From Normalcy to New Deal," 87–92.

Table 5.3. *Average state support for Democratic presidential candidates,*
1932-1940

Over 70%	60-70%	55-60%	50-55%
Alabama	Arizona	Idaho	Colorado
Arkansas	California	Kentucky	Connecticut
Florida	Maryland	Minnesota	Delaware
Georgia	Montana	Missouri	Illinois
Louisiana	Nevada	North Dakota	Indiana
Mississippi	New Mexico	Oregon	Iowa
North Carolina	Oklahoma	West Virginia	Massachusetts
South Carolina	Tennessee	Wisconsin	Michigan
Texas	Utah	Wyoming	Nebraska
	Virginia		New Hampshire
	Washington		New Jersey
			New York
			Ohio
			Pennsylvania
			Rhode Island
			South Dakota

class, and national themes. The breadth of Democratic support is illustrated in Table 5.3, which lists Roosevelt's share of the presidential
vote in 1932, 1936, and 1940. The Democratic presidential campaigns
secured large majorities in states where Democratic candidates had done
well in the prior political order (such as the South) and created powerful
streams of support in new states and regions (as in industrial states in
the North and Midwest). In this phase of regime politics the Democratic
bloc combined themes and measures that primarily favored the working
class with others cast in broad popular and national terms.[15]

15. For a sophisticated view of class voting in Western Europe as class-based, see Adam
    Przeworski and John Sprague, *Paper Stones: A History of Electoral Socialism* (Chi-
    cago, Ill.: University of Chicago Press, 1986). In the mid-1930s, depicting the Demo-
    cratic upsurge as purely a class phenomenon is precluded by the persistence of ethnic,

Democratic gains in the Senate and House were also dramatic. Between 1916 and 1930, Democratic Senators on average made up 44 percent of the Senate; the average from 1932 to 1940 rose to 67 percent. In the House, the comparable shift was from a Democratic average of 187 to 300 seats. Democrats gained ninety-seven seats in the House of Representatives in 1932, the largest shift in the twentieth century.

The 1936 campaign

The New Deal's management of the country's crises was popular, given vivid memories of the Republican alternative. Roosevelt faced his reelection campaign confidently after the passage of major social reform legislation in 1935. Both in the party platform (more explicitly and ardently reformist than in 1932) and the campaign, Roosevelt claimed to have addressed the nation's crises by taking all necessary measures. The Democratic platform strongly asserted the responsibilities of government: "(1) Protection of the family and the home. (2) Establishment of a democracy of opportunity for all the people. (3) Aid to those overtaken by disaster."[16] Roosevelt stressed that Hoover's refusal to expand state action and related policies caused danger and suffering:

> It is my belief that the people of Detroit, like the people of the rest of the country, are going to ask on November 3rd that the present type of Government continue rather than the type of Government which in its heart still believes in the policy of laissez faire and the kind of individualism which up to only three and a half years ago, frankly, put dollars above human rights.[17]

The campaign fused progressive, democratic, and populist themes in denouncing selfish elites for blocking national progress. This mix of themes was dynamic and expansive, reaching new groups and areas.

The conflicts of 1936 were basically about whether the new Democratic order would be a lasting replacement for the Republican order. The result was a stunning Democratic success against Republicans, conservative Democrats, and business groups who did not expect such a defeat.[18]

regional, and racial bases of Democratic voting. Ladd and Hadley, *Transformations of the American Party System*, 66–70.
16. "Democratic Platform of 1936," in Johnson, *National Party Platforms*, 360.
17. Franklin D. Roosevelt, Campaign Address at Detroit, Michigan, October 15, 1936, in *The Public Papers and Addresses of Franklin D. Roosevelt*, vol. 5, *The People Approve – 1936*, compiled by Samuel I. Rosenman (New York: Random House, 1938), 499.
18. The administration had relatively accurate information both from polling work done by Emile Hurja and from the ceaseless efforts of James Farley to gain information

Party organization and activities

Roosevelt's major speeches and public statements in 1936 made no reference to the Democratic Party.[19] He did not campaign mainly as a Democrat nor credit his accomplishments to the party. He offered a national, progressive, and popular-democratic program and vision, always trying to attract Republicans and independents.[20] Obviously voters knew Roosevelt was a Democrat, and that Democratic candidates were apt to support his programs.[21] The lack of reference to the party reflected a desire to broaden support for the New Deal and an awareness of popular views. In terms of appeal, Roosevelt's popularity came first, including his political persona and policies; then came approval of the administration. Support for the Democratic Party per se was mainly derivative of these other preferences, especially for new Democratic voters.

about local and state situations. It was known that populist forces outside the Democratic Party were in electoral decline in the summer of 1936. Yet even the administration underestimated the extent of its victory, probably because it insufficiently appreciated the role of new voters. On the results, see David, *Party Strength*, 53–6. On the decline of populism, see Letter, Henry Briggs to Farley, 7/27/36, Folder California #1, Correspondence of James Farley, Papers of the National Committee of the Democratic Party, 1928–48, FDR Library. Several campaign polls asked the choices of prospective 1936 voters about their 1932 preference without asking about new voters. Folder Polls, OF 300 (Democratic National Committee), FDR Library.

19. Leuchtenburg claims that Roosevelt referred to the party no more than three times. Given the volume of campaign materials, it's hard to be sure of that figure. Leuchtenburg, *Roosevelt and the New Deal*, 190.

20. Roosevelt's campaign retained his 1932 support while mobilizing previously nonvoting groups, who were disproportionately poor, first- or second-generation immigrants, and of the working class. Landon received more votes than Hoover (16.7 to 15.8 million), the third-party vote remained roughly the same (1.3 million), and Roosevelt's vote increased more than 20 percent, from 22.8 to 27.8 million. Since some Democratic voters in 1932 switched to the Republican Party, and others had died, the overall Democratic upsurge was on the order of 6 to 7 million voters. These votes came from previously Republican and third-party voters, previously nonvoting members of the electorate, and young people for whom 1936 was the first election in which they could vote. Democrats did well with the latter group (over 60 percent). It seems likely that 50 to 60 percent of the increase in Roosevelt's support, perhaps as much as 75 percent, came from new voters. Burnham's claim that 40 percent of new Democratic voters in the 1930s were converted Republicans is probably a high estimate. See Walter Dean Burnham, *The Current Crisis in American Politics* (New York: Oxford University Press, 1982), 147. See also Kristi Andersen, *The Creation of a Democratic Majority, 1928–1936* (Chicago, Ill.: University of Chicago Press, 1979), 53–82.

21. Roosevelt often attacked specific Republicans or the Hoover administration without attacking the party as such, given his aim of securing support from progressives who had until recently been (or remained) Republicans, such as those discussed in John E. Miller, *Governor Philip F. La Follette, The Wisconsin Progressives, and the New Deal* (Columbia: University of Missouri Press, 1982), 10–60.

In 1936 the organized Democratic Party was closely associated with a very popular administration. The party as a distinct organization, however, remained relatively weak.[22] The political capacities of the party certainly increased, yet even so it was not a very vital force. This is the moment when one would expect a major party-based initiative, if the Democratic Party were the key agent in building a new political order. But it is hard to credit the party with responsibility for Democratic electoral successes. And the question remains, why did Democratic electoral successes not mean more for developing the party as an organization?

To locate the Democratic Party in the new order, I will first consider two routes through which a basic reordering of the party might have occurred: by the president and the administration, or by the party itself.[23] While Roosevelt argued for developing the party in the 1920s, in 1935–7 he made no major commitment to such a project. Asked whether he would have welcomed such a result he doubtless would have said yes. But pressures to win and implement a national political agenda took precedence over party matters.[24] To achieve his political aims Roosevelt took the Democratic Party as he found it. The leadership of the new political order was open to compromise with any Democrats willing to support the main direction of its national policies. Southern Democrats who offered such support in the mid-1930s did not have to worry about a federal challenge to segregationist race relations, though

22. In 1935–7 this weakness is clear in correspondence about the Democrats' condition in various parts of the country. Such records as exist are in Roosevelt's Presidential Papers and in the files of the Democratic Party in the Papers of the Democratic National Committee. Relevant materials are in Official File 300 (Democratic Party National Committee); President's Secretary's File (DNC), (Conventions), (Platform); and Papers of the National Committee of the Democratic Party – all at the FDR Library.

23. In examining archival and press materials for the 1930s and 1940s, I focused on several important and representative states: California, Georgia, Illinois, Iowa, Michigan, and New York. The relative scarcity of secondary work on party organizations may be due partly to the predictability of the result of most such inquiries: Party organizations suffered from high leadership turnover, unclear procedures for the conduct of their work, and uncertain relations between national and local units.

24. Sean Savage claims Roosevelt was a dedicated party builder, while his account shows that in organizational terms this was far from the truth. Roosevelt was a skilled political leader in dealing with Democrats in Congress, with urban Democratic organizations – and with Republican progressives. Savage gives little evidence of the vibrant party organization that he claims Roosevelt helped build. Sean J. Savage, *Roosevelt: The Party Leader* (Lexington: The University Press of Kentucky, 1991), 3, 17–47. Also see Ronald A. Mulder, *The Insurgent Progressives in the U.S. Senate and the New Deal, 1933–1939* (New York: Garland, 1979).

they reasonably feared that the New Deal would mean a major long-term decline in their power in the Democratic Party. Cooperative local machines, even if corrupt, were relatively safe from assault.[25] This openness also extended to the left, as Roosevelt cooperated with local Democratic parties in which socialists played a significant role.[26]

Where compromise was difficult, the Roosevelt administration often found it less costly and hazardous to bypass rather than try to transform the organized Democratic Party.[27] With good reason the administration leadership suspected many state and local Democrats of sabotaging New Deal programs. One way to bypass the least promising Democratic partners was to create pro-New Deal networks that were not controlled by local Democratic powers, without claiming to build alternative party forms per se. And the administration could focus on building direct links with mass constituencies through public appeals and the work of new

25. On relations between the emergent political order and the South, see James T. Patterson, *Congressional Conservatism and the New Deal: The Growth of the Conservative Coalition in Congress, 1933–1939* (Lexington: University of Kentucky Press, 1967); and Harvard Sitkoff, *A New Deal for Blacks: The Emergence of Civil Rights as a National Issue* (New York: Oxford University Press, 1978). See also James C. Cobb and Michael V. Namorato, eds., *The New Deal and the South* (Jackson: University of Mississippi Press, 1984), which includes valuable essays by Harvard Sitkoff, Alan Brinkley, Wayne Flint, and Frank Freidel. Roosevelt's effort to defeat anti-New Deal Democrats in 1938 took as one of its key texts the National Emergency Council's *Report on Economic Conditions of the South*, which painted a highly critical picture of Southern social and economic backwardness. On relations with urban machines, see John Allswang, *Bosses, Machines, and Urban Voters*, revised ed., (Baltimore, Md.: Johns Hopkins University Press, 1986), and Lyle Dorsett, *Franklin D. Roosevelt and the City Bosses* (Port Washington, N.Y.: Kennikat Press, 1977).

26. The administration would accept support from socialists and communists if it could define the public identity of the project in question. When this condition was violated things went differently. Roosevelt intervened in California in 1934, making clear that Upton Sinclair's quasi-socialist EPIC campaign was to the left of what he deemed politically acceptable. Materials on the EPIC campaign are in OF 300 (California 1933–6), FDR Library. Also see Upton Sinclair, *The Way Out: What Lies Ahead for America* (New York: Farrar & Rinehart, 1933).

27. Administration interests in bypassing recalcitrant party organizations occasionally converged with local forces to the left of those organizations to establish labor-populist third parties. Such efforts aimed to ratify the national Democratic direction, not to build a new political party. Richard Valelly argues that the national evolution of the New Deal closed off prospects for state-level radicalism, mainly by allowing such efforts to enter or affilliate with the national Democratic Party. His account underlines the flexibility of the progressive liberal leadership and its lack of commitment to previous partisan ties. Richard Valelly, *Radicalism in the States: The Minnesota Farmer-Labor Party and the American Political Economy* (Chicago, Ill.: University of Chicago Press, 1989), 170.

federal agencies.[28] Both courses meant relying on the resources of an expanding state without any full-scale rebuilding of the party.

As for a transformation by the Democratic Party itself, the party had neither the capacity nor the inclination. It was led by James Farley, Roosevelt's Postmaster General and campaign manager in 1936. Farley, chairman of the Democratic National Committee, was committed to Roosevelt but to his right politically; he was also to the left of many leaders of Democratic organizations in cities and states.[29] Farley tried to mediate endless conflicts in the party in which pro- and anti-New Deal factions battled.[30] His own ambivalence – loyalty to Roosevelt, plus close ties to an often conservative party – signified that the Democratic Party was unlikely to lead any major transformation of its own forms.[31]

The main political divisions of these years had a logic that would have undermined any attempt to make the party a coherent and autonomous center of power. Pro-New Deal Democrats were drawn to the expanding public activities linked to the new state – and had no interest in opposing the administration. Democrats to Farley's right who worried about the state's encroachment and New Deal tolerance for popular radicalism faced a tough decision. They could compromise basic principles and

28. Martin Shefter, "Party, Bureaucracy, and Political Change in the United States," in Louis Maisel and Joseph Cooper, eds., *Political Parties: Development and Decay* (Beverly Hills: Sage, 1978), 211–65. Also see Martin Shefter, *Political Parties and the State: the American Historical Experience* (Princeton, N.J.: Princeton University Press, 1994).

29. Farley's campaign speeches stressed national unity with fewer democratic and popular emphases than Roosevelt's. His correspondence and speeches are prominent in the Papers of the Democratic National Committee and OF 300 (Democratic National Committee), FDR Library. He outlines the terms of his support for the New Deal in James A. Farley, *Behind the Ballots: The Personal History of a Politician* (New York: Harcourt, Brace, 1938).

30. Reports of such conflicts appear over and over in letters outlining local political situations, in response to a 1936 Farley letter soliciting judgments of Roosevelt's reelection prospects. The questionnaire is in Folder, Farley's Forms for Campaign Correspondence, Miscellaneous Democratic Papers 1932–48, Papers of the Democratic National Committee, FDR Library. Among the accounts of conflict are: Letter, Edward C. Purpus to Farley, October 2, 1934; and Letter, James Meeks to Farley, August 17, 1936 – all in Correspondence of James Farley, Papers of the National Committee of the Democratic Party, FDR Library.

31. The Democratic organizations that seriously claimed to organize effectively were atypical. Mayor Edward Kelly of Chicago wrote Farley that the "intensive drive" of the last part of the 1936 campaign would involve the efforts of his organization's almost 50,000 employees. This was likely an overstatement, perhaps including large numbers of city workers whose campaign efforts were not especially zealous. Letter, Edward Kelly to Farley, n.d., Folder Illinois #2, Correspondence of James Farley, Papers of the National Committee of the Democratic Party, FDR Library.

reluctantly follow the administration, or go into full opposition and risk marginality. Sometimes this tension resulted in passive Democratic resistance, but trying to overhaul the entire Democratic Party to oppose the New Deal was out of the question for conservative Democrats outside the South. As the failures of Al Smith showed, such an effort would yield isolation without creating a new Democratic Party. Conservative Democrats were better off making grudging compromises with the new order and trying to slow its reformist dynamic.

If political alignments made an organizational transformation unlikely, patronage issues had similar effects.[32] Most sections of the Democratic Party wanted to place their members in new federal positions and control future patronage. These desires muted any aspirations toward the formation of a party center distinct from, much less opposed to, the administration.[33] It is unsurprising that no party-based Democratic force capable of acting autonomously and powerfully emerged in 1935–7.[34]

A mass Democratic Party?

If neither the administration nor Democratic elites sought to transform the Democratic Party into the leading political force, could another route be opened by the entry of masses of new Democratic voters? Could a

32. It is easier to find detailed memos about patronage procedures, with long discussions of how the party hierarchy should be involved, than to find similar memos about party organization (much less policy matters). The idea was that party support should be a preliminary screen after which agencies should be able to exercise discretion. One memo, from 1940, went so far as to divide up most of the government into agencies that "mean something to us on patronage" and others. The former group included the Treasury Department, the War Department, the Department of Justice, the Interior Department, the Department of Agriculture, and among smaller agencies, the NLRB. Letter, Paul H. Appleby to Oscar Ewing, 12/20/40, Folder DNC Patronage Policies; Memo, Dick Durham to Chairman, n.d., Folder Patronage – Letters and Memos, Papers of the National Committee of the Democratic Party, FDR Library. Vast amounts of patronage correspondence exist in Patronage Correspondence and Letters, 1933–40, Papers of the National Committee of the Democratic Party, FDR Library.

33. Other centrifugal forces arose from local alignments, as when some "old" Progressive elements in the early-to-mid 1930s were suspicious of the New Deal. They feared that the growing political power of unions and other mass political forces would create corrupt new machines, while they watched the administration make deals with old ones. On progressive ambivalence in Detroit in the early 1930s, see Raymond R. Fragnoli, *The Transformation of Reform: Progressivism in Detroit, 1912–1933* (New York: Garland, 1982), 373–80.

34. David Mayhew's study of party organizations as of the late 1960s suggests the modest reach of effective organizations three decades earlier. According to Mayhew's analysis, roughly 45 percent of the population in the 1930s lived in states that contained "traditional party organizations," to use his term. If one takes into account that a

renovated Democratic Party be built "from below"? Workers, young people, blacks, and others poured into the voting booths to vote Democratic, and deep political attachments were created. This provided resources for improving Democratic organizational capacities and expanded the base for conventional party forms. Yet these changes rarely produced durable new party forms (either formal organizations or informal networks) that could sustain extensive public involvement.

New Democratic organizations appeared mainly at the city level, based on local electoral shifts and support for New Deal policies. Their links with the national state, commitment to much of the New Deal program, and diminished reliance on white ethnic identifications distinguish them from prior party organizations. In a modest number of cases, Democratic activists tried something more novel – to increase public participation in party affairs, in effect trying to build local mass parties. Such organizations arose where labor was strong and well-organized, especially when a Republican administration was removed and previous Democratic forces were weak. They took shape mainly in industrial states in the North and East and in urban areas with large middle-class progressive constituencies, such as Los Angeles. These efforts were fluid and not highly institutionalized. Even where these organizations were mainly led by labor, they were conceived as popular parties, combining laborist, populist, and radical democratic elements. They were usually short-lived though they influenced labor political efforts and more conventional Democratic organizations.[35] To imagine them as able to dominate or even seriously influence the party at the national level would be unrealistic.

Here a comment on terms is necessary. In the mid-1930s, the Democratic Party as a formal association of affiliated state party organizations certainly existed. But even the term "Democratic Party" can be mis-

large part of the population lived in rural areas and small towns, where such organizations were less likely to be present, and that some of the "traditional" party organizations were Republican, it seems unlikely that more than 25 percent of the population lived in areas with strong conventional Democratic organizations, and the figure was probably lower. David Mayhew, *Placing Parties in American Politics* (Princeton, N.J.: Princeton University Press, 1986), 196–200.

35. These local mass party efforts accompanied a smaller number of efforts to create quasi-independent state and local parties that supported the New Deal but were at odds with Democratic Party organizations. See R. Alan Lawson, *The Failure of Independent Liberalism, 1930–41* (New York: Putnam, 1971); and Steven Fraser's account of the American Labor Party and the CIO's relation to the Democratic Party in *Labor Will Rule: Sidney Hillman and the Rise of American Labor* (New York: The Free Press, 1991), 363–72.

leading, especially when it is linked to "party organization," because it suggests more coherent and disciplined organizations than existed. The "Democratic Party" in cities and states often meant a hodgepodge of small formal organizations, informal networks linked to those organizations, and masses of unorganized Democratic voters. The "Democratic Party" certainly looks much larger and stronger if one uses the term to include all three of these elements. But using it so broadly as to include all pro-Democratic sections of the electorate obscures the limits of the party as a political organization. Instead I use "Democratic Party" mainly to refer to the formal organizations plus the most closely related informal networks.

One indication of the weakness of the new party structure is that voting rates did not increase significantly after 1936, going from 61 percent that year to 62.5 percent in 1940 and then decreasing (partly due to wartime conditions) to 55.9 percent in 1944.[36] Had the mobilization of 1936 yielded durable new mass political organizations on a wide basis, it might have been feasible to increase voting rates significantly by 1940, especially given the low base figures. While there doubtless would have been a wartime decline, it might have been less steep, and postwar voting might have soon returned to prewar levels.[37]

The upsurge of Democratic voters and partisans resulted in major changes in the Democratic Party – it was greatly expanded without being deeply transformed. The Democratic electorate grew and Democratic state and local power increased, extending into areas where it had been marginal for decades. Growth resulted mainly in increasing the resources of existing Democratic organizations and creating new Democratic organizations of relatively conventional types where none had existed. Much of the limited organizational innovation in efforts to create new party forms for pro-New Deal voters originated outside regular party structures, building on labor ties, networks among farmers,

36. Bureau of the Census, *Historical Statistics of the United States – Colonial Times to 1970*, Y 27-78, "Voter Participation in Presidential Elections, by State: 1824 to 1968" (Washington, D.C.: Government Printing Office), 1071–2.

37. One way to gauge the mass character of parties is to calculate the ratio of party members to the party vote – a higher ratio implies a party with more mass features. In the United States it is not possible to perform such a calculation because no equivalent category of party membership exists. Party registration is a status that signifies less practical commitment than party membership (and records on that status vary greatly in quality by state). Democratic Party records contain little information on the number, size, and form of party meetings and other local activities; no overall party center cared to collect and save such information. Yet even with poor record keeping, substantial mass party forms would have left many traces.

and progressive Republicans.[38] Alongside Democratic electoral triumphs there was much complaining about factionalism and organizational weakness in the party in 1935–7.[39]

New mass forces could not change the party on their own. Yet despite the forces discouraging deep innovation in party organization, one still might imagine that electoral competition would have produced greater changes than took place. Why wouldn't Democratic interests in winning elections encourage organizational change beyond what occurred? There were several reasons. Everyone claimed to want to win elections, but for different purposes and with different means.[40] For more than a few leaders of Democratic organizations, there were worse fates than occasionally losing an election, if winning would jeopardize their power. North and South, local Democratic elites were not enthusiastic about encouraging mass Democratic organizations that might threaten them. Politically, regular Democratic forces were often well to the right of the administration, as was evident in the failure of the administration to defeat anti-New Deal Democrats in 1937–8.[41]

Party organizations cooperated with the administration enough to reduce the already small prospect that serious national efforts would be made to set up new party institutions. State and local Democratic

38. On Progressive parties, see Miller, *Governor Philip F. La Follette;* Valelly, *Radicalism in the States;* and Millard L. Gieske, *Minnesota Farmer-Laborism: The Third-Party Alternative* (Minneapolis: University of Minnesota Press, 1979).

39. A campaign memo from 1944 outlines the campaign structure in 1936, which seems to have involved fewer than twenty national staff. Another memo from the same year reports that "during the past twelve years the party organization in many Democratic states has become somewhat inactive for the simple reason that the Democratic majorities have been heavy and party workers have not felt the necessity of doing a regular organization job." Memos, "Background for 1936 and 1940 Campaigns," and "Organization – County and Precinct Party Officials," both in Folder – Organization of Party, Papers of the National Committee of the Democratic Party, FDR Library.

40. Virtually all Democrats would have affirmed commitments to winning and strengthening the party. Yet many actions indicate that factional imperatives were given priority over the electoral interests of the party. As with most economic accounts of political action, the concept of party as a seeker of electoral victory works best when the agent in question is unified and coherent. See Joseph A. Schlesinger, "On the Theory of Party Organization," *The Journal of Politics* 46 (1984): 374–5; and *Political Parties and the Winning of Office* (Ann Arbor: University of Michigan Press, 1991).

41. Burns criticizes the lateness of Roosevelt's party reform effort, while Leuchtenburg portrays him as mainly reactive. Leuchtenburg, *Roosevelt and the New Deal*, 252–74. In the South, regular party forces combined openness to some New Deal economic and social measures with a deep commitment to maintaining the racial order. See Patterson, *Congressional Conservatism and the New Deal*, 65.

organizations had good reasons to cooperate – they needed to find potential new voters and to maintain the security of organizations that were often legally and politically vulnerable.[42] Local Democratic organizations could also act as patronage bureaus with regard to new national agencies and social welfare projects.[43]

Cooperation with the New Deal would tend over time to weaken local party organizations, although it was probably their best alternative. Transferring social provision to the federal government promised eventually to reduce the influence of local organizations with urban working-class and lower middle-class voters. The growth of federal government agencies and of national and local civil service mechanisms would also make positions with local political organizations less attractive to those interested in combining politics, public service, and professional activities. It is hard to know if the ambivalence of local party organizations about the New Deal expressed an awareness that the long-term effects of the new political order would be corrosive. Their anxious and qualified support of the national administration was more likely based on political disagreement about reform measures and immediate fear of federal intrusion into their political territory.

In sum, the Democratic Party was in no sense the central agent in building the Democratic order. Rebuilding the party was limited by the weight of prior party forms and by the administration's need for immediate support. The course taken yielded major political benefits but reduced the extent to which new electoral support could be translated into durable party institutions. The Democratic Party relied on Roosevelt's political persona as a means of winning elections. It benefited from

42. In the 1930s urban machines remained significant, especially in the East and Midwest. But their political importance had declined from the early twentieth century and was continuing to decline. The weakening of machines and the obstacles to building new ones had several sources: the political effects of progressivism, modernizing social and economic changes, and demographic shifts that reduced the proportion of the population living in cities dominated by machines. Harold Gosnell stressed that machines shifted from controlling resources to mediating between local clients and branches of the federal government in *Machine Politics, Chicago Model*, second edition (Chicago, Ill.: University of Chicago Press, 1968), 90. One can miss the force of these tendencies if the definition of political machines is loosened so that weaker forms of local political organization qualify over time; "machines" finally become defined only as enduring political organizations. Thus, Banfield and Wilson's definition of machines – as party organizations that depend on specific and material inducements – allows many organizations to count that may not be very successful. Edward C. Banfield and James Q. Wilson, *City Politics* (Cambridge, Mass.: Harvard University Press, 1963), 118–20.

43. See Richard Polenberg, *Reorganizing Roosevelt's Government – The Controversy over Executive Reorganization* (Cambridge, Mass.: Harvard University Press, 1966).

new patronage arrangements organized by the national state, which it did not control.[44]

In these years an expanding state and an electorally successful Democratic Party were closely tied, with the party clearly subordinate. Few among the leadership of the administration – as in Roosevelt's Cabinet and top advisers – came from the Democratic Party organization. Administration proposals reached the party via national public appeals, or administration allies in Congress, or through party chairman James Farley – while major political issues at a state or local level often went directly to the national administration, bypassing the Democratic organization.

As in passing and implementing the NLRA, the crucial leadership in constructing the new order did not come from the Democratic Party per se. It came from progressive liberals who, although mostly Democrats, had their roots in nonparty professional and administrative settings. The progressive liberal leadership expanded to include the most sympathetic parts of the organized Democratic Party and sections of emerging movements. It built a framework, centered on the state, in which compromises could be made with many regular Democratic forces.

Labor as a new political force

In 1935–7 major nonparty political forces appeared. Movements of the urban and rural poor were sporadically powerful, a germinal youth movement briefly emerged, and new civil rights efforts surfaced. Among these forces I focus on the labor movement, in its double emergence as a powerful industrial force and a significant political actor. Political conflicts were crucial in shaping a new framework for labor politics: As the labor movement helped build the Democratic order, it was constructed as a legitimate political force. I am addressing two questions: What caused durable unions to emerge, and what caused labor to become a significant political force? The answers overlap. Unions were produced by major and unprecedented political reforms, which were the core of the progressive liberal response to a widespread labor mobilization. And labor's political role was built through political interaction among progressive liberals, new labor leaders, and highly mobilized sections of

44. Lines between political and civil service appointments were indistinct as the state grew rapidly. In 1936 civil service positions made up a smaller part of federal employment than before Roosevelt's election, because federal employment was expanding rapidly while the major civil service reforms of the decade were not yet in place. Bureau of the Census, *Historical Statistics*, Y 308–317, "Paid Civilian Employment of the Federal Government: 1816 to 1970."

the working class. The outcome was a powerful interest group support-ive of and intertwined with the Democratic order.

The formation of durable unions was in large part a political story – NRA, 1934 election, NLRA, 1936 election, sit-down strikes, court deci-sions. The protagonists were progressive liberals and the labor move-ment; without working class mobilization, progressive liberals would not have created unions as a gift to workers. Yet the key political measures did not recognize a de facto state of affairs in the economy. Even by 1937 secure unions existed in relatively few settings, and a diligent use of coercion might still have resolved most conflicts on terms favorable to antiunion employers. For a new direction to be taken, political measures were essential in constituting and protecting the unions.

The political dimension of unionization

The political dynamic between emergent labor and progressive liberal forces helped construct a new labor movement. By the last years of the Republican order, the labor movement was small and weak.[45] This weakness was most recently due to ardent antiunion efforts from World War I through the 1920s and the disorganizing effects of the Depression. In 1930 unions organized little more than 10 percent of the nonagricul-tural labor force.[46] There were regional and sectoral strongholds (coal and railroads) but little growth. The labor movement was mainly the AFL; in 1930 roughly 3 million of 3.6 million unionized workers were enrolled in AFL unions.[47] The disruption and suffering caused by the Depression helped spur workers to attempt to unionize, and the militant and creative efforts of unorganized workers were central to building new unions.[48] Yet respect for the dignity and frequent heroism of these efforts should not mean overstating their effects. Even after the organiz-

---

45. Melvyn Dubofsky underlines the antilabor normal times of the post-1896 Republican order in "Abortive Reform: The Wilson Administration and Organized Labor, 1913–1920," in James E. Cronin and Carmen Sirianni, eds., *Work, Community, and Power: The Experience of Labor in Europe and America, 1900–1925* (Philadelphia: Temple University Press, 1983), 197–220.

46. Bureau of the Census, *Historical Statistics of the United States – Colonial Times to 1970*, D 952-969, "Labor Union Membership, by Industry: 1897 to 1934," 178.

47. Bureau of the Census, *Historical Statistics, of the United States – Colonial Times to 1970*, D 940–945, "Labor Union Membership, by Affiliation: 1897 to 1934," 177.

48. My discussion of the labor movement focuses on industry rather than on services or agriculture, and within industry on mass-production sectors. This focus is warranted by the economic importance of those sectors and their perceived importance vis-à-vis the prospects of the labor movement.

ing efforts and strikes of 1933–4, unionization was limited and the labor movement fragile.

The high unemployment and residential dislocation of the Depression weakened unions, which were preoccupied with sustaining their fragile organizations. The fragmented and often impoverished work force of the early Depression was less capable of collective action than it would become after the New Deal programs and modest economic recovery.[49] Yet prior changes in the work force and the structure of production had increased the prospects of new labor organization based on urban workers in mass production industries.[49] Union growth in the 1930s was enhanced by growing familiarity with the new industrial settings and by generational and cultural changes that made previous ethnocultural and occupational rivalries less salient.[50] The workforce in these industries opposed restrictive and often demeaning labor relations, and resented the urban hardships to which it was subjected.[51]

By the early 1930s several decades of experience with work conditions and management strategies in the new industries had set the stage for a new labor movement. Yet given the economic weakness of the working

49. With a few notable exceptions – centrally the mineworkers – unions grew most rapidly in larger metropolitan areas. See Milton Derber, "Growth and Expansion," in Milton Derber and Edwin Young, eds., *Labor and the New Deal*, (Madison: University of Wisconsin Press, 1957), 38–42.

50. The mobilization of the working class is richly documented in local and industry-based labor histories, oral histories, memoirs, and ethnographies. See Staughton Lynd and Alice Lynd, *Rank and File: Personal Histories by Working Class Organizers* (Boston: Beacon Press, 1973); Peter Friedlander, *The Emergence of a UAW Local, 1936–39: A Study in Class and Culture* (Pittsburgh, Pa.: University of Pittsburgh Press, 1975); Ewa Morawska, *For Bread with Butter: Life-Worlds of East Central Europeans in Johnstown, Pennsylvania, 1890–1940* (New York: Cambridge University Press, 1985); John Bodnar, *Workers' World: Kinship, Community, and Protest in an Industrial Society, 1900–1940* (Baltimore, Md.: Johns Hopkins University Press, 1982); and David Gartman, *Auto Slavery: The Labor Process in the American Automobile Industry, 1897–1950* (New Brunswick, N.J.: Rutgers University Press, 1986).

51. These views did not mean opposition to expanded mass production or urban life, or general opposition to social and economic modernization. The new unionism and the CIO in the mid-1930s represented and developed modernizing currents within the working class. In his biography of Hillman, Fraser emphasizes the modernizing sympathies of the CIO leadership in the 1930s. He also stresses the extent to which the mass-production industries after World War I eroded a prior world of smaller enterprises, craft and skilled positions, and ethnocultural divisions. He is cautious about imputing Hillman's full views on modernization and mass production to the mass working-class forces of the 1930s. But his account makes clear that those forces were less gripped by the combination of ethnocultural politics and craft allegiances that had shaped the world of industrial work in the late nineteenth and early twentieth centuries. Fraser, *Labor Will Rule*, 337–40.

class, widespread unionization is hard to imagine without major political shifts.[52] Though the AFL often allied locally with Democratic organizations in the 1920s and early 1930s, its influence in the party was modest, while many in the party mistrusted the unions.[53] A number of important AFL leaders were Republican in the early 1930s, as were many in the union rank-and-file.[54] Another Hoover administration or a conservative Democratic government might have permitted enough political and economic repression to restrict greatly, if not prevent, the growth of industrial unions.

Labor's support for Roosevelt was not central to his election in 1932.[55] In creating a new dynamic, the legitimation of union organization that began with the NIRA early in Roosevelt's first term was very important. A key political event was the government response to the dramatic strikes of 1934, when serious efforts at conciliation were undertaken along with the usual defense of order. These uprisings did not immediately produce unions; union membership in 1935 was only 13 percent of the nonagricultural labor force, having increased by less than 200,000 from 1930.[56] But national political forces were pressured to take the labor movement more seriously.

The midterm election in 1934 produced a Democratic sweep that emboldened progressive liberals to propose labor law reform and made others in Congress much more open to such measures. In 1935 the NLRA was passed with an eye on the turbulence of the previous year, at a time when union activism was linked to wide strata among the urban working class and poor. Yet the Wagner Act did not immediately establish unions with the power to negotiate wages and working conditions, as it was fiercely resisted by employers. Further political conflicts were required for major increases in union membership. The 1936 election

52. By the 1930s external political pressures and rethinking within the AFL had reshaped voluntarism to admit positive state measures, such as the Norris-La Guardia Act, by considering them as enabling acts that would allow voluntarist relations to flourish. Ruth Horowitz, *Political Ideologies of Organized Labor: The New Deal Era* (New Brunswick, N.J.: Transaction, 1978), 80.

53. Bernstein, *Lean Years,* 334–57; David Brody, *Workers in Industrial America: Essays on the 20th Century Struggle* (New York: Oxford University Press, 1980), 44–5, 82; and Horowitz, *Political Ideologies of Organized Labor,* 55, 73.

54. James Sundquist emphasizes Republican strength among urban workers in *Dynamics of the Party System: Alignment and Realignment of Political Parties in the United States* (Washington, D.C.: Brookings Institution, rev. ed. 1983), 200.

55. Leuchtenburg, *Roosevelt and the New Deal,* 10–17.

56. Bureau of the Census, *Historical Statistics of the United States – Colonial Times to 1970,* D 946-951, "Labor Union Membership and Membership as Percent of Total Labor Force and of Nonagricultural Employment: 1930 to 1970," 178.

expressed popular approval of the New Deal and thereby reduced employers' options for resisting unions. In 1936 the AFL and the emergent CIO rallied to support Roosevelt. Much of labor's effort went through Labor's Non-Partisan League, which was dominated by the CIO.[57] The AFL also acted through the labor division of the national campaign committee and its ties with local Democratic organizations. The labor movement could take significant credit for Roosevelt's victory.

The next key political shift came with the government response to the sit-down strikes in Flint, Michigan, in late 1936 and early 1937. The refusal of Roosevelt and Governor Murphy to use force against those occupying the automobile factories was highly unconventional. A torrent of letters and cables arrived at the White House demanding that Roosevelt deal harshly with the strikes.[58] His refusal to take action was taken to mean support for labor's right to organize, even tolerance of extralegal measures when management refused to bargain. Introducing his 1937 public statements, he later wrote:

> Enemies of labor were quick to condemn in 1937. From familiar circles came the old cry of the Tories: "Something drastic must be done to curb labor; it is getting too powerful." Of course what these people really want and strive for is to return to the good old days when labor was unorganized and weak, and starving for jobs. You could always reason with a starving applicant for a job. But it is so inconvenient to bargain with a strong, united group of employees who know that they are entitled to a fair share of the profits of an industry.[59]

In 1936 the question of how to win court acceptance of New Deal legislation was discussed in administration circles. The election was perceived as a choice between the Court's and the administration's

---

57. Most local labor involvement in politics in the mid-1930s meant campaign rallies, registering voters, and getting out the vote at election time. See Schlesinger, *Politics of Upheaval,* 592–5; C. K. McFarland, "Coalition of Convenience: Lewis and Roosevelt, 1933–1940," *Labor History* 13, no. 1 (Winter 1972): 400–14; and Thomas T. Spencer, " 'Labor Is with Roosevelt': The Pennsylvania Non-Partisan League and the Election of 1936," *Pennsylvania History* 46, no. 1 (January 1979): 3–16.

58. Governor Murphy of Michigan and Roosevelt were also pressured by the AFL not to encourage a settlement of the auto disputes that would benefit the CIO and weaken AFL units. Telegram, William Green to Franklin Murphy, February 6, 1937; Summary of Franklin Murphy telephone call to White House, February 8, 1937, Folder Auto Strike 37, OF 407-B (Strikes) FDR Library.

59. *The Public Papers and Addresses of Franklin D. Roosevelt,* vol. 6, *The Constitution Prevails – 1937,* compiled by Samuel I. Rosenman (New York: Random House, 1941), 7, 20, 23, 274.

views of the Constitution.[60] The resulting political pressure probably influenced opinion within the Court.[61] Supreme Court decisions upheld the NLRA, crucially in 1937 in *NLRB v. Jones & Laughlin Steel Corp.*:

> Thus in its present application, the statute goes no further than to safeguard the right of employees to self-organization and to select representatives of their own choosing for collective bargaining or other mutual protection without restraint or coercion by their employer. That is a fundamental right. Employees have as clear a right to organize and select their representatives for lawful purposes as the [company] has to organize its business and select its own officers and agents.[62]

The legal recognition of unions as public, representative entities provided a crucial condition for their existence. Without such intervention, the likelihood is that the labor movement would still not have been able to establish durable new unions on a large scale. In fact, union membership surged in 1937 and 1938, from 4.0 million members in 1936 to 8.0 million in 1938.[63]

The limits of an economic account

Union growth closely followed critical political victories for prounion forces in 1936 and 1937. This does not prove a causal link but the case is strengthened by considering an alternative view. The lag between the onset of the Depression and the spread of unions might be explained as the effect of the economic cycle on working class organization: As

60. Attorney General Cummings proposed a platform plank calling for an amendment to affirm social and economic regulation as a governmental aim. Felix Frankfurter made similar proposals. Letter, Homer Cummings to Roosevelt, June 20, 1936, Folder Justice Department 1933–7, PSF, FDR Library. Letter, Frankfurter to Roosevelt, May 29, 1935, Folder Frankfurter 1933–5, PSF, FDR Library.

61. Bruce Ackerman depicts the Supreme Court's shift in this manner: "Like its Reconstruction predecessor, the New Deal Court rejected simplistic solutions to the problem of synthesis. It refused to find that popular support for the New Deal amounted either to a comprehensive reworking of the entire Constitution or to the enactment of a few superstatutes that changed nothing fundamental. Instead, the Court treated the popular repudiation of *Lochner*'s property-oriented jurisprudence as a transformative amendment expressing a profound, but not total, change in American constitutional identity." Bruce Ackerman, *We the People – Foundations*, vol. 1 (Cambridge, Mass.: Harvard University Press, 1991), 114–15.

62. Chief Justice Hughes, cited in Karl Klare, "Judicial Deradicalization of the Wagner Act and the Origins of Modern Legal Consciousness," *Minnesota Law Review* 62, no. 3 (March 1978), 311–12.

63. Bureau of the Census, *Historical Statistics*, D946-951, "Labor Union Membership."

Table 5.4. *Union growth and economic growth in the 1930s*

Year	GNP growth (%)	Union membership growth (%)
1934	9.1	14.8
1935	9.9	16.1
1936	13.9	11.3
1937	5.3	75.5
1938	-5.0	14.8
1939	8.6	9.1
1940	8.5	-5.2

Source: Bureau of the Census, <u>Historical Statistics of the United States --
Colonial Times to 1970</u> (Washington, D.C.: Government Printing Office,
1975), F 31, "Average Annual Growth Rates of Gross National Product:
1909-1970," and O 946-951, "Labor Union Membership and Membership as
Percent of Total Labor Force and of Nonagricultural Employment: 1930-
1970."

conditions improved, the working class grew more capable of collective
action. Karen Orren argues:

> . . . most of the activity, as well as its ebb, can be explained by the strategi-
> cally favorable business upturn of 1935 and the recession of 1937. . . . The
> delaying tactics of business – refusal to bargain, refusal to sign a written
> contract – were effectively eliminated only after 1938 when the most dra-
> matic gains had already been registered.[64]

Orren's account captures a basic pattern in American labor relations –
significant union growth occurs in brief, intense moments. But the limits
of an economic account are suggested by figures on the rates of increase
of union membership and gross national product (Table 5.4). Variance
in economic conditions does not readily explain variance in union mem-

64. Orren also claims that at the beginning of the twentieth century unionization occurred
in another phase of economic improvement following a severe depression, but without
a friendly government – which indicates that developments in 1933–8 were economically determined. Karen Orren, "Liberalism, Money, and the Situation of Organized
Labor," in J. David Greenstone, ed., *Public Values and Private Power in American
Politics* (Chicago, Ill.: University of Chicago Press, 1982), 183.

bership. Unions grew more rapidly in 1934 and 1935 than in 1936, when economic conditions were improving most rapidly. Then the poor economic year of 1937 saw a huge increase in union membership. The slump of 1938 was accompanied by further strong union growth.

If one took union growth as a function of the prior year's economic course, the dramatic union growth of 1937 could be linked to the strong economic growth of 1936. But what purely economic dynamic could explain how a 4 percent increase in the rate of growth of gross national product from 1935 to 1936 would cause a 64.2 percent increase in union growth between 1936 and 1937 – while a much greater GNP increase between 1938 and 1939 (13.6 percent) accompanied a sharp decline in the rate of union·growth from 1939 to 1940?[65]

Economic circumstances were important; had conditions remained as terrible as in 1930–3, unionization prospects would have been worse throughout the decade. Without the partial recovery of 1935–7, broad labor action would have been more difficult, and the recession of 1937–8 certainly had a negative effect. Yet political sources of union growth were crucial, as in the unprecedented changes of 1937. The major strikes of that year were spurred by the Democratic triumph of 1936 and the expectation of a favorable political climate for labor activity. Had they been attempted in a hostile political context, sit-down strikes and other industrial actions would probably have met extensive force. Coercion, including federal troops, could have been used against strikers until the strikes were broken and further efforts blocked by intimidation. Force might not have settled all disputes on employers' terms, but had it been appealing to the administration and politically acceptable, the outcome in labor relations would have been very different.

Even with the sympathy of Governor Murphy and Roosevelt for union organization, the use of force against the sit-down strikes in Michigan was not entirely out of the question. The size and force of the labor actions per se were not sufficient to compel the government to abstain from force at the moment of protest (much less prevent anti-union efforts by employers and local authorities thereafter). Thus to explain why unions appeared in the automobile industry, and then in other major industries, one has to return to political reasons why coercion was not employed. That such repression did not occur hinged on the choices of Roosevelt and many state and local officials, all of whom

65. Bureau of the Census, *Historical Statistics,* D946-951, "Labor Union Membership"; F 31, "Gross National Product, Total and Per Capita, in Current and 1958 Prices: 1869–1970," 178, 224.

were urged to use force.[66] Their choices and the resulting break with the normal coercion against industrial union activities allowed the establishment of a new model of labor relations.

In these conflicts the effort to obtain unions did not mean diluting any essential radicalism of the labor movement. Labor's aims, among both leaders and members, did not go far beyond establishing durable unions capable of gaining wage increases and challenging factory despotism. More radical aims inspired numerous organizers of the new industrial unions, and parts of the membership. But these radical currents cannot be equated with the labor movement as a whole, much less the entire working class.

Because of fluctuations in union size and the fluidity of political tendencies, it is hard to make quantitative estimates of the size of political currents in the labor movement in the mid-to-late 1930s. The labor left, defined broadly to include those in favor of some version of "industrial democracy" and committed to a broad social reform program, included perhaps a fifth of the AFL leadership and between half and three quarters of the CIO leadership. By this broad definition, the center of the CIO and figures such as Sidney Hillman of the Amalgamated Clothing Workers should be included in the labor left. If we define "left" restrictively to include socialists and communists along with militant unionists who were social democratic or radical democratic in their politics, it might have included a third of the CIO leadership and a small fraction of the AFL leadership.

This narrower definition, which would limit the labor left to those distinctly to the left of the CIO center, is analytically valuable. But it is important to remain aware of the modest size and influence of the force that is thus defined, even within the labor movement as a whole, not to speak of the working class more broadly. Building the labor movement always entailed a double fight: Against employers, who in 1935–7 opposed the unions' existence and thought they could win, and among workers, many of whom needed to be persuaded of the merits of the unions.[67]

66. Roosevelt received many complaints about disorder and demands for the use of force against strikes (not only the sit-down strikes) from 1934 through 1937. Management groups conveyed their disappointment and eventual antagonism. See Folder 1934, Folder 1935, and Folder Auto Workers' Strike, OF 407B (Strikes), FDR Library.
67. See Bert Cochran, *Labor and Communism: The Conflict That Shaped American Unions* (Princeton, N.J.: Princeton University Press, 1977); Harvey Levenstein, *Communism, Anti-Communism, and the CIO* (Westport, Conn.: Greenwood Press, 1981); Ronald Schatz, *The Electrical Workers: A History of Labor at GE and Westinghouse, 1923–60* (Urbana: University of Illinois Press, 1983); and Joshua B. Freeman, *In Transit: The Transport Workers Union in New York City, 1933–66* (New York: Oxford University Press, 1989).

Strengthening labor's political action

The successful establishment of new unions was due largely to political factors, notably the initiatives of progressive liberals. How did the new labor movement become a significant political force?[68] A dynamic among progressive liberal leaders of the emerging order, labor leaders who sought political influence, and mass working-class forces produced this result.

By 1936, before the unions were securely established, the labor movement entered politics in new and more powerful ways to become a major component of the Democratic order. Labor's appearance on the political scene required working-class and popular mobilization and a split in the unions. With leaders drawn from sections of the AFL, the political left, and previously unorganized groups, the new labor movement became a substantial political force that helped elect Roosevelt and other Democrats in the mid-1930s. Its central objective was to obtain state intervention to compel unwilling employers to recognize unions. The new labor movement fought politically to establish its right to exist in a union form. It waged this fight as a powerful part of an emerging Democratic political bloc. Labor's political initiatives were radical in the 1930s, as independent unions faced fierce resistance.[69] The labor movement aimed to extend effective citizenship rights to sections of the working class that had been denied them; this meant major political shifts and changes in relations in production.

How did labor enter politics in these years? Labor helped organize and mobilize, urging its membership and supporters to vote Democratic (or for Roosevelt on a labor line).[70] Labor was active and dynamic in

---

68. For the 1930s, by labor movement I mean existing unions; prospective union members undertaking action aimed at improving wages and working conditions, as well as unionization; and those who supported labor's aims actively but were not actual or prospective union members.

69. In the 1930s it was politically radical to defend industrial unionism and a substantial political role for labor. A more stringent definition of labor radicalism in these years would designate advocacy of a greater shift toward egalitarian and participatory labor relations than proposed by the Wagner Act, along with redistributive government social and economic policies. Radicalism in this sense was a significant minority force in the CIO, but given its weakness in the AFL and lesser standing among unorganized workers, it never gained majority support in the working class.

70. Leuchtenburg credits the labor movement with carrying Ohio, Illinois, Pennsylvania, and Indiana for Roosevelt in 1936, and for swinging a number of previously Republican cities into the Democratic column. Leuchtenburg, *Roosevelt and the New Deal*, 189. Lubell also stresses the effects of the unions' mobilization in *The Future of American Politics*, third edition (New York: Harper & Row, 1965), 46–55.

recruiting pro-New Deal voters, and in educating workers and the public about the policies of the Roosevelt administration. In 1936 labor contributed roughly $750,000 to the Democratic campaign.[71] This aid was important because some sources of campaign funding previously available to Democratic nominees were not obtained, due to Depression difficulties and the hostility of business to Roosevelt.

Yet in 1936 the labor movement was still fragile and insecure. Its choice to make a major political commitment suggests that labor was trying to create a new institutional position through its political intervention. For the CIO unions in 1936, the elections took priority over new organizing – because the fate of the labor movement was understood to depend on the political outcome.[72] The labor movement needed a prounion political outcome. To attain that outcome labor had to build a viable political force, as there was no predefined labor vote that merely needed to be signaled.

While the labor movement's efforts were invaluable to the Democratic Party, it lacked direct power in the national party organization. Few members of the national committee or other leading figures in the party emerged from the labor movement or were identified mainly with it. Very few Democrats in Congress came directly from the movement.[73] One reason for the absence of labor representatives at the top of the party and in Congress may have been suspicion of large organized groups in politics. (This absence is another indication of the distance of the Democratic order from a social democratic regime.) Not many progressive liberals wanted union leaders to have a powerful formal role in the party, much less the state. The absence of labor from high positions in the party and the administration also reflected a progressive

71. In 1932, bankers and brokers alone contributed 24 percent of all sums of $1,000 or more; in 1936 that figure fell to 4 percent. Louise Overacker, "Labor's Political Contributions," *Political Science Quarterly* (1939): 60.
72. Piven and Cloward stress the role of economic disruption in forming the unions and downplay the importance of the 1936 election. Yet they acknowledge the key point – the millions who were to join the CIO had not done so prior to the election. Piven and Cloward, *Poor People's Movements: Why They Succeed and How They Fail* (New York: Vintage, 1979), 160–1. See also J. David Greenstone, *Labor in American Politics* (Chicago, Ill.: University of Chicago Press, rev. ed., 1977), 49–50.
73. While many representatives considered that they owed their election partly to labor's efforts, labor leaders and activists did not become elected officials. Democratic officials and party leaders in 1936 were first of all lawyers, then other professionals and career politicians, and (less prominently) businessmen. J. David Greenstone formulates the issues judiciously but overstates the extent to which Democratic Party–labor ties resembled a social democratic entity, in *Labor in American Politics*, 79–80.

liberal preference that decision making on public issues go through the
state rather than private associations.

It is hard to know how the role of large labor organizations would
have been defined in a Democratic Party controlled entirely by progressive liberals, though labor would probably have been more powerful.
No such party existed. In the actual party, significant forces opposed the
new unions or wanted them to function in a restricted manner. The
Democratic Party was not tempted to turn over formal leadership positions to the labor movement, especially to the new industrial unions. In
1936 labor organizations did not play anything like a leading role at the
Democratic convention, and the labor division of the party's campaign
committee was small, poorly funded, and caught up in labor's factional
conflicts.[74]

In local political settings, especially in urban industrial areas where
the new unions were strongest and pro-New Deal Democratic forces
were most influential, the power and involvement of the unions in the
party was greatest. As unions became stronger they became more involved in party affairs. Yet labor usually became an important partner
in state and local coalitions, rather than seeking to transform party
forms and practices. In a few cities the labor movement helped to create
party organizations resembling those of European mass parties. In Los
Angeles, Detroit, Minneapolis, and New York, for example, labor-based
party structures coexisted with more conventional party forms. The
modest extent of labor-based party forms is indicated by the small
number of places which met the apparent preconditions: that the city be
Democratic, that the CIO be at least as strong as the AFL, and that there
not exist a strong traditional Democratic organization able to block new
efforts. Such organizations emerged in less than a quarter of major cities
and almost never predominated for a sustained period.[75]

In national election campaigns union political influence went through

---

74. See Democratic Party, *Official Report of the Proceedings of the Democratic National
Convention – 1936*. The head of the labor committee, Daniel Tobin, often found
himself trying to persuade AFL leaders that Roosevelt's closeness to the LNPL did not
signify a choice for the CIO. Letter, Tobin to James Farley, August 20, 1936, Folder
8/14-21, 1936, OF 300 (Democratic National Committee), FDR Library.

75. A useful way to get at the shape of interest-group and mass-party organization is to
read voting studies of the mid to late 1940s and monographs on labor's political
involvement in that period. These studies suggest a narrow scope for mass forms in
the earlier years. See Paul F. Lazarsfeld et al., *The People's Choice* (New York:
Columbia University Press, 1948); and Fay Calkins, *The CIO and the Democratic
Party* (Chicago, Ill.: University of Chicago Press, 1952).

labor organizations directly to the administration.[76] At the top of the Democratic order the labor movement had access to the president and top administration officials to an extent unprecedented in American politics.[77] Yet even on matters of great concern, this access never meant veto power over administration policy or personnel choices. Nor did it include a capacity to compel new administration initiatives. Even appointments of labor figures to major federal public positions were rare.[78]

The political power of the labor movement grew as the state expanded. Labor built important relations with new state agencies, some of which included support for the new unions in their founding aims. Prolabor individuals were widely placed in the emerging state and often believed that their work entailed supporting the new labor movement. Strong sympathy with unionization was of course central to the NLRB; it could also be found in many relief agencies, in cabinet departments (such as Labor and Interior), and among policy advisers.[79]

New political forces and interest groups

In the mid-thirties a wide range of new political forces took shape. Elements of the labor model were repeated, though no other movement became nearly as powerful. As in forming the labor movement, political

76. George Berry's reports on the activities of Labor's Non-Partisan League went directly to the administration and Roosevelt, rather than through the Democratic Party. He claimed that LNPL had organized in every state and most congressional districts, but it is hard to know how far this organizing went. While labor political action influenced outcomes and officials' actions, any image of a coherent, mass, disciplined force turning out voters everywhere would greatly overstate that action. Letter, George L. Berry to Steven Early, 9/9/36, and Memo, "Notations for the President," OF 2251 (Labor's Non-Partisan League), FDR Library.

77. Democratic leaders acknowledged labor's prominent new role. In 1936, Roosevelt wrote to a meeting of LNPL state chairmen: "I should like to have you know that I am sincerely proud that you are gathering in support of my candidacy. This could not be the case if you did not know, out of the experience of the past three years, that the present Administration has endeavored to promote the ideal of justice for the great masses of America's wage earners and to make that ideal a reality." Letter, Roosevelt to George L. Berry, August 3, 1936, Folder Labor '36, OF407, FDR Library. See also Burns, *Roosevelt*, 276–7.

78. After the election, Lewis and others pressed Roosevelt on patronage issues, but they were disappointed by the result. Report of meeting, Lewis et al. with Roosevelt, n.d., 1937, OF 2251 (Labor's Non-Partisan League), FDR Library.

79. The close ties between the NLRB and the unions are noted in virtually every work on labor in the 1930s, as in Fraser, *Labor Will Rule*, 350–2.

practices were central in defining new groups.[80] The intervention of progressive liberals helped constitute new forces in agriculture, in racial and ethnic relations, and among the professional middle classes. These forces contributed to Democratic successes, and their links with the state were at least as important as any formal party ties.

Several new movements arose mainly outside the emerging political order, sometimes partly opposed to it. Some, such as Upton Sinclair's "End Poverty in California" (EPIC) movement, drew on socialist themes.[81] More often, as with Huey Long, these movements relied on populist themes. Most independent efforts reached their height by 1935, and then large parts of these movements found a place in the new political order.[82] Efforts to sustain autonomous forces opposed to the old Republican order and critical of the New Deal did not fare well.

Nonparty political forces were encouraged by the emergence of new federal agencies to which groups could appeal in Washington and locally.[83] They were stimulated by the national administration's commitment to regulatory state intervention, which expanded points of contact between the government and social and economic activities. Every point of contact could become a site of group formation. New state agencies grew out of specific administration initiatives and when new forces entered politics they first focused on distinct sectoral concerns, even if their arguments were cast broadly and they shared the overall perspective of the new order.

Economic and occupational criteria were increasingly important for defining the aims and boundaries of interest groups. There was a decline in the role of regional and cultural divisions, compared with the shape of Democratic politics in the prior political order. The economic focus

---

80. Thus, in agricultural policies in the 1930s, the modern definition of "farmers" as an interest group came into being. This was not the only possible definition, and it resulted partly from state policies favoring a coalition among more prosperous farmers. See Theda Skocpol and Kenneth Finegold, "State Capacity and Economic Organization in the Early New Deal," *Political Science Quarterly* 97, no. 2 (Summer 1982): 255–78.

81. Greg Mitchell, *The Campaign of the Century: Upton Sinclair's Race for Governor of California and the Birth of Media Politics* (New York: Random House, 1992).

82. In 1935, polling conducted for James Farley by Emil Hurja indicated that Huey Long was supported by roughly 8 percent of voters, while the category of "misc. left" was supported by 2 percent. Farley expected the Long vote to become Roosevelt's. Letter, Farley to Roosevelt, and Memo, Hurja to Farley, September 26, 1935, PSF 143 (DNC), FDR Library.

83. In agriculture, the professions, and quasi movements of "youth" and "consumers," progressive liberal efforts helped give direction, notably when such groups had little

made certain questions, such as the position of women, difficult to raise, as Nancy Gabin indicates:

> The CIO ... did not accord the organizing of women a high priority in the 1930s. Its principal concern was to unionize the heretofore unorganized basic industries, and in none of them did women represent more than a minority of production workers. The CIO did not exclude women, but neither did it actively and conscientiously recruit them.[84]

Ironically it was easier in the more conservative Republican order than in the 1930s to develop political initiatives explicitly concerned with the position of women in American politics and society. Women's organizations were not very important in the main battles of the decade, though a number of women with roots in the social feminist efforts of previous decades were important progressive liberal leaders.[85]

In the mid-1930s new political forces mainly supported Democratic policies and candidates. But they were not formally integrated into the party, which contained only rudimentary means for including them, such as token recognition through divisions of the party campaign organizations. New forces in and close to the Democratic order took shape mainly as interest groups. Although they did not aspire to become political parties, they were nonetheless politically aggressive. New groups aspired to become part of a new political order, seeking recognition and their leaders' entry into the progressive liberal leadership group. When new groups sought to shape national policy they turned to the state and the administration.[86]

prior history and needed state aid to sustain their fragile initiatives. See the discussion of efforts to organize "youth" in John A. Salmond, "Aubrey Williams: Atypical New Dealer?" in John Braeman, Robert H. Bremner, and David Brody, eds., *The New Deal – The National Level* (Columbus: Ohio State University Press, 1975), vol. 1, 218–45.

84. Nancy F. Gabin, *Feminism in the Labor Movement: Women and the United Auto Workers, 1935–1975* (Ithaca, N.Y.: Cornell University Press, 1990), 17.

85. In 1935–6, close working relations evolved among the Women's Division of the Democratic Party and the Consumer and Women's divisions of the Department of Labor. There was a circulation of ideas and personnel, and support for common projects. Could more significant efforts to increase attention to gender inequities have been made in the 1930s without endangering the prospects of the new order? In my view such efforts were feasible. On women in the 1930s and in the New Deal, see Carolyn Ware, *Beyond Suffrage: Women in the New Deal* (Cambridge, Mass.: Harvard University Press, 1981); and Winifred D. Wandersee, *Women's Work and Family Values, 1920–1940* (Cambridge, Mass.: Harvard University Press, 1981).

86. This orientation toward the national state was also true of the political mobilization of blacks. The explicit racism of the southern Democratic Party and many northern organizations provided little practical choice. Weiss, *Farewell to the Party of Lincoln*; Sitkoff, *New Deal for Blacks*.

We are so accustomed to this framework that it seems natural, but of course it is not. People can be organized and mobilized in many ways – as individual citizens, as members of classes, as members of ethnic and national groups, and more. If interest groups are not natural or automatic, why did this model predominate? First, the idea of interest groups in the 1930s had deep roots in American politics and was available for those seeking to make new claims. Progressive liberals who built the new order believed that interest groups were an appropriate means of reconciling democratic principles with the size and complexity of American society. Second, the shape of the regime-building process in the United States also contributed. The Democratic order waged a sequence of fights with opposition forces, often focused on particular legislative measures and agencies; this encouraged new Democratic forces to appear as in a mirror-image, proceeding group by group rather than in a coordinated expansion of political action. Third, the expansion of the state created contact with diverse social groups, providing many chances for group formation aimed at shaping state policies. Social differentiation and complexity increased the number of potential groups and reduced the likelihood that their differences could be articulated through any single division, such as class or region.

What did the predominance of interest group conceptions among new political forces mean for the emerging political order? It has been charged that the interest group framework limited the prospects of durable or principled political agreement, owing to competition among groups. Yet the interest-group model was effective in expanding the Democratic political order at its formation – labor, farmers, citydwellers, blacks, youth, consumers, and more groups could be included. In this conception diverse forces could make alliances, or at least view their relations as nonantagonistic. Thus blacks were conceived as an ethnic interest group rather than as one side of a racialized social division, and labor was taken to signify a major group of occupations and communities, rather than a class opposed to others. The core image was of a long chain of legitimate groups, all expressing popular and democratic aspirations.

Interest-group conceptions also enhanced the appeal of a new order by limiting the efforts of any single component of its leading bloc to establish their domination. If all interest groups were legitimate, none had intrinsic priority. Labor, to take the key example, could make serious claims about industrial relations and the political system – but there was little conceptual space in which labor could claim the right to guide other groups and determine their strategic choices.

Labor could "only" claim to be the leading popular force in a Democratic political bloc. In principle this construction certainly limited the prospects of social democracy. But in the actual context its primary effect was to allow a progressive liberal bloc to expand further than it otherwise would have, by allaying fears that a new regime would be dominated by labor or any other single group. Had the labor movement sought to assert a commanding leadership in this context it might have disrupted wide sections of the Democratic bloc, given the diversity of popular forces and the continuing strength of populist suspicion of large organized groups.

Political leadership

Despite these advantages, the hazards of interest-group politics are clear enough. How could an interest-group regime keep from disintegrating amid conflicts among its components? To answer this question requires examining Democratic leadership, which was not the purely pragmatic brokering that has often been claimed. In the formative years of the Democratic order there were two main ways of talking about political leadership. One was a language of coalition-building, envisioned as adding up diverse groups like bricks to a wall. Such formulations did not attend sufficiently to the problems of sustaining cooperation among self-interested actors. The other way to talk about leadership in the mid-1930s was to consider it as a virtuous and energetic activity. Proponents of the new order cited the heroic efforts of Roosevelt and other Democratic leaders while critics charged the new regime's leaders with conspiratorial maneuvers. Such charges by Republicans and conservative Democrats were at least partly sincere, and their frequency reveals the extent to which these forces failed to grasp the new political situation.

The Democratic leadership made creative efforts that cannot be understood adequately in either way. Their flexible and fluid leadership style was rooted in progressive liberal commitments, which defined basic choices and justified tactical maneuvers. It was pragmatic, not unprincipled. The political themes of the new Democratic bloc allowed the inclusion of new groups without the regime exploding. Conflicts among Democratic groups never disappeared, but many potential conflicts were muted because the aims of relevant groups were reinterpreted. For example, nativist and racist themes among whites, especially in the lower middle and working classes, were a source of potentially disastrous conflict. Yet their political weight declined as the aims of working-class organizations were redefined to focus on economic improvement and active citizenship. Competition between professional and working-class groups was reduced as significant currents within major professional associations emphasized public service on behalf of relatively egalitarian forms of modernization. The political rhetoric and iconography of the mid-1930s often portrayed diverse groups advancing separately, yet unified in spirit.

In normal political times, when groups and the framework for their competition are established, relations among interest groups can often be fruitfully analyzed in terms of a quasi-economic logic of coalition-building and maintenance. The core concept has been that of a minimum winning coalition, beyond which members will be ejected or prospective members barred in order to maximize returns to winners.

At moments of regime formation, political leadership means creating not only an expansive political bloc but building flexible alliances well beyond that bloc. It is common that explicit support for central measures at the outset of a political order is much larger than would be predicted by the size of the groups most apt to benefit directly. It is hard to imagine a new political order being created by a series of minimum winning coalitions, and this concept cannot be applied in any strict sense to such dramatic events as Roosevelt's first two sweeping electoral victories, or the large majority by which the Wagner Act passed.[87]

Hegemony – as forceful leadership, not pure domination – is an appropriate term for this process. Leaders were aware of their possible role in shaping a new political order, and they were aware that such a course required them to achieve and maintain broad popular support. Part of the work of Democratic leadership took place through dialogues with actual and prospective mass political forces, in which changes of position occurred on all sides. Democratic leaders did not regard themselves as formalists engaged in following rules and filling offices. Nor did they yearn to enact statist programs for total social transformation, despite the charges of Republican critics. The Democratic leadership acted boldly to achieve progressive liberal aims.

87. In regime politics, actors tend to have relatively broad rather than narrow objectives. This increases the likelihood that they will be uncertain about the size of the coalition needed at a specific moment and be willing to expand it, because they will engage in one conflict with their eye on a subsequent conflict in which an expanded alliance may be necessary. The minimum winning coalition concept relies on a zero-sum premise. Modern regime politics instead presumes that systemic changes can secure enlarged benefits for both the polity as a whole and a majority of groups within it. The main economic account of political coalitions is William Riker's *The Theory of Political Coalitions* (New Haven, Conn.: Yale University Press, 1962).

6

Progressive liberalism as pragmatic common sense

When it became necessary for the Government to fill gaps in the national structure in which private business enterprise was an obvious failure, the myths and folklore of the time hampered practical organization at every turn. Men became more interested in planning the culture of the future – in saving posterity from the evils of dictatorship or bureaucracy, in preventing the American people from adopting Russian culture on the one hand, or German culture on the other – than in the day-to-day distribution of food, housing, and clothing to those who needed them.

– Thurman Arnold, 1937[1]

Thurman Arnold's commentary illustrates core themes identified with New Deal political and social thought – skepticism about received wisdom, disbelief in the conventional public/private distinction, and a practical focus on immediate problems. This image of what progressive liberal leaders thought is too simple. Arnold and colleagues thrived on a self-presentation as realistic and pragmatic. Yet if they deserved recognition for these virtues, it was largely due to how they established a new framework for political argument.

Previous chapters have examined the construction of the Democratic order in terms of the choices of emerging political forces in a turbulent and challenging political and social setting. I have often referred to the themes of the Democratic leadership and of new political and social movements – it is not possible to explain the decade's main events without doing so. This chapter elaborates previous claims about Democratic themes. My argument draws on presidential speeches and statements, public statements by major administration figures, reports and

---

1. Thurman Arnold, *The Folklore of Capitalism* (New York: Yale University Press, 1937), 46–47.

administrative histories of government agencies, congressional proceedings, party convention proceedings and public statements, major court cases, and the public record of the labor movement (at conventions, in the labor press, in organizing campaigns, in administrative and judicial hearings).[2]

It would be unimaginable to find a repetition of identical formulations throughout these materials. And that was never the aspiration of Democratic leaders. The aim was a new thematic framework – Democratic progressive liberals sought to establish a reformist progressive liberalism as a new common sense, and they succeeded.

Progressive liberalism?

Why use "progressive liberalism" to name the main discourses of the Democratic order? First, it emphasizes the basic liberal commitments of Democratic discourses. Second, "progressive" suggests the combination of modernizing and democratic themes that distinguished the Democratic reworking of American liberalism. It points to the Progressive movement two decades earlier, with its rationalizing drive, and to the subsequent use of that term to indicate a concern for democratic reform. Third, "progressive liberalism" is not a familiar term, though its two words are – linking these words is meant to suggest the active process through which diverse thematic elements were integrated in building the Democratic order. Fourth, both parts of this term are mainly political in their referents, and direct attention to the crucially political character of Democratic efforts.[3]

---

2. The ample writings of major political and intellectual figures of the new regime are also a major source. Among the many valuable works are Franklin Delano Roosevelt, *Roosevelt and Frankfurter: Their Correspondence, 1928–1945*, annotated by Max Freedman (Boston: Little, Brown, 1968); Felix Frankfurter, *Law and Politics: Occasional Papers of Felix Frankfurter, 1913–1938* (New York: Harcourt Brace, 1939); Arnold, *The Folklore of Capitalism;* and Adolf A. Berle and Gardiner C. Means, *The Modern Corporation and Private Property* (New York: Macmillan, 1933).
3. Two valuable studies of labor politics in the 1930s, by Gary Gerstle and Lizabeth Cohen, understate the political coherence achieved by the new order, via the concepts of "working-class Americanism" and "moral capitalism" that they respectively use to designate popular views. Both terms lack specifically political referents and suggest that workers were less interested in and involved with national political conflicts than was the case. Gary Gerstle, *Working-Class Americanism: The Politics of Labor in a Textile City, 1914–1960* (Cambridge University Press, 1989), 9, 155, 170–5; Lizabeth Cohen, *Making a New Deal, Industrial Workers in Chicago 1919–1939* (Cambridge University Press, 1990), 315.

The efforts of Democratic leaders to create a new thematic framework have often received insufficient attention, even from analysts who see progressive liberal themes as virtually constitutive of modern political wisdom. Moreover, the common emphasis on pragmatism has often obscured from view a good part of what progressive liberals were doing.

Democratic leaders liked to consider themselves as realistic and flexible, as nonformalist regarding institutional and legal arrangements, and as open to revising policies in the light of practical experience. They rejected what they took to be doctrinaire political methods. This approach can be fairly termed pragmatic as an approach to gaining political knowledge and as a way of making political decisions.

But the term "pragmatic" has gained a further common meaning in writing about American politics. It often signifies a lack of strong substantive commitments, so that all principles are open to compromise. The notion that political life can be expected to overturn received principles and generate new ones leads to disinterest in principles, in this view. This shift of meaning has been encouraged by ardent proponents of the New Deal: In their eagerness to defend the new order from critics who charge that it lacked principles, they have tended to make a virtue of that lack. Thus Schlesinger's depiction virtually empties Roosevelt's project of political content:

> Rejecting the platonic distinction between "capitalism" and "socialism" he led the way toward a new society which took elements from each and rendered both obsolescent. It was this freedom from dogma which outraged the angry, logical men who saw everything with dazzling certitude. Roosevelt's illusion, said Herbert Hoover, was "that any economic system would work in a mixture of others. No greater illusions ever mesmerized the American people." "Your president," said Leon Trotsky with contempt, "abhors 'systems' and 'generalities' . . . Your philosophic method is even more antiquated than your economic system." But the American President always resisted ideological commitment. His determination was to keep options open within the general frame of a humanized democracy; and his belief was that the very diversity of systems strengthened the basis for freedom.[4]

This passage, in a book published in 1960, is itself an instance of Democratic political argument. It locates Roosevelt's position as democratic common sense, reasonably positioned between Hoover and Trotsky. Rather than analyzing Democratic themes it affirms them.

4. Arthur M. Schlesinger, Jr., *The Politics of Upheaval* (Boston: Houghton Mifflin, 1960), 651.

If Democratic leaders had been as vague as Schlesinger and other commentators claim, they would probably have been unable to win the vigorous political battles they waged. In the (misleading) sense of lacking a strong thematic core, Democratic progressive liberals were not pragmatic at all. They had strong commitments, developed over decades, which they sought to realize in flexible and responsible ways. They were not willing to compromise about everything or with anyone, even while they made important deals with dubious allies.

In the quite different sense in which "pragmatic" usefully describes the new political order in the 1930s, the proper antonyms are "formalist" or "doctrinaire." The opposite of pragmatic is not principled. Without strong commitments to a distinctive set of views about politics and society, it is doubtful that a new political order would have been built. And Democratic progressive liberals could not have succeeded in establishing so large a part of their core principles as a new common sense.

Democratic discourses

Democratic discourses were imbedded in the efforts of Democratic leaders, new political forces, and state agencies.[5] These discourses appeared in presidential speeches, speeches by important cabinet officers and other major administration figures, and statements by national and local Democratic politicians. They appeared in the arguments and programs of the labor movement and in the procedures and announcements of new government agencies.[6]

In the 1936 campaign the administration and Roosevelt stimulated and shaped a new popular Democratic identification. Roosevelt's political persona fused a patrician liberalism, an ardent reform progressivism,

5. What about the risk of claiming too much continuity between official statements and popular discourses? The most complex Democratic themes were not always reproduced in everyday speech. Yet they were publicly present at the top of the Democratic order and widely disseminated. The many confrontations between Democratic and other discourses had the effect of enhancing consistency. Consistency never meant identity – Democratic discourses differed from California to Iowa to Georgia. The analogy is to a national language with regional dialects whose speakers can recognize each other and communicate directly by returning to the official form of the language – even if they have difficulty communicating between their own dialects.

6. Again, by discourses I mean ensembles of meaningfully related ideas and symbols; they are structured, and can be sustained past the moment of their origin. They shape behavior through framing and delimiting possible courses of action and providing criteria of choice.

and democratic concern for the fate of the nation. A distinctive new position was articulated, which, as Roosevelt and others said, was slightly to the left of center. What they said less often and less clearly was that their efforts had redefined the political spectrum. Thus the new "center" was very different from that of the previous political order.

The Democratic order was proposed as a popular and national project for economic and political renewal. The claim was that an aggressive modernizing approach, conducted within the boundaries of basic liberal commitments, could defend "the people" and the nation against economic disasters and the threat of social collapse. When new groups took shape in this framework their legitimacy and their capacity to gain important goals strengthened Democratic claims.

Popular identification with the New Deal state and Roosevelt surpassed identification with the Democratic Party. Thus Democratic Party registration and identification lagged behind Democratic presidential voting, rather than carrying it forward.[7] Roosevelt and other Democratic leaders argued extensively and persuasively for their overall policies. If Democratic support had been built only through a sequence of immediate responses to problems, the Democratic order would have been ripped apart by frequent policy mistakes and by severe conflicts of interest among prospective supporters.

The concepts used most positively in Democratic discourses – liberal, democratic, progressive, modern, popular – gained wide acceptance in 1935–7. They designated particular Democratic projects and the general orientation of the regime. "Liberal" was redefined to designate progressive liberalism and reject the conservative liberalism of the previous political order.[8] In responding, Republican and conservative Democratic opponents of Roosevelt were off balance, often reduced to attacking the Democratic use of new media and Roosevelt's skilled efforts as devilish and fraudulent. Unused to sharp criticism from sources that could not be stigmatized as marginal, conservative political and business leaders failed to grasp how building a new Democratic framework entailed defining them as antagonists in 1935 and 1936. Instead, they attributed Democratic success to crafty and sinister manipulation of the public. Meanwhile, Democratic speeches rang with attacks on Hooverism and economic royalists, heralding the Democratic order as a national effort

7. Everett Carll Ladd and Charles D. Hadley, *Transformations of the American Party System: Political Coalitions from the New Deal to the 1970s* (New York: W. W. Norton, 1975), 69–73.
8. Ronald Rotunda, *The Politics of Language – Liberalism as Word and Symbol* (Iowa City: University of Iowa Press, 1986), 52–87.

in opposition to the selfish and narrow concerns of the elites of the old order.

Democratic discourses were widely disseminated through radio, press, and newsreel accounts of political developments.[9] This further tied the Democratic order to a modernizing course that was generally popular. Even when the editorial stance of a paper or radio station was hostile, Roosevelt and the progressive liberal leadership used the media to convey their messages so effectively that Democratic themes and the social diffusion of the new communications technologies were intertwined. The use of these media took place mainly outside of party channels. Thus listeners to Roosevelt or other administration figures on the radio might not participate in any organized Democratic Party activities.[10] They could still identify themselves as part of a new political force, linked with interest groups and other individuals.

Democratic discourses marked the practices of new government agencies. First, when state benefits and services were delivered effectively, this validated Democratic political claims about the virtues of the new order. Second, as government employment expanded, supporters of the new order often regarded their new jobs as entailing the energetic application of Democratic principles, rather than seeing their positions as offices to be filled according to fixed rules. Third, state policies were cast and defended in Democratic terms – claims of technical competence were cited to show the modern, flexible character of the Democratic order. Sometimes Democrats charged branches of government with restraining popular progress, though Roosevelt's attack on the Supreme Court showed this could be risky.[11]

9. In the 1936 national Democratic campaign, expenditures for radio were already almost as great as a separate overall figure for publicity ($340,000 to $382,000), and much larger than expenditures on club or interest organizations (the Division of Clubs received $25,000). "Budget for the Democratic National Campaign of 1936," Folder – Democratic National Committee, President's Secretary's File, Franklin D. Roosevelt Library.

10. The effectiveness of Roosevelt's direct appeals was widely recognized: "President Roosevelt's mass appeal was so superior it practically took care of those who would listen over the radio." Memo, Mary Dewson, "Campaign of 1936, Work of the Women's Division," n.d., Folder – Campaign of 1936, Papers of Mary Dewson, FDR Library.

11. I say risky rather than disastrous because the results of this effort were mixed. When Roosevelt and other advocates of reshaping the Court seemed insensitive to constitutional constraints, they were attacked for overstepping liberal boundaries, and a countermobilization took place. When they instead appeared to be calling for a reinterpretation of the Constitution in the light of changed social and economic conditions, their efforts probably helped persuade the Court to consider the major

The state reached far and often into the lives of citizens, through relief and unemployment policies, social security, agricultural policies, urban and housing policies, public works efforts, and support for new unions. When policies were described, benefits delivered, and alternatives discussed, government officials acted as political agents. They explained and advocated Democratic aims, and were often compelling. The multiplication of contacts between citizens and the federal state in the 1930s – in relief agencies, labor policies, urban policies, and elsewhere – had a strong political content.[12] Democratic discourses gained a durable reality in the normal practices of agencies and the frequent interactions of millions of citizens with the state.

Opponents of the Democratic order raged against what they saw as the illicit and corrupt political role of a newly expanding state.[13] Their attacks were largely ineffective. While Democratic practices contained instances of conventional corruption, imbedding Democratic discourses in state agencies and activities was mainly about political change rather than spoils. The core of this process eluded charges of corruption or legislative proposals to cut back patronage.

Reshaping liberalism

The Democratic order was committed to liberal political and economic principles, as Roosevelt repeatedly affirmed:

> It is the self-reliant pioneer in every enterprise who beats the path along which American civilization has marched. Such individual effort is the glory of America. The task of government is that of application and encouragement.[14]

shifts it made in the late 1930s. The attempt to influence the Supreme Court was part of the institutionalization of the Democratic order. On the Court in the late 1930s see Bruce Ackerman, *We the People – Foundations*, vol. 1 (Cambridge, Mass.: Harvard University Press, 1991), 105–30.

12. For descriptions of what new government agencies did and how their professional employees saw their work see Grace Abbott, *From Relief to Social Security: The Development of the New Public Welfare Services and Their Administration* (Chicago, Ill.: University of Chicago Press, 1941); Josephine Chapin Brown, *Public Relief, 1929–1939* (New York: Holt, 1940); and Edwin E. Witte, *Development of the Social Security Act* (Madison: University of Wisconsin Press, 1962).

13. Liberty League, "Report on the Constitutionality of the National Labor Relations Act" (Washington, D.C.: American Liberty League, 1935) and "Seventeen Months of the American Liberty League" (Washington, D.C.: American Liberty League, 1936).

14. Franklin Roosevelt, San Diego, 10/3/35, in Samuel Rosenman, ed., *The Public Papers and Addresses of Franklin D. Roosevelt*, vol. 4, *The Court Disapproves – 1935*, compiled by Samuel Rosenman (New York: Random House, 1938), 406–7.

There was no question of creating a state-owned economy or replacing representative political institutions.[15] And calls for political and social mobilization presumed that after crises had been resolved, politics would not routinely supplant the work, family, and community concerns of most Americans. The depth of enduring liberal commitments was frustrating to some on the New Deal left, such as Rexford Tugwell, who regretted their regime's inability to produce and act on a new integral theory of society:

> It would not be inaccurate to describe what went on in the inner circles of the early New Deal as a struggle between old-fashioned and new-fashioned progressivism. . . . To the collectivists it was clear enough, however, that Roosevelt could be persuaded to depart from the old progressive line only in the direst circumstances and then only temporarily. Even then he felt it necessary to make for himself a satisfactory rationalization.[16]

Left intellectuals like Tugwell underestimated the thematic changes made by those who were building the Democratic order. The progressive liberal leadership and other parts of the Democratic bloc were reshaping American liberalism in basic ways.

The Democratic order articulated a new progressive liberalism distinct from the main themes of the previous Republican order and from earlier Democratic Progressivism. As I outlined in Chapter 4, three main themes were expressed by Democratic leaders. Together they provided a basic framework for political action. One was a positive view of the role of groups in political and economic life; the second was a positive view of the state's role in regulating social and economic life. The third theme advocated governmental responsiveness to the claims of the less advantaged, if necessary through expanding democratic political participation. In shaping these themes into a durable framework, progressive liberals fused progressive and democratic elements. Modernization, national coordination, administrative reform, and efficiency were linked with demo-

---

15. The limits on state economic activity were clear by 1935, given the failures to establish the legitimacy of ambitious planning approaches. Limits to state economic action were also evident in the vehemence of congressional antistatism, and the inability of left political forces to make headway when they stressed going beyond regulation to governmental control of economic and social life. See Ellis W. Hawley, *The New Deal and the Problem of Monopoly: A Study in Economic Ambivalence* (Princeton, N.J.: Princeton University Press, 1966); and Richard Polenberg, "The Decline of the New Deal, 1937–1940," in John Braeman, Robert H. Bremer, and David Brody, eds., *The New Deal – The National Level* (Columbus: Ohio State University Press, 1975), vol. 1, 246–66.

16. The quote is from Rexford G. Tugwell, *In Search of Roosevelt* (Cambridge, Mass.: Harvard University Press, 1972), 282.

cratic notions of governmental responsiveness, equity in policy outcomes, and the right to a meaningful political voice.

Politics as group activity

The Democratic order treated politics as group activity in ways that broke not with individualism per se but with the modes of individualism that dominated the prior Republican order. Groups – composed of individuals – were conceived as unavoidable components of complex societies, and as legitimate starting points for political action. Democratic constituencies were addressed as groups by the state and party. The stated aim was not to displace but to sustain individualistic values.[17]

The early Democratic order expressed a strong commitment to coordinate the conditions under which groups would interact in the economy and politics.[18] Defenses of the Wagner Act asserted that state action should ensure collective bargaining not merely to cope with underconsumption problems but to create a new social and political balance. Yet there was little enthusiasm for national decision making by new institutions made up of official representatives of designated social interests (corporatism). Nor was there enthusiasm for government planning that would dictate the outcomes of group interaction. Labor law illustrates these limits. It was understood that the NLRA would reshape labor relations and help to establish unions. It was also understood that this result would increase workers' incomes. But there was no intention that the government specify particular outcomes in firms or regions, much less produce binding national agreements about wages or production.

In law and policy, progressive liberals expanded the prevalent concept of the public. They also recognized differences in the extent to which social activities were public. Most of those engaged in building the new order did not think that defining an activity as relevant to public concerns or in need of regulation meant defining it as wholly public.[19]

17. Thus, Felix Frankfurter's draft of the 1936 Democratic platform aimed to restate American liberal themes – stressing competition and enterprise – in the context of modern large-scale organizations. See Roosevelt, *Roosevelt and Frankfurter: Their Correspondence, 1928–1945*, 347–54. There was little real corporatism in the New Deal in 1935–37. Corporatist themes were expressed by sections of the labor movement strongly influenced by Catholic social thought.
18. The seconding speeches on behalf of Roosevelt's nomination in 1936 relied extensively on group-based conceptions in enumerating the sources of Democratic support. *Official Proceedings of the Democratic National Convention, 1936*, 248–93.
19. Nonetheless, progressive liberals – including many legal realists – did not have a clear theoretical account of how to distinguish among different types of public and private activity. See Joseph William Singer, "Legal Realism Now," *California Law Review* 76

Progressive liberals wanted to expand the commonly understood boundaries of the public, but not by considering all activities with public elements to be equally and fundamentally public. The latter move was unattractive both for reasons of principle and out of sensitivity to the antistatist critiques continually made of their efforts.

The Democratic order's encouragement of group organization and participation in politics had a democratic character. Given the extensive prior organization of business elites and middle-class groups and associations, Democratic themes meant expanding the range of legitimate entrants onto the political scene. Many nonelite social groups had previously found it difficult even to sustain political interest groups and other associations, especially at the national level. The democratic shift is striking when one compares the political position of industrial workers in the mid-1920s with their position a decade later. Long after the building of the Democratic order, it is easy to take its democratic achievements for granted. The florid and dramatic tone of some of its protagonists appears quaint:

> It is an issue of whether the working population of this country shall have a voice in determining their destiny or whether they shall serve as indentured servants for a financial and economic dictatorship which would shamelessly exploit our natural resources and destroy the pride of a free people. On such an issue there can be no compromise for labor or for a thoughtful citizenship.[20]

John L. Lewis's tone was not really so hyperbolic considering the intensity and stakes of the conflicts over whether subordinate social groups could build and sustain important interest organizations.

An expanding state

After the failure of the NRA and the decline of aspirations toward comprehensive planning, Democratic themes stressed that an active state should energetically confront economic and political crises.[21] Govern-

---

(1988): 482–95. In some contemporary critiques of the concepts of public and private, this problem is unsuccessfully dealt with by trying to show that these concepts have no determinate meaning. See Duncan Kennedy, "The Stages of the Decline of the Public/Private Distinction," *University of Pennsylvania Law Review* 130, no. 6 (June 1982): 1349–57.

20. John L. Lewis, "Industrial Democracy in Steel," Radio Address, 7/6/36.

21. In the mid-1930s it was argued that antitrust and fiscal policy could provide the core of a workable full employment program. Full employment in turn would enhance the position of the United States internationally. Report, Executive Committee on Economic Foreign Policy, "Formulation of a Full Employment Program with Reference to Economic Foreign Policy," 2, Folder Labor Department 1933–45, PSF, FDR Library.

ment should take responsibility for arresting the downward slide of the economy and for preventing economic disaster from tearing society apart. State economic action was all the more necessary in a mature economy whose internal sources of growth had diminished.[22] The state should maintain the general conditions of group organization and protect the rights of the weakest groups.

Between 1935 and 1937 Democratic conceptions were far more committed to active state intervention than the Republican order had ever been. Government now had responsibility for sustaining and enhancing overall economic performance, securing social and political order, and maintaining at least modest levels of social security for the majority of the population. This conception of government responsibility developed via the political battles of the 1930s. It was suggested in Democratic campaign themes in 1932, and in Roosevelt's speeches:

> The government should assume the function of economic regulation only as a last resort, to be tried only when private initiative, inspired by high responsibility, with such assistance and balance as government can give, has finally failed. As yet there has been no final failure, because there has been no attempt; and I decline to assume that this nation is unable to meet the situation.[23]

One could regard this formulation of stringent requirements for government regulation as a skilled way to propose expanded state activity in a difficult political setting. It would also be accurate to say that the administration's initial inclination toward government regulation – in itself a sharp break with Hoover – over time became a broad and ambitious conception of what government action might accomplish.

Much debate has occurred about whether the new economic policies were Keynesian.[24] The answer is no if one means an explicit strategy of massive spending aimed at promoting a recovery, regardless of immedi-

22. This strand of economic thinking supported both regulatory and spending commitments. See Alvin H. Hansen, *Full Recovery or Stagnation?* (New York: W. W. Norton, 1938).
23. Franklin D. Roosevelt, Speech at the Commonwealth Club in San Francisco, September 23, 1932, in *The Public Papers and Addresses of Franklin D. Roosevelt*, vol. 1, *The Genesis of the New Deal*, compiled by Samuel I. Rosenman (New York: Random House, 1938), 756. For a discussion of this speech that emphasizes its effectiveness as pragmatic liberal argument, see Robert Eden, "On the Origins of the Regime of Pragmatic Liberalism: John Dewey, Adolf A. Berle, and FDR's Commonwealth Club Address of 1932," *Studies in American Political Development* 7, no. 1 (Spring 1993): 74–150.
24. The role of Keynesian ideas in the policies of the administration is treated in Hawley, *New Deal and Monopoly*, 283–7; and Herbert Stein, *The Fiscal Revolution in America* (Chicago, Ill.: University of Chicago Press, 1969), 11–17.

ate budgetary consequences. A full strategy of deficit spending aimed at leaving the Depression never dominated the administration in the mid-1930s. Budget-cutting in the face of recession persisted, probably intensifying the downturn of 1938. The better answer is yes, however, because there was a deep political shift toward efforts to counteract the economic cycle, sustain demand, and expand employment. Progressive liberals accepted activist approaches to fiscal policy, public employment, and social spending. Relief policies increased effective demand and linked popular consumption to economic recovery. Keynes thought the New Deal had adopted perspectives similar to his, though he regarded Democratic policies as inadequate. In 1938 he wrote:

> It is true that the existing policies will prevent the slump from proceeding to such a disastrous degree as the last time. But they will not by themselves – at any rate, not without a large scale recourse to [public works and other investments aided by Government funds or guarantees] – maintain prosperity at a reasonable level.[25]

Accounts of the 1930s often note that economic recovery was not really achieved between 1935 and 1937, absent a stable renewal of production and a steady reduction of unemployment. Yet political success was defined by Democratic leaders as preventing the economic collapse from continuing on a downward path and leading to social chaos. By this standard, Democratic policies were on balance successful.

Here it is worth quoting Roosevelt at length. His 1937 State of the Union Address presents the Democratic case about relations among political and economic problems. The emphasis on sustaining democratic commitments is too often neglected in accounts of the New Deal as economic crisis management:

> In March 1933 the problems which faced our nation, and which only our national government had the resources to meet, were more serious even than appeared on the surface. It was not only that the visible mechanism of economic life had broken down. More disturbing was the fact that the long neglect of the needs of the underprivileged had brought too many of our people to the verge of doubt as to the successful adaptation of our historic traditions to the complex modern world. In that lay a challenge to our democratic form of government itself.
>
> The times required the confident answer of performance to those whose instinctive faith in humanity made them want to believe that in the long run democracy would prove superior to more extreme forms of government as

25. Letter, John Maynard Keynes to Roosevelt, 2/1/38, in Howard Zinn, ed., *New Deal Thought* (New York: Bobbs-Merrill, 1966), 405–6.

a process of getting action when action was wisdom, without the spiritual sacrifices which those other forms of government exact.

That challenge we met. To meet it required unprecedented activities under Federal leadership – to end abuses – to restore a large measure of material prosperity – to give new faith to millions of our citizens who had been traditionally taught to expect that democracy would provide continuously wider opportunity and continuously greater security.[26]

This statement notably lacks exaggerated claims about economic improvement in Roosevelt's first term. The crucial point is to justify strong national action to stop the economic and social unraveling. This step would enhance democratic prospects by strengthening public confidence in the responsiveness of the political process. The political efforts of the administration and wide sections of the new Democratic bloc were successful to such an extent that the most severe forms of the economic crisis were resolved by the end of 1937 – even if the economic situation remained tenuous.

Expanding democratic themes

Proponents of the new political order linked their advocacy of state intervention with a major expansion of democratic themes.[27] They called for government policies more responsive to the needs and concerns of a majority allegedly victimized by the Great Depression and Republican indifference. They also urged increasing the range of individuals and groups who could participate significantly in politics. This meant opening up the party system as well as reforming the political side of mainly nonpolitical institutions.

The democratic themes of the new political order were taken seriously by the progressive liberal leadership and its core elite. As the Democratic order was formed, further democratic views surfaced. Social democratic, populist, and radical democratic themes appeared widely in the mid-1930s.[28]

26. Franklin Roosevelt, State of the Union Address, 1/6/37, in Fred L. Israel, ed., *The State of the Union Messages of the Presidents, 1790–1966*, vol. III, 1905–66 (New York: Chelsea House, 1967): 2827–8.

27. Efforts to find compassion and concern for social bonds in Hooverite Republicanism miss this turn. Such arguments confuse a conservative liberal interest in social integration and community with a progressive liberal interest in expanding the field of political agents and projects.

28. On the Socialist Party see David Shannon, *The Socialist Party of America* (New York: Macmillan, 1955); on left tendencies among intellectuals, see Daniel Aaron, *Writers on the Left* (New York: Harcourt, Brace & World, 1961), as well as Richard H. Pells, *Radical Visions and American Dreams: Culture and Social Thought in the Depression*

American social democracy?

What we would now call social democratic themes were important in the new labor movement, in reform groupings allied with it, and among intellectuals. They appeared in calls to increase the political and socio-economic power of an organized working class, and in calls for dramatic and sustained government action against unemployment and for large increases in social services. Parts of the labor movement called not only for union rights and expanded social welfare provision but for increased political power. Those influenced by social democratic themes in and near the labor movement thought that attaining their aims would require sustained high levels of political organization by labor in conjunction with a transformed Democratic Party. They saw union organization as both a valued goal and a way to encourage a more egalitarian income distribution, expand social welfare provision, and reduce unemployment.

These aims were highly radical in the American context. The center and left of the CIO made proposals that might have been made by an American social democratic party. Yet even this qualified analogy should be treated carefully. The aims of European social democratic parties changed during the twentieth century, so references to "social democracy" have different meanings over time. In the 1930s most European socialist and social democratic parties still called for state control of the economy and for radical political transformation. They were mainly gradualist in their view of how such changes would occur, but affirmed the need for systemic change. Thus they often debated whether particular reforms, as in social welfare policies, would hasten the achievement of socialist objectives.

Several political platforms in the United States at the state level resembled European socialist and social democratic platforms with respect to their short-term objectives. But the American proposals were not posed as steps on a road to socialism. They were conceived as measures that would bring about a more democratic and decent industrial society. This basic distinction marked even such radical American platforms as that of the Minnesota Farmer-Labor Party in 1934, whose objectives were not framed as part of a process of socialist transformation. (And this

Years (New York: Harper & Row, 1973). A valuable collection of short pieces representing many left currents in and outside the Democratic order is Richard Polenberg, ed., *Radicalism and Reform in the New Deal* (Reading, Mass.: Addison-Wesley, 1972). It contains selections from writings and speeches by Adolph Berle, Ralph Bunche, Earl Browder, Huey Long, Norman Thomas, and Rexford Tugwell.

platform in the 1930s was well to the left among the programs of local state and party efforts partly independent of the Democratic Party.)

If the term "social democratic" is used in the American context, it must be done cautiously, to indicate modest areas of programmatic overlap. It would be a mistake to consider this intersection between parts of the Democratic order and European social democratic parties as an overall political convergence. With these qualifications, one can find social democratic themes in and near the new Democratic political bloc, but as subsidiary elements of its discourses. Social democracy did not appear as an autonomous political force. Instead, social democratic themes influenced the views and activities of a large part of the CIO, a portion of the progressive liberal leadership, and elements of state and local Democratic Parties. The limited role of even moderate social democratic themes indicates that efforts to establish autonomous labor parties in opposition to the Democratic Party had no chance of success.

Even in the mid-1930s, with strong popular movements and widespread antibusiness sentiment, socialist programs for state ownership of productive resources and central planning were not politically significant. When small political parties advancing state socialist objectives did intervene significantly in public political life – as in the Farmer-Labor Party in Minnesota or the American Labor Party in New York – their contributions were often negative. Broader reform political forces and organizations were in danger of being ripped apart by fights among socialist and Communist organizations whose long-term goals were unattractive in American politics (especially the Communist aim of a Soviet-style socialism). The central issues of the international socialist and Communist movements arose from the development of the Soviet regime or from national settings where these movements had a mass character and often confronted fascist adversaries. The American Communist and socialist left translated these issues into destructive struggles for organizational power and sectarian advantage. Socialists were less illiberal than Communists or Trotskyists in these matters, but that was not much of an accomplishment.

Populism

Populism, to a much greater degree than social democracy, permeated the new political order, including the unions. The strong presence of populist themes sharply differentiated the new regime from the Republican order, which was partly defined in opposition to the turn of the century Populist movement.

Populism takes the subject of political action as the "people" rather than a sectoral group, class, or nation. Populism counterposes the "people" to an external dominating force whose actions are held responsible for grave problems. Populist formulations vary according to how they characterize the "people," how they designate the enemy ("business," "big government," etc.), and how severe they consider the antagonism between the two.

In the United States in the 1930s, populism defined the "people" as productive, energetic, and oppressed by the Great Depression. The people were counterposed to the privileged and wealthy, to economic elites who wielded vast power with indifference to suffering. The sharp antagonism posed between the people and the privileged did not imply an irreconcilable struggle, occasional claims to the contrary. The aim voiced by most populist forces was to resolve wrenching crises on terms that would provide the "people" with dignity, while forcing the "rich" to compromise on economic questions and modify their social and political arrogance.

The Roosevelt administration used populist themes in 1935–7 in harsh attacks on business and on conservatives in both parties. There were elements of calculation in the Democratic use of populist themes – as in maneuvers to stay in contact with the mass discontent amplified by Huey Long and organized populist groups. But Democrat leaders were sincere in reciprocating the antagonism of business elites in the mid-1930s, and populist sentiments were too widespread to be reduced to any single group's stratagem.[29]

Populist themes often depicted the people as constituted by an ensemble of close-knit communities. Thus the activist national emphases of the Democratic order could be seen as dangerous. But compared with antagonism to national economic elites, antistate sentiment was secondary – and many populist proposals presumed a national state strong enough to engage in significant redistribution and programmatic innovation. In his insightful history of populism in the 1930s Alan Brinkley says that populists addressed:

> economic issues of genuine importance; they denounced men and institutions who bore no little responsibility for the problems of the era; and they offered solutions that, whatever their many failings, represented rational, concrete approaches to knotty problems. . . . [H]owever, the movements were failures, not only as quests for political power but as efforts to articulate a consistent, persuasive, and enduring vision of reform. They were

29. Populist themes even shaped policy choices in Congress and the administration. On "soak the rich" tax reform proposals see Mark Leff, *The Limits of Symbolic Reform: The New Deal and Taxation, 1933–39* (Cambridge University Press, 1984), 67–92.

doomed, ultimately, by their own timidity; and perhaps, too, by their growing irrelevance in a modern, consolidated nation in which basic choices had long since been made.[30]

This ambivalent judgment understates the influence of populism in shaping the themes of the Democratic order. As a distinct movement, however, populism did not construct coherent alternatives to address the main issues of the 1930s. Its economic programs centered on redistributive taxation and deconcentration, but neither idea was put forward in novel or persuasive ways. Its political programs affirmed both a localist suspicion of national political elites and institutions and a strong federal government to achieve economic goals. The denunciation of the corruption and malfeasance of political and economic elites was stirring and popular. Yet populist forces did not propose attractive ways of making the large choices that did exist about forms of economic and social regulation and modes of popular political participation.[31]

Radical democracy

Radical democratic themes emerged in several contexts, though they were rarely predominant. Their participatory emphasis was not typical of populist themes. Populist attacks on the wealthy and privileged focused more on distributing resources and on protecting communities and families. In the labor movement radical democratic themes appeared in calls for thorough reforms of work relations so that workers could gain a real measure of participation. Such themes emerged at high points of mobilization, as in the sit-down strikes, when calls for democracy and participation went beyond the main demands of the labor movement for reforming authoritarian work practices and securing real bargaining between labor and management.[32]

In agriculture, radical democratic themes appeared in the activism of

30. Alan Brinkley, *Voices of Protest: Huey Long, Father Coughlin, and the Great Depression* (New York: Alfred A. Knopf, 1982), 168.
31. Perhaps Brinkley's sympathy for populist efforts leads him not to dwell on the limits of populism as a view of how to reorganize American society. Thus the weakest chapter in his book is his discussion of populist program and vision, "The Dissident Ideology," in Brinkley, *Voices of Protest*. For a broad view of populism in the United States, see Michael Kazin, *The Populist Persuasion: An American History* (New York: Basic Books, 1995).
32. These impulses are apparent in most accounts of labor radicalism in the mid-1930s, including Sidney Fine, *Sit-down: The General Motors Strike of 1936–37* (Ann Arbor: University of Michigan Press, 1969); and Art Preis, *Labor's Giant Step, Twenty Years of the CIO* (New York: Pioneer, 1964), in addition to the works by Cochran, Fraser, Lynd and Lynd, Piven and Cloward, and Richmond cited previously.

poor farmers and farm laborers. These themes also arose in black opposition to racism. Democratic themes about race relations were not taken up by most of the administration, because of fear of breaking ties with Southern Democrats. In 1936 and 1937 Democratic progressive liberals made no frontal attack on racism (North or South). Even leading Democratic figures sympathetic to racial reform, such as Harold Ickes, were sensitive to conservative disapproval:

> The general social and civic status of Negroes reveals a picture quite as unsatisfactory as those which portray the economic and educational phases of their lives. . . . Under our new conception of democracy, the Negro will be given the chance to which he is entitled – not because he will be singled out for special consideration, but because he preeminently belongs to the class that the new democracy is designed especially to aid. . . .
>
> I congratulate you on your patience, and on the fact that you have worked while you waited. I believe that your cheerful disposition, your faith, your loyalty and your lack of resentment are some of the qualities that have brought you the success that already is yours.[33]

Emerging civil rights forces were growing less cheerful and patient, as when Walter White wrote in 1935: "The Department of Justice in Washington may lay claim to a 100 per cent performance in at least one branch of its activities – the evasion of cases involving burning questions of Negro rights."[34] If the administration rarely challenged images of the "people" as white, openly racist themes declined. Relief efforts reached many blacks, and there was a less discriminatory implementation of federal social and economic policies than in preceding decades. The severely discriminatory character of the racial order meant that when new federal programs were not explicitly racist they put elements of that order in question. Ickes was wrong to suggest that such an approach would be very effective in overcoming racial discrimination. But it did open political space for challenges to conventional racial practices. The comprehensive and stringent character of racial domination made racial and economic issues intertwined in emerging black efforts.[35]

Social democratic, populist, and radical democratic political currents did not provide programs and political visions that made them plausible

---

33. Harold Ickes, Address to the 27th Annual Convention of the NAACP, June 1936, reprinted as "The Negro as Citizen," *Crisis* 18 (August 1936): 230–53.
34. Walter White, "U.S. Department of (White) Justice," *The Crisis* (October 1935): 309.
35. For an interpretation of black political and social action in the 1930s that emphasizes emergent civil rights issues, see Harvard Sitkoff, *A New Deal for Blacks: The Emergence of Civil Rights as a National Issue* (New York: Oxford University Press, 1978); for an economic emphasis, see Nancy J. Weiss, *Farewell to the Party of Lincoln* (Princeton, N.J.: Princeton University Press, 1983).

competitors with Democratic progressive liberals in efforts to create a new political order. These currents encountered major problems even in presenting themselves as serious autonomous political projects, rather than as mainly loyal critics of the Democratic order. Of these currents, social democracy had the clearest and most stable institutional location, in parts of the CIO – but in the mid-1930s, with the turmoil in labor relations, that was not such a stable place. And there were major thematic problems – even the most temperate formulations of social democratic positions retained a class emphasis that was not easy to reconcile with core progressive liberal commitments to individualism and social cooperation. Other radical currents were more fragile in their organized forms and had less developed programs. There were also significant tensions between some of their themes and those of the new Democratic order. Thus populist efforts not infrequently had an antimodernizing cast at variance with the main orientation of the new Democratic bloc. Nonetheless, progressive liberals drew frequently on social democratic, populist, and radical democratic themes. The assimilation of parts of these themes helped distinguish Democratic discourses sharply from those of the preceding political order.

An expansive reworking of liberal discourses was a crucial part of constituting and developing the new political order. There are several ways to miss the novelty of the political framework that was built. One is to stress what the new order failed to be – social democratic or radical democratic. This obscures the extent to which liberalism was reformulated, so that views and positions beyond the pale only a decade before were now near or partly within a new centrist common sense. Another way to miss what happened is to emphasize diversity and heterogeneity in the 1930s to the point of failing to see the overall conception of a liberal market society capable of expanding both democratic practices and economic capacities. Democratic discourses linked progressive and modernizing themes with popular and democratic themes in producing this conception, which provided a solid framework for political action and argument.

A progressive liberal framework

To grasp the distinctiveness and political effectiveness of Democratic progressive liberalism, consider two major questions of the 1930s:

Should state intervention expand beyond regulation toward full planning?
Should state policies encourage the political and social organization of nonelite groups?

Table 6.1. *New Deal political currents*

	No government aid to popular organization	Government aid to popular organization
State Regulation	Conservative Democrats	Brandeisians
State Planning	Business corporatists	Left planners

The common sense of the Republican order implied negative answers to both questions and made them hard even to raise as serious issues, especially the first. The arrival of these questions as central issues in public life was an indication that the old order had been shattered. What might replace it?

If one combines the preceding two questions to produce four cells, as in Table 6.1, the resulting positions can be given the familiar names of political currents in and around the New Deal: business corporatists, left planners, conservative Democrats, and (left) Brandeisians.

Where does what I call progressive liberalism fit in? If one takes these cells to define fixed and unchanging positions, there is no space for it. The space for Democratic progressive liberalism was not found so much as it was opened, by reconfiguring the political terrain. A dominant progressive liberalism took shape by cutting across these cells to combine parts of each into a new formation. Tensions did not disappear, but new Democratic formulations redefined questions in ways that reduced them and assembled much wider support than any single prior position could achieve.

To visualize this process first consider Table 6.1 as a transparent map – then think of progressive liberalism as a colored transparency superimposed on it. The new map – depicted in Table 6.2 – would include most of the upper right cell (left Brandeisians) and most of the lower right cell (left planners), along with small but significant portions of the other two cells (conservative Democrats and business corporatists). These new boundaries marked an area of broad agreement on the core progressive liberal themes – (popular) interest group formation, expanded state action, and egalitarian commitments.

To redraw the post-Republican map of political positions in this way

Table 6.2. *Emergent progressive liberalism*

	No government aid to popular organization	Government aid to popular organization
State Regulation	Conservative Democrats	Brandeisians
State Planning	Business corporatists	Left planners

Table 6.3. *Marginalizing Republican positions*

	Oppose government aid to popular organization	No government aid to popular organization	Government aid to popular organization
Cooperation	Hoover, Liberty League	Moderate Republicans	
State regulation		Conservative Democrats	Brandeisians
State planning		Business corporatists	Left planners

a progressive liberal perspective had to be developed and vigorously advocated. It was not a matter of reminding the appropriate people and groups that they really agreed. Creating a progressive liberal framework was a disruptive process that involved redefining the questions that mark off the cells in Table 6.1. The disruption meant marginalizing conservative and Republican alternatives. To illustrate what was done, Table 6.3 expands Tables 6.1 and 6.2 to include influential perspectives during the Republican order that were still present in the 1930s but had no chance of winning major debates. These perspectives are summarized

Figure 6.1. *The Democratic political order (DPO) on a new spectrum of responses to the question "What forms of state economic intervention are appropriate?"*

DPO

State Planning	"Keynesianism"	Cooperation	Libertarianism

Figure 6.2. *The Democratic political order (DPO) on a new spectrum of responses to the question "How should popular organizations be aided?"*

DPO

Statism	Legal Support	Neutrality	Opposition

as government hostility to popular organization, and a preference for voluntary cooperation among economic agents rather than government regulation of their relations.

A positive redefinition of the political terrain occurred in three analytically distinct steps. First, progressive liberals rejected what was taken to be the far left position on each question, as represented in Figures 6.1 and 6.2. They rejected full planning of economic and social life, and explicit state sponsorship and direct subsidies for interest groups and movements. Communist – as distinct from Popular Front – positions often provided key negative referents in these moves.

Having rejected a far left alternative, progressive liberals next moved to stigmatize influential conservative positions, such as those of Hoover Republicans in Table 6.3. The rejection of these positions sometimes included claims that they were effectively the same as far right positions. These exclusionary moves were greatly resented by more moderate opponents of the emerging regime, who denounced attacks that paired them with extremists. But the vitriolic and hyperbolic denunciations of Roosevelt and the New Deal by so many of its opponents made such a move plausible.

In these bitter arguments, Democratic political and intellectual leaders were making claims about the practical political meaning of conservative positions on central issues. One claim was that in Depression conditions, Hoover's conceptions of public-private cooperation and self-regulation were an abication of public responsibility on such a scale as to converge with extremist opposition to government action aimed at even the most urgent public goals. A second claim was that the severe hostility of leading business groups and allied political and social forces to popular organization made a stance of legal neutrality by the federal government a de facto capitulation to the extremist antiunion sentiment of intransigent employers.

Democratic progressive liberals did not ask whether under some imaginable circumstances Hoover's view of organizations and associations and a Democratic pluralist view might be reasonably close. Their question was instead: *What did conservative Republican positions mean politically in the mid-1930s?* To stigmatize those positions as uncompassionate, antidemocratic, and irresponsible was a strong move in a rough political conflict.

This second step, marginalizing conservative positions, meant positing a new political spectrum. This spectrum is presented in two parts in Figures 6.1 and 6.2. The third step was to locate a point to the left of center on that new spectrum and propose it as the reasonable way forward.[36] Thus progressive liberals affirmed the merit of legal and political assistance to popular organizations, as with the NLRA. In doing so they appealed to notions of political and economic balance and equity. They argued that an extensive role for the state in economic development and social welfare provision would enhance economic and social security.

This third step made previously radical stances into temperate and responsible answers to new questions: How could an active regulatory program best be conducted? What were the most responsible and effective means of aiding popular organization? On a political spectrum defined by those questions, Democratic leaders could in good faith locate themselves moderately to the left of center among legitimate political options, while pushing the official right close to the edge and sometimes partly outside of the range of acceptable positions.

The resulting stance of pragmatic moderation was vigorously represented by Democratic leaders as an accurate depiction of their style and aims. This plausible representation was not a trick, but the effect of a dynamic political effort. The three steps outlined were accomplished through fierce arguments against determined adversaries. When Republicans assented to parts of the new Democratic course it meant that dramatic political changes had occurred. Positions that a decade before would have been on the very edge of the legitimate political spectrum were becoming a new common sense.

---

36. The movement from planning toward regulation accompanied an overall shift to the left: Left Brandeisians were more powerful relative to conservative Democrats by the middle of the 1930s than left planners had been with respect to business corporatists. See Hawley, *New Deal and Monopoly*, 130–46; and Otis Graham, *Toward a Planned Society* (New York: Oxford University Press, 1976), 1–68.

Many critics – and defenders – have portrayed the New Deal as cautiously experimental or even reactive, as at most weakly ideological. This account is mistaken: It does not take seriously the many statements of progressive liberal principle by Roosevelt and Democratic leaders. These statements identified enemies on the left and right and attacked them, and counterposed a view of how best to govern and develop an advanced industrial society.[37] Views of the New Deal as purely flexible and even opportunistic are misled by the resilient and adaptive political style of the new leadership, and perhaps by Democratic claims to have rejected doctrinaire formulations. Such claims should not be taken to show a lack of strong commitments. Nor should they be identified only with rejections of Communist and Fascist political styles, though such rejections were intended. Democratic avowals of pragmatic moderation were an important part of highly charged political arguments against Hoover Republicans and conservative Democrats. As the Democratic order was built, predefined political tendencies were not merely added together. A new political force assimilated elements of diverse prior views and reshaped them within a distinctive perspective.

A related misconception has long influenced accounts of the cultural politics of the early Democratic order, leading to a view of the new regime as more conformist and conventional than was the case. The Democratic order did not propose to repudiate "American values," but – as many conservative intellectual and political opponents charged – cosmopolitan, nationalizing, and egalitarian themes were central to Democratic practices. These themes were bound to be disruptive.[38]

Arguments in the 1980s and 1990s that the Democratic Party would succeed in presidential politics by combining economic liberalism and social conservatism often claimed that such an approach was at the root of Democratic successes in the 1930s and 1940s. However one gauges end-of-the-century prospects, the historical claim is basically wrong. If

37. For an interesting discussion of New Deal thought that regards progressive liberal views as less coherent than I have claimed, see Daniel Rodgers, *Contested Truths: Keywords in American Politics since Independence* (New York: Basic Books, 1987), 204–6.

38. The Southern conservative intellectual and cultural opposition in the 1930s associated these attributes with the onrush of "civilization" against culture. Major themes of this opposition were expressed by a group of writers in 1930 in *I'll Take My Stand*, which appears as Twelve Southerners, *I'll Take My Stand: The South and the Agrarian Tradition*, with an introduction by Louis D. Rubin, Jr., and biographical essays by Virginia Rock (Baton Rouge: Louisiana State University Press, 1977). Also see Eugene D. Genovese, *The Southern Tradition: The Achievement and Limitations of an American Conservatism* (Cambridge, Mass.: Harvard University Press, 1994).

one compares the cultural themes of the early Democratic order with the cultural radicalism before World War I or the broader cultural radicalism of the 1960s, it is certainly true that the former were more conventional. But these are not the appropriate referents. The proper comparison is with the cultural politics of other major tendencies in American political life in the late 1920s and early 1930s. In the 1920s the main Democratic themes were parochial, defensive, sectional, and not infrequently racist. In that decade and well into the next, Republican themes articulated a mainly Protestant conservative nationalism. The Democratic order was modernizing and egalitarian – its cultural politics broke with pre-1932 Democratic themes and redefined Americanism in far more open forms.[39]

An emerging Democratic order

Out of the crises and conflicts of the 1930s a new political order emerged. Its main features became clear in 1935–7. To return to the image of a Democratic triangle: In party-state relations the party aided in gaining electoral support. It provided employees for an expanding state (though the most powerful state figures were not recruited out of the party organization). The party gained a new popular definition through its association with state programs and policies.

Relations between new movements and groups and the Democratic Party also benefited both. The party could not claim to have organized them, but it did support key demands, as with the Wagner Act. The movements broadened the party when they entered it and on balance helped it electorally.

In this triangle the new Democratic state was crucial in encouraging electoral support for the party and building new political forces. The state was itself built out of political conflicts in which a Democratic political bloc predominated. Progressive liberals in the administration,

39. The modernizing and egalitarian elements of Democratic cultural themes are discussed with insight in Cohen, *Making a New Deal*. One of the best books on the 1930s has been a source of confusion in this area. Richard Pells chose "The Decline of Radicalism, 1935–39" as the title for a key chapter. He saw national cultural shifts through the lens of a critical view of the Popular Front. Pells powerfully restated the *Partisan Review* critique of the conformist and sentimental elements of Popular Frontism. But his claim that the late 1930s saw a deep shift toward conservative themes celebrating nation, family, and region has often been read as a general account of the new political culture of that decade, rather than as a claim about cultural politics on the left. This depiction encourages a view of the Democratic order as much more culturally conservative than it was, given previous Democratic commitments and the overall national context. Pells, *Radical Visions and American Dreams*, 292–329.

Congress, the Democratic Party, state agencies, and professional associations led in building this political bloc.

It might seem easier to use a conventional term to name what happened. But this new political bloc was unconventional. Progressive liberals were not a party, though they had considerable power in the Democratic Party; the Democratic bloc included progressive Republicans. Nor was this new bloc equivalent to the state, though progressive liberals controlled major components of an expanding state.

A dramatic displacement of activities from conventional locations signaled a regime politics of creating new institutions and commitments. Popular movements and their interest group political forms played some of the roles of a political party in representing their constituents. The Democratic Party often acted like an interest group, battling for the demands of party notables and loosely linked political and social groupings (rather than supplying a broad program and policies). And the state and administration played major party roles in nourishing popular identification with a new political direction.

The new Democratic bloc cut across normal institutional lines. Perhaps because of its complex location there has been a tendency to describe programmatic and institutional changes in the 1930s as less coherent and more reactive than was the case. Thus if one asks whether state, party, and movements were unified agents capable of generating a new political order – taking one at a time, the answer is no. Comparative referents confirm this impression: If one compares the Democratic Party of the mid-1930s to a European mass party, it looks weak and fragmented. Or if one compares the activities of the state in the United States with those in some nations in Western Europe, the American state seems modest. Yet the Democratic order could resolve the main political and social crises it confronted. It won and sustained a popular consensus for its policies. The strength of the Democratic order was linked to its unconventional configuration. As they took shape, emerging forces could escape the constraints of established institutions (the Republican state, conventional Democratic state and local party organizations, the AFL, etc.) and innovate.

Democratic capacities can be summarized in the terms used in Chapter 2. The state recruited and educated individuals through its policies and agencies. By encouraging interest group activity, the state assisted mobilizing and organizing efforts on behalf of the political order. The party's identification with the new state strengthened its position. In turn it supported state/administration policies by organizing and mobilizing political support for the new order and played a (modest) role in recruiting and educating supporters. New political movements and groups, notably labor, organized and mobilized political support for the Democratic order. They also recruited important new political support.

A Democratic start

Although the Republican order was deeply in crisis by late 1932, one could not be sure of the direction or success of the new administration. The central cause of the formation of the Democratic order was the political effort made by progressive liberals in alliance with new mass political forces to resolve the crises that dominated the first half of the decade. Progressive liberal leaders in conjunction with new mass political forces, previous Democrats, progressive Republicans, and many prior nonvoters built a Democratic political bloc. This bloc was the dominant force in American politics. In forming the Democratic order, many elements of the Democratic political bloc and its progressive liberal leadership were themselves changed.

Crises and the transition to a new political order were intertwined. The most serious crisis – of the state's legitimacy – was resolved in the measures taken by the first Roosevelt administration to make a political commitment to maintaining economic and social order. This meant an extensive national redeployment of coercion, as in partially protecting protests against dire Depression conditions. Social and political order were redefined to include much wider popular organization than in prior decades. For recalcitrant political and economic elites, the national shift made it likely that without major changes – in labor relations, or local welfare provision, or police practices – they would be increasingly vulnerable to popular protest.

In building the Democratic order new mass political forces were both a cause and a solution of the crises. As a cause, they challenged the inability of the Republican order to guarantee social order and decency after the Depression and tried to overcome its exclusive system of political representation. As a solution, they helped shift the balance of party forces toward a new Democratic Party, assisted in expanding state responsibility for social and economic crisis management, and increased political participation.

Forming the Democratic order was both a modernizing and a democratizing process. The Democratic leadership claimed to have accomplished crucial national tasks, not merely to have served its most ardently supportive constituencies. These claims accompanied the building of a more powerful state with a growing capacity to undertake ambitious projects. This capacity was directed toward domestic objectives in 1935–7, but the basis was being created for an expanded international role. At the same time, Democratic progressive liberalism grew to include a much wider array of democratic (and populist) elements than before 1932.

Among the feasible outcomes in the 1930s – from a more flexible Hooverism to a more radical and popular-democratic version of the New Deal – the result was close to the left boundary. What emerged was well outside the limits of the prior political order, and more energetically reformist than Roosevelt and other progressive liberal leaders anticipated in 1932. Yet this new order might have been only a moment of reform, made possible by dire hardship and reliant on Roosevelt's personal appeal. The next chapters look at what happened after the Depression and after Roosevelt's death.

7

Surprising years: electing Truman and sustaining the Democratic order, 1947–9

> If you wanted to compare it to the field of battle, let's say that President Roosevelt conducted a constant offensive for twelve years, and finally then he left and President Truman came in. I think President Truman found that maybe we had advanced to a point where it was not a good idea to advance further. Stop and establish a line at that point, bring up your supplies, bring up your lines of communications, reorganization, and reevaluate, and then gradually, and slowly, start a gradual new offensive under the name of the Fair Deal.
>
> – Clark Clifford[1]

From 1947 through 1949 the Democratic order was sustained through the defense of position Clark Clifford described. Truman's presidential victory surprised many participants in the postwar political conflicts; few believed he would win and few presumed the Democratic order would continue.[2] Yet the main story of American politics in the late 1940s was Democratic persistence, despite factional conflicts and con-

1. Transcript, Clark Clifford Oral History Interview (Washington, D.C., March 23, April 13, April 19, May 10, July 26, 1971; March 16, 1972; and February 14, 1973), Harry S. Truman Library, 67.
2. On the late 1940s see Alonzo L. Hamby, *Beyond the New Deal: Harry S. Truman and American Liberalism* (New York: Columbia University Press, 1973); John Patrick Diggins, *The Proud Decades: America in War and Peace, 1941–1960* (New York: W. W. Norton, 1988); and David McCullough, *Truman* (New York: Simon and Schuster, 1992). For a good review of the literature as of the early 1970s see Richard S. Kirkendall, ed., *The Truman Period as a Research Field: A Reappraisal* (Columbia: University of Missouri Press, 1972). See also Barton J. Bernstein, ed., *Politics and Policies of the Truman Administration* (Chicago, Ill.: Quadrangle Books, 1972). The oral history interviews at the Harry S. Truman Library are a valuable source, including those of William Batt, Andrew Biemiller, Samuel Brightman, Oscar Chapman, Clark Clifford, India Edwards, George Elsey, Oscar Ewing, William Hastie, Leon Keyserling, Charles Kindelberger, James Loeb, John McEnery, Edwin Nourse, Samuel Rosenman, Harold Seidman, James Sundquist, and Raymond Vernon.

servative pressures.[3] New reform accomplishments were limited, but the Democratic order was not overturned or fundamentally transformed.

The political conflicts of 1947 through 1949 could have led to the end of the Democratic order.[4] Much of the Republican and conservative Democratic opposition sought this objective after the war. Yet no such end occurred. How and why did the Democratic order persist after World War II? To answer this question, I focus first on the 1948 election (in this chapter) and next examine conflicts over the Taft-Hartley Act (Chapter 8), which was passed over Truman's veto in 1947. These events refer to the claims about the Democratic order made in Chapter 2: "Major institutional and discursive continuities marked the four decades of the Democratic political order. These continuities registered the capacities of the party, state, and movements to recruit, organize, mobilize, and educate political support for the Democratic order." A negative judgment of these claims would be appropriate if, after Roosevelt, there were basic institutional and discursive shifts in the state-party-movement relations at the core of the Democratic order.

The most likely practical alternatives to the Democratic course taken by the Truman administration and its allies involved major political shifts well to the right. The political victory of Republican moderate opponents of the Democratic order was a strong possibility – there was also a chance of a victory by a right-center coalition in which Taft Republicans had a leading role. Given these prospects, it is wrong to consider the postwar years as primarily a missed chance to expand the most ambitious reform efforts of the prior decade (even to convert the Democratic order into a social democratic regime). A full deployment of Democratic capacities was required to avert plausible outcomes well to the right of what happened.[5]

3. To recall the earlier discussion, for a political order to persist in advanced industrial settings, support has to be recruited from existing political forces or socioeconomic groupings not represented on the political scene. For such support to matter past the moment of recruitment, these forces have to be organized. Mobilization realizes the potential of organized support. Education – with dialogic elements – is crucial for these activities. In advanced industrial societies, frequent changes in socioeconomic and political conditions require a flexible application of basic perspectives for a political order to continue. Thus, a modern political order is more likely to endure if its supporters participate in interpreting and responding to new developments.

4. I have distinguished among routine crises of adjustment in a political order, crises that put a regime in question, and crises that jeopardize basic institutional and cultural features of a society. In the late 1940s crises of the third type were not present.

5. For the view that a social democratic opportunity was lost after World War II, see Ira Katznelson, "Was the Great Society a Lost Opportunity?" in Steve Fraser and Gary Gerstle, eds., *The Rise and Fall of the New Deal Order, 1930–1980* (Princeton, N.J.: Princeton University Press, 1989) 185–211.

A number of political figures who helped build the Democratic order in the 1930s were disappointed with the course of the Truman administration. Many analysts have cited this discontent to bolster their claim that there was basic discontinuity between the New Deal and the Truman years. Some cite political factors: the failure of new reform initiatives, the waning of ambitious economic planning schemes, the onset of McCarthyism, and the emergence of the Cold War. Others claim that postwar economic growth took political reform off the agenda, separating the politics of the late 1940s from the preceding decade.[6] Both interpretations are wrong. Those who stress political aspects of an alleged shift tend to see the Democratic order of the 1930s as much further to the left than was the case, and thus misconceive Truman's policies as a rupture with prior Democratic efforts. Those who claim that an economic break occurred wrongly attribute a determining role to economic growth in shaping political alignments. In reality, the central result of the late 1940s was to confirm the key political and legal shifts of the 1930s, including the national state's active regulatory role. Democratic efforts blocked the opposition to the point that even major counter-reforms, such as the Taft-Hartley Act, also entailed a reluctant settlement with the Democratic order.

The persistence of the Democratic order was due in the first instance to Democratic political capacities, through which diehard opponents of the regime were defeated or partially incorporated. The Democratic order in the late 1940s again centered on a triangle among an interventionist state, movements and interest groups (especially labor), and the Democratic Party. In institutional terms, the state and the presidency were central, while the party and the main interest groups and movements relied on the state as they made their own contribution to Democratic power. In this triangle a progressive liberal group continued to exercise overall leadership. Both the founding years and the postwar maintenance of the Democratic order involved a turn to the left by leading political forces and a substantial popular mobilization.

6. Several articles that posit a break between the late 1940s and the prior decade appear in Michael J. Lacey, ed., *The Truman Presidency* (Cambridge University Press, 1990): Robert Griffith, "Forging America's Postwar Order: Domestic Politics and Political Economy in the Age of Truman," 57–88,; Nelson Lichtenstein, "Labor in the Truman Era: Origins of the 'Private Welfare State,' " 128–155,; and to a lesser degree, William H. Chafe, "Postwar American Society: Dissent and Social Reform," 156–173. These articles make useful critiques of the conservative aspects of the Truman administration's policies, but the authors do not demonstrate that a real political break occurred vis-à-vis the regime established in the previous decade.

The international setting

During the formation of the Democratic order, debates over foreign policy were not central. If Roosevelt gradually advanced internationalist positions, reticence about foreign involvement was widespread late into the 1930s, when fascist expansion in Europe and Asia was well under-way.[7] After World War II, with the defeat of Germany and Japan, the weakening of the old colonial empires, and the strengthened position of the Soviet Union, international matters demanded the full attention of the Truman administration. Clark Clifford later claimed:

> I believe historians will look back at the period of Mr. Truman's administra-tion and take the position that for the first time the United States did step up and meet the responsibility of world leadership, and that is the brightest star in President Truman's crown.[8]

Some have argued that the Cold War and the expanded American international presence meant a rupture with the main reformist political tendencies of the prior decade. International economic opportunities reduced pressure for domestic reform (growth replaced equity) and Cold War conflict incited domestic anti-Communism and weakened prospec-tive reform coalitions.[9] Such accounts of how postwar international relations reshaped American politics aim to explain something that did not occur, a fundamental shift away from the Democratic order as it was built in the 1930s. Conservative pressures were substantial but did not destroy the Democratic order. Without the Cold War's conservative effects, reform would otherwise not have been boundless.

The Democratic order shaped a distinctive international political course that cannot be reduced to imperatives of the international system or needs of the American economy. The American postwar role required

7. William E. Leuchtenburg, *Franklin D. Roosevelt and the New Deal, 1932–1940* (New York: Harper & Row, 1963), 193–230.
8. Clark Clifford Oral History Interview, Truman Library, 453–4.
9. See Fred Block, "Empire and Domestic Reform," *Radical History Review* 45 (Fall 1989): 98–114; and Alan Wolfe, *America's Impasse: The Rise and Fall of the Politics of Growth* (New York: Pantheon, 1981). In an exaggerated version of this sort of argument, Gabriel Kolko and Joyce Kolko claim that the Cold War *originated* in the domestic economic and political needs of conservative elites. They argue that the American postwar role in both economic expansion and conflict with the Soviet Union derived from the conservative impulses of domestic American politics: "Unable to alter its internal economic priorities, American capitalism could only turn outward, not with disinterested aid but with new designs to save itself." Joyce Kolko and Gabriel Kolko, *The Limits of Power: The World and United States Foreign Policy, 1945–1954* (New York: Harper & Row, 1972), 383.

a domestic political order that could sustain a high level of military preparation.[10] It also needed a democratic political ideology for competition with the fading colonial powers and the Soviet Union. While the Democratic order met these requirements, it was not determined by them.[11]

The defining experience for relations between the Democratic order and international politics was World War II. Democratic internationalism provided the political basis for the arduous task of organizing domestic support for alliances with the antifascist allies and then for military intervention. The leadership of the Democratic order emphasized the military and political urgency of an international antifascist campaign.[12]

World War II had a strongly ideological character, as leaders of the Democratic order declared a democratic antifascist campaign. The war received extensive public support.[13] Democratic conduct of the war had several distinctive elements: the U.S. aim of unconditional surrender by the fascist regimes of Germany, Italy, and Japan; the political destruction of these regimes as an objective; and the alliance with the Soviet Union and acceptance of its legitimacy as a participant in postwar international politics.[14]

10. While military spending fell drastically from 1945 to 1947, it was more than ten times higher in 1948 than a decade earlier. Bureau of the Census, *Historical Statistics of the United States – Colonial Times to 1970*, Y 533–566, "Federal, State, and Local Government Expenditure by Function: 1902–1970" (Washington, D.C.: Government Printing Office, 1975), 1120.

11. For a liberal vision of an expansive American international role, see Arthur Schlesinger, Jr., *The Vital Center* (Boston: Houghton Mifflin, 1949). For a revisionist account see William Appleman Williams, *The Contours of American History* (Chicago, Ill.: Quadrangle, 1966), 451–78.

12. On the American war effort, see John Morton Blum, *V Was for Victory – Politics and American Culture during World War II* (New York: Harcourt Brace Jovanovich, 1976); James MacGregor Burns, *Roosevelt – 1940–45 The Soldier of Freedom* (New York: Harcourt Brace Jovanovich, 1970); and William L. O'Neill, *A Democracy at War: America's Fight at Home and Abroad in World War II* (New York: Free Press, 1993).

13. To gauge the support for World War II, it is useful to consider the forms of popular resistance that have been made to American military efforts in the nineteenth and twentieth centuries: draft evasion and resistance, tax resistance, labor unrest, public demonstrations and civil disobedience, and electoral campaigns against the war. None of these activities occurred on a large scale or in a sustained form compared with the resistance to the Civil War, World War I, the Vietnam war, or even the Spanish-American war. On wartime propaganda in the United States, see Blum, *V Was for Victory*, 16–52.

14. The democratic political aims of the war effort were one source of the ferocity of the military conflict. The Allied purpose was not to block the further expansion of fascist

The war effort strengthened Democratic internationalism among both the progressive liberal leadership and wide sections of the population. The experience of the war stamped Democratic views of international politics in ways that endured for decades: It encouraged strong beliefs in the legitimacy of American power, in the evil of the main opponents of the United States, and in the possible international force of democratic and liberal commitments. Democratic leaders saw expanded American power as much preferable to the main perceived alternative, a return to conventional balance-of-power arrangements. They believed the latter would provide the basis for new military conflicts, block initiatives toward stable security arrangements, and increase the domestic power of isolationist currents in the United States by giving up the ideological basis of World War II.[15]

A major feature of the politics of these years is often obscured by the post-1960s focus on the Cold War (early and late) and the Vietnam debacle. Isolationism was very powerful in the United States well into the 1930s, preventing serious efforts to oppose the fascist regimes until late in the decade. In the late 1930s isolationism predominated in the Republican Party and had significant support from Democrats.[16]

From the late 1930s to the early 1950s, Democratic leaders suggested that Republican foreign policy was so compromised by isolationist tendencies that Republican administrations in the 1930s and early 1940s would have been insufficiently ardent in opposing fascism. In all likelihood the United States would have been drawn into war sooner or later, but Democratic charges of Republican equivocation and timidity are worth taking seriously. A different political order might well have fought a war that was more conventional in form and less ideological in its

regimes or achieve a modus vivendi with their leaders but to destroy those regimes. The links between antifascist aims and military brutality are clear regarding the American use of nuclear weapons against Japan. Part of the rationale for their use was the commitment to destroying the Japanese regime rather than negotiating a peace that would have allowed its leaders to stay in or near power without any deep institutional transformation. It has not been shown that using nuclear weapons was essential to antifascist goals. But the contemporary discussion mainly ignores this element of American strategy, which simplifies the case against using nuclear weapons after Japan was clearly no longer an immediate threat to American territory. In a stringent and in my view persuasive critique of the American decision, John Rawls makes little distinction between the aims of achieving a military settlement with the country of Japan and destroying Japan's fascist regime. John Rawls, in "Fifty Years After Hiroshima: A Symposium" *Dissent*, Summer 1995, 323–7.

15. For a recent defense of Democratic postwar internationalism, see Arthur M. Schlesinger, *The Cycles of American History* (Boston: Houghton Mifflin, 1986), 170–80.

16. This configuration is clear in Leuchtenburg's account in *Roosevelt and the New Deal*, 219–30, 297–325.

aims. A Republican or conservative Democratic war might have taken place later, and it might have focused more on American and hemispheric territorial security and less on destroying the fascist regimes.

With Landon's election in 1936, or even Willkie's in 1940, it is less likely that a persistent effort to implement internationalist positions would have been made, given the strength of isolationist currents in and around the Republican Party.[17] It is conceivable that the sequence leading toward fascist attacks on American territory would have changed, as the Japanese regime might not have regarded an isolationist United States as a barrier to attaining many of its objectives in Asia. Even if one imagines roughly the same sequence, resulting in Pearl Harbor, would a Willkie administration (much less a more conservative and isolationist administration) have mobilized the American people for an extended antifascist war? There are reasons to doubt this. American military and political involvement for a war aimed at destroying fascism rather than blocking its expansion would have been a matter for debate. So would the domestic coordination of economic and military activities, given the hostility of large sections of the Republican Party to the New Deal. And Republican leaders would surely have been hesitant about forming the strong alliance with the Soviet Union required for an antifascist effort. Reasonable judgments of these matters could be translated into claims that Republican commitments to democracy internationally were weak and that Republican isolationism was insufficiently patriotic.

During and after World War II, Democratic leaders claimed to be democrats and antifascists on a global scale. They claimed to have overcome the historic divide between a foreign policy based on democratic principles and one based on concern for American national security. Democratic war efforts created intense strategic dilemmas for the Republican and conservative opposition, because the latter's positions risked handing over all the force of national and patriotic attachments to the Democratic order. Yet isolationism persisted, with repeated warnings from Robert Taft and others of the dangers of American international engagement. Then in the late 1940s and early 1950s parts of the opposition sought to outflank the Democratic order with heightened demands for international efforts to confront the Soviet Union.

The political legacy of World War II was to identify Democratic policies with antifascist and democratic international initiatives and to provide a durable reference point for Democratic claims to international

17. The strength of these currents is indicated in Blum, *V Was for Victory*, 265–80; and Diggins, *Proud Decades*, 7–10.

competence and effectiveness. The war was crucial in shaping how the Democratic order approached Soviet-U.S. relations in the late 1940s. From the end of World War II through the end of the Democratic order, core themes derived from the wartime experience were linked together: Democratic order/internationalism/antifascism/anticommunism.[18] These associations had the effect of strengthening the Democratic order; they also affirmed continuity between World War II and postwar Democratic foreign policies. Thus Democrats could claim to represent both democratic and national values in American political life, while stigmatizing opponents as parochial and nondemocratic. Yet defining American commitments through the lens of World War II would lead to serious problems: when that war was not a sufficient framework of interpretation, when American power had to be more modest in its reach, when tensions between American national interests and progressive liberal norms were greater, and when resolute opponents were more ambiguous figures than the Nazis.

The domestic meaning of World War II

Fighting a war can have varied political meanings for the nations engaged, depending on the prior alignment of forces and the course of the war. For the United States the central domestic result of World War II was to cement the Democratic order. In World War II the exigencies of fighting a global war, especially of the type pursued by the Democratic leadership, required rapid and extensive mobilization. There was broad popular support for this war effort, whose forms on balance helped to consolidate major Democratic reforms and spurred expansion of the state.[19] David Brody correctly argues that: "if World War II did not generate new departures, it did consolidate older achievements. The reform wave of the 1930s stopped at the war's edge, but did not recede."[20] The main changes of 1935–7 suffered no reversals, while some assaults on the New Deal were rejected as disruptive of national unity.

18. These themes, referred to by critics as cold war liberalism, are discussed in Hamby, *Beyond the New Deal;* Schlesinger, *Cycles of American History;* and Wolfe, *America's Impasse.*
19. These effects are emphasized in David Brody, "The New Deal and World War II," in John Braeman, Robert H. Bremner, and David Brody, eds., *The New Deal – The National Level* (Columbus: Ohio State University Press, 1975), vol. 1; and Otis L. Graham, Jr., "The Democratic Party, 1932–45", in Arthur M. Schlesinger, Jr., ed., *History of U.S. Political Parties: 1910–1945: From Square Deal to New Deal* (New York: Chelsea House, 1973).
20. David Brody, "The New Deal and World War II," 297.

Wartime coordination of economic and social activities built on the expanded state action of the 1930s.[21]

The war had mixed consequences for new efforts at progressive liberal reform – for example, wartime industrial relations agreements spurred union growth while encouraging bureaucratic tendencies within the labor movement. But few Democratic leaders believed that wartime conditions ought to be used as an opportunity for major new reform initiatives, even among those insistent on equity in sharing the burdens of wartime sacrifices. An exception was the work of the National Resources Planning Board, a wartime source of left-progressive policy themes.[22] In the 1944 election campaign and then as the end of the war approached, Democratic leaders argued that victory in an antifascist war should be followed by the recognition of broad social rights after the emergency ended.[23]

Agreements among government, management, and labor allowed a massive expansion of unions during the war. Labor union membership grew from 8.7 million in 1940 to 14.3 million in 1945.[24] Labor's wartime growth was based on the political and economic strength gained in the previous decade as well as the sympathetic stance of the administration. Wartime formulas expanded union membership, especially in already organized industries. New union growth occurred mainly without mass strikes and militant actions such as those of 1936–7, and often without much mass participation of any type. The popularity of World War II made the labor movement reluctant to initiate or sharpen industrial conflicts that might jeopardize national military and political objec-

21. The war sustained the ideological themes of the later New Deal while renewing institutional formulas partly reminiscent of its earlier years. See Hamby, *Beyond the New Deal*, 1–28.

22. Proposals for expanded government economic regulation and service provision were justified in terms of severe problems that would appear after World War II, due not only to postwar economic conversion and adjustment but to secular tendencies toward stagnation in American capitalism. On the NRPB see Marion Clawson, *New Deal Planning – The National Resources Planning Board* (Baltimore, Md.: Johns Hopkins University Press, 1981); and Ira Katznelson and Bruce Pietrkowski, "Rebuilding the American State: Evidence from the 1940s," *Studies in American Political Development* 5 (Fall 1991): 301–39.

23. Roosevelt's Economic Bill of Rights, Four Freedoms, and other programmatic statements made strong declarations of postwar progressive liberal aims. Brody terms Roosevelt's 1944 state of the union address, which proposed an economic bill of rights, the most radical statement Roosevelt ever made. David Brody, "New Deal and World War II," in Braeman et al., eds., *The New Deal*, 283.

24. Bureau of the Census, *Historical Statistics of the United States – Colonial Times to 1970*, D 946–951, "Labor Union Membership and Membership as Percent of Total Labor Force and of Nonagricultural Employment: 1930 to 1970," 177.

tives. But this restraint was not just a strategic response to perceived public support for the war – it reflected workers' judgments about the merit and requirements of the war effort.[25] Factional conflicts in the labor movement and wartime restrictions on labor action further limited mobilization and helped mute the participatory themes articulated by labor in the 1930s.[26]

During the war business elites entered the federal government and especially the war-related agencies, such as the Office of Production Management and the War Production Board. They tended to favor wartime policies at odds with the strongest reformist aims of the New Deal. Yet the involvement of business in the war effort also had an important unintended consequence: It weakened the unqualified opposition that business elites so often expressed toward the new Democratic state in the late 1930s. A subtle process of business incorporation took place within the framework of the Democratic war effort.[27] And the war effort spurred economic improvement. With increased employment, wages and family incomes rose. Productivity grew, and gross national product more than doubled from 1940 to 1945.[28]

Marking the Truman years

With Roosevelt's death, whatever immediate advantages his successor might enjoy were not guaranteed to last beyond the war. Postwar unity

25. The popularity of the war is downplayed or ignored in many critical accounts of wartime industrial relations. Doubtless these authors want to avoid sentimental accounts of patriotic unity. Yet a strong and extensive political unity was constructed regarding the war's conduct and goals. The force of this unity, especially compared with prior and subsequent American experiences of war, was distinctive.

26. These points are emphasized by Nelson Lichtenstein in *Labor's War at Home* (Cambridge University Press, 1982), 178–202. C. Wright Mills criticized the unions for similar reasons in *The New Men of Power: America's Labor Leaders* (New York: Harcourt, Brace, 1948).

27. Fraser and Lichtenstein emphasize the conservative effects of wartime shifts. These shifts are claimed to have incorporated labor elites in arrangements with business and government officials in which labor ultimately had little power – while diminishing democratic initiatives in the trade unions and the broader labor movement. These authors minimize the ways in which wartime pacts compelled business to recognize labor and to acknowledge principles of state intervention they previously had refused. They understate the importance of wartime agreements in permitting a large growth of unions that employers would otherwise have fought vigorously. See Steven Fraser, *Labor Will Rule: Sidney Hillman and the Rise of American Labor* (New York: The Free Press, 1991), 482; and Nelson Lichtenstein, *Labor's War at Home*, 74–110.

28. Bureau of the Census, *Historical Statistics of the United States – Colonial Times to 1970*, F 32–46, "Gross National Product – Summary in Current and Constant (1958) Prices: 1929 to 1970," 228.

was by no means guaranteed in an uncertain atmosphere marked by gloomy economic forecasts.[29] Truman's firmest supporters would not have imagined that he could sustain Roosevelt's popularity and authority.[30] Chosen as a compromise candidate for vice president, he was a relatively consistent supporter of New Deal measures in the Senate, although he never led reform fights.[31] Truman did not join the conservative opposition to the New Deal, and his support for the administration could rarely be assumed of senators from border states. While he was not the choice of the Democratic left as vice-presidential nominee in 1944, those who preferred Henry Wallace accepted Truman.[32]

Truman defended the legacy of the New Deal in major statements on postwar aims. He stressed his commitment to new reform policies, as when in September 1945 he endorsed a full-employment bill, called for comprehensive housing legislation, and proposed increasing the minimum wage and unemployment compensation.[33] Such policies had strong advocates in and around the administration. Although many important progressive liberal officials left, the Democratic order attracted new groups of professionals during and after the war whose political identification was with the progressive Democratic state. There were early reform accomplishments, notably the 1946 passage of the Employment Act.[34]

29. See Fred L. Block, *The Origins of International Economic Disorder: A Study of United States International Monetary Policy from World War II to the Present* (Berkeley: University of California Press, 1977), 34–5.

30. Personal attachment to Roosevelt frequently intensified liberals' criticisms of Truman, as Hamby indicates in *Beyond the New Deal,* 53–85.

31. Truman's career in the Senate thus receives little notice in the main treatments of the New Deal, such as those by Burns, Leuchtenburg, and Schlesinger cited previously. See also Robert J. Donovan, *Conflict and Crisis: The Presidency of Harry S. Truman, 1945–1948* (New York: W. W. Norton, 1977), 26–33.

32. These consultations are discussed in Hamby, *Beyond the New Deal,* 30–33; and Fraser, *Labor Will Rule,* 531.

33. Truman's 21-point message was sent to Congress on September 6, 1945. Much of its content was inspired by Roosevelt's speeches on the need for a postwar economic and social bill of rights, as in his 1944 state of the union address. Truman's message is discussed in Donovan, *Conflict and Crisis,* 110–15.

34. See Stephen Bailey, *Congress Makes a Law – The Story Behind the Employment Act of 1946* (New York: Columbia University Press, 1950), 9–13, 35–40, 92–125. The title of Bailey's book is misleading. Congress – with Robert Wagner again playing a crucial role – was obviously involved. But the main inspiration for the measure came from administration liberals who composed versions of it in 1944 and 1945 and were active in organizing the passage of a weakened form in 1946. The measure was motivated by fear of a postwar relapse into economic stagnation. Business elites did not support any version of this measure. The National Association of Manufacturers opposed it strongly, arguing that it would promote statism and inflation.

Yet after the war Truman at times veered to the right, as Harvard Sitkoff observes: "Indecisiveness and an extreme reliance on conservative advisors also marked Truman's efforts to work with big business during reconversion. . . . Almost an idle spectator, he did little to minimize or counter the governmental influence of corporate power."[35] For some New Deal supporters, Truman's inconsistent policies threatened prior Democratic achievements. Midterm elections in 1946 reduced the size of the progressive liberal group in Congress as Republicans made a strong antistatist case, capitalizing on fatigue with wartime restrictions.[36] By 1947 Truman's position seemed very weak.

Labor relations were a source of trouble for the Truman administration. Near and after the war's end, workers were less willing to accept workplace and wage discipline for the sake of national security. Massive strikes in 1946 involved a larger proportion of workers than those in 1937.[37] These strikes met strong opposition, especially from large companies who renewed their determination to reshape and perhaps eliminate the Wagner Act. The Truman administration opposed strikes in sectors closely related to defense and the process of conversion, such as railroads and mines.[38] When railway unions struck in May 1946, Truman drafted a speech in which he invited his prospective audience to "come along with me and eliminate the Lewises, the Whitneys, the Johnsons, the Communist Bridges and the Russian Senators and Representatives and really make this a government of, by and for the people."[39]

35. Harvard Sitkoff, "Years of the Locust: Interpretations of the Truman Presidency since 1965," in Kirkendall, *The Truman Period as a Research Field*, 84. On Truman's appointment of conservatives, see Hamby, *Beyond the New Deal*, 177–84.

36. The Democratic percentage of all votes cast in House races fell from 57.6 percent in 1944 to 53.4 percent in 1946. Paul David, *Party Strength in the United States, 1872–1970* (Charlottesville: University Press of Virginia, 1972), 302. See also Susan Hartmann, *Truman and the 80th Congress* (Columbia: University of Missouri Press, 1971), 3–11.

37. The increase from 7.2 percent of workers in 1937 to 10.5 percent in 1946 partly reflected the greater resources of the labor movement in 1946. Bureau of the Census, *Historical Statistics*, D 970–985, "Work Stoppages, Workers Involved, Man-Days Idle, Major Issues, and Average Duration: 1881 to 1970," 179. See also Irving Howe and B. J. Widdick, *The UAW and Walter Reuther* (New York: Random House, 1949), 126–8.

38. Truman's responses to the postwar strikes appear in General Motors folder and Coal folder, President's Secretary's File 137 (Strikes), Truman Papers, Truman Library. His labor policies are discussed in Sitkoff, "Years of the Locust," 85; and Arthur F. McClure, *The Truman Administration and the Problems of Postwar Labor, 1945–48* (Rutherford, N.J.: Fairleigh Dickinson University Press, 1969).

39. Cited in Hamby, *Beyond the New Deal*, 77.

Along with public acceptance of unions there was widespread apprehension about labor's use of its new power, a large part of which had been gained through wartime agreements. After the war employers and major currents in the Republican Party fanned antiunion sentiment:

> Management representatives had been so abused and so hampered by government rules and regulations that they had long since discarded the human tendency to exaggerate to prove their points. What they had to say was documented and, if anything, understated. Labor has been permitted and encouraged to grow into a monster supergovernment. The Taft-Hartley law is the first step towards an official discouragement of that trend. . . . As a result, the vote for the Taft-Hartley bill was not a vote against union labor. It was a vote against the tactics of the *leaders* of union labor.[40]

The Taft-Hartley Act was passed in June of 1947.[41] It shifted government policy away from active encouragement of trade union organization. Proponents of the measure defended it in terms of the need for balance, claiming to accept the commitment of the National Labor Relations Act to independent unions. Yet Taft-Hartley's main provisions all restricted union activities, in designating unfair union practices (including refusal to bargain and secondary boycotts), allowing national injunctions against strikes, requiring union officials to sign a non-Communist affidavit, and permitting states to enact laws prohibiting closed shops.[42] Labor fought hard against Taft-Hartley, but Truman's veto was overridden.

The 1948 presidential election promised to break the line of political development initiated in the 1930s. Dewey had done well against Roosevelt four years earlier.[43] The rebellion of the South against Democratic civil rights and social policies was underway. Disaffected Southern Democrats formed a States' Rights Party and ran Senator Strom Thurmond for president.[44] To Truman's left, former vice president Henry Wallace challenged Truman's claim to represent the legacy of the New Deal.

40. Fred A. Hartley, Jr., *Our New National Labor Policy: The Taft-Hartley Act and the Next Steps* (New York: Funk and Wagnalls, 1948), 47–8.
41. The Hartley bill passed the House on April 17, 308 to 107. It was opposed by 22 Republicans, 1 American Laborite, and 84 Democrats. It was supported by 93 Democrats, 79 of them from the South. Taft's bill passed the Senate soon after by a vote of 68 to 24. The final measure passed on June 23, 1947, as H.R. 3020 and Public Law 101. Hartmann, *Truman and the 80th Congress*, 82–90.
42. For a good summary of Taft-Hartley, see R. Alton Lee, *Truman and Taft-Hartley: A Question of Mandate* (Lexington: University of Kentucky Press, 1966), 75–6.
43. George H. Mayer, "The Republican Party, 1932–52," in Schlesinger, *History of U.S. Political Parties*, 2284–7.
44. Robert A. Garson, *The Democratic Party and the Politics of Sectionalism, 1941–48* (Baton Rouge: Louisiana State University Press, 1974), 232–314.

Thurmond and Wallace campaigned energetically, while Dewey concluded that Truman's weakness recommended a cautious approach in
order not to jeopardize a likely Republican victory.[45]

Truman responded with a turn to the left, proposing to defend and
extend the New Deal and sharply attacking the Republicans.[46] As he
took the initiative, the lesser candidates faltered. Thurmond's regional
effort was too stridently a defense of racial privilege to be acceptable
even in parts of the South. Wallace's support dwindled to small left
groups whose links with New Deal constituencies were being severed,
while Truman had the support of most Democratic and progressive
liberal forces and major figures.[47] Toward the end of the campaign it
was clear that Truman would make a much better showing than had
been expected, yet his victory was still a surprise. Truman showed that a
campaign run as a referendum on the Democratic order could win
against major obstacles. After his election Truman failed to achieve
the reform program proposed in 1948, including an alternative labor
law measure.[48]

Winning in 1948

Truman's victory in 1948 resulted from the decision of progressive
liberal forces to conduct an aggressively reformist and populist campaign
in defense of the Democratic order. This choice allowed an energetic use
of Democratic capacities and resources. The 1948 campaign really began

45. A *Newsweek* poll of political writers shortly before the election produced a unani-
   mous prediction of a Dewey victory. *Newsweek* (November 1, 1948): 12.
46. On the 1948 campaign, see the works cited previously by Robert Donovan and
   Alonzo Hamby, as well as Cabell Phillips, *The Truman Presidency: The History of a
   Triumphant Succession* (New York: Macmillan, 1966); and Irwin Ross, *The Loneliest
   Campaign: The Truman Victory of 1948* (New York: New American Library, 1968).
   At the Truman Library, much relevant material appears in the papers of William
   Boyle, India Edwards, Oscar Chapman, Clark Clifford, George Elsey, J. Howard
   McGrath, and John Redding, as well as the papers of the National Committee of the
   Democratic Party.
47. For analyses sympathetic to Wallace see Richard Freeland, *The Truman Doctrine and
   the Origins of McCarthyism* (New York: Alfred A. Knopf, 1971); and Richard J.
   Walton, *Henry Wallace, Harry Truman and the Cold War* (New York: Viking, 1976).
   Views more sympathetic to Truman and the ADA appear in Hamby, *Beyond the New
   Deal*, 147–246; and Stephen Gillon, *Politics and Vision: The ADA and American
   Liberalism, 1947–1985* (New York: Oxford University Press, 1987). On the role of
   the Communist Party, see Robert Starobin, *American Communism in Crisis, 1943–
   1957* (Berkeley: University of California Press, 1972), 155–94.
48. See Hamby, *Beyond the New Deal*, 330–51; and Richard Neustadt, "Congress and
   the Fair Deal: A Legislative Balance Sheet," *Public Policy* 5 (1954): 349–81.

with Truman's veto of the Taft-Hartley Act in 1947. The press opposed his veto of Taft-Hartley and many party leaders preferred to downplay labor issues.[49] But Truman staked out a political position in strong defense of labor and the New Deal legacy.[50]

When Truman proclaimed his intention to renew the reformist dynamic of the New Deal, this crucial shift was not inspired by the Democratic Party per se. In 1947 progressive liberal advisors in the Truman administration met frequently to discuss strategy and policy questions. The central figures were Clark Clifford, the president's adviser, and Oscar Ewing, an administration official who organized the group. Other members were Leon Keyserling of the Council of Economic Advisors, David Noyes of the Labor Department, C. Girard Davidson of the Interior Department, and Charles Murphy of the White House staff.[51] This group was defined by its progressive liberal political outlook. Its members had never been major Democratic Party officials; most entered government service in the 1930s or during World War II.

Even while remaining semi-secret through 1948, this group functioned as a crucial part of the leadership of the Democratic order. Its members helped shape Clark Clifford's long "Memorandum for the President," which proposed an overall political strategy for 1948. This document is one of the crucial texts of the Democratic order. Presented to Truman in November, 1947, it was written under the pressure of the difficult situation that faced the administration. Clifford argued that Truman's election required a turn to the left to counter threats posed by the disaffection of many liberals, only part of which was registered in Henry Wallace's candidacy.[52] Clifford urged Truman to mobilize Democratic constituencies, especially labor: "President Truman and the Democratic Party cannot win without the active support of organized labor. It is

---

49. When the head of the Democratic Party, Senator Howard McGrath of Rhode Island, gave a major speech at the Democratic Pre-Convention Conference in late 1947, he focused Democratic campaign themes on inflation and Soviet expansion. Speech, J. Howard McGrath, Democratic Pre-Convention Conference in Bangor, Maine, 11/30/47, 10/31/47-2/48 folder, DNC File, John M. Redding Papers, Truman Library.

50. Hartmann, *Truman and the 80th Congress*, 85–9.

51. Hamby, *Beyond the New Deal*, 182; and Hartmann, *Truman and the 80th Congress*, 71. Clark Clifford dates the formation of this group as late 1946 or early 1947. Clifford Oral History Interview, Truman Library, 187–205. William L. Batt, Jr., Director of the DNC Research Division, indicates there was little interchange between this group and DNC leaders. Transcript, William L. Batt Oral History Interview, July 26, 1966, Truman Library.

52. Clifford, "Memorandum for the President," 1948 Confidential Memo, Political File (Part 3), Clark Clifford Papers, Truman Library, 10.

Figure 7.1. *Truman, Dewey, and the political spectrum in 1947-1948*

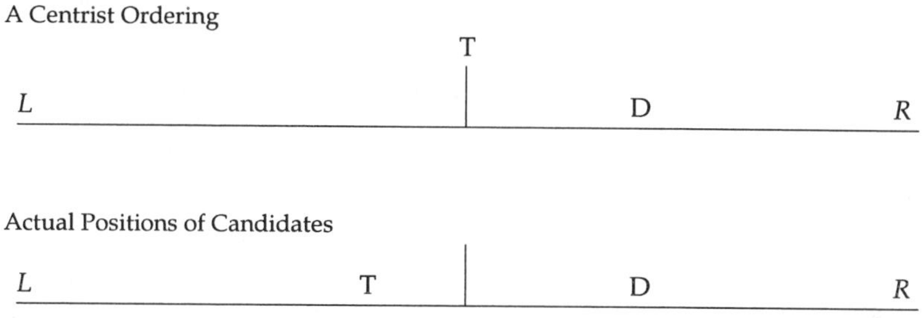

A Centrist Ordering

```
                        T
                        |
L _____|_____ D _____ R
```

Actual Positions of Candidates

```
                        |
L _____ T _____|_____ D _____ R
```

dangerous to assume that labor now has nowhere else to go in 1948. *Labor can stay home.*"[53] He argued for assembling interest groups – Jews, liberals, Catholics, labor, farmers, blacks – based on liberal positions on inflation, housing, taxes, conservation in the West, and civil rights.

Truman had more conservative advisers whose advice he might have heeded. He might well have chosen to fight Dewey for the center by moving to the right. Instead he sought to win by moving to the left and reshaping the political spectrum in that direction, rather than trying to place himself just to the left of Dewey. The aim was to reshape the political spectrum and in doing so to place Dewey farther to the right, near the fringe of political legitimacy. Truman could then draw support extending all the way from a point to the left of but close to Dewey – while placing himself slightly left of the center of the new spectrum he had defined. For this approach to work, Truman's campaign had to draw a line close to Dewey on his left and through political argument give that line two properties. First, Dewey could not cross it without placing his candidacy in jeopardy by alienating supporters on his right. Second, a significant number of people relatively close to Dewey on his left would judge that despite their apparent proximity to Dewey, Truman's basic direction was more acceptable. (See Figure 7.1.)

The campaign adopted Clifford's approach in contrasting dynamic interest groups to a weak Democratic Party:

> The truth is that the old "party organization" control is gone forever. Better education, the rise of the mass pressure group, the economic depression of the 30's, the growth of government functions – all these have contributed to the downfall of "the organization." Tammany, Hague, Kelley and the

53. Clifford, "Memorandum for the President," 8.

rest of the straight party leaders, while still important, are no longer omnipotent, no longer able to determine the issues. For practical political purposes, they are moribund; they cannot be relied on to do the job alone. They have been supplanted in large measure by the pressure groups.[54]

Clifford proposed bypassing much of the organized Democratic Party. Instead, a progressive liberal administration would rely on mobilized interest groups and friendly party and Congressional forces. His memorandum was not always right: "It is inconceivable that any policies initiated by the Truman administration no matter how 'liberal' could so alienate the South in the next year that it would revolt."[55] Its core insight was to see the promise of a Democratic course centered on linking a progressive national administration and popular interest groups and movements – this approach would persist throughout the Democratic order. The campaign should start from the administration – Clifford recommended that leadership of the 1948 campaign be taken by a small working committee in the administration that would not be public (much less a formal part of the Democratic Party).[56]

The early campaign aimed to establish Truman's legitimacy as a presidential candidate by identifying him with the state and the New Deal. In 1946 and 1947 and well into the election year many sections of the Democratic Party and closely-linked political groups were eager for a substitute. James Loeb, head of the new Americans for Democratic Action, complained: "Harry Truman is ADA's great frustration." In April, 1948, the ADA commended Truman while calling for an open convention:

> We honor President Truman for his unswerving support of the European Recovery Program, for his courageous advocacy of civil rights, and for his wise recommendations for domestic economic policy. We appreciate his brave rearguard action in defense of our social and labor legislation against the onslaughts of a reactionary Congress. But we cannot overlook the fact that poor appointments and faltering support of his aides have resulted in a failure to rally the people behind policies which in large measure we wholeheartedly support. The ADA feels that an open Democratic convention will serve the best interests of the country. We feel strongly that this Nation has a right to call upon men like Dwight D. Eisenhower and William O. Douglas if the people so choose.[57]

---

54. Clifford, "Memorandum for the President," 6–7.
55. Clifford, "Memorandum for the President," 3.
56. Clifford, "Memorandum for the President," 40–3.
57. Loeb is quoted in Hamby, *Beyond the New Deal*, 225. Many Democrats hoped Eisenhower would be their candidate both in 1948 and 1952. ADA "Statement on

The lack of party support could not deny Truman the nomination. No coherent Democratic Party could deliberate autonomously and decide to replace him. Thus no feasible means of replacing Truman existed even when much of the Democratic Party preferred to do so.

In facing a disaffected party and an uncertain electorate, Truman's efforts to survive drew him toward affirming basic Democratic commitments. He made several major appointments of individuals identified with the New Deal, and his 1948 State of the Union Address pledged to renew and expand Democratic reformism.[58] Truman rarely made his party affiliation the center of appeals for support, and political leadership was not in the hands of the party.[59] The campaign was organized by the administration and led by Truman's political advisors.[60] They were mainly employees of the executive, with careers in business or law, who campaigned for Truman and what they understood as the legacy of the New Deal. No one in this leading group – continuous with the 1947 group described above – was mainly a Democratic Party figure, though several were associated with the Democratic Party Research Division.[61] The campaign was run largely as a referendum on Truman's record and its links to the New Deal, against the Republican 80th Congress. It was less a battle of party against party than the campaign of an administration and a broader progressive liberal leadership against the leadership of a minority Republican Party. Truman denounced "special privileges" and defended the New Deal:

Political Policy," April 11, 1948, in Political File 1948 (2), W. L. Batt folder, Papers of Clark Clifford, Truman Library.

58. *Public Papers of the Presidents of the United States – Harry S. Truman, 1948* (Washington, D.C.: Government Printing Office, 1964), 3. The appointments included David Lilienthal and Samuel Rosenman; Rosenman helped draft the Democratic platform and Truman's 1949 state of the union message.

59. The Democratic Party focused on attacking Republicans; beyond that, DNC press releases amounted to lists of federal programs in important states, attributing those programs to the recent progressive administrations. Press Release, Publicity Division, Democratic National Committee, n.d., Folder Presidential Campaign '48 (2), Box 8, Redding Papers, Truman Library. Clark Clifford later claimed that a lackluster DNC effort on Truman's behalf was caused partly by the belief that he was sure to lose. Clark Clifford Oral History Interview, Truman Library, 317.

60. George Elsey, Clifford's assistant, later recalled that links between the White House and the DNC were informal and went through Truman's appointment secretary, Matt Connelly. The DNC had no means of monitoring the actions of the progressive leadership group in the administration, much less controlling it. Transcript, George Elsey Oral History Interview, 1964, 1969, 1970, Truman Library, 52–60.

61. Hamby lists the main participants as Oscar Chapman, Jonathan Daniels, Samuel Rosenman, Charlie Murphy, David Bell, David Lloyd, Leon Keyserling, David Noyes, Albert Carr, Clark Clifford, and George Elsey, in *Beyond the New Deal*, 248.

There is just one big issue: it is the special interests against the people. And the President, being elected by all the people, represents the people. You have now a special interests Congress.[62]

The Republican politicians don't like the New Deal. They never have liked the New Deal, and they would like to get rid of it – repeal it – put it out of existence.[63]

William Batt, Director of the Research Division of the Democratic National Committee, urged a progressive pro-New Deal focus similar to what Clifford proposed. The campaign should strive:

. . . to gain and solidify support from three large groups in the nation which can swing the election one way or the other, and are already predominantly Democratic in their inclinations – the working people, the veterans, and the Negroes. . . . To present the President as a crusader rallying the people to save the tremendous social gains made under the New Deal and carried forward by his administration in a difficult postwar period.[64]

A new popular campaign

In the dominant image of the 1948 campaign Truman spoke up for the common man and denounced Republicans from a railroad car in a small town. Many accounts treat Truman's campaigning as stirring and attractively reminiscent of an era of extensive direct contact between candidates and voters.[65] This image has been brightly redrawn in David McCullough's biography of Truman:

"I want to see the people," [Truman] had said. There would be three major tours: first cross-country to California again, for fifteen days; then a six-day tour of the Middle West, followed by a final, hard-hitting ten days in the big population centers of the Northeast and a return trip home to Missouri. . . . No President in history had ever gone so far in quest of support from

62. Speech, June 17, 1948, Jefferson City, Missouri, Harry S. Truman – Western Trip, Speeches folder, Political File 61, PSF, Truman Papers, Truman Library.
63. From a speech in Akron, Ohio, October 11, 1948, cited in Hamby, *Beyond the New Deal*, 249.
64. Memo, William L. Batt, Jr., to Clark Clifford, August 11, 1948, Folder W. L. Batt, Political File 1948 (2), Clark Clifford Papers, Truman Library.
65. Robert Donovan dissents from what might be called the romantic-popular view: "It was the same old Truman campaign: sharp speeches fairly criticizing Republican policy and defending New Deal liberalism, mixed with sophistries, bunkum piled higher than haystacks, and demagoguery tooting merrily down the track. Truman's attacks were rough. Still a good deal of his rhetoric smacked of the blarney of old campaigns for Board of Alderman." Donovan, *Conflict and Crisis*, 425.

the people. . . Nor would any presidential candidate ever again attempt such a campaign by railroad.[66]

Of course Truman wanted to make his case as widely as possible. But the last sentence quoted above suggests the need for a less literalistic reading of the campaign.

Truman's campaign was a modern popular (and populist) effort, relying on the administration's use of state capacities and modern media (mass circulation newspapers and magazines, radio, telephones, and television).[67] Incumbency was a resource to be used in ratifying Truman and his administration as the modern and popular-democratic course.[68]

Was Truman's touring simply an effort to talk directly with the citizenry? He claimed to have traveled 31,700 miles, during which he delivered 356 speeches heard by 12 to 15 million people.[69] The last figures were exaggerated. Yet even if as many people saw and heard Truman's campaign as he claimed, much of the basic character of Truman's railroad tours was a stylized representation of a certain kind of American campaign effort.

A major aim of these tours was to present to the nation the image of a combative popular politician. Stories about Truman's efforts (in the press, on the radio, and now on television) reached far more people than the trips themselves. The political images conveyed by these stories were important purposes of events directed at the entire population. Even those who actually attended one of Truman's speeches were watching Truman reenact an old-fashioned popular campaign. His tours were a means of overcoming two obstacles: weak or recalcitrant party organizations, and highly critical press accounts. Extensive party work was not

66. McCullough, *Truman*, 654–5.
67. Opinion studies done in 1948 and 1952 were motivated partly by concern about whether the use of mass media in political campaigns might replicate some features of fascist regimes. The main studies minimized the effects of mass media on citizens, arguing that any such effects were mediated first through personal networks and then through party forms. Given the diverse forms of political participation in a complex society, the argument went, media do not have major effects. See Bernard Berelson, Paul Lazarsfeld, and William McPhee, *Voting: A Study of Opinion Formation in a Presidential Campaign* (Chicago, Ill.: University of Chicago Press, 1954).
68. Here Richard Neustadt's famous formulations understate the power of the presidency. He argues that because American political institutions are multiply divided the president cannot much command; he must seek to persuade. This downplays the crucial forms of power that lie between issuing commands and seeking to persuade – including much of what an incumbent like Truman did in renewing the Democratic order. Richard Neustadt, *Presidential Power: The Politics of Leadership from FDR to Carter* (New York: Wiley, 1980), 26–43.
69. Harry S. Truman, *Memoirs: Years of Trial and Hope*, vol. 2, (New York: Time, 1956), 219.

required for the railroad tours. And they presented a positive image of his campaign and personality to a wide national audience, even in the same papers that attacked him.[70] Such tours would not be repeated, as McCullough notes, but for reasons he misses. Future presidential candidates facing time and resource pressures turned more directly to the rapidly growing national electronic media. And the full simulation of a genuine old-fashioned campaign, once done in earnest, populist high style, could not be duplicated without taking the risk of seeming to be purely cynical.

In 1948 the Truman administration's presidential campaign relied on regional and national media. The Democratic National Committee devoted more attention to radio broadcasts than to organizing precinct activities or sustaining links with state parties. The national convention garnered substantial television coverage, and the campaign relied heavily on radio publicity. Via such efforts the Democratic order was represented as popular – it proposed direct contact unmediated by conventional political forms – and modern: the Democratic use of new campaign technologies signified a general commitment to progress.[71]

The Democratic Party in 1948

The Democratic Party was fragmented in 1948 as factional conflicts arose in states where powerful left-liberal forces opposed Truman and where a strong segregationist conservatism was moving into political opposition.[72] By "Democratic Party" I refer to its formal national structure, state and local party organizations, Democratic elected officials,

70. The weakness of the Democratic Party organization and the hostility of much of the press to Truman also encouraged reliance on radio in the campaign. These issues are discussed in a memoir of the 1948 campaign by John Redding, the publicity director of the Democratic National Committee, in *Inside the Democratic Party* (New York: Bobbs-Merrill, 1958), 244.

71. William Batt argued, "The President can maintain continuous contact with the people through the one wide channel of communication always open to him – the radio." Memo, William L. Batt to Clark Clifford, July 22, 1948, Folders – Miscellaneous Political File 1948, Political File 20, Clifford Papers, Truman Library. Democratic campaign materials emphasize radio and then press relations, with far less attention to Democratic Party organization. Radio coverage was national, television coverage included Washington, Baltimore, Philadelphia, New York, and several New Jersey cities. Radio Coverage Democratic Convention (1948) folder, Television Coverage of Convention folder, Nationwide NBC Broadcast (1/25/48) folder, all in Publicity Division Files, Democratic National Committee: Records Pertaining to Appointments, Publicity, and Research, 1943–52, Truman Library.

72. When political records were kept by state in Truman's papers, Clifford's papers, and Democratic National Committee papers, I again devoted primary attention to California, Georgia, Illinois, Iowa, Michigan, and New York.

and the most active supporters of the party at all levels. I do not include all registered Democrats or all likely Democratic voters – the party was not a mass membership organization.

By definition all Democratic members of the Senate and House were as elected officials part of the party. Yet Democrats in Congress were politically divided and not constrained to act together on crucial questions. Some Democrats in Congress were mainly identified with that institution and sought to increase and coordinate Democratic power within it. Others were linked primarily to the administration (and to federal agencies); yet others were linked primarily to state and local Democratic Party organizations. These institutional divisions intersected ideological differences, which by 1948 guaranteed conflict among loyalist Democrats and placed part of the Southern Congressional delegation outside the boundaries of the Democratic order.[73]

There were such sharp divisions in the party that it had difficulty in acting as a unified agent. In major states such as California, state Democratic Parties seemed ready to explode. Former California attorney general Robert Kenny supported Henry Wallace in 1948; in 1947 he addressed a Democrats for Wallace Caucus in Fresno:

> Will a fight for Wallace split the Democratic Party? The answer is no, it will strengthen the Democratic Party! The Democratic Party was united in 1944 – and in 1940. It was united within itself, and united with the independent liberals who hold the balance of power on Election Day. What has destroyed the unity of the Democratic Party is Mr. Truman's abandonment of the policies of Franklin Roosevelt. Party unity can only be restored by a return to the Roosevelt principles, as enunciated by Henry Wallace.[74]

Factionalism on the right was at least as consequential. Conflicts in Southern states sharpened after a relatively strong civil rights plank

73. Southern Democrats who were generally sympathetic to the New Deal and even supportive of some of Truman's Fair Deal proposals moved outside the Democratic order when they made clear a willingness to destroy Truman's candidacy on grounds that the national Democratic Party and federal government were intruding into race relations with aims that were unacceptably egalitarian. Thus Thurmond and many of his supporters crossed into active opposition. See Garson, *Democratic Party and Sectionalism,* 241–60.

74. Robert W. Kenny, Speech to Democrats for Wallace Caucus, Fresno, July 19, 1947, Press Releases and Statements, 1946–48 folder, Political File 19, Clifford Papers, Truman Library. In 1946 Kenny ran for governor in California and failed to win even the Democratic primary, which Earl Warren captured with over 55 percent of the vote. Much additional material on the deep and bitter splits in the California party is in Political File, Box 54, PSF, and Political Business by State, Boxes 976–7, Official File 300. Splits in the Democratic Party in New York fill up many pages of correspondence in New York, Political Business by State, Official File 300. In New York,

passed at the Democratic National Convention.[75] Calls for more "responsible" parties appeared after 1948 when the Fair Deal foundered in a recalcitrant Democratic Congress due to Southern resistance and the inconsistent support for administration efforts by many non-Southern Democrats.[76] Thus some liberal complaints that the party was weak and divided meant calling for procedural changes that would weaken Southern conservatives, especially in Congress. Many liberals who were not in deep disagreement with Truman simply felt he could not win; loyalty to the Democratic order meant finding another leader.

The national party was not a force capable of directing the political order. No major efforts were made to build a more powerful national Democratic party apparatus in the late 1940s.[77] Top party positions

factional conflict was more likely to appear as organizational division, linked to the American Labor Party and Liberal Party, while in California, factions remained in the Democratic Party until the Wallace campaign.

75. William Berman recounts the platform amendment conflict in *The Politics of Civil Rights in the Truman Administration* (Columbus: Ohio State University Press, 1970), 107–12. The Rhode Island delegation, led by Senator McGrath, opposed the civil rights plank proposed by Hubert Humphrey. The plank passed was stronger than Truman preferred, though acceptable to him. For accounts of the splits in Southern states, see Garson, *Democratic Party and Sectionalism*, 255, 279–301. Sharp political divisions in Georgia are recorded in Political Business by State, Official File 300, Boxes 976–7, Truman Library.

76. The idea was that stronger, more disciplined parties would be more apt to yield sustained reform. The classic statement is *Toward a More Responsible Two-Party System*, a report of The Committee on Political Parties, American Political Science Association (New York: Rinehart and Company, 1950). The drafting committee included Clarence Berdahl, Bertram Gross, Louise Overacker, E. E. Schattschneider, and Fritz Morstein Marx. The argument for responsible parties was connected with a critique of the Democratic Party in the South as a particularly nonresponsible organization, regarding both the national party and the citizens of its states. Thus in 1952, Bertram Gross, then Research Director of the DNC, gave Truman a report on the presidential vote in the 1930s and 1940s, emphasizing that "in all but the 1948 election, the Democrats had an 'excess' of electoral votes considerably larger than the total Southern electoral vote." The implication was that Southern political pressure on a national Democratic administration could be rejected without great risk. This point would have been valid if the gulf between Southern Democrats and non-Southern conservative Democrats were much greater than it really was, and if the Democratic position in non-Southern states could be presumed to remain as secure as in Roosevelt's landslides. Letter, Bertram Gross to Harry S. Truman, May 16, 1952, Research folder, Political File, PSF, Truman Library.

77. No evidence of such efforts appears in the popular histories or monographs on Democratic politics in 1947–8. Nor is there evidence of them in the state-level party records of the Democratic Party; the records of the Democratic National Committee; the memoirs and records of leading Democratic officials, such as J. Howard McGrath and John Redding; and Truman's own political files at the Truman Library.

were far behind administration positions and elected offices in terms of power and prestige. There is little evidence of party-based efforts at new organizing or mobilization. Local and state Democratic Party organizations persisted yet there was a decline in the number and strength of organizations able to distribute large amounts of patronage and determine electoral outcomes reliably. The nationalizing tendencies of the New Deal, complemented by those of the war, were weakening local Democratic organizations. Where they survived, or where new ones had developed in the 1930s, their dependence on the state increased and their capacity to recruit new support was modest.[78]

In the 1948 campaign the Democratic Party was mainly a publicity and organizational committee for the presidential campaign. It sent out press releases, distributed information about issues to party activists, and conducted a get-out-the-vote operation. Its distinct political contribution was modest.[79] The national party was a small, poorly funded organization acting as a subordinate campaign administrator. Where the party had a public voice, it argued for a Democratic vote to support programs imbedded in the Democratic state, stressing that recent Democratic administrations had produced economic and social recovery.[80]

The Democratic Party was also narrow in the composition of its leadership. There were few nominations of trade unionists, women, or blacks for major national positions in the party (or for Senate seats or Cabinet positions). The Women's Division of the national party had several important leaders, notably India Edwards. But the national leaders in the Democratic National Committee and its Research Division were men.[81] Democratic leaders in the organized party and Congress were typically white lawyers and businessmen. There is little reason to

78. Most accounts of party organization complained that it was terrible, without making clear what could be done. Internal reports indicate that Democratic precinct organization and statewide organization were poor. Memo, "Precinct to President – Confidential," Publicity Division Files 12, Precinct to President folder, Records of the Democratic National Committee, Truman Library.

79. Truman's memoirs give little credit to the work of the Democratic Party. Truman, *Memoirs,* vol. 2, 206–22.

80. This is the main message of the campaign materials compiled by John H. Redding, Presidential Campaign Material #2, Publicity Division folder, Democratic National Committee File, Papers of John H. Redding, Truman Library.

81. Truman appointed no women to Cabinet positions. After the departure of Frances Perkins, one of her replacements as Secretary of Labor, Maurice Tobin, was the only unionist at that level. There were certainly a sufficient number of qualified women – and union leaders – to allow several plausible nominations. On the lack of women nominees, see Cynthia Harrison, *On Account of Sex: The Politics of Women's Issues, 1945–1968* (Berkeley: University of California Press, 1988), 56.

expect a party leadership to replicate the social features of its electoral support, but it is worth noting that people from several of the major popular constituencies of the Democratic order were strikingly absent from the top of the Democratic Party.

The party's reliance on the state

The Democratic Party's limited political role was linked to its dependence on the state. The centralizing elements of World War II had weakened nonstate political forms, and the population movements of the war years eroded Democratic networks. During the war millions of people moved to enter military service, and many did not return to take up permanent residence in the cities they left. Within regions the massive departures for military service caused many further relocations, as with those who moved to take positions vacated by departing workers, or with families whose loss of wage-earning members led to a change in residence. The demand for labor to replace departed workers and to meet the needs of war production encouraged major interregional migrations, as into Southern California.

The party's reliance on the state derived mainly from Democratic efforts to retain power, as turning toward the state so often seemed the most effective way to win important political conflicts. Across the country in 1947–8 Democratic forces faced a choice. They could try to reinvigorate (or create) local party organizations. Or they could rely on Democratic officials' arguments in favor of a Democratic vote, and on the practices of state agencies that could be highlighted to show the virtues of Democratic rule. Given limited time and resources, reasonable immediate choices about the most effective options led to relying on the Democratic state (both its officials and agencies). Democratic activists needed to use whatever resources were available to fight their battles.[82]

Party reliance on the state was consistent with progressive liberal commitments that approved an energetically interventionist state. This course gained support from the top – in the leading strategic role of the Clifford group – and in cities and states where Democratic officials sought to publicize national achievements and call favorable attention to their local implications. State-oriented choices seemed to be reasonable ways to address urgent political dangers – thus relying on the state arose mainly out of reasonable strategic behavior by Democratic and

---

82. State Democratic Party records, Democratic National Committee records, and the campaign accounts of Hamby, Miller, Phillips, and Redding show no serious efforts to build local Democratic organizations.

progressive liberal actors. These choices increased the relative strength of the state. Democratic actors defined their interests in terms of a political commitment to Democratic progressive liberalism. They did not set out to produce an enervating reliance on the state; they were trying to defeat their opponents. They aimed to defend progressive liberal achievements and to protect and advance their own positions and careers.

The shape of the Democratic victory

The Democratic victory in 1948 had the same basic electoral shape as previous Democratic presidential successes, although Truman's victory was much narrower.[83] Thurmond and Wallace together gained almost 5 percent of the national vote. Even had Truman gained all their votes, the result would have been closer than Roosevelt's narrowest win. Yet Democratic campaigning along with Republican incapacity limited Democratic defectors and put them out of Republican reach when the core of the New Deal was in question, even though the voting rate declined. No major Democratic constituencies outside the South were lost.[84] The Democratic advantage in the working class remained substantial; because of reduced support in other classes, 1948 appears as a moment of sharp class polarization (in American if not comparative terms).[85] There

83. Truman won the popular vote by 8.1 percent; Roosevelt's margin was 14.9 percent in 1944. Assuming that two-thirds of the 5 percent of the vote received by Thurmond and Wallace would have gone to Truman had they not run, and the remainder to Dewey (all from Thurmond), Truman's margin would have been about 10 percent. Thurmond received thirty-nine electoral votes; Wallace's votes probably cost Truman New York. Paul David, *Party Strength*, 302. Bureau of the Census, *Historical Statistics of the United States – Colonial Times to 1970* Y 79–83, "Electoral and Popular Vote Cast for President, by Political Party: 1789 to 1968"; Y 135–186, "Popular Vote Cast for President, State and Political Party: 1836 to 1968," 1073, 1077–8.

84. The Wallace vote was not potentially Republican, but with Thurmond the situation was more complicated. Where Thurmond did not have the official ballot identification of the Democratic Party, he lost; in states where he did, he won. After 1948, some Thurmond voters remained Democrats in state and local races but voted Republican for president. See Everett Carll Ladd and Charles D. Hadley, *Transformations of the American Party System: Political Coalitions from the New Deal to the 1970s* (New York: W. W. Norton, 1975), 135–41.

85. The election of 1948 occurred prior to full-scale public opinion research on national elections at the University of Michigan. Thus it is hard to establish a consistent series from 1948 to the present. Robert Alford's analysis of class and party, based on a manual/nonmanual dichotomy, found that the extent of "class voting" – the preference of manual workers for Democratic candidates – was similar in 1944, 1948, and 1952, though somewhat larger in 1948. Even so it remained modest in comparative terms. Alford's analysis risks overstating class voting by grouping black and white

was also a Democratic edge in the urban professional middle classes. Blacks increasingly identified with the Democratic order, partly because Truman's civil rights policies promised to oppose some flagrant forms of racial inequality.[86] Democratic candidates continued to do better among Catholics than among Protestants. Even with Thurmond's candidacy, the Democratic Party did better in the South than did the Republicans.

How did Democratic voters make their choice? They did so mainly out of political commitment to a new regime. That commitment was often organized through identification with groups that had benefited from the policies of the Democratic order. To distinguish between the Democratic Party and the broader political order provides a framework for assessing studies that surveyed American citizens from the late 1940s on and found stable voting patterns linked to durable party identities. The most influential accounts argued that politics was organized by deep partisan commitments rather than ideological divisions.[87] But these studies had trouble explaining the origins and substance of party identification. In the University of Michigan study of the 1948 election, two questions yielded responses that are not easy to reconcile with the core claims of the famous later studies. When asked, "What made you decide to vote the way you did?", 27 percent mentioned party allegiance – a significant figure, but less than the 36 percent who emphasized Truman's issue positions. When the entire sample was asked why people voted for Truman, only 3 percent mentioned party allegiance. Voters identified Truman with (in order) "the common man," labor, farmers, and "Negroes."[88] People whose vote was defined mainly by Democratic Party commitments almost certainly made up more than 3 percent of the electorate, but such responses make one doubt that their numbers were large.

voters together. Over the course of the Democratic order, increases in black voting also appeared as increases in Democratic affiliation within the working class, given the class position of most blacks. The question is whether this should be understood as class voting by black members of the working class or as racial voting by working-class blacks. If the latter formulation is partially correct, then even Alford's formulations about the modest extent of class voting in the United States should be trimmed. See Robert Alford, *Party and Society: The Anglo-American Democracies* (Chicago, Ill.: Rand McNally, 1963), 225, 234–5, 289–90.

86. A large black majority turned out for Truman in urban areas, where he gained almost 70 percent of the black vote and Wallace less than 10 percent. Berman, *Politics of Civil Rights*, 128–9.

87. It was further argued that party loyalty was a lens through which issues were perceived and even defined. Angus Campbell et al., *The American Voter* (Chicago, Ill.: Midway Reprint, University of Chicago Press, 1980), 135.

88. Angus Campbell and Robert Kahn, *The People Elect a President* (Ann Arbor: Survey Research Center, Institute for Social Research, University of Michigan, 1952), 44, 51, 53.

Voting and opinion data suggest that Democratic voting signified political identification with the direction of successive Democratic administrations, although no such question was asked directly. This sort of Democratic identification – with a political order rather than the party per se – meant support for the social security and welfare measures of the 1930s, for growth-oriented economic policies concerned with sustaining demand, and for the right of independent unions to exist. Democratic commitments mainly referred to the political order, often in conjunction with group attachments. Such people as union members and professionals in occupations closely linked to the state voted Democratic as members of groups they regarded as having benefited from Democratic practices.

It is misleading to blur the distinction between identification with the regime and with the party, and then consider both attachments as "partisan" in a narrower party sense. But this approach often appears in analyses of the late 1940s, as in *The American Voter:* "It is likely, then, that in 1948 the electorate responded to current elements of politics very much in terms of its existing partisan loyalties."[89] Yet Democratic loyalties were new for many voters, either because they had changed their views in the previous decade or had entered the electorate in the 1930s or 1940s. In becoming Democratic voters the attraction of the party was subordinate to the appeal of the programs and public principles of Democratic administrations. Thus many people voted for the Democratic Party as a way to approve crucial elements of recent Democratic administrations. A grudging recognition of this reality encouraged parts of the opposition to accept basic Democratic positions on social security and labor relations. The political order had built an asymmetrical terrain of conflict; those who rejected its premises could be defined as agents of disorder (in the economy and labor relations) and destruction (of the progressive state).

Survey questions in the late 1940s did not name and ask about a Democratic order, but asked about the president, the parties, and major interest groups. The results were often interpreted by analysts of public opinion and electoral behavior to mean that in voting, the driving political force was party attachment. This attachment was conceived as basic affective ties gained in a relatively unreflective manner. Without a concept of regime or political order, claiming a key role for affective party loyalties was at least as plausible as proposing that voters were self-conscious adherents of the party, given the latter's weakness.

The main voting and opinion studies of the 1940s and 1950s also argued that partisan commitments were not articulate or coherent

89. Campbell et al., *American Voter*, 532.

enough to be deemed ideological. American voters were regarded as far more affectively partisan than ideological, as they seemed to lack explicit, structured views of politics that shaped their positions on particular issues.[90] This argument was misconceived. Relating ideological consistency to party rather than regime commitments made it likely that the thematic content of voters' judgments would be understated. If there were a significant degree of ideological consistency, it would be unlikely to emerge in questions about a factionalized party organization (with which many voters had little direct contact). How could one have an ideologically consistent loyalty to a sharply divided party? Some Democratic Party forces were on the verge of leaving the Democratic order while others argued for major new reform measures. The Democratic order's discourses were much less about party than about the appropriate role of government. They advocated government efforts to provide social security and encourage growth, and openness to new political group efforts. After Roosevelt, Democratic loyalty meant identification with policies and principles that had taken shape as agencies, programs, and organized groups. Moreover, the standards that political judgment had to meet to be considered "ideology" were too stringent: Even if a question about regime commitments had been asked, assent to the overall direction of a political order would not have qualified as an ideological view.[91]

If Democratic Party attachments were longstanding and deep in the late 1940s, and the party was headed by reasonably competent political

90. Campbell et al., *American Voter*, 192–216. This argument is summarized clearly in Norman H. Nie, Sidney Verba, and John R. Petrocik, *The Changing American Voter* (Cambridge, Mass.: Harvard University Press, 1976), 16–20.

91. Commitment to a political order does not appear among the ways in which political affiliations are conceived in *The American Voter*. The choices are depicted as (primordial) affective party ties, systematized political ideology, or (primitive) self-interest. These choices make it hard to navigate a political reality in which individuals did not adhere self-consciously to a fully elaborated group of principles, but did make political judgments according to general criteria that included substantive elements. A key move in the Michigan studies limits the concept of ideology to systematic programmatic formulations: "An 'ideology' may be seen as a particularly elaborate, close-woven, and far-ranging structure of attitudes." Given this exclusive definition, political commitments were separated into party loyalties and self-interest: "In sum, then, the pattern of responses to our domestic issues is best understood if we discard our notions of ideology and think rather in terms of primitive self-interest." This approach misses most of what the concept of ideology (whether or not that term is used) can illuminate in calling attention to a structured discursive order. A discourse exists whether or not all individuals replicate its elements precisely in their own speech; it is interwoven with and helps to define self-interest. Campbell et al., *American Voter*, 192, 205.

entrepreneurs, one would expect major efforts to build new forms of party organization. There would be attempts to squeeze every possible organizational and electoral benefit out of strong Democratic loyalties – to win presidential elections, win local elections, increase party resources, and expand influence when party and administration policy preferences diverged. The lack of serious efforts at party renewal indicates that the Democratic vote was linked to substantive political aims and could not readily be transformed into active support for the Democratic Party per se. No very deep reservoir of Democratic affective ties seems to have existed apart from political support for the Democratic order.

The centrality of the Democratic state

From 1947 to 1949 the national state was central to preserving the programmatic and policy direction established in the 1930s. It also served the immediate aims of Democratic officeholders and leaders. The Democratic order was sustained through links between party and state that tended to merge the former into the latter, under the direction of the federal executive. Progressive liberal Democratic forces in the party organization identified with and were often tightly connected to this Democratic state. State officials and agencies guided the work of sustaining political support, acting as the general staff of the political order.

The state's central role grew out of the substantive commitments and strategic choices of Democratic elites and supporters discussed previously. The negative side of these choices was the inability of nonstate Democratic forces to replace the state in supplying political resources. The fragmentation and political weakness of the national Democratic Party meant it could not be a workable political alternative to relying on the state. Other nonstate Democratic forces were also drawn toward the state. With labor, this was in large part a result of its accomplishments over the previous decade. With civil rights forces, the weight of explicit and legal modes of racial discrimination and the hostility of large parts of the Democratic Party made engagement with the courts and the administration essential.[92]

92. For a critical view of the unions' reliance on the state, see Christopher Tomlins, *The State and the Unions: Labor Relations, Law, and the Organized Labor Movement in America, 1880–1960* (Cambridge University Press, 1985), 285–318. On the centrality of an ambivalent state in civil rights politics, see Berman, *Politics of Civil Rights* 67–77; on the NAACP's legal strategy to desegregate education, see Mark V. Tushnet, *The NAACP's Legal Strategy against Segregated Education, 1925–1950* (Chapel Hill: University of North Carolina Press, 1987).

Building the Democratic order had yielded a national state that was a key location for political leadership and a continual pole of attraction for Democratic elites. Efforts to maintain the reforms of the 1930s enhanced the state's predominant role.[93] One might even say that much of the Democratic bloc had become institutionalized as the national state. Thus in the late 1940s the Democratic order no longer appears as a regime-in-formation, but as a network of agencies, political currents, and organizations within and close to the state.[94] Beyond the growth of the state during the 1930s, the wartime experience and changed international situation were important in expanding it. The war entailed a broad expansion of (Democratic) state activity in allocating labor and resources, organizing military participation, and coordinating production. Wartime economic needs justified increased taxation. The success of the war under Democratic auspices created new reserves of political legitimacy that were partly passed on to Truman. The postwar growth of American international power entailed a further expansion of the state.[95]

In the late 1940s three features of this Democratic state stand out. First, it reached widely into social life. Truman achieved few of the major reforms he proposed before or after his election, although significant postwar efforts in housing and urban policy did occur. But the main programs of the New Deal persisted and often grew, although the sweeping wartime proposals for social welfare provision and labor market regulation made by the National Resources Planning Board and other left progressives were not enacted.

Moreover, major programs tied to the war were initiated, including veterans' benefits programs. The G.I. Bill, passed in 1944, entitled veter-

---

93. The identification of the state with a popular Democratic order even reduced the force of antistatism, though the latter flared up dramatically in the late 1940s. Southern opposition to the Democratic order had a strongly antistatist character in the 1940s, especially when the Truman administration began to take up civil rights issues. See Numan V. Bartley and Hugh D. Graham, *Southern Politics and the Second Reconstruction* (Baltimore, Md.: Johns Hopkins University Press, 1975), 24–80.

94. On postwar state agencies see Louis Galambos, ed., *The New American State: Bureaucracies and Policies since World War II* (Baltimore, Md.: Johns Hopkins University Press, 1987).

95. International pressures for the growth of the state ranged from the need for enlarged military capacities to the need for refined means of making policy on questions that were not priorities before World War II (e.g., what to do about Greece). Pressure for expansion is clear in accounts by critics and defenders of the postwar role of the United States. In addition to the works by Barton Bernstein and Joyce Kolko and Gabriel Kolko cited previously, see John Lewis Gaddis, *The United States and the Origins of the Cold War, 1941–47* (New York: Columbia University Press, 1972).

ans to federal assistance with education, housing, and health care.[96] As roughly 16 million people served in the war effort (of a total population of 130 million), such programs extended widely across the population. They had deep effects on the lives of recipients. Postwar veterans' programs were not universalistic social welfare programs. But they did expand the national state's role in providing crucial public goods. New federal commitments in education and the housing market outlasted and grew beyond the provision of special benefits to veterans, and had major effects on economic and social institutions. Thus veterans' benefits in housing encouraged demographic shifts and the restructuring of the housing industry, and accelerated suburbanization. And veterans' benefits contributed to a major expansion of higher education that aided the construction of new institutions and reshaped older ones.

On several occasions Truman gave in to antistatist pressure after the war, as when he dismantled price controls more rapidly than many progressive liberals would have liked.[97] Yet such concessions occurred in a framework defined by his commitment to maintaining a new Democratic state. Nondefense federal spending totalled roughly 14 billion dollars in 1945 and 23 billion dollars in 1948.[98] Truman never tried to dismantle the New Deal state. Federal civilian employment had increased from 953,000 in 1939 to 3,816,000 in 1945, and the postwar decline to 2,111,000 in 1947 still left twice as many federal employees as before World War II.[99] (On state employment and expenditures see Tables 7.1 and 7.2).

Second, presidential power continued to grow. The Democratic order

---

96. As many have noted, veterans' benefits have often provided a means by which the federal government provides major economic and social benefits to large parts of the population without establishing programs that provide general entitlements to those benefits. The scale of World War II was so large, and participation so broad, however, that benefits granted in this way were bound to have significant distributive and institutional effects. See Theodore R. Mosch, *The G.I. Bill: A Breakthrough in Educational and Social Policy in the United States* (Hicksville, N.Y.: Exposition Press, 1975); and Keith W. Olson, *The G.I. Bill, the Veterans, and the Colleges* (Lexington: University Press of Kentucky, 1974).

97. See Joel Seidman, *American Labor From Defense to Reconversion* (Chicago, Ill.: University of Chicago Press, 1953); and the critical judgments of Barton Bernstein in Bernstein, ed., *Towards a New Past: Dissenting Essays in American History* (New York: Pantheon, 1968).

98. Bureau of the Census, *Historical Statistics of the United States – Colonial Times to 1970*, Y472–487, "Outlays of the Federal Government, by Major Function: 1940 to 1970."

99. Bureau of the Census, *Historical Statistics of the United States – Colonial Times to 1970*, Y 308–317, "Paid Civilian Employment of the Federal Government: 1816 to 1970."

Table 7.1. *Growth of state employment: government employees, 1930-70*

Year	Total	Federal civilian	State and local
1930	3,223,000	601,000	2,622,000
1940	4,474,000	1,128,000	3,346,000
1950	6,402,000	2,117,000	4,285,000
1960	8,808,000	2,421,000	6,387,000
1970	13,028,000	2,881,000	10,147,000

Source: Bureau of the Census, Historical Statistics of the United States --
Colonial Times to 1970 (Washington, D.C.: Government Printing Office,
1975), 332-4, "State and Local Government Employment: 1929-1970."

Table 7.2. *Growth of state expenditures: federal government outlays,*
1940-70

Year	Total (millions)	Health	Income security	Education and manpower
1940	9,589	48	1,460	73
1950	43,147	252	4,707	219
1960	92,223	756	18,203	1,060
1970	196,588	12,907	43,790	7,289

Source: Bureau of the Census, Historical Statistics of the United States --
Colonial Times to 1970 (Washington, D.C.: Government Printing Office,
1975), 472-87, "Outlays of the Federal Government, by Major Function:
1940-1970."

was stamped from the first by Roosevelt's presidency. Truman was
obviously a less compelling figure, but that did not mean any radical
decline in the presidency's power. Truman's isolation in 1946–7 encouraged efforts to strengthen the executive, as he had so few allies elsewhere – thus his campaign illustrated and further developed the
president-centered character of the regime. In relations with Congress
the administration took the initiative. While major legislative successes
were infrequent, the executive increasingly organized proposals and programs.

Third, the progressive liberal leadership that persisted at the center of the Democratic political bloc remained in the federal state. Despite loud disagreements and significant departures no general purge of pro-New Deal elements occurred under Truman.[100] And many progressive liberal professionals were willing to replace those who left. Progressive liberals in and near the state saw their domestic political role as defending the New Deal and advancing new progressive programs.[101] As in the previous decade, most lacked involvement in local or state Democratic Party politics, and few were seriously involved with the national party organization.

In 1947–9 state-based progressive liberals were active in the decision to veto the Taft-Hartley bill. They shaped Truman's decision to call a special session of the 80th Congress (aiming to expose Republican campaign pledges). They were largely responsible for new reform efforts and were crucial in defining Truman's campaign and his program to extend the New Deal.[102] From the perspective of leading progressive liberals, maintaining order and developing the Democratic regime were interwoven aims.[103]

These elements of the Democratic state – its expanded role, the growth of presidential power, and its progressive liberal leadership – provided support for an initially weak Democratic administration. Truman's political efforts were most successful when his own fate was closely tied to sustaining that state and the Democratic order. Although

---

100. The distinction between departures – even angry ones – by administrators who were involved in the New Deal and an overall purge is important. The former would register argument and factional conflict in the Democratic order; the latter would call into question whether the regime persisted. Hamby provides a good account of progressive liberal criticism of Truman in 1945–8 in *Beyond the New Deal*, 53–85.

101. Clifford's oral history interview makes clear his commitment to preserving and extending the New Deal as progressive liberal reform. The similar commitment of key political actors engaged in campaigning and running the state is clear in the oral history interviews of Samuel C. Brightman, Oscar L. Chapman, George M. Elsey, Oscar R. Ewing, and Samuel I. Rosenman, all at the Truman Library.

102. Hamby, *Beyond the New Deal*, 293–310.

103. Of course, progressive liberals preferred order to disorder. But they sought order and a more powerful state within the terms of Democratic commitments. Thus, the actions and outlook of this leadership group cannot be explained adequately by treating them as an interest group of state managers, although this explanation does better with the normal times of the 1940s than with the regime politics of the previous decade. Considering progressive liberals as state managers seeking to maximize power and personal income does not provide a convincing account of the basic choices of the individuals in question. Many of them would have done far better as maximizers of income and perhaps also as maximizers of power had they chosen other pursuits after World War II, such as the practice of corporate law, for which a number of them were well-qualified.

he was weak and vulnerable in 1945 and 1946, Truman managed to take command of the presidency, was firm in contesting Taft-Hartley, and in 1947–8 waged a lively political defense of the new state.

The state – now the focal point of political leadership – was also crucial in maintaining the popular electoral dimension of the Democratic order. Had the maintenance of the regime relied on the organized party in 1947–9, the Democratic order might well have ended. The state could not institute its own forms of organization and mobilization, but it made a major indirect contribution as the progressive liberal leadership guided the national campaign. The state played a more direct role in recruiting and educating political support: in the practices of state agencies; through the many contacts between citizens and the state, via local offices of federal agencies; through mass media and public appearances by Democratic government officials; and through expanding benefits and opportunities. Thus social security, the NLRB, veterans' programs, and housing programs all conveyed pro-Democratic messages as they were publicized and put into effect. To take one example from the massive number of government publications and messages, in 1946 the National Housing Agency distributed a pamphlet whose content and political message were both clear in its title: "Home loans under the G.I. Bill of rights: How your Government will help you finance the building or buying of a home."[104] Appeals of this type enraged Republicans who charged the Democratic order with corruption and political manipulation. Yet recruiting political support by such means was not corrupt by conventional standards. And if voters responded in a pro-Democratic fashion partly out of narrow self-interest, Republicans were not innocent of proposing policies that offered benefits mainly to particular groups. After years of bitter attacks on the New Deal, and many cases of special pleading for business groups, it was not easy for Republicans to claim to defend civic virtue.

Progressive liberals asserted that there was nothing wrong with drawing attention to Democratic accomplishments, and argued that civil service and administrative reform were making the federal government more professional. During and after the war administrative procedures were redefined, notably in the Administrative Procedures Act of 1946, which specified norms of fairness for administrative agencies. This reform did not disturb the deeper identification of an expanded and activist national state with Democratic projects for progressive liberal reform,

---

104. U.S. National Housing Agency, *Home Loans Under the G.I. Bill of Rights: How Your Government Will Help You Finance the Building or Buying of a Home* (Washington, D.C.: Government Printing Office, 1946).

an identification that greatly benefited the Democratic order.[105] Opponents of the New Deal and the Democratic order in Congress charged that the state had been politicized – they tried to restrict the political action of state employees and to break up particularly offensive agencies. Yet they lacked sufficient strength to realize their goals.

Critics of the Democratic state found themselves in a position they had not expected and for which they were not prepared. They could influence Democratic practices when they acknowledged the regime's premises – and thus restricted their capacity to gain more basic changes in the political situation. Some anti-Democratic forces were able to adapt to a new setting and limit Democratic reform impulses. This was a much more modest role than anti-Democratic forces hoped to play a decade earlier, when they tried to block the consolidation of the Democratic order even while Roosevelt dominated the political scene.

105. Brian Balogh identifies four features of the convergence between professionals and the postwar state: (1) organizational and professional maturity, (2) recognition of mutual advantage, (3) public legitimation, and (4) new sources of demand for the products of federal-professional collaboration. See Brian Balogh, "Reorganizing the Organizational Synthesis: Federal-Professional Relations in Modern America," *Studies in American Political Development* 5 (Spring 1991): 119–72; and James O. Freedman, *Crisis and Legitimacy: The Administrative Process and American Government* (Cambridge University Press, 1978).

8

Passing Taft-Hartley: what the losers won (and what the winners lost)

Judging from experiences in Southern California, the provisions that have occasioned greatest criticism are those governing the conduct of employers prior to certification elections, the use of injunctions in the course of labor disputes, and the priority treatment given cases against unions. In a number of critical situations, these aspects of the Act have been used with telling effect to nullify the safeguards still supposedly enjoyed by unions under the law and to rob the unions of any real effectiveness as bargaining representatives of the workers.

> – Dr. Frank Pierson, UCLA Institute of Industrial Relations,
> December 21, 1948.[1]

Dr. Pierson's negative judgment of the Taft-Hartley Act less than two years after its passage would surely have been rejected by that measure's proponents as hyperbolic and premature. Who would have been closer to the truth? To ask this question, given the centrality of political conflict about labor relations in the 1930s and 1940s, is virtually to ask whether the Democratic order survived the passage of a measure that all parties saw as significantly restricting trade unions. In the late 1940s what would a political rupture have looked like?

In terms of political support, a break with the Democratic order might have been achieved by the defection of core Democratic constituencies in several regions, or by an aggressive anti-Democratic mobilization of wide sections of the population who were not voting or otherwise participating in politics in the 1940s. In policy terms a break with the Democratic order would have been made by successful attempts not merely to restrain unions but to undermine the CIO in its strongholds and to reject the core aims of the NLRA. A break with the Democratic

---

1. Dr. Frank Pierson, UCLA Institute of Industrial Relations, "The Effects of the Taft-Hartley Act on Labor Relations in Southern California," 12-31-48, Taft-Hartley 1949–53 folder, Official File 407 – Taft-Hartley, Harry S. Truman Library.

order would have meant repealing at least some of the main social welfare measures of the 1930s, blocking government efforts at demand-oriented economic regulation, and preventing further progressive liberal reforms, as in housing and civil rights.

Any of these changes would have destroyed central features of the regime. Taken together they would have ended it, and in the late 1940s some opposition currents wanted to do precisely that.[2] But they failed, and the Democratic order persisted.

To assess the more modest changes that actually took place I will examine the conflicts over labor relations in the late 1940s. I focus on the passage of the Taft-Hartley Act and the failure to sustain Truman's veto or to repeal the measure.[3] These events reveal the main features of labor's role – both its strength and limits – as well as the resilience of the Democratic order. The labor movement was central in sustaining the Democratic order in 1947–9. While the passage of the Taft-Hartley Act was a major defeat, that measure did not destroy the new unions, and labor's strength precluded the more stringent measures that many employers and Republicans envisioned.

Who passed Taft-Hartley?

The Taft-Hartley Act was proposed and passed by a coalition of intractable opponents of the Democratic order with less hostile Democrats and Republicans anxious about the postwar role of the labor movement.

The measure resulted from three changes that had taken place in the years since the passage of the NLRA in the mid-1930s. First, business was stronger economically and politically than it had been during the Depression. The ability of business to build and sustain its associations and undertake political action had increased. This was partly due to the

---

2. On Republican perspectives in the late 1940s, see James T. Patterson, *Mr. Republican: A Biography of Robert A. Taft* (Boston: Houghton Mifflin, 1972); David Green, *The Language of Politics in America: Shaping Political Consciousness from McKinley to Reagan* (Ithaca, N.Y.: Cornell University Press, 1987), 171–201; and Stephen E. Ambrose, *Eisenhower: Volume One: Soldier, General of the Army, President-Elect, 1890–1952* (New York: Simon and Schuster, 1983).

3. The choice of Taft-Hartley as a lens for examining the Democratic order in 1947–9 asserts the importance of labor relations in defining and sustaining the Democratic order. This importance was accepted by most observers and participants at the time. With the long decline of labor politics as a crucial national site of political conflict has come a decline in attention to these issues, even in studies of years when they were important. Thus, David McCullough's thousand-page biography of Truman discusses Taft-Hartley for only two pages! David McCullough, *Truman* (New York: Simon and Schuster, 1992), 565–6.

wartime experience of cooperation across firms and sectors; the resulting links could be developed and turned to new purposes after the war.[4] Wartime and postwar economic growth furnished business with resources that could be used to develop associational ties and pursue political aims.[5]

Public views of business and labor had changed in ways generally to the advantage of business. Popular attitudes toward business were highly and unusually negative in the 1930s. Wartime national unity (in which business participated) and economic growth combined to mute antibusiness sentiment, so that proposals advocated by business and its political allies had better prospects than a decade earlier. While critics of wartime labor relations have focused attention on the influence that business gained via its participation in the war effort, they have underestimated the degree to which business cooperation encouraged an improvement in public views of business elites. Antibusiness sentiment in the 1930s had contained strong national elements, based on the idea that business elites acted only for narrow gain rather than as guardians of national economic resources; business involvement in the war effort provided a patriotic counterpoint. Moreover, labor was no longer regarded as purely disadvantaged and thereby deserving of political sympathy to the extent that had been the case in the mid-1930s.

Second, business elites and parts of the Republican Party were more willing to accept the premises of the Democratic order in 1947–9 than they previously had been. The change was hesitant and qualified, but it enhanced the ability of conservative forces to shape policy. This change had a major cost: Proponents of Taft-Hartley were obliged to state their acceptance of large independent unions and a state that would protect their right to exist. While this acceptance was always grudging and sometimes insincere, it helped limit antiunion attacks. Thus while labor and progressive liberals correctly regarded Taft-Hartley's passage as a defeat, the political battles that surrounded the legislation also constrained antilabor employers and political forces. The first preference of

---

4. Some of these links were mainly political; others were economic, via the networks built among large firms and the Pentagon. See Gregory Hooks, *Forging the Military-Industrial Complex: World War II's Battle of the Potomac* (Princeton, N.J.: Princeton University Press, 1991).

5. Howell John Harris, *The Right to Manage: Industrial Relations Policies of American Business in the 1940s* (Madison: University of Wisconsin Press, 1982); Sanford Jacoby, *Employing Bureaucracy: Managers, Unions, and the Transformation of Work in American Society* (New York: Columbia University Press, 1985); and Gabriel Kolko, *Main Currents in Modern American History* (New York: Harper & Row), 310–16.

much of American business and large parts of the Republican Party after the passage of the NLRA and for a number of years thereafter had been to smash these unions. The gradual and unhappy recognition that this hope was unrealistic provided the basis for reconciling these currents to a Democratic order toward which they remained hostile.[6]

Third, the labor movement had political trouble articulating a coherent and persuasive opposition to Taft-Hartley. Although the movement was larger and more institutionally developed in the 1940s than in the previous decade, its achievement of basic objectives (wide unionization and a legitimate political role) made continued mobilization and new programmatic initiatives problematic. The labor movement could not make major inroads in the South; nor could it formulate a clear and attractive vision of its postwar role as a political and economic actor. Labor did not create an effective public political voice or provide a cogent political vision of its postwar role beyond reasserting the right of unions to exist. That assertion was neither empty nor irrelevant, given the widespread antiunion sentiment. Yet once the new industrial unions were established, labor's practical claims were mainly interest-group demands backed up by economic power.[7] The previous decade's thematic and organizational links among union growth, economic security, and a wide range of progressive reforms were in great need of creative restatement.

Owing to these three changes labor lost a major legislative battle. Sharp conflicts involved a divided labor movement, the national Democratic leadership, their political opponents, and business groups. Taft-

6. The hostility of business toward unions at the end of World War II is widely noted, as in Harris, *Right to Manage;* and Christopher Tomlins, *The State and the Unions: Labor Relations, Law, and the Organized Labor Movement in America, 1880–1960* (Cambridge University Press, 1985), 249. Business may even have listened to its critics. In an article published at the end of World War II, William Leiserson wrote that managers continued to behave as though they wanted to get rid of unions; he suggested they might do better with "equalizing" amendments to the NLRA. William Leiserson, "To Strengthen the Act," in Louis G. Silverberg, ed., *The Wagner Act: After Ten Years* (Washington, D.C.: Bureau of National Affairs, 1945), 117.

7. This judgment may seem harsh, as labor, especially the CIO, declared its views on many public policy issues. Starting in 1944, the PAC program outlined a reform perspective located on the left edge of the Democratic order. But the PAC program was not crucial for the bulk of labor's economic and political activity in the late 1940s. See Steven Fraser, *Labor Will Rule: Sidney Hillman and the Rise of American Labor* (New York: The Free Press, 1991), 503–6. On the postwar narrowing of union concerns, see C. Wright Mills, *The New Men of Power: America's Labor Leaders* (New York: Harcourt, Brace, 1948), and Irving Howe and B. J. Widdick, *The UAW and Walter Reuther* (New York: Random House, 1949).

Hartley meant a conservative political shift. Despite this shift, labor retained its historically unprecedented position, maintaining large independent unions and a major role in national politics. *From World War II to 1949, labor's great political success was to prevent sharp political attacks from turning into an all-out assault on the gains it had won in the previous decade and during the war.* This point deserves emphasis because many accounts minimize labor's continued economic and political strength, focusing instead on the limits imposed on its power in these years. But American employers' economic and political hostility to labor unions can rarely be underestimated. The postwar desire of many among them to produce much weaker unions or get rid of them altogether was strong.[8]

The labor movement during and after World War II

The unions – members and leaders – supported the war effort. Workers disliked wartime hardships and management efforts to take advantage of the truce in production, but most were willing to make sacrifices. There was only a limited presence of the antiwar sentiment that existed in previous and subsequent American wars in the twentieth century, such as refusals to enlist, publication of antiwar materials, and opposition by major political forces. Popular support for the war effort in 1942–5 was apparent in massive enlistment in the armed forces, the acceptance of wartime restrictions on consumption, and willingness to adapt to the demands of war production. Strikes to win union recognition were reduced by formulas for securing unionization that reflected federal acceptance of unions.[9] In the wartime political climate outright

8. Fraser's account of failed efforts at labor-management cooperation near the end of the war makes clear the extent of management hostility to independent unions. Fraser, *Labor Will Rule*, 565.
9. The number of strikes did not fall dramatically early in the war. There was even an increase from 1940 to 1941, when many strikes concerned union recognition. This early pressure was partly responsible for wartime agreements that allowed unions to expand without recognition strikes. The overall percentage of workers involved in strikes then declined in part because of the rapid increase in employment. From 1941 to 1944 the average duration of strikes fell sharply, and work stoppages focused on wages and working conditions. Bureau of the Census, *Historical Statistics of the United States – Colonial Times to 1970*, D946–951, "Labor Union Membership and Membership as Percent of Total Labor Force and of Nonagricultural Employment: 1930 to 1970," D970–985, "Work Stoppages, Workers Involved, Man-Days Idle, Major Issues, and Average Duration: 1881–1970" (Washington, D.C.: Government Printing Office, 1975), 178, 179.

employer antagonism to unions risked seeming unpatriotic. While the unions would not have grown nearly as fast without government support, features of the wartime social pact were in tension with the more democratic aspects of the new labor movement.[10]

Soon after the war conflicts between unions and employers exploded in strikes focused on wages and work rules. When management threatened to undermine union gains, the restraint labor had shown during the war disappeared – workers were unwilling to continue making wartime sacrifices, and they anticipated new postwar challenges.[11] Massive strikes showed that the new unions could assert themselves at the firm and industry levels. Without these strikes, numerous employers would have been much less likely to make major wage concessions, and many would have reverted to authoritarian management practices. Yet the strikes had the unintended effect of enhancing efforts to revise the Wagner Act. They made political action seem more urgent to employers, while the thinness of public support for the postwar strikes showed labor's vulnerability. The powerful efforts of railway workers, mineworkers, and others mainly appeared to be strong economic moves on behalf of immediate interests. Arguments such as Walter Reuther's were not typical:

> The road leads not backward but forward, to full production, full employment, and full distribution in a society which has achieved economic democracy within the framework of political democracy. We shall not attain these positive goals by a single-minded concern for the contract-termination pains of business or by grudging, belated, and negative action calculated to take care of the "human side of reconversion."[12]

Even the most serious efforts to give the strikes public appeal, as in the UAW efforts to link union demands with broad political and economic

10. Critics of labor's wartime role exaggerate the extent to which labor's policies marked a sharp conservative turn, and minimize the extent of business concessions. They provide no persuasive argument that unions could have grown as much as they did without agreements to stabilize labor relations, or that such agreements were regarded as wrong in principle by the labor movement. See Fraser, *Labor Will Rule*, 471–82.

11. Strikes in 1946 exceeded those of any single year in the 1930s. Several took on a political character, such as the UAW strike against General Motors and the general strike in Oakland. See Bert Cochran, *Labor and Communism: The Conflict That Shaped American Unions* (Princeton, N.J.: Princeton University Press, 1977), 248–58; and Joel Seidman, *American Labor from Defense to Reconversion* (Chicago, Ill.: University of Chicago Press, 1953), 214–40.

12. Walter Reuther, "Our Fear of Abundance," *New York Times Magazine* (September 16, 1945), in Henry M. Christman, ed., *Walter P. Reuther, Selected Papers* (New York: Macmillan, 1961).

issues, had little success.[13] If the UAW failed to convince the public of its message, there is little evidence that other unions even expressed any such message.

In responding to the postwar strikes Truman began with a belief that workers had a right to unionize. He also saw the labor movement as a major source of political support (not an equal partner with the state or Democratic Party). Truman had supported most New Deal labor measures and viewed labor's cooperation as essential for growth, with government helping to balance interests:

> We are relying on all concerned to develop, through collective bargaining, wage structures that are fair to labor, allow for necessary business incentives, and conform with a policy designed to 'hold the line' on prices. . . . In this country the job of production and distribution is in the hands of businessmen, farmers, workers, and professional people – in the hands of our citizens. We want to keep it that way. However, it is the Government's responsibility to help business, labor, and farmers do their jobs. There is no question in my mind that the Government, acting on behalf of all the people, must assume the ultimate responsibility for the economic health of the Nation.[14]

Truman was suspicious of employers' claims about the dire negative effects of independent unions and took up what might be called an anti-antilabor stance. Yet his sympathy for labor waned when he felt that union activities jeopardized the government's ability to manage the economy (or affronted the authority of his office). In early postwar statements, he called for changes in the Wagner Act to limit union action. Several times he threatened to use force to compel labor to settle disputes, especially when they allegedly endangered national security. On

13. In 1945 the UAW demanded that General Motors and other auto companies "open the books" to demonstrate their claims about the need to raise prices. Partly because of lack of public support, the UAW failed to gain open books or any other objective regarding pricing policy. Howell Harris cites a December 1945 poll conducted in northeastern industrial states in which 42 percent of respondents blamed the UAW for the strike, while 19 percent blamed GM. Howell Harris, *Right to Manage*, 141. Howe and Widdick make clear the lack of public sympathy with the political dimension of the UAW's activity in *The UAW and Walter Reuther*, 136–48. Substantial material on the strike is in Strikes – General Motors File, Political File, President's Secretary's File, Truman Library. The president's commission, headed by Milton Eisenhower, recommended a moderate wage increase to cope with problems linked with the end of the war, and did not endorse the UAW's effort to broaden the issues raised by the strike.

14. *Public Papers of the Presidents of the United States – Harry S. Truman, 1948* (Washington, D.C.: Government Printing Office, 1964), 51. See also Arthur F. McClure, *The Truman Administration and the Problems of Postwar Labor, 1945–48* (Rutherford, N.J.: Fairleigh Dickinson University Press, 1969), 35–44.

May 24, 1946, he condemned the railway strike a day after requesting legislation to allow drafting strikers.[15]

Formulating Taft-Hartley

After the war almost all Republicans wanted to revise the Wagner Act (NLRA) substantially, and many remained unreconciled to strong, independent unions. Still mainly hostile to the new unions, business was willing to accept the Wagner Act and NLRB only when there was no politically feasible alternative. The firm anti-NLRA stance of the National Association of Manufacturers was more typical than the critical but somewhat flexible views of the American Management Association and the Committee for Economic Development.[16] The mixed outcome of the postwar strikes and the Republican victory in congressional elections in 1946 invited serious efforts to change labor law. Proposals to revise the NLRA circulated in 1946 and 1947.[17]

Though much of business and large sections of the Republican Party were deeply hostile to the NLRA, it seemed unlikely that they could effect major changes by opposing unions altogether. A public stance of fundamentalist opposition might have prevented forming a broad coalition in favor of restraining unions through more "balanced" labor laws, while stimulating ardent mobilization by labor and its supporters. Thus anti-NLRA forces accepted core elements of the new model of labor relations developed in the 1930s. Such acceptance meant recognizing the barriers to dismantling the new system, appreciating that it might be compatible with economic growth, and trying to reshape it to limit union power. The process can be described as strategic adjustment, if one focuses on the views of business leaders and allied Republican elites, or as forced conversion, if one focuses on the strength of efforts to

15. Alonzo L. Hamby, *Beyond the New Deal: Harry S. Truman and American Liberalism* (New York: Columbia University Press, 1973), 77. Yet he vetoed the Case Bill on June 11, 1946, and disapproved of what he regarded as punitive antiunion legislation.

16. Employers were typically more open toward unions in public statements by business associations than in the practices of their firms. Opposition to the Wagner Act in the decade after its passage is detailed in Harry A. Millis and Emily Clark Brown, *From the Wagner Act to Taft-Hartley: A Study of National Labor Policy and Labor Relations* (Chicago, Ill.: University of Chicago Press, 1950), 281–96.

17. On the legislative antecedents of Taft-Hartley, see James A.Gross, *The Reshaping of the National Labor Relations Board – National Labor Policy in Transition 1937–47* (Albany: State University of New York Press, 1981), 209–15, 241–51. In 1946 Democrats lost many seats in the House and Senate, including many progressive liberals. Bureau of the Census, *Historical Statistics*, Y 204–210, "Political Party Affiliations in Congress and the Presidency: 1789–1970."

retain the NLRA and block antilabor policies. There remained great antagonism to unions, and more than a few opponents of the Democratic order saw Taft-Hartley as part of a process that would lead to a full return to a pre-Wagner state of affairs. Yet in 1947–9 Republicans and business elites made a key shift by claiming to accept the right of unions to exist and to seek to modify rather than overturn the NLRA. This shift is captured in the text of the Taft-Hartley Act:

> Industrial strife which interferes with the normal flow of commerce and with the full production of articles and commodities for commerce, can be avoided or substantially minimized if employers, employees, and labor organizations each recognize under law one another's legitimate rights in their relations with each other, and above all recognize under law that neither party has any right in its relations with any other to engage in acts or practices which jeopardize the public health, safety, or interest.[18]

Proponents of the bill argued for limiting union power, not denying union rights. Balance was needed, as the Wagner Act had encouraged unions to grow rapidly into large and sometimes irresponsible organizations that required discipline.[19] The Taft-Hartley bill would place reasonable restraints on union activities; its advocates stressed that unions had responsibilities and obligations as well as rights.[20] The measure was presented as an effort to protect the public from undesirable actions by large unions, whose existence was accepted as legitimate. This approach resonated with popular ambivalence about powerful new unions and made it hard to depict the bill as purely destructive. It gained wide support in the press and from public figures who could not be portrayed as pure enemies of labor. Thus Mariner Eccles wrote on behalf of the Board of Governors of the Federal Reserve System:

> Conceding that this measure is a compromise, that the machinery and procedures entailed are cumbersome, and that it will be difficult to administer, nevertheless, we believe that it will facilitate settlement of labor-management disputes and minimize industrial stoppages without infringement of the rights of either side. If that expectation is realized, this bill would be of positive benefit to the public and in the long run to workers. ... We do not think the bill will affect adversely the legitimate functioning

---

18. Public Law 101 (H.R. 3020), *Public Laws* (June 23, 1947): 136.
19. This characterization of the debate on Taft-Hartley relies on the accounts of the legislative history of the act in the works cited previously by Alonzo Hamby, James Gross, Susan Hartmann, and Christopher Tomlins. It also relies on records of the congressional debates in 1946 and 1947, and on contemporary press coverage.
20. See R. Alton Lee, *Truman and Taft-Hartley: A Question of Mandate* (Lexington: University of Kentucky Press, 1966), 28–30.

of unions in their efforts to protect the living standards and rights of their members.[21]

Academics advised Clifford and Truman that the measure would protect the public:

> Under existing statutes, the trade union organization, as such, has gained very considerable power at the expense of the freedom of the individual wage earner. The Taft-Hartley Bill, in principle, seeks to correct this unbalance. . . . The bill gives some protection to the general public against excessive loss and inconvenience arising from paralyzing strikes in public service industries.[22]

The Taft-Hartley Act emphasized prohibitions on labor actions that were deemed coercive. Key prohibitions targeted what were called secondary boycotts (efforts by strikers in firm X to compel that firm to take some action by putting pressure on firm Y in its business relations with firm X and jurisdictional strikes aimed at forcing employers to recognize one union rather than another. In terms of the principles of the NLRA, a good argument can be made against an overall prohibition of secondary boycotts. Some secondary boycotts might be reasonable efforts to compel obdurately antiunion employers to recognize unions and bargain. Others might be coercive efforts to produce outcomes that could not be fairly achieved or justified. Thus the problem of boycotts called for careful legal distinctions and context-sensitive forms of adjudication. Jurisdictional strikes are on much weaker ground in NLRA terms. The text of the Taft-Hartley Act rejected any such distinction, as it closely and effectively linked the two types of labor action as unfair and coercive labor practices.[23]

---

21. Letter, Mariner Eccles to Truman, June 16, 1947, Official File, Truman Library.
22. Letter, J. Douglas Brown (Department of Economics, Princeton) to Clark Clifford, June 13, 1948, Labor File, Taft-Hartley #2, Papers of Clark Clifford, Truman Library.
23. Restrictions on boycotts and jurisdictional strikes were linked: "It shall be an unfair labor practice for a labor organization or its agents . . . to engage in, or to induce or encourage the employees of any employer to engage in, a strike or a concerted refusal in the course of their employment to use, manufacture, process, transport, or otherwise handle or work on any goods, articles, materials, or commodities or to perform any services, where an object thereof is: (A) forcing or requiring any employer or self-employed person to join any labor or employer organization or any employer or other person to cease using, selling, handling, transporting, or otherwise dealing in the products of any other producer, processor, or manufacturer, or to cease doing business with any other person; (B) forcing or requiring any other employer to recognize or bargain with a labor organization as the representative of his employees unless such labor organization has been certified as the representative of such employees under the provisions of section 9; (C) forcing or requiring any other employer to

In a provision that became a focus of extended political controversy, Taft-Hartley asserted:

> Nothing in this Act shall be construed as authorizing the execution or application of agreements requiring membership in a labor organization as a condition of employment in any State or Territory in which such execution or application is prohibited by State or Territorial law.[24]

This provision (Section 14b) was not effective in weakening existing unions, because employees in unionized firms gave strong support to union shops when employers put the matter to a vote. In 1948 Arthur Goldberg, then general counsel of the CIO, reported:

> The overwhelming vote which has been accorded in favor of the presentation and the retention of a union-shop provision in collective-bargaining contracts has to my estimation been a most salutary demonstration of the fact that the union-shop provisions have not been imposed upon union membership. . . .[25]

Section 14B did help strengthen barriers to unionization in states where the labor movement was weak. It encouraged opponents of unions to pass "right to work" laws that blocked union shops.

Other major provisions were likely to weaken labor. Taft-Hartley denied the legal standing of unions led by officials who were members of the Communist Party.[26] It allowed injunctions against strikes deemed to jeopardize the national interest, a provision that could be read as a threat to bring back the systematic use of injunctions against labor. It complicated the NLRB's operation and thus disadvantaged labor, because labor usually needed a rapid adjudication of disputes in order to limit the costs of sustaining its mobilization.

Opposing Taft-Hartley

As the bill proceeded through Congress in early 1947, political opposition was mobilized by the unions through mail campaigns and public meetings. William Green of the AFL wrote Truman:

> recognize or bargain with a particular labor organization as the representative of his employees if another labor organization has been certified as the representative of such employees under the provisions of section 9" (Public Law 101, 141–2).

24. Public Law 101, 151.

25. Arthur J. Goldberg, general counsel, CIO, Testimony, *Hearings Before the Joint Committee on Labor-Management Relations, Congress of the United States, Second Session on the Operation of the Labor-Management Relations Act, 1947* Part Two, June 4–12, 1948 (Washington, D.C.: Government Printing Office, 1948), 594.

26. The barring of Communists was not achieved by declaring membership in the Communist Party illegal, but by refusing government recognition to unions whose leaders refused to disavow membership in that organization. Public Law 101, 146.

[T]he operation of a law such as the Taft-Hartley Bill would promote class hatred, industrial chaos, unsound management-labor relations, and the creation of a political controversy which will run indefinitely. . . . [It] would render unions weak and impotent, would impose on labor a form of involuntary servitude, create a highly objectionable bureaucracy, and provide methods by which labor-hating employers could destroy unions through the institution of civil damage suits.

Philip Murray of the CIO wrote:

H.R. 3020 is the keystone in a program to legislate a new depression. . . . It seeks to accomplish its objective by the suppression of fundamental democratic rights of economic self-defense against exploitation. It deliberately seeks to create an atmosphere of fear and repression so as to make possible a widespread cancellation of civil and political rights.[27]

Taft-Hartley, it was charged, would return the country to the economic circumstances of the Depression, encourage industrial disorder, and jeopardize political liberties. The first two claims are continuous with the defenses of the Wagner Act discussed earlier; the third warns of a repressive dynamic likely to follow from vigorous enforcement of Taft-Hartley. The unions regarded the NLRA as the foundation of their existence and feared the proposed changes both for their direct effects and as signals of an unrestricted assault that might follow.

Economists opposed to the measure argued that the unions would be important in postwar conversion and growth. Taft-Hartley was also charged with being too intrusive, as the Council of Economic Advisors wrote Truman: "[I]t would, however, inject the Government into almost innumerable details in the internal affairs of labor organizations of all sizes and in the collective bargaining process."[28] Academics and state administrators claimed Taft-Hartley would increase strikes and poison labor relations. As pluralist collective bargaining weakened, litigation would increase. The measure would be disruptive, as E. Wright Bakke warned Clifford:

Unions will be driven to the development of new pressure tactics to compensate for those which are now to be limited or forbidden. . . . [Taft-Hartley]

27. Letter, William Green to Truman, June 7, 1947; Letter, Philip Murray to Truman, June 9, 1947 – both in Labor, H.R. 3020, President's Correspondence folder, Clifford Papers, Truman Library.

28. The authors continued: "If subsequent legislation were to inject the Federal Government as sweepingly and deeply into the affairs of employer organizations as the present bill does for labor organizations, we would substantially have abandoned our concept of free enterprise and moved far toward a controlled economy." Letter, Edwin G. Nourse, Leon H. Keyserling, and John D. Clark, to Truman, June 16, 1947, Labor, H.R. 3020, President's Correspondence folder, Clifford Papers, Truman Library.

imposes restrictions on the great body of responsible and reasonably inclined group of labor leaders which will put them in a fighting mood and
stimulate their convictions that labor relations is a class struggle.[29]

Harry Millis and Emily Clark Brown concluded that the measure was ill
conceived and harmful:

> Taft-Hartley, with its confusion and division of purposes, its weakening of
> all unions rather than carefully directed restraint of specific abuses, its
> weakening of restraints upon employers who still seek to avoid a democratic
> system of labor relations, its interference with collective bargaining, its
> encouragement of litigation rather than of solving problems at the bar-
> gaining table, its administrative hodgepodge, was a bungling attempt to
> deal with difficult problems.[30]

Labor defended the experience of labor relations under the Wagner Act
by arguing that the NLRB had been charged with allowing unions to
organize – *it was supposed to be fair but not neutral in its effects*. That
the NLRB had treated employers fairly was shown by most of its decisions having been upheld in court. Defenders of the unions also argued
that they were relatively democratic and that federal intervention would
not resolve remaining problems.[31]

In critiques of Taft-Hartley there was little clear political argument
about what role unions should play and why – in firms, industries,
or national politics. Dramatic warnings that Taft-Hartley would yield
economic disorder and resurrect industrial tyranny were central in labor's arguments, before and shortly after Taft-Hartley passed. Thus
Thomas Johnstone, assistant director of the General Motors Department
of the UAW, warned in 1948:

> We have not yet experienced the full evil of the act. If allowed to stand, the
> clock may be turned all the way back to the days before the enactment of
> the Wagner National Labor Relations Act, to the days of the open shop and
> industrial labor.[32]

Another key theme was fairness. But as the following passage from
the 1948 Democratic Platform indicates, there was not much clarity
about what fairness meant:

29. Letter, E. Wright Bakke (Yale University) to Clark Clifford, June 14, 1947, Labor –
Taft-Hartley #2, Papers of Clark Clifford, Truman Library.
30. Millis and Brown, *From the Wagner Act to Taft-Hartley*, 665.
31. For a defense of the NLRA written in anticipation of postwar attacks, with essays by
Leon Keyserling, Henry Millis, Robert Wagner, and other major figures in the passage
and administration of the Wagner Act, see Louis G. Silverberg, *Wagner Act: After
Ten Years*.
32. Thomas A. Johnstone, Assistant Director, General Motors Department, UAW-CIO,
Testimony, *Hearings Before the Joint Committee on Labor-Management Relations*,
Part Two, June 4–12, 706.

We advocate such legislation as is desirable to establish a just body of rules to assure free and effective collective bargaining, to determine, in the public interest, the rights of employees and employers, to reduce to a minimum their conflict of interests, and to enable unions to keep their membership free from communistic influences.[33]

The suspicion – fanned by business elites and conservative Republicans – that what labor meant by fair treatment was privileges for powerful unions and their leaders was encouraged by labor's strident yet often opaque denunciations of Taft-Hartley.

Skepticism about labor's course was increased by the unions' preoccupation with jurisdictional strikes, in which a union tries to block the activities of a firm in order to gain the right, against an existing union making a similar claim, to represent that firm's workers. Labor's claims about the dangers of governmental restriction of strikes over jurisdiction had merit, given the chance that union recognition might become a favor bestowed by government in return for political allegiance. Yet the focus on these conflicts suggested a narrow concern for the welfare of union leaders, as interunion strikes over members and dues seemed to have little function beyond reallocating resources among unions.[34]

For all their passion, labor and other opponents of Taft-Hartley could not stop Republicans and Democrats in Congress from supporting the measure. The bills proposed in the Senate and House by Robert Taft and Fred Hartley, respectively, passed overwhelmingly. The key role was played by Taft, who maneuvered the bill through a Senate that was somewhat to the left of the House. Taft mediated between fundamentalist forces wholly opposed to the Wagner Act and an array of conservative and centrist forces who wanted to modify it substantially. While the first group found the Taft-Hartley Act insufficiently stringent, it seemed the best that could be attained then and a step in the right direction. The Senate bill, milder in its antilabor elements, predominated in the final version.[35] Conflict then moved to the administration, where the domi-

33. "Democratic Party Platform of 1948," in Donald Bruce Johnson, ed., *National Party Platforms,* vol. 1, *1840–1956* (Urbana: University of Illinois Press, 1978), 430.
34. Tomlins notes the negative effects of the preoccupation with jurisdictional strikes in *The State and the Unions,* 308. A partial defense of such strikes might be constructed by analogy with arguments in favor of corporate takeovers; the strikes send signals regarding the efficiency of unions in securing workers' objectives and the loyalty of workers to them. But such an argument could not make much headway (then or now), given the weak standing of unions in the United States: The negative externalities of these strikes are weighted more heavily in public political argument than their possible advantages to workers.
35. The more stringent House bill was probably in part an effort to make the Senate bill seem more reasonable. Hartmann claims that the Senate bill prevailed in conference, while Lee claims the House version prevailed. Susan Hartmann, *Truman and the 80th*

nant liberal group opposed Taft-Hartley while others had mixed or even positive feelings toward it.[36] The labor movement put as much political pressure on the administration as it could, recognizing that quasi-legal mass action, such as large political strikes, would have been counterproductive.

Truman's failed opposition

Truman opposed the final form of Taft-Hartley, though he had earlier indicated support for revising the NLRA.[37] He claimed the bill would increase government intervention in economic life and increase labor strife, that it would be unworkable, and that it threatened basic labor rights: "[T]he bill is a clear threat to the successful working of our democratic society."[38]

How should we judge such statements? Despite angry arguments with labor during the postwar strikes, Truman believed his claims. Denouncing Taft-Hartley also made strategic sense. A reasonable concern for his political future meant relying on the core institutions and commitments of the Democratic order. Vetoing Taft-Hartley could gain support for his candidacy from progressive liberal forces and labor at a time when he faced daunting problems in the Democratic Party and with the electorate. To refrain from a veto would risk a complete rupture with major Democratic groups, without compensating gains. Thus principle and strategic needs combined to recommend a veto. Oscar Ewing, an organizer of the progressive liberal group in the administration, combines these elements:

> In organizing the group it was my idea that we should try to develop a pattern of things for the President to do that would convince the various groups of voters that President Truman was pitching on their team, just as

Congress (Columbia: University of Missouri Press, 1971), 86; Lee, *Truman and Taft-Hartley*, 77.

36. Support for vetoing the bill was first restricted to a minority of the Cabinet, though after debate most of the cabinet supported the veto. Division in the Democratic Party is indicated by a poll of national committee members that found 103 in favor of a veto and 66 against, with 4 suggesting it be allowed to become law without Truman's signature. Hartmann, *Truman and the 80th Congress*, 87.

37. In his memoirs, Truman says that in early 1947 he was committed to "the early enactment of legislation to prevent certain unjustifiable practices, such as jurisdictional strikes, secondary boycotts, and the use of economic force by either labor or management to decide issues arising out of existing contracts." Truman, *Memoirs: Years of Trial and Hope*, vol. 2 (New York: Time, 1956), 29–30.

38. Quoted from his veto message in Millis and Brown, *From the Wagner Act to Taft-Hartley*, 390.

those Harlem Negroes felt toward President Roosevelt in 1940. For instance, one of the early subjects that we considered was whether or not President Truman should veto the Taft-Hartley Bill. He was under great pressure from the leaders in Congress and I think from all of his Cabinet, except the Secretary of Labor, to go along with that bill and approve it. Our group, after discussing it, felt very strongly that it was unwise for him to approve the bill. We argued that labor was very much opposed to it, that the chances were the bill would be passed over his veto anyhow and thus become law so that he would lose nothing by the veto. Our view finally prevailed and the President vetoed the bill. Congress promptly overrode the veto but Truman had greatly increased his popularity with labor thereby.[39]

The maneuvering after Truman's veto resulted in a veto override. The final Senate vote was 68–25. It could have been closer; when it became apparent that the administration could not win, several senators switched to approve the measure.[40] Was the Truman administration willing to allow Taft-Hartley to pass, hoping to gain new powers in labor relations while reaping the political benefits of a veto? While Truman was able to live with this result, evidence that he aimed for it as a deliberate strategy has not appeared.[41] The strongest indication of administration complicity is the failure to propose a workable compromise in 1947–9. But this stance probably shows miscalculation rather than a clever plan to permit Taft-Hartley to pass while seeming to oppose it. Some who urged a veto thought compromising would encourage congressional conservatives to enact further restrictive measures while undermining labor's support for the administration.

The Truman administration was inept in organizing the Senate fight, and Truman was unable or unwilling to bring his power fully to bear on recalcitrant senators.[42] While Truman cannot be fairly charged with plotting to allow the passage of Taft-Hartley, the administration did not act effectively. Truman and the administration misread the situation. They overestimated the chances of sustaining the veto (and later overestimated the prospects of a new bill in 1949). The failure to sustain the veto reflected poor organizational ability and a degree of ambivalence in the administration as well as the weakness of Democratic progressive

39. Oscar R. Ewing Oral History Interview, April 29–May 2, 1969, Truman Library, 137.
40. On the vote see Lee, *Truman and Taft-Hartley*, 102; and Samuel Brightman Oral History Interview, December 7–8, 1966, Truman Library.
41. There is no evidence of such a plan in the monographs by Hartmann, Lee, McClure, or Seidman. Nor does evidence appear in the papers of Truman, Clifford, or other administration figures.
42. The final effort to persuade senators to change their vote was poorly organized, and last-minute attempts to assemble support were sloppy. Millis and Brown, *From the Wagner Act to Taft-Hartley*, 392.

liberalism in Congress.[43] The outcome also indicated the limits of the unions' power, as they were unable to win over crucial sections of public opinion or prevent a number of centrist Democrats from approving Taft-Hartley.

Labor's campaign in 1948

Truman's veto of Taft-Hartley improved his chances of gaining the Democratic nomination in 1948 and made him likely to get labor's support in the presidential campaign.[44] After Taft-Hartley passed, labor denounced Congress and praised the administration.

In the late 1940s diverse political tendencies existed in American labor, from voluntarism combined with pro-Republican politics to Communism. The center of gravity was a progressive liberal view of a dynamic pluralist market society in which labor unions were legitimate industrial and political participants. To the left of this view, often intertwined with it, was a conception that incorporated elements of social democratic and Catholic social thought within a progressive liberal framework. This conception, prominent in Walter Reuther's formulations and those of a number of other CIO leaders, did not dominate the overall labor movement.

Part of the CIO remained resolutely critical of the administration from the left. In 1947 such forces included at most a sixth of total union membership (AFL and CIO). At the end of World War II the Popular Front left led unions that made up roughly 25 to 30 percent of the membership of the CIO. The left led no major AFL unions at the national level, but locally it influenced perhaps 10 percent of the AFL. By 1947–8 these figures were halved, and they soon declined further.[45]

43. Labor overestimated the prospects of sustaining the veto. A memo from Truman to Charles Murphy in June 1947 asked Clark Clifford to check on a list, provided by George Harrison of the Railroad Brotherhood, of Senators likely to support the veto. Harrison listed 29 Senators as committed to it, 3 as possible, and 8 as requiring attention from Truman. This total of 40 potential votes was 15 higher than the actual result. Memo, Truman to Charles S. Murphy, June 16, 1947, Official File, Truman Library.

44. James Loeb, national director of the ADA in 1948, assessed Truman's course in these terms: "The fact that there was a Dixiecrat candidate on the right, and there was a Wallace candidate on the pretty far left, made the all-out liberal position of Harry Truman seem a middle position, and the middle is a very attractive position for the great mass of American voters." James I. Loeb Oral History Interview, Truman Library, 44–5.

45. It is hard to attach precise figures to political tendencies in the labor movement in 1945–50. The size of unions was in flux, as was the political composition of their

Many on the labor left favored the candidacy of Henry Wallace early in 1948. But the CIO rejected this third-party course, and in August its endorsement of Truman gained a large majority. By the time of the election very few unions supported Wallace, partly because of the bitter struggles that took place within – and against – unions that refused to support Truman.[46] The Wallace campaign in effect solidified Truman's labor support. Many of Wallace's early labor supporters left when it became clear he had no prospect of winning and a good chance of aiding the Republicans.[47] After the veto of Taft-Hartley, supporting Wallace

leaderships, and both influenced the orientation of the membership. The least unreasonable way to estimate the strength of political currents is to construct categories with reference to views among the leadership, and then assign proportions of the labor movement to those categories as a function of the strength of leadership groups. For estimates of the size of political currents in the labor movement, see Bernard Karsh and Phillips L. Garman, "The Impact of the Political Left," in Charles M. Rehmus and Doris B. McLaughlin, eds., *Labor and American Politics* (Ann Arbor: University of Michigan Press, 1967), 190; William Riker, "The CIO in Politics 1936–1946" (Ph.D. dissertation, Harvard University, 1948), 53; and Bert Cochran, *Labor and Communism*, 300–14.

46. The *Washington Post* reported a 35-to-12 endorsement of Truman and Barkley by the CIO's national board. Those who opposed Truman included representatives of United Electrical Workers; American Communications Association; Farm Equipment Workers; Fishermen and Allied Workers; Food, Tobacco, and Agricultural Workers; Fur and Leather Workers; United Furniture Workers; Marine Cooks and Stewards; Mine, Mill, and Smelter Workers; United Office and Professional Workers; and United Public Workers. *Washington Post* (September 1, 1948). These unions' membership added up to perhaps one-sixth of the CIO. No key CIO union of the 1930s supported Wallace, and no AFL union supported Wallace. The AFL did not formally endorse Truman, but worked through the Labor League for Political Education to support him. J. David Greenstone, *Labor in American Politics* (Chicago, Ill.: University of Chicago Press, 1977), 54–5.

47. From 1946 to the 1948 Democratic convention, many progressive liberals, social democrats, and Popular Front leftists wished for a political alternative to Truman. Yet the forces that eventually led the Wallace candidacy, in which the Communist Party played a key role, acted in a way that was sectarian and maladroit. The decision to wage a third-party campaign rather than pursue other means of expressing criticism of Truman from the left was a disaster – with no real chance of success, it put unbearable stress on already fragile alliances. Wallace's positions on the key domestic questions that separated Truman from Dewey or more conservative Republicans were much closer to those of Truman. The major differences were on foreign policy, where Wallace allowed his positions to be perceived as (and sometimes become) uncritical defenses of the Soviet Union. One result was that in 1948 much of the Wallaceite and Communist left relentlessly attacked people with whom they had worked for years. This stance helped destroy the links that had made Popular Frontism somewhat politically viable during and just after World War II. On the Wallace campaign see Joseph Starobin, *American Communism in Crisis, 1943–1957* (Berkeley: University of California Press, 1972), 155–92.

against Truman seemed untenable even for many pro-Communist union leaders.[48]

In the presidential campaign the labor division of the Democratic National Committee was not a major center of activity. The unions mainly acted through the AFL's Labor League for Political Education and the CIO's Political Action Committee. Labor managed impressive contributions of funds, staff, and offices. Union efforts to organize and mobilize their own members to vote Democratic were relatively success-ful, especially in major industrial states.[49] But labor's ability to mobilize broader groups had declined somewhat, as suggested by the close vote and the low rate of voter turnout. Even compared with difficult wartime conditions in 1944, voter turnout dropped by 3 percent in 1948 to reach its lowest point from 1932 to 1964.[50]

CIO strength and CIO involvement with the Democratic Party went together. Yet even in highly unionized regions, labor typically did not dominate local parties. The extent of labor's power in the Democratic Party has been exaggerated by the pattern of studies of labor politics in the 1940s and 1950s. Studies of labor in politics are skewed toward one industry, city, and union – the auto industry, Detroit, and the UAW.[51] As the Detroit area had a large union movement and a formerly weak Democratic organization, this focus overstates labor's political role. It

48. In their oral history interviews at the Truman Library, Clark Clifford and James Loeb insist that Wallace's campaign had this effect. Historians sympathetic to the Popular Front are ambivalent about this claim, recognizing its merit as to strategic maneuver-ing in 1948 but preferring to emphasize that an overall shift to the right allegedly accompanied the failed Wallace campaign and anti-Communist policies in the unions.

49. A positive judgment of labor's role appeared in the press at the time and in many later accounts, such as Robert J. Donovan, *Conflict and Crisis: The Presidency of Harry S. Truman, 1945–1948* (New York: W. W. Norton, 1977), 416–19. That view, which I believe is correct, is not unanimous. Hamby gives little credit to the labor movement's role in 1948, and Berelson and his coauthors emphasized the demoralization of New Deal constituencies. Hamby, *Beyond the New Deal*, 241–65; Bernard Berelson, Paul Lazarsfeld, and William McPhee, *Voting: A Study of Opinion Formation in a Presi-dential Campaign* (Chicago, Ill.: University of Chicago Press, 1954).

50. Bureau of the Census, *Historical Statistics*, Y 27–78, "Voter Participation in Presiden-tial Elections, by State: 1824 to 1968."

51. Arthur Kornhauser and his coauthors studied Detroit and its automobile industry workers in the early 1950s and found what they described as a weak labor party, with considerable political apathy among the workers and a modest role for the union in political education. See Arthur W. Kornhauser, Albert J. Mayer, and Harold L. Sheppard, *When Labor Votes – A Study of Auto Workers* (New York: University Books, 1956). Studies not focused on Detroit usually examine other eastern industrial cities and convey an impression of a major union role in local politics, as with Gary Gerstle's study of Woonsocket, Rhode Island, *Working-Class Americanism: The Politics of Labor in a Textile City, 1914–1960* (Cambridge University Press, 1989).

also exaggerates the role of social democratic elements in the Democratic Party and the role of the socialist left in the labor movement.[52]

In a study of labor politics in the Midwest in 1950, Fay Calkins found varied forms of labor political involvement in the states of Ohio and Michigan and in the cities of Chicago and Rockford, Illinois, and Steubenville, Ohio. In Ohio the CIO supplemented the party's effort from the outside. In Steubenville, the CIO was poised between the two parties and able to extract concessions from the Democrats. In Chicago, the CIO was in conflict with the Democratic machine. And in Rockford and Michigan the CIO was very influential in the party – 40 percent of the members of the Michigan State Central Democratic Committee in 1950 were members of the CIO. The contemporary studies of Calkins and William Riker depict the labor movement as the leading force mainly in local parties, rather than the dominant grouping in whole states and regions.[53]

The lack of labor appointees to high administration positions and the infrequency of labor candidacies for major public offices suggest the limits of labor's power – and further distinguish the Democratic order from most social democratic regimes.[54] In contests for mayor in large towns and cities, statewide office, and Congress, the number of CIO candidates was small, no more than several dozen from the end of World War II to 1949. A familiar social democratic career path was rarely traveled in the United States in the 1930s and 1940s: from local or

52. Thus, Walter Reuther is sometimes depicted as a labor centrist (or even a conservative). This is plausible in the context of factional conflicts in the UAW and in Michigan. But overall Reuther's position can be depicted as centrist only by misjudging the overall shape of the labor movement, either by eliminating most if not all of the AFL from consideration or inflating the weight of currents to the left of Reuther in the CIO.

53. William Riker outlines three common patterns linking labor to the local parties. In one mode, labor – mainly the CIO – took over and operated a local party organization. In another, where a Democratic organization was stronger, labor acted as a coalition partner. In a third, labor made little effort at formal political organization but tried to aid the election efforts of the local Democratic Party. Riker found that where CIO members and their families comprised more than 10 percent of the vote in a congressional district, an equivalent number of members of other unions existed, and Democratic organization was weak; labor dominated the Democratic Party. These were demanding criteria. William Riker, "CIO in Politics," 339–40; Fay Calkins, *The CIO and the Democratic Party* (Chicago, Ill.: University of Chicago Press, 1952). State-level Democratic records at the Truman Library show no greater labor influence than Calkins and Riker estimate.

54. Riker cites a reference volume that listed only fourteen CIO leaders in California and fifteen in Michigan as holding significant Democratic Party positions, including positions as club officers. Riker, "CIO in Politics," 334. Calkins's account suggests similarly low figures in *The CIO and the Democratic Party*.

regional activism in the labor movement to major public appointive and elective offices. The organizational weakness of the Democratic Party per se and progressive and populist concern about the dangers of corruption arising from powerful interest groups pushed labor leaders to remain in or near the labor movement. Where popular hostility to the left was politically important, such sentiment further discouraged CIO leaders from running for office.

Labor's stance after 1948

Despite labor's importance in the Democratic victory in 1948, there was no repeal of Taft-Hartley. In 1949 measures were proposed that would have repealed much or all of it and returned to the Wagner Act.[55] Labor backed the effort at repeal, which had significant support in Congress and the administration, but it did not come close to succeeding. By the early 1950s repeal of Taft-Hartley was only a symbolic Democratic platform statement. What prevented the outcome labor preferred – to repeal Taft-Hartley and return to the Wagner Act? Failing in that aim, why were compromises more favorable to the unions not reached?[56]

First, Democratic support for the labor movement (by which I mean the support of the Truman administration and the progressive liberal leadership of the Democratic order) was tested much more severely by the demand for a new labor law than by the attractive prospect of a preelection veto of an antilabor bill. Truman would not make repeal his main priority; without such a focus its prospects were limited, given his administration's modest ability to achieve any of its legislative aims.[57]

---

55. The course of the main measure is recounted in Lee, *Truman and Taft-Hartley*, 168. Gerald Pomper analyzes the post-1948 maneuvering in "Labor and Congress: The Repeal of Taft-Hartley," *Labor History* 2, no. 3 (Fall 1961): 323–43. It was widely anticipated that there would be significant labor law reform in 1949, given Truman's victory and the new Congress. A *Business Week* editorial even suggested that Taft-Hartley would be revised because it had gone too far. *Business Week* (December 18, 1948).

56. On this failure, see Pomper, "Labor and Congress," 323–5.

57. On the Truman administration's relations with Congress, see Richard Neustadt, "Congress and The Fair Deal: A Legislative Balance Sheet," *Public Policy* 5 (1954). Neustadt was involved in an effort to strengthen relations between the White House and Congress so that a coherent administration program would have a better chance at passage. These efforts are documented in Chronological Files, 1948 and 1949, Richard Neustadt Papers, Truman Library, notably in a memo from Neustadt to Staats, Legislative Progress Reporting for the President, August 20, 1946. The rudimentary character of the administration's liaison with Congress is underlined in Dr. Harold Seidman's Oral History Interview, July 29, 1970, Truman Library. Seidman was on the staff of the Bureau of the Budget in the late 1940s.

Second, progressive liberal forces in Congress after 1948 had not recovered from the defeat of 1946 insofar as initiating major new reforms was concerned. The new Democratic majority was politically heterogeneous and not ardently prolabor.[58] Here some of labor's problems were rooted in the relation between its concentration in industrial states and districts and the decentralized shape of American political institutions. More than two-thirds of union membership was concentrated in ten states: Because of single-member districts in the House and the allocation of Senate seats by state, any such concentrated force has great trouble gaining political representation proportionate to its weight in the national population.[59]

Third, the course of economic events after the war made it difficult for labor to expand its political power. There was no return to Depression conditions, and growth was underway. This improvement was welcomed by labor, since it benefited union members. *Yet when neither labor leaders nor their allies could argue that decline was imminent, economic improvement did not appear to require major new social and political reforms.* The economic dynamism of the wartime experience and the postwar course of events weakened stagnationist views and shifted attention toward how to sustain growth.[60] The immediate economic effects of Taft-Hartley were not so negative for labor as to compel those who had supported the measure with reservations to reconsider that support.

Fourth, labor's own limits played an important role in the failure to repeal or revise Taft-Hartley. One limit was labor's inability to sustain high levels of mobilization. In 1947–9 labor fought hard against Taft-Hartley, yet after the initial postwar strikes most labor leaders saw continued high levels of mobilization as unworkable and undesirable. Their perception was correct, even if it was sometimes employed to justify unduly cautious or narrowly self-interested choices by union leaders. There were numerous barriers to a permanent mobilization of labor. The central aims of the labor movement – union recognition, grievance procedures, and job security – had been won or seemed within reach through a combination of union and government action. This

---

58. The coalition in favor of Taft-Hartley retained strength after 1948, and it cut through the Democratic Party in Congress. After 1948 there were 263 Democrats in Congress, near the figure of 280 Democrats Mayhew has estimated was necessary for postwar reform legislation to pass. David R. Mayhew, *Party Loyalty among Congressmen: The Difference between Democrats and Republicans, 1947–1962* (Cambridge, Mass.: Harvard University Press, 1962), 167.

59. Riker, "CIO in Politics," 316–30.

60. Hamby, *Beyond the New Deal,* 328–34.

reduced the impetus for high levels of mobilization. And large parts of the population, including actual and potential union members, were exhausted by more than a decade of economic hard times, social and political conflict, and war.

Some have suggested that intensive efforts against Taft-Hartley could have been continued on an expanding scale (or that the South could have been flooded with organizing efforts to whatever extent was required for large-scale unionization to succeed). There is no reason to think that unions could have sustained collective action at any level they desired or deemed politically necessary.[61] The routinization of state-labor relations derived partly from labor's recognition of daunting obstacles to a permanent labor mobilization. And labor leaders and members realized that employers were capable of an even stronger counteroffensive than the one they had launched.

Labor's problems with and without Taft-Hartley

To explain fully why labor could not gain repeal of Taft-Hartley or get a better compromise, it is important to examine the political limits of the labor movement itself.

The labor movement misjudged the overall situation and its own prospects in refusing to accept or devise compromise measures that might have eased Taft-Hartley's restrictions and provided a basis for future reform efforts. In 1948 and 1949 the Democratic order was reaffirmed, but little basis for major new reforms existed. The unions claimed a right to exist, charged that Taft-Hartley jeopardized it, and demanded repeal. Yet labor and its allies were neither clear nor compelling about what should replace Taft-Hartley. Nor was labor able to

---

61. Sometimes the mass upsurge of the 1930s is taken to show that the postwar stabilization was almost by definition a conservative involution in labor politics, with the implication that a renewed postwar mobilization was in principle available and blocked by the interests of conservative labor elements. For such a view, see Frances Piven and Richard Cloward, *Poor People's Movements: Why They Succeed and How They Fail* (New York: Vintage, 1979), 167–75. A similar suggestion is made by Nelson Lichtenstein, regarding the failure of new organizing efforts after World War II, in "From Corporatism to Collective Bargaining: Organized Labor and the Eclipse of Social Democracy in the Postwar Era," in Steve Fraser and Gary Gerstle, *The Rise and Fall of the New Deal Order, 1930–1980* (Princeton, N.J.: Princeton University Press, 1989), 135–8. Yet in another article Lichtenstein notes the strength, sophistication, and antiunion attitudes of large employers after World War II, surely a reasonable source of caution for unions with much to lose. Nelson Lichtenstein, "Labor in the Truman Era: Origins of the 'Private Welfare State,' " in Michael J. Lacey, ed., *The Truman Presidency* (Cambridge University Press, 1989), 134–7.

formulate a medium-term political strategy in which a compromise or repeal of Taft-Hartley would have made sense.[62]

In 1935 the unions were institutionally much weaker than in 1947, yet they acted in the context of growing mass movements that concerned Congress. In the late 1940s the unions' objectives were uncertain. They could not assume majority support for expanding their size or power. For a major new burst of growth or a redefinition of their economic role they needed to make an effective political case about two issues: How would larger and stronger unions enhance the performance of the economy, and what would such unions contribute to improving American political life?

What about a simpler explanation of the unions' actions in 1949 – they expected repeal, and saw no reason to compromise? This would portray the labor leadership as wholly unobservant of political realities. It is more likely that the unions did not want to compromise because they did not want to tie their hands with regard to anticipated future struggles over labor law. Even this view underlines the political underdevelopment of the labor movement and its allies, who seem not to have considered how to compromise while creating possibilities for future debate.[63]

Labor's problems flowed from the themes of its industrial and political action. The argument for replacing Taft-Hartley in 1949 lacked a clear statement of the economic or political role that unions should play. The official aim was a balance between employers and unions, and peaceful, stable labor relations, as when Paul Douglas insisted: "Our aim is to restore the processes of collective bargaining and to encourage the parties to settle disputes by themselves aided by government machinery and an informed public opinion."[64]

But what was the *content* of this balance supposed to be? After World War II the unions had trouble communicating a positive meaning of their struggles, even among their membership. They increasingly behaved as a powerful economic interest group aiming to protect and increase its resources. Yet the central role of labor relations in the mass-production industries for the national economy made it implausible to consider industrial relations as a setting in which private groups would

---

62. Pomper, "Labor and Congress," 335, 343.

63. In referring to labor's views after the passage of Taft-Hartley and the 1948 election, I draw on a wide range of sources: narratives of Taft-Hartley cited previously; general histories of the labor movement and of the Truman administration; and the labor press.

64. Paul Douglas, Radio Broadcast, February 8, 1949, Labor-General-Speeches, Papers of Clark Clifford, Truman Library.

compete as the government watched disinterestedly. Ironically, arguments for the Wagner Act had effectively depicted labor relations as too important for public life for such a conception to be politically viable.

Union successes had created a new context. Before World War II, when unions sought basic recognition, their immediate needs were a positive reference point and even a source of inspiration to poor and working-class groups who could not themselves organize effectively. The upsurge of the 1930s fused democratic and progressive conceptions of labor politics. In the late 1940s, advocating support for whatever union leaders considered their most urgent aims was much less attractive to large sections of the population. Now it was less clear that the interest-group demands of labor had a distinctively democratic character, that what was good for the unions was good for many other groups.

In this setting proponents of Taft-Hartley turned the case for public regulation against the unions. Advocates of Taft-Hartley stressed the need for balance between labor and management and argued that this required powerful unions to be restrained in the public interest. After 1948 pro—Taft-Hartley arguments were mainly consistent with the pre-passage case for the measure. Many opponents of the new unions were coming to accept their presence (with great reservations), and in that light Taft-Hartley made sense. Polemics against union bosses were more powerful when framed by a distinction between legitimate and illegitimate union activity. Of course, the legitimate and responsible role for unions now posed as the alternative to an abuse of union power was a much larger role than employers were willing to grant in the mid-1930s.[65]

Labor's thematic problems

The postwar debate about industrial relations was difficult for labor. When unions insisted on retaining or expanding their economic power, they were labeled irresponsible, although they employed an interest-group language of justification similar to that which accompanied their legal recognition in the 1930s and their wartime growth. Both the New Deal view of labor and the voluntarism that preceded it considered unions as one group among others in the American political economy. For proponents of voluntarism, unions were autonomous agents contracting with others in the market; in the more political conception of

---

65. Many polemics of this type appear in Taft-Hartley 1949–53, Official File 407 (Taft-Hartley), such as a radio broadcast by Mahlon Ensinger, President of Union Wire Rope Corporation in Kansas City, March 28, 1949.

the New Deal, workers chose unions to attain their interests in an economy regulated by a progressive liberal state.

Once the core of the New Deal labor program was achieved, political questions arose anew and with force. The new unions were located at the center of the American political economy. How should that realm be organized? Given the reality of these unions as government-supported representative agencies, it was not feasible to consider labor relations as purely private matters. In addition to their size, which far exceeded that of most other interest groups, they had distinctive financial and organizational capacities. It was unrealistic to think that unions would for long be accepted as only another interest group, such as an association of dentists or a regional farm group. Labor needed to present a persuasive political account of its aims and efforts not only to mobilize support on behalf of that conception but to resist immediate attacks.

The main arguments against Taft-Hartley from outside labor's ranks emphasized the virtues of pluralist collective bargaining. Thus Paul Herzog argued that the NLRB's primary commitment to free collective bargaining entailed a responsibility to enforce both the NLRA and Taft-Hartley, and he urged employers not to take excessive advantage of their new powers under the latter measure. Labor had no effective conception that went much beyond such sympathy.[66] This was an inadequate basis for deflecting attacks when critics of unions claimed to seek a proper balance among legitimate interests.

How could American unions, recently built, create a compelling new discourse and program about labor relations in the late 1940s? Beyond voluntarism, two main conceptions of labor relations were readily available. The labor movement could adopt Communist notions of unionism as economic class struggle whose eventual political leadership resided in the Communist Party. Communist views clearly subordinated nonparty forces to the party's strategic priorities – this instrumental view of unions was sufficient to prevent widespread acceptance of Communist views in the labor movement. Communist views of labor action could justify militant struggles against employers and for new unions. But they could not supply a plausible view of union action in a growing market economy, beyond insisting that strikes and other means of resisting employers' initiatives should be used often.

66. Paul M. Herzog, "The NLRB Today," Speech, 4/23/48, San Francisco, in Speeches and Articles, 1948 folder, Papers of Paul M. Herzog, Truman Library. Herzog's testimony in 1949 on the Thomas Bill, which would have replaced Taft-Hartley, was equivocal. Paul Herzog, NLRB Statement before the Senate Committee on Labor and Public Welfare, February 2, 1949, Speeches and Statements 1947–50 folder, Papers of Paul M. Herzog, Truman Library.

A far more attractive and realistic alternative was for unions to continue to develop pluralist views of industrial relations, relying on progressive liberal themes. Unions could promote industrial stability through effective representation of workers. Given the actual choices, most of labor embraced pluralist and progressive liberal views, with some CIO unions adding social democratic elements. Yet by the 1940s these views were more effective in reaffirming the right of unions to exist than in defining a positive role for them. Such affirmation was inadequate when unions faced attacks in the name of fairness, balance, and efficiency, and when antiunion proposals allegedly aimed only to temper unions' excesses.

Without a persuasive view of the power unions ought to have, and why, unions and their supporters made hyperbolic claims that Taft-Hartley would destroy collective bargaining and yield grave instability. Such claims were an implicit acknowledgment of the political hollowness of a pure interest-group stance – we reject Taft-Hartley because we don't want our power reduced. Thus an understandable but ineffective labor move was to denounce Taft-Hartley as an all-out assault on labor:

> The Taft-Hartley Law attempts to take us back in the direction of the old evils of individual bargaining. . . . It has strengthened the hands of the most arrogant, the most anti-labor portion of American industry in its determination to destroy labor organizations. These misguided employers are now using the provisions of the law as a weapon for union-busting, for provocation, and for economic aggression against working people.[67]

The CIO's loud alarm had little content:

> Our program has met with bitter opposition from the forces of privilege and reaction. These forces are motivated by deep hostility to organized labor. These are the same forces whose purpose it is to wipe out the program of social legislation which we proudly call the New Deal and which has been won in the past 16 years.[68]

Many powerful Republicans and a large section of the national business elite did remain fundamentally opposed to the Democratic order after World War II. Yet claims such as those above left the labor movement vulnerable to the key move made when critics of the NLRA claimed to recognize the new realities of labor relations and seek "balance" within them.

---

67. Philip Murray, Speech on "Issues Facing the Special Session of Congress," ABC Broadcast, July 29, 1948, Political File, Press Releases 1948, Papers of Clark Clifford, Truman Library.
68. CIO Executive Board, "Political Action in the 1948 Campaign," August 31, 1948.

Curbs on union power portrayed as moderate restraints were accepted by much of the public, including many union members. The idea of enhancing social welfare by balancing interest groups was comfortably familiar. While public support for unions' right to exist was strong, there was opposition to several union practices, notably secondary boycotts and jurisdictional strikes.[69] And there was widespread suspicion of union political power.

The unions needed to define a reasonable course of self-restraint regarding such matters as jurisdictional strikes. More broadly, the labor movement needed to present a positive conception of how its further growth would improve American political and economic life. Progressive liberal views of labor relations were not adequate to this task. Social democrats in the labor movement partially recognized these issues, without having any real answers. Moreover, Walter Reuther's early postwar course was viewed critically by many in the labor movement, who judged from the failure of the General Motors strike that it would be safer to maintain an interest-group approach than to risk highly visible public defeats while engaging large political issues.[70]

Where the labor movement did make a major effort to build new unions, as in the South in 1946–7, broad political questions received little attention. Instead, the unions seemed to proceed as though new unionization would result from astute maneuvers by already-defined forces. Thus the labor movement tried to replicate the strategies of its successes in the industrial North and Midwest in the 1930s. Leaders gave little thought to what it would mean to win the equivalent of the political victories that had shaped the industrial setting in the mid-1930s, victories that were essential given fierce Southern resistance to

69. In public opinion polls, when people were asked about particular union practices – jurisdictional strikes, secondary boycotts, and some closed or even union shop situations – they responded with strong objections. When asked if they wanted to destroy unions, they said no. Thus, restrictions on labor could gain popular support if they were convincingly presented as intended to moderate union behavior and reduce objectionable practices rather than to undermine unions per se. A Gallup Poll in the spring of 1947 found that 66 percent of those polled agreed with the general idea of new legislation to control labor unions. See Lee, *Truman and Taft-Hartley*, 52.

70. Near the end of the war the UAW and Walter Reuther proposed notions of industrial democracy that relied on extensive government economic regulation and high levels of government spending. To a large degree the proposals were justified as vital for renewed growth. When this soon appeared not to be true, no clear case was made about their virtues on other grounds. Unsurprisingly, business was not interested. On the UAW's postwar political role, see Stephen Amberg, *The Union Inspiration in American Politics: The Autoworkers and the Making of a Liberal Industrial Order* (Philadelphia: Temple University Press, 1994), 110–15, 165–70.

unions. The large CIO effort to build industrial unions in the South was a disaster in 1946 and 1947. Local governments and employers smashed the organizing drives.[71]

It would have been remarkable if the postwar labor movement had created a new conception of American labor politics beyond the interest-group notions of progressive liberalism – decades later such a conception remains absent. Who would have conducted such dramatic and risky innovation? To advocate an expanded political and economic role for unions while retaining a commitment to strong economic growth was a difficult conceptual and practical project. An explicit turn toward social democratic formulations would not have provided answers in the late 1940s. The premises of such positions were not widely accepted in American politics. Social democratic conceptions of economic development in the late 1940s were far more statist than would have been politically viable. Social democratic parties generally advocated substantial public ownership of industry, extensive economic planning measures, levels of public social welfare provision well beyond those in the United States, and significant efforts to redistribute income. Such positions had support from no more than small minorities of the American electorate. Even if there had been a radical shift in American politics so that the way was much more open for social democratic arguments, the latter did not have clear answers to the problems the labor movement faced in the United States in defining its political aims and linking them with programs for growth and modernization. (In Europe social democratic conceptions were themselves troubled and changing, as social democratic and labor parties moved uneasily away from the socialist orthodoxies of the interwar years.)

Democratic interest in repealing Taft-Hartley vanished after labor led an unsuccessful effort to defeat Senator Taft in his bid for reelection in Ohio in 1950. Truman attributed this outcome to misjudgment and intrusiveness by national labor organizations:

> I am sorry to say that our national labor leaders used very poor judgment in their approach to the campaign in Ohio, Illinois and Indiana. The most remarkable thing about the Ohio returns was the fact that every labor

71. In addition to the inhospitable Southern political setting and the conservative paternalism of many of the main industrial settings, labor's setback resulted from employers' coercion and racial divisions among Southern workers. See Barbara S. Griffith, *The Crisis of American Labor: Operation Dixie and the Defeat of the CIO* (Philadelphia: Temple University Press, 1988), 62, 97, 101, 139, 161. I have also benefited from reading chapters of Daniel Marien's dissertation-in-progress at the Graduate Faculty of the New School for Social Research. His project is a comparative study of labor relations in the postwar American South and the province of Quebec.

center voted for Taft and from the best information I can get they were expressing their disapproval of the attempt of the national leaders to tell them what to do.[72]

The outcome in 1947–9 was to impose Taft-Hartley's burdens on the labor movement while forcing employers to accept large independent industrial unions. The Democratic order remained the only American regime in which unions were relatively secure in their legal and industrial standing and could exercise sustained political influence nationally.[73]

Conclusion

In passing Taft-Hartley, the crucial factors were labor's political difficulties in opposing it, the increased postwar power of business and conservative political forces, and the flexibility of the latter groups in partly accepting the premises of the Democratic order and then proposing to modify that regime. Five main factors explain the failure to replace Taft-Hartley with a new measure in 1948–9: the administration's decision not to make repeal a central project, the limited power of progressive liberal forces in Congress, economic conditions that made it difficult to claim that Taft-Hartley meant disaster, the limited capacity of labor for mobilization, and labor's difficulty in developing and advocating a positive conception of its postwar political and economic role.

Taken as a whole, the passage of Taft-Hartley and the failure of its opponents to repeal or modify it amounted to a conservative reshaping of the New Deal transformation of American labor relations. Conservative Republicans (and Democrats) along with business groups initiated Taft-Hartley and won its passage and retention. Their actions were the primary cause of this outcome. Thematic shifts were key in enabling them to act effectively, as anti-NLRA efforts would almost certainly

---

72. Letter, Harry S. Truman to Cliff Langsdale, November 29, 1950, PSF Political File, Truman Library. See also Lee, *Truman and Taft-Hartley*, 204.
73. On labor law in the nineteenth century, see Victoria Hattam, *Labor Visions and State Power: The Origins of Business Unionism in the United States* (Princeton, N.J.: Princeton University Press, 1993); Morton Horwitz, *The Transformation of American Law, 1780–1860* (Cambridge, Mass.: Harvard University Press, 1977); and Karen Orren, *Belated Feudalism: Labor, the Law, and Liberal Development in the United States* (Cambridge University Press, 1991). The Republican regime after the 1960s alternated between active and passive hostility toward labor unions. See Richard B. Freeman and James L. Medoff, *What Do Unions Do?* (New York: Basic Books, 1984); Michael Goldfield, *The Decline of Organized Labor in the United States* (Chicago, Ill.: University of Chicago Press, 1987): and Paul Weiler, "Promises to Keep: Securing Workers' Rights to Self-Organization under the NLRA," *Harvard Law Review* 96, no. 8 (June 1983): 1769–1827.

have failed had they aimed at the total destruction of the new unions and the new labor relations system. The anti-NLRA offensive was not a sufficient cause of the result – more adroit responses by the labor movement and the Truman administration might have resulted in more modest changes in labor relations. While some changes in the Wagner Act framework were likely, less stringent formulations of the main restrictive provisions (regarding secondary boycotts, jurisdictional strikes, and even section 14b) were feasible.

The limits of the labor movement also played a major causal role. The lack of a compelling account of unions' postwar role severely hampered the labor movement's efforts.[74] Labor's limitations – and strengths – helped to select the actual outcome from a range of possibilities. Labor's militancy and tenacity blocked any effort to go beyond Taft-Hartley in weakening labor's position and resulted in a more moderate practical interpretation of that measure than its critics expected. Yet labor's political weaknesses prevented it from stopping or reshaping a measure it strongly opposed.

The administration's political hesitation and misjudgment also played a significant role. Truman and other progressive liberals wanted to stop Taft-Hartley. But the administration's weakness was clear in its failure to organize support for the 1947 veto of Taft-Hartley and its inability to lead an effective fight for new reform measures in 1949. Labor law reform deserved more attention than it got from an administration that had trouble winning any major reform victories. While leaders of the Democratic order sustained their regime against strong challenges, they could not block a conservative shift within that framework.

What the losers won (and the winners lost)

What were the effects of the Taft-Hartley process? It did not destroy existing unions or make it impossible to build new ones.[75] The act served further to institutionalize the new unions. Most of the labor movement was eager for greater security and did not yearn for the

74. For an interesting account that attributes too much of the responsibility for Taft-Hartley to the unions, especially via the strikes of 1945–6, see Joel Seidman, *American Labor from Defense to Reconversion.*

75. Tomlins interprets New Deal labor policy in a manner that leads him to argue that Taft-Hartley encoded practices already under way. He is correct to reject a view of Taft-Hartley as a radical break with the NLRA, but his eagerness to indict the state leads him to depict its intervention as always the same negative force. This view leads him into difficulties similar to those that labor encountered in the late 1940s – an inability to suggest a politically viable and normatively attractive model of labor relations in a large, complex market economy. Tomlins, *State and Unions,* 251.

unions to be a permanently mobilized force seeking to transform American industry and politics. Permanent mobilization was the basic view of parts of the pro-Communist labor left in the late 1940s, but this perspective would have failed to gain support even had there been no Cold War. It offered images of endless militancy (no limits on strikes even during the time when contracts were in effect) whose benefits were uncertain and whose costs were likely to be great.

Taft-Hartley did not lead to a sweeping reduction in union power (as some supporters hoped it would) or to extended new rounds of turbulent conflict about labor relations (as some critics feared).[76] While no legislative compromise occurred in 1949, a practical compromise in labor relations did take place. Labor was confirmed in its recently gained rights to organize and maintain unions; to strike over wages, hours, and working conditions; and to initiate grievance actions. Management retained the right to organize production according to its own criteria and to make price and investment decisions.

This compromise was distinctively favorable to labor, given the long-standing resistance of business to unions. After World War II many employers and the most conservative sections of the Republican Party preferred to eliminate unions or radically limit their power and scope of action. The political conflicts of 1947–9 showed that both aims were out of reach, and employers could not even achieve such objectives as gutting grievance procedures where unions were already in place. Employers made real concessions in accepting the new labor relations model of large independent unions, serious wage-bargaining, and meaningful grievance procedures. Their reluctant consent resulted from a sequence of political defeats from the passage of the NLRA through Truman's election in 1948.[77]

76. Nor did Taft-Hartley undermine the NLRB to the extent that some of that measure's supporters hoped, and some of its critics have charged. Gross overstates the damage done to the NLRB in *The Reshaping of the National Labor Relations Board*, 264–7.
77. This arrangement resembles what several authors have described as a postwar accord. I do not use this term, though I have benefited from analyses that use it. "Postwar accord" suggests that the framework for postwar labor relations was devised after the war – but the new labor relations framework was built in the 1930s. In this context the term "accord" has most often been used to indicate an agreement in which labor acquiesced to a new mode of subordination, as when Bowles and Gintis claim: "The accord granted workers the possibility of real distributional gains, while at the same time ensuring the continued dominance of capital within the site of capitalist production. By an accord we do not mean a balance of class forces, less still a cessation of class conflict. Rather an accord is a restructuring of class relations." The authors choose to use a word that implies agreement and balance, but then reject those meanings. Given the mainly antilabor character of the political orders that preceded

Labor's political mobilization in 1947 and 1948 played a large role in ensuring that Taft-Hartley was not implemented in the most stringently antilabor fashion. Direct attacks on the main centers of union power did not follow. There was no major increase in strikes; there was even a decline in some indices of strike activity, rather than the predicted turbulence.[78] Unions had difficulty responding when their bleak predictions failed to materialize (although they rightly claimed that some of Taft-Hartley's provisions were unfair). Thus when Taft-Hartley did not spell disaster, this result had the ironic effect of disproving labor's warnings about the dire consequences of the measure.

Antilabor political forces now found they had reached a barrier to their own further success. Having won Taft-Hartley, they could not easily claim a compelling need for a new round of legislation to constrain unions. Employers sometimes found themselves defending Taft-Hartley on grounds that it had not greatly changed an industrial relations framework that they mostly opposed in the 1930s and that many of them hoped to replace after World War II. In 1948, Raymond Smethurst, counsel for the National Association of Manufacturers, countered criticism of Taft-Hartley in this way:

> Obviously, employees have not been enslaved, nor have labor organizations been weakened. In thousands of plants throughout the country, the process of collective bargaining has been carried on without serious obstacles or disruption.[79]

No labor legislation close to Taft-Hartley in its range and significance was passed for the remainder of the Democratic order. The overall result was far short of what large parts of business and militantly anti–New Deal sections of the Republican Party had hoped for from the late 1930s to the end of the 1940s. The foes and critics of labor were reconciled to the Democratic order to a substantial and surprising extent.

After Taft-Hartley, the rapid and large increases in union strength of the 1930s and 1940s were not repeated. Relative to the work force, the unions soon stopped growing. In 1949, 32.6 percent of nonagricultural employees were unionized. This figure increased modestly to 34.7 per-

and followed the Democratic order, it is more useful to stress labor's gains in the 1930s and 1940s. Samuel Bowles and Herbert Gintis, "The Crisis of Liberal Democratic Capitalism: The Case of the United States," *Politics & Society* 11, no. 1 (1982): 65.

78. Bureau of the Census, *Historical Statistics*, D 970–985, "Work Stoppages, Workers Involved, Man-Days Idle, Major Issues, and Average Duration: 1881 to 1970."

79. Testimony of Raymond S. Smethurst, counsel, National Association of Manufacturers, *Hearings Before the Joint Committee on Labor-Management Relations*, Part One, May 24–28, June 1–3, 1948, 131.

Table 8.1. *Union membership, 1930-1970*

Year	Total union membership (thousands)	Percentage of labor force	Percentage of nonagricultural labor force
1930	3,401	6.8	11.6
1935	3,584	6.7	13.2
1940	8,717	15.5	26.9
1945	14,322	21.9	35.5
1950	14,267	22.3	31.5
1955	16,802	24.7	33.2
1960	17,049	23.6	31.4
1965	17,299	22.4	28.4
1970	19,381	22.6	27.3

Source: Bureau of the Census, <u>Historical Statistics of the United States -- Colonial Times to 1970</u> (Washington, D.C.: Government Printing Office, 1975).

cent in 1954, and then began to decline. (On union membership, see Table 8.1.)[80] Taft-Hartley reshaped the NLRA framework to make industrywide action more difficult and channel conflict into individual workplaces and companies. This accentuated the likely pattern of postwar union growth, which mainly included workers in already unionized industries and areas. Taft-Hartley helped make it more efficient for unions to seek to expand into nearby firms and areas rather than into previously nonunion sectors and regions.

The act made it harder (or illegal, as with secondary boycotts) to undertake forms of labor action that might aid a qualitative expansion of unions. Yet even had Taft-Hartley not passed, further qualitative expansion of unions would have been difficult, owing both to political and industrial opposition and to the weaknesses of the labor movement itself. Taft-Hartley hurt labor, but it was not the primary cause of the declining rate of union growth. It cannot be blamed for failures to unionize in the postwar South, for example, when the main failed efforts to do so preceded its passage.

Half a century after the passage of Taft-Hartley, unions are relatively smaller than at any point in the intervening decades. It is tempting to see

80. Bureau of the Census, *Historical Statistics*, D 946–951, "Labor Union Membership and Membership as Percent of Total Labor Force and of Nonagricultural Employment: 1930 to 1970."

the long decline of trade unions as caused by the NLRA framework, including the Taft-Hartley Act. This view wrongly conceives unions' decline as a determined sequence in which the legal forms and institutions built in the 1930s and 1940s were bound to weaken labor over time. Audit diverts attention from the political inability of the unions to work more effectively within the NLRA framework, and from the inability of both unions and their Democratic allies to achieve desired reforms in labor law.[81]

In the late 1940s the new unions were concerned with securing their positions. In pursuing that reasonable aim, they increasingly relied on the state in efforts to defeat powerful opponents. It made sense for unions facing dangerous immediate political and economic conflicts with employers to turn toward the Democratic state, rather than risk efforts to remobilize their membership in a postwar setting where the appetite for mass action was far from insatiable. Thus unions appealed to the National Labor Relations Board to redress their grievances rather than trying to engage in more and more militant strikes. This course limited employers' counterattacks and was less apt to alienate an ambivalent public. Yet labor could not persuade a majority of the population of the merits of stronger and more militant unions, and it lacked the economic and political resources simply to force that result.

In sum, postwar labor politics yielded a conservative turn *within the Democratic framework*. The result was to sustain labor's main achievements from the prior decade while limiting new labor efforts. Employers could not use Taft-Hartley to destroy large independent unions; indeed, they were, in effect, required to cooperate with them to an unprecedented extent in the context of the history of American labor relations.

This outcome cannot be deduced from any economic logic. Postwar

---

81. Interpretations of the meaning of the NLRA framework for unionization have varied considerably since Taft-Hartley was passed. From the 1950s to the early 1970s, industrial pluralist views considered the NLRA framework mainly as enabling a large and durable union presence in the American economy. From the late 1960s on, and especially in the 1980s and 1990s, critics of that framework have blamed it for labor's decline. To decide precisely how much responsibility Taft-Hartley and the NLRA arrangements should be assigned for the course of the labor movement from the 1950s on is a complex problem that lies beyond the scope of this book. For influential statements of industrial pluralism, see Derek Bok, "Reflections on the Distinctive Character of American Labor Laws," *Harvard Law Review* 84, no. 6 (April 1971): 1394–1463; and David E. Feller, "A General Theory of the Collective Bargaining Agreement," *California Law Review* 61, no. 3 (May 1973): 663–856. For an argument that attributes much of the unions' decline to Taft-Hartley, see Joel Rogers, "Divide and Conquer: Further 'Reflections on the Distinctive Character of American Labor Laws,' " *Wisconsin Law Review* 1 (1990): 1–147.

economic growth did not require the results of these battles about labor relations. In the late 1940s several models of labor relations were feasible. Expansion could have taken place with a weaker or stronger labor movement. Growth could have occurred if more stringent terms had been imposed on labor – for example, if union growth had been stopped cold, some unions broken up, and labor's power in industrial relations substantially diminished. While such shifts might have produced instability in large, nonunionized industrial settings, a combination of coercion and paternalism could have reduced the costs of disruption.

Nor did postwar growth require new restrictions on union activity. It was compatible with fuller unionization of the mass-production industries, an expansion of unions into the urban South, and at least a modest emergence of unions in growing white-collar occupations, both in manufacturing and in industries such as banking and insurance. Growth in these areas might have increased unionization by as much as an additional 10 to 15 percent of the labor force by the mid-1950s. Such an increase might have had significant political consequences in the 1950s and later.

9

New political fronts? growth and civil rights in the 1940s

The Government must work with industry, labor, and the farmers in keeping our economy running at full speed. The Government must see that every American has a chance to obtain his fair share of our increasing abundance. ... We cannot maintain prosperity unless we have a fair distribution of opportunity and a widespread consumption of the products of our factories and farms.

— Harry Truman, State of the Union address, January 5, 1949[1]

After World War II, Democratic leaders wanted to maintain a reformist progressive liberalism and mainly did so. They adapted to pressures from a renewed and more sophisticated opposition, so that a conservative shift was channeled within the framework established in the 1930s. While the popular mobilization of the 1930s could not be sustained through the 1940s, new areas of political debate and potential reform were opened. This chapter first evaluates postwar relations between the Democratic order and the economy. I then examine movements and interest groups that arose in and around the Democratic order beyond labor, focusing on the emergence of civil rights as a major public issue. The chapter concludes by assessing the thematic shifts that occurred from the mid-1930s to the end of the 1940s.

Democratic policies and economic performance

Postwar growth did not create a new political order. The Democratic order had been built a decade earlier.[2] The Democratic order benefited in

1. "State of the Union," January 5, 1949, *Public Papers of the Presidents of the United States – Harry S. Truman, 1949* (Washington, D.C.: Government Printing Office, 1964), 1.
2. This sequence does not support an economic periodization of politics in these decades, including the conception that Gordon, Reich, and Edwards propose in considering the

the late 1940s from economic outcomes that it had encouraged through political decisions in the 1930s and early 1940s.[3] Efforts to increase demand and alleviate unemployment encouraged the growth of mass-production industries in the late 1930s, though it was not until 1939 that the gross national product exceeded that of 1929. While gross national product virtually doubled between 1930 and 1950, much of the growth occurred soon before and during the war.[4] In these decades employment grew significantly – from 1930 to 1950 the number of operatives (a census category including mainly semiskilled and unskilled production workers in industry) increased from 6.2 to 8.3 million.[5]

postwar period in terms of a social structure of accumulation built between 1935 and 1947. To mark a new period as beginning in the late 1940s, the authors combine acts of fundamental importance – Wagner and Social Security – with measures such as Taft-Hartley and the 1946 Employment Act. The latter were not equivalent to the former, but reshaped the framework established in 1935–7. David Gordon, Richard Edwards, and Michael Reich, *Segmented Work, Divided Workers: The Historical Transformation of Labor in the United States* (Cambridge University Press, 1982), 169–70. In a work with a similar perspective, Bowles, Gordon, and Weisskopf refer to a postwar social structure of accumulation with four elements: "One involved U.S. capital's dealings with foreign suppliers of goods imported into the United States and foreign buyers of goods exported from the United States. A second featured new and much more structured relationships between corporations and a substantial segment of the work force in the United States. A third managed the continuing domestic conflicts between the business quest for profits and popular demands for the social accountability of business. And the fourth limited the extent to which U.S. firms were exposed to product market competition." Thus a new social structure of accumulation emerged after World War II. As this "ssa" resulted from a search for answers to mainly economic problems, the implication is that through the requirements of a broadly defined "ssa," economic pressures shaped most major political and social institutions. In the actual sequence, a new political order began in the 1930s. This order was less a functional response to economic needs than a distinctive political project. Samuel Bowles, David Gordon, and Thomas Weisskopf, *After the Waste Land: A Democratic Economics for the Year 2000* (Armonk, N.Y.: M. E. Sharpe, 1990), 48.

3. Major socioeconomic changes from the Great Depression through the postwar years were partly the effect of political conflicts on socioeconomic relations. To assert economic determination would mean conceiving the Depression as entailing economic crises that caused the emergence of a new political order. The latter would then be understood as expressing economic pressures. This account presumes an economy with one clearly most efficient overall course of development – the political actors who find and pursue it are rewarded. Yet when there is more than one feasible choice to sustain a politically acceptable economic performance, explaining the actual political course must refer to the aims and capacities of political and economic actors.

4. Bureau of the Census, *Historical Statistics of the United States – Colonial Times to 1970*, F 32–46, "Gross National Product – Summary in Current and Constant (1958) Prices: 1929 to 1970" (Washington, D.C.: Government Printing Office, 1975), 228.

5. Despite extensive female labor force participation in World War II, most of this increase was in male workers. Bureau of the Census, *Historical Statistics of the United States –*

By the late 1940s there was a coherent and plausible story about Democratic economic management from the early 1930s. Democrats first stopped the horrible collapse of the Depression from proceeding further, and produced a gradual and partial recovery in the later 1930s. Democrats then organized a wartime economic mobilization that was militarily and economically successful. After the war they avoided a return to Depression conditions while leading the nation toward substantial growth. The popular perception was of major increases in welfare after World War II because resources were shifting rapidly from military to domestic sectors – consumption increased even if overall production fell below wartime levels.

This account allowed Democratic leaders to take credit for avoiding a return to crisis, minimizing the most extreme forms of dislocation in the transition, and providing a framework for growth. This pro-Democratic story was a reasonable interpretation of economic developments by 1948, even if the large role it accorded Democratic policy choices was often overstated. Silences about Democratic mistakes, as in the economic downturn of the late 1930s, were an unsurprising feature of such political argument. For this story to be plausible, economic development had to occur – had there been a severe and protracted downturn after the war, Truman would probably have lost the 1948 election.

After the initial postwar economic contraction, Democratic efforts to sustain demand encouraged further expansion. Pledges of full employment were qualified in practice, and high employment was not seen as a means of increasing working-class political strength or radically redistributing income. Democratic policies aimed at expanding employment through demand-oriented strategies with welfarist elements – they were Keynesian but not social democratic. Postwar recovery affirmed Democratic capacities to manage the economy.[6]

Colonial Times to 1970, D 182–232, "Major Occupation Group of the Experienced Civilian Labor Force, by Sex: 1900 to 1970," 139–40.

6. Keynesian themes were important for practical efforts to sustain demand, reduce employment, and encourage growth. Herbert Stein emphasizes the Democratic break with pre-New Deal policies and stresses the Keynesian side of the Democratic order's policies in *The Fiscal Revolution in America* (Chicago, Ill.: University of Chicago Press, 1969), 197–240. A more recent volume asks whether Keynesian approaches were adopted due to the analytical force of the theories, the shape of state structures, or the logic of political coalitions. Its essays give too little attention to the causal force of the theories, because they blur together two different questions: Why were Keynesian perspectives adopted at all in the 1930s and 1940s? And why were they adopted at different rates and in different formulations across nations? The structural factors that deserve considerable weight in answering the second question receive undue importance in answering the first. See Peter A. Hall, ed., *The Political Power of Economic Ideas: Keynesianism across Nations* (Princeton, N.J.: Princeton University Press, 1988).

The Democratic achievement was to build and sustain positive links among mass production, mass consumption, and a pluralist industrial relations system. These policies avoided a return to Depression conditions and encouraged postwar growth.[7] Reforms in labor relations were essential to provide stability and regular means of increasing wages. The Democratic order reshaped labor relations to yield an industrial setting that in the late 1940s was much less authoritarian and potentially more stable and productive than the prevalent forms of industrial relations in the late 1920s or early Depression. In the major industrial firms a routinized labor relations system emerged, with internal labor markets, grievance procedures, and unions.[8]

Democratic economic policies in the 1930s also sought to address the disasters in cities. In the late 1940s urban policy was linked to growth-oriented macroeconomic policies. As Truman said

> I have today approved the Housing Act of 1949. This far-reaching measure is of great significance to the welfare of the American people. It opens up the prospect of decent homes in wholesome surroundings for low-income families now living in the squalor of the slums.[9]

Federal policies encouraged movement out of urban centers through assisting the housing industry and making credit widely available for families to purchase houses.[10] The housing industry preferred to build single-family units on cheap land, a form that was widely popular, since many urban residents wanted to leave cities, which they identified with poor housing and services. New units were available at moderate rates, jobs grew in construction, and profits were abundant for banks and the housing industry.

Postwar growth also depended on socioeconomic factors for which

---

7. Aglietta terms the economic side of this complex a regime of intensive accumulation. Michel Aglietta, *A Theory of Capitalist Regulation: The US Experience* (London: New Left Books, 1979), 116–17.
8. Gordon, Reich, and Edwards periodize the structure of the working class in this way: The 1890–1930 period saw the homogenization of labor alongside the emergence of mass-production forms. On this basis, the unions of the 1930s arose. The response from capital was an elaborate segmentation of labor in the 1940s on the basis of qualifications, job definitions, and sector. In their terms, Democratic efforts to spur growth in 1947–9 enhanced the position of workers in the primary sector, especially the "subordinate primary" group in mass-production industries. Gordon et al., *Segmented Work, Divided Workers*, 189.
9. Truman, July 15, 1949, *Papers of Truman, 1949*, 381.
10. Mollenkopf emphasizes postindustrial economic transformation as a crucial postwar force in reshaping cities. John Mollenkopf, *The Contested City* (Princeton, N.J.: Princeton University Press, 1983), 15, 43. On suburbanization see Kenneth T. Jackson, *Crabgrass Frontier: The Suburbanization of the United States* (New York: Oxford University Press, 1985), 267–93.

the Democratic order was much less responsible. First, American industry enjoyed a wide technological lead over other nations, linked with high rates of education and investment in research and development. Labor-saving mass-production forms had widened the gap between the United States and European nations. Second, the war had spurred a rapid expansion of production while American industry had suffered no significant military damage. Third, wartime restraints on top of the long Depression had created a powerful desire for consumer goods of all types in the United States. And fourth, the wartime devastation of Europe created a vast demand for American products there. Democratic policies were not the main cause of these sources of economic growth, but they were responsive to new postwar possibilities.[11]

The Democratic order benefited greatly in the early postwar years from open international economic institutions that it had helped to build. The story of expanding American involvements, from Bretton Woods to the Marshall Plan, has often been told.[12] The key political move was the Truman administration's choice of an internationalist economic course after World War II; the result was to spur domestic economic growth, which in turn strengthened the Democratic order. After World War II – and over the next two decades – expanded trade accompanied growing overseas investment by American firms. The international economic order helped sustain Democratic power in the United States by encouraging high employment and rising wages.

The construction of an open international economic order was due to political choices by the United States and its allies, choices based partly on the judgment that the Depression had been worsened by protectionist

---

11. On economic growth in these years, see Stephen A. Marglin and Juliet B. Schor, eds., *The Golden Age of Capitalism: Reinterpreting the Postwar Experience* (New York: Oxford University Press, 1990); and Gavin Wright, "The Origins of American Industrial Success, 1879–1940," *American Economic Review* 80, no. 4 (September 1990): 651–68. These accounts respectively emphasize the roles of class and industrial relations, and access to raw materials, in postwar growth. Abramovitz emphasizes three features of the role of knowledge in economic growth: (1) close relations among science, technology, and business; (2) risky and expensive investment; and (3) the conditions of deploying knowledge. His argument provides a good basis for evaluating the economic contribution of organizational changes in the United States after World War II. Moses Abramovitz, *Thinking about Growth* (Cambridge University Press, 1989), 28–45.
12. See Fred L. Block, *The Origins of International Economic Disorder: A Study of United States International Monetary Policy from World War II to the Present* (Berkeley: University of California Press, 1977); Charles Kindleberger, *Marshall Plan Days* (Boston: Allen and Unwin, 1987); and Susan Strange, *Sterling and British Policy: A Political Study of an International Currency in Decline* (New York: Oxford University Press, 1971).

policies. Postwar progressive liberals had little interest in ambitious forms of state economic planning that implied nationalist and protectionist strategies. Given the prospect of expansion, emergency arguments that could justify a large increase in state economic regulation were not plausible.

The new international economic order had the effect of strengthening Democratic power in the postwar years. And some who helped to shape American policies after World War II were aware of the prospective domestic gains of an open international economy led by the United States. Yet Democratic international policies were not simply determined by domestic economic pressures. Although international trade and markets were attractive to many business groups, their interest in open markets is not enough to explain the outcome. The positive links between domestic economic performance and an open international economy were mediated by the Democratic order. Its leaders believed that expanded American production and open international economic relations were interdependent goals and that both would enhance international political stability and the prospects of liberal democracy. Here Democratic views provided a basis for partial agreement with those business groups whose domestic policy orientation was much closer to that of Republican opponents of the Democratic order, but who wanted an open international economy. Democrats who helped to establish a more open international economy believed this effort would foster growth in many regions and enhance prospects for international peace. This coincided with the views of important business groups but is irreducible to their perceived immediate interests. Postwar Democratic economic policies were formulated as a broad political initiative, whose success framed the interest-group bargaining that occurred.[13]

Growth and the eclipse of planning

The Democratic combination of demand-oriented domestic policies and open international policies coincided with and aided a phase of rapid expansion. This expansion strengthened the political position of the Democratic leadership. One casualty of this process was a cluster of left-

13. For a similar argument about business politics in the 1970s, see David Plotke, "The Political Mobilization of Business," in Mark P. Petracca, ed., *The Politics of Interests – Interest Groups Transformed* (Boulder, Colo.: Westview Press, 1992), 175–98. For a different approach, in which the expected results of exposure to international trade define interest-group coalitions in domestic politics, see Ronald Rogowski, *Commerce and Coalitions: How Trade Affects Domestic Political Alignments* (Princeton, N.J.: Princeton University Press, 1989).

oriented Democratic economic conceptions framed by the dual notions of stagnation and planning. From the time of Roosevelt's first election, some in the Democratic leadership had been attracted by notions of planning, such as that implemented by the NRA and then during the war. Most planning conceptions were rooted in doubts that a mature capitalist economy could produce sustained growth without a strong and growing role for government.

Given this understanding, parts of the left of the Democratic order expected that after the war a return to economic stagnation was likely. What had been changed so deeply from the 1930s as to avoid a relapse? Facing such a prospect, parts of the Democratic left and the left outside the regime argued that interventionist and egalitarian economic policies would be needed to avoid stagnation tendencies. This stance reflected skepticism about whether the moderate, demand-oriented economic policies attractive to Democratic leaders would prove effective, a judgment that underestimated the positive role that modest doses of Keynesian policies could play. It also entailed a misreading of the political situation, one that has lingered among left-Democratic and social democratic critics of postwar economic policies. Even if stagnation had followed the war, the public would not have called for planning, especially after a decade of controversy about the legitimacy and effectiveness of dramatically expanded levels of government intervention in economic relations.

If there had been a return to anything like Depression conditions, the likely result would not have been a political turn to the left, to left-progressive and social democratic policies. Instead, conservative criticism of the Democratic order would have gained sufficient force to produce Truman's defeat in 1948. And that might have led to political battles in which the entire Democratic order was dismantled.

Because major new forms of government planning and related reforms were proposed as a means of coping with deep stagnation tendencies, substantial wartime growth weakened the case for them. So did the promising course of the economy in the first postwar years. Unemployment had fallen below 2 percent of the civilian labor force during the war. In 1946 it more than doubled, to 3.9 percent. But this was not the prelude to a new depression. Instead, unemployment remained under 4 percent for the next two years, roughly a quarter of what it had been in the final prewar years. Gross national product fell sharply in 1946 but then stabilized and in 1948 grew by over 4 percent.[14] The absence of a

14. Bureau of the Census, *Historical Statistics of the United States – Colonial Times to 1970*, D 85–86, "Unemployment: 1890 to 1970"; F 31, "Average Annual Growth Rates of Gross National Product (Percent): 1909 to 1970"; 135, 226–7.

prolonged downturn, combined with the massive transfer of resources from military to domestic activities, weakened arguments that policies more interventionist than the demand-oriented Keynesianism of the Democratic leadership were required to meet a new emergency. Why undertake major new state interventions if postwar economic growth seemed feasible without them?

Given significant economic progress, advocates of expanded state intervention had to make a case for which they had neither compelling evidence nor persuasive arguments. They had to show that greatly increased economic regulation – headed toward extensive planning – would generate substantially more growth and greater equity than was likely to result from the recovery that was apparently underway. Because they lacked compelling arguments, it was not possible to propose initiatives toward planning and major redistribution as pragmatic adaptations to economic exigencies from within a progressive liberal framework.[15]

Fred Block uses the term "national capitalism" to designate a scheme of extensive political regulation of market relations, which he considers to have been a reasonable economic option unfairly excluded from the postwar political agenda. In debates about postwar economic policy, participants were not unaware of such alternatives. Yet such alternatives never came close to playing a dominant role in Democratic policies. Block portrays opposition to "national capitalism" as driven by business fears of extensive state management and broad redistribution. These fears existed, but alongside a widespread progressive liberal belief that the regulatory and planning approaches in proposals such as those of the National Resources Planning Board (NRPB) were unnecessary and apt to be counterproductive. Rather than being suppressed, strongly interventionist approaches were defeated by a combination of persuasive counterarguments and improving economic circumstances.[16]

Growing postwar opportunities for foreign trade along with the do-

15. I base this judgment on my reading of the publications of the National Resources Planning Board and on several recent efforts to claim that a viable interventionist program was available to Democratic leaders after the war. Katznelson and Pietrkowski take the NRPB to represent this course, in its advocacy of active and growing government intervention to define and regulate markets to achieve full employment and significant economic redistribution. A similar case is made by Brinkley, who also emphasizes the NRPB vision of a broad and encompassing welfare state. See Ira Katznelson and Bruce Pietrkowski, "Rebuilding the American State: Evidence from the 1940s," *Studies in American Political Development* 5 (Fall 1991): 301–39; and Alan Brinkley, *The End of Reform: New Deal Liberalism in Recession and War* (New York: Alfred A. Knopf, 1995).

16. Fred Block, *Origins of International Economic Disorder*, 34, 50, 70–7; "Empire and Domestic Reform," *Radical History Review* 45 (Fall 1989): 122.

mestic stimulus of military programs tended to reduce pressures for major new progressive liberal economic reforms. But to consider these factors as having caused a detour – via growth – away from left-progressive or social democratic economic policies is doubly wrong. This view understates the strength of domestic growth tendencies. And it misunderstands the real postwar choices, in which the main alternative to Democratic policies was not social democracy but a combination of Dewey and Taft.[17] Growth helped to consolidate Democratic practices and institutions by demonstrating the good judgment of progressive liberal policies; without growth, the clamor for change would have mainly given the advantage to powerful antistatist political forces.

The ironies of growth

Economic growth always has disruptive elements, even when it seems mainly to realize the promise of an established economic model. Postwar growth seemed to achieve the promise of a mature mass-production market economy that had been signaled by economic changes from the turn of the century onward.

Yet if the economic successes of the postwar years helped sustain the Democratic order, the forms of growth contained elements that would eventually weaken it. This growth, which occurred amidst a rapid expansion of mass production, has come to be called postindustrial.[18] Postindustrial growth meant social and economic change that would eventually disrupt networks that were politically important to the Democratic order. Postwar growth also tended to become nonunion growth – this was so much a political as well as an economic process that I will discuss it later as one of the political problems that were arising for the Democratic order.

The Democratic order was a modernizing economic and political project (not a way back to the prosperity of the 1920s). Modernization, given the maturity of the mass-production system in the 1940s, meant policies that encouraged postindustrial growth without that aim being specified. From macroeconomic policy to research subsidies (as via defense spending) to urban and housing policies, Democratic policies had

17. Thus Katznelson and Pietrkowski are wrong to claim that the key choice in the 1940s was between two versions of a New Deal state, developmental and fiscalist: The key choice was whether or not a New Deal state would be retained. See Ira Katznelson and Bruce Pietrkowski, "Rebuilding the American State"; and Marion Clawson, *New Deal Planning – The National Resources Planning Board*, (Baltimore, Md.: Johns Hopkins University Press, 1981).

18. I use "postindustrial" to indicate the relative decline of labor directly engaged in producing material goods in an advanced economic setting.

the effect of stimulating postindustrial change. This meant a growth in professional, scientific/technical, and service occupations; a relative decline in manual occupations in mass production; and sectoral shifts from manufacturing toward services. Even in the decade ending in 1950, white-collar occupations grew faster than blue-collar positions.[19]

While postindustrial change was visible in the late 1940s, the most obvious tendency was the rapid growth of mass production. The backlog of demand for consumer durables spurred an expansion of industrial employment. Exports also buoyed manufacturing employment in the United States. The postwar exclusion and withdrawal of women from wartime jobs in production, along with claims that this was a natural process, made less visible the declining relative capacity of goods production to absorb labor. Had women workers resisted their displacement from industrial jobs, this might have been more evident.[20]

Economic and social modernization meant a relative shift of labor away from goods production, even at the high tide of industrial mass production. This shift was likely to erode social groups from which the Democratic order drew support, notably industrial workers. In 1947–9 political discourse on the economy had other primary concerns, mainly finding a way to sustain growth.

Who were "consumers"?

In the late 1940s Democratic policies encouraged movements and interest groups to take shape. When such new forces made claims for resources or access to political power, they were drawn toward the Democratic order. This was due both to Democratic power and to Democratic themes of participation and equity.

No force equivalent to the labor movement appeared, and labor re-

19. Bureau of the Census, *Historical Statistics*, D 182–232, "Major Occupation Group of the Experienced Civilian Labor Force." On postindustrial change, see Daniel Bell, *The Coming of Post-Industrial Society* (New York: Basic Books, 1976); and Fred Block, *Postindustrial Possibilities: A Critique of Economic Discourse* (Berkeley: University of California Press, 1990).

20. Claims about postindustrial change in these years refer to changes in rates of growth, not to an absolute decline in labor in goods production. Thus despite the postwar exclusion of many women from industry, the number of women employed in manufacturing increased from 2.3 million in 1940 to 3.6 million in 1950. The *rates* of increase for women's employment in transport and communications, wholesale and retail trade, and finance were larger – 100, 80, and 70 percent respectively, as against 57 percent in manufacturing. Table 131, "Detailed industry of employed persons, by sex, for the United States: 1950 and 1940," Bureau of the Census, *Census of Population: 1950*, vol. 2, *Characteristics of the Population* (Washington, D.C.: Government Printing Office, 1950).

mained preeminent among popular groupings. Its leading position was recognized in links with the party and state and in routine Democratic practices, even if its size and strength made for an uneasy fit with the progressive liberal idea that popular interest groups are basically equal. Democratic discourse affirmed the legitimacy of interest-group formation and of political efforts by groups that had been politically excluded or severely underrepresented. This opened political space for new efforts to a far greater degree than had been possible before the 1930s. Although no group could challenge labor's position, several emerging groups were potentially powerful.

Yet there was already a tension in Democratic approaches to new political forces. The democratic side of Democratic themes encouraged the development of new forces. But the Democratic leadership was cautious about any course that might be destabilizing, by disrupting alliances or jarring Democratic routines of governance. Major new political forces were likely to mean disruption. A simultaneous encouragement and hesitation can be observed in postwar conflicts about consumers and civil rights.

Regarding "consumers," the Democratic leadership could not generate major organized groups despite its interest in doing so. The Truman administration faced an explosive situation after the war regarding prices and wages. If wartime restrictions on consumption were relaxed, inflation might soar. There was a brief effort to mobilize support for price controls, and Democratic appeals for lower prices continued for several years.[21] Amidst great concern about prices, consumers were often recognized as a group by the administration and by Democratic leaders. Such recognition reflected progressive liberal commitments to cope with social and economic problems by linking state intervention and interest-group action. The appeal to consumers also aimed to find a new route to middle-class electoral support at a point when economic recovery was undermining arguments that hardship required Democratic governance.

While Democratic leaders claimed success when the 1948 victory seemed partly due to Truman's concern about "average" families, little was accomplished in building a political force of consumers.[22] Consumers were often addressed as women managers of the domestic econ-

21. Joel Seidman, *American Labor from Defense to Reconversion* (Chicago, Ill.: University of Chicago Press, 1953), 214–53.

22. Consumer groups do not figure in Alonzo L. Hamby's account of the main liberal forces in 1948, in *Beyond the New Deal: Harry S. Truman and American Liberalism* (New York: Columbia University Press, 1973), nor are they important in the campaign accounts by Donovan, Miller, and Phillips cited previously. Consumer groups are not among those with which the DNC maintained major ongoing relations in the

omy.[23] Encouraging consumer action thus meant building an interest group based on women's domestic responsibilities. In this conception, women's interests should be identified with Democratic policies that would improve the economic side of domestic life. This emphasis was continuous with the social feminist themes of the 1930s, though it meant a relatively conservative formulation of them.[24]

Not surprisingly, few people mainly identified as "consumers" achieved high positions in the political order; even had consumers been much more active and organized, the attempt to mobilize them was not an invitation to share power. Women were addressed as domestic managers and urged to support a political order whose centers of power were far from their grasp. Democratic leaders combined "women" and "consumers," but their efforts did not spur enduring major efforts by groups of consumers. Why not?

Seen from the center of the regime, the political landscape seemed full of actual and prospective interest groups whose support might prove beneficial. Yet the leadership of the Democratic order could not simply call forth substantial new movements and interest groups. Even if Democratic efforts had been more astute with regard to "consumers," it required more than state action to produce powerful new forces. It also required that a germinal group or movement take shape on its own, which was not occurring. And there was a need for a compelling and plausible set of ideas, if not a full program. With consumers, these ideas might have provided a fuller and richer account of what organized

1948 presidential campaign. "4/20–7/1/48" folder, "7/2/48–9/1/48" folder, "9/2/48–10/7/48" folder, File DNC, Redding Papers, Truman Library.

23. Recording, July 27, 1948, "The High Cost of Living," India Edwards and Mrs. Clark Clifford, "Script of Recording, India Edwards and Mrs. Clifford," folder, Papers of the Democratic National Committee, Truman Library. See also India Edwards, Oral History Interview at the Truman Library, January 16, 1969, and November 10, 1975.

24. By social feminism I mean the view that the position of women could and should be improved through expanded social welfare provision and labor law reform, and that a broader political and social participation of women should be encouraged – without insistence on egalitarianism in law or politics, without equal rights measures, and without an effort at an independent mobilization of women. Social feminism did not reject the notion of primary female responsibilities for childrearing and domestic work but sought to enable women to carry out those tasks in more comfortable circumstances while widening the range of opportunities available to women in work and public life. On social feminist currents in the 1920s and 1930s, see Nancy Cott, *The Grounding of Modern Feminism* (New Haven, Conn.: Yale University Press, 1987); Susan Ware, *Beyond Suffrage: Women in the New Deal* (Cambridge, Mass,: Harvard University Press, 1981); Susan Ware, *Partner and I: Molly Dewson, Feminism, and New Deal Politics* (New Haven, Conn.: Yale University Press, 1987); George Whitney Martin, *Madam Secretary: Frances Perkins* (Boston: Houghton Mifflin, 1976); and Blanche Wiesen Cook, *Eleanor Roosevelt* (New York: Viking, 1992).

consumers might do in an advanced market economy than Democratic leaders were able to suggest. This thematic absence was not surprising – defining such a role for consumers would probably have meant proposing major new forms of economic regulation. Such an expansion was not very appealing for Democratic leaders who saw little room to maneuver in this area.

"Consumers" were a partly imaginary interest group, despite their frequent presence on Democratic lists alongside labor and urban ethnic groups. A real consumers' group would have met several Democratic political needs in the late 1940s, and might have provided anti-Republican pressure to back up Democratic economic and social policies. Yet since most "consumers" were women and addressed as such by Democratic leaders, we can understand the weakness of consumer efforts as a failed substitute. What the Democratic leadership failed to do about consumers was much less disruptive and difficult than what they did not even consider doing with respect to women!

Does this mean the Democratic order should have tried to mobilize women as consumers on the basis of a feminist appeal? Democratic leaders would have had little conception of how to proceed, and it is unlikely that a sufficient nonstate basis for such a movement existed to allow the political order to help it develop rapidly. Rather than a nascent feminist movement merely in need of Democratic support in the late 1940s, there were small political groups of women in or close to the Democratic order who were concerned with improving the political and social position of women. Their views of how to achieve that improvement – and what it should include – were often in conflict. This was partly due to strategic differences between advocates of involvement in party politics and advocates of other modes of political activity. And there were sharp differences of principle between social feminists and equal rights advocates.

In the debate on equal rights approaches and an equal rights amendment, social feminists and the labor movement generally opposed such measures on protectionist grounds, while equal rights advocates insisted on their potential for alleviating inequities between men and women. The Truman administration did not support an equal rights amendment. The Women's Bureau of the Labor Department remained a stronghold of social feminism, and it made little or no effort to assist women who wanted to remain in the industrial work force after the war.[25] Serious

25. On postwar debates about equal rights see Cynthia Harrison, *On Account of Sex: The Politics of Women's Issues, 1945–1968* (Berkeley: University of California Press, 1988), 24–30. On women, the labor movement, and reconversion, see Ruth Milkman,

efforts by the Democratic leadership to forge unity among these currents or to provide decisive support to one of them would have been costly and difficult. As an indication of how much remained to be done in overcoming divisions among political currents concerned with women's status, one can read a proposal by the League of Women Voters in 1947 advocating that "in law and its administration no distinctions on the basis of sex shall be made except such as are reasonably justified by differences in physical structure, biological, or social function."[26]

The Democratic order had more choices than trying to promote a full-scale feminism or addressing women only as consumers. The extraordinary economic and social mobilization of women during World War II followed their substantial political involvement in the prior decade. While many women (and men) wanted to reestablish stable families after the war, they also wanted to stay involved in work and public life.[27] The Democratic approach to women as consumers had little to say about these complex choices. Truman presumed women could be politically defined as domestic managers and mothers, a restricted view given their recent activities:

> I say the Democratic Party has relied on you women. And I must turn this sentence around and say that you women have relied on the Democratic Party. As mothers and homemakers, you must be concerned with the prices you pay in the stores and with the proper schooling of your children. And you have learned through bitter experience that the Republican Party cannot be relied upon to bring your children a better tomorrow. For proof

Gender at Work: The Dynamics of Job Segregation by Sex during World War II (Urbana: University of Illinois Press, 1987), 128–52. See also Susan Hartmann, *The Home Front and Beyond: American Women in the 1940s* (Boston: Twayne Publishers, 1982).

26. League of Women Voters, Pamphlet, 4/1/47, "Bill on the Status of Women": 4, in Subject File, General Correspondence 1947, Papers of India Edwards, Truman Library.

27. Claims about women's preferences after the war are hard to prove. Women were rarely asked, either in opinion polls or the popular press, but were often lectured on their domestic obligations. When the issue of women's postwar roles was debated, the typical categories made it difficult to express what may have been prevalent sentiment. Women did want to build or rebuild families; it also seems that many women wished to continue elements of their expanded economic and social involvement from the Depression and war years. At the time, these preferences were often presented as exclusive choices, with the presumption that the first was morally proper. See Harrison, *On Account of Sex;* Milkman, *Gender at Work;* Nancy F. Gabin, *Feminism in the Labor Movement: Women and the United Auto Workers, 1935–1975* (Ithaca, N.Y.: Cornell University Press, 1990), 134–42; and Leila Rupp and Verta Taylor, *Survival in the Doldrums: The American Women's Rights Movement, 1945 to the 1960s* (New York: Oxford University Press, 1987).

of that, you have only to look at the record of the Republican 80th Congress.

You are the housewives of our country. What is the campaign issue foremost in your minds? We all know the answer. Day after day, when you do your marketing, you must face the soaring prices the 80th Congress has forced upon you.[28]

A similar approach was taken by other prominent Democratic leaders.[29]

In an election waged over the legacy of the New Deal and major foreign policy issues, Truman's approach – the dominant Democratic approach – was condescending and even exclusionary. The Democratic order was unable to build on the modest reform efforts some of its leaders had made in the 1930s. At that time women with social feminist views influenced Democratic policies in several areas.[30] Eleanor Roosevelt, Frances Perkins, Mary Dewson, and numerous others aimed to improve the political and social position of women.

Postwar conservative opposition to the Democratic order rarely attacked its social feminism. There certainly would have been attacks on a more assertive reform policy, given the flowering of conservative discourses on women's obligation to home and family.[31] Yet the continued involvement of women in public political and economic activities sug-

28. Truman, "Remarks Recorded for Broadcast on Democratic Women's Day," September 27, 1948, *Public Papers 1948,* 580.

29. J. Howard McGrath asserted: "I am convinced that the great majority of [women] will vote for Harry S. Truman. . . . [A] vast majority of women consistently voted for the Democratic Party during the administration of Franklin Delano Roosevelt. They did so because the social and economic programs of the Democratic Administration reached into their homes, touched them and their husbands and families directly and intimately, and gave them a sense of greater security and a more abundant life." Press Release, J. Howard McGrath, Democratic National Committee, Monday, February 9, 1948, DNC File, Publicity Division, Papers of John Redding, Truman Library. A Democratic Party radio show contained the following exchange in July, 1948:

> India Edwards: "Of course, everybody knows that prices have gone up . . .
> Mrs. Clark Clifford: "Yes, but most of us are too busy – just getting our daily work done – to study the problem very carefully. But I'm convinced that if the women of America knew *all* the facts – if they knew just how *high* prices have gone, how *fast* they have climbed and *why* – something would be done about it, and quickly."

Recording, "The High Cost of Living," India Edwards and Mrs. Clark Clifford, July 27, 1948, Records of the Democratic National Committee, Truman Library.

30. See Ware, *Beyond Suffrage;* Frances Perkins, *The Roosevelt I Knew* (New York: Harper & Row, 1964); and Martin, *Madam Secretary.*

31. Elaine Tyler May, *Homeward Bound: American Families in the Cold War Era* (New York: Basic Books, 1988).

gests that Democrats could have taken new initiatives without risking much. Instead, women who in 1935–7 had been addressed not only as family members but also as citizens and occasionally as workers were in 1947–9 addressed almost exclusively as wives and mothers concerned with home management. The postwar Democratic effort to reach women as consumers and domestic managers was unimaginative and restrictive, and both features were probably connected to its lack of success. Given tensions between social feminist and equal rights perspectives, there would have been problems in formulating a broadly agreed-on course of reform. But the Democratic leadership never got to the point of considering how those problems might be overcome.[32]

Efforts to build on the social feminism of the 1930s – there were available leaders and institutional points of departure – might have produced significant benefits. There might have been Democratic electoral gains among women. And ties between social feminist currents and the Democratic order might have been strengthened in ways that would have been valuable to both.

Regarding gender and family, there were policies worthy of consideration both on their merit and in terms of their political viability. Perhaps what in Western Europe is called family policy – combinations of family allowances, health care, child care, and early education – might have been proposed in the United States after World War II.[33] A family

32. Discussions of the Fair Deal make little or no reference to policies directed primarily toward women. This absence indicates the marginality of the debate about equal rights and social reform with regard to the main concerns of the leadership of the Democratic order at that time. Hamby, *Beyond the New Deal,* 311–51. India Edwards, a Democratic official, repeatedly complained about the failure to take women seriously within the DNC. India Edwards folder, Political File, President's Secretary File, Truman Library.

33. On postwar family policies see Gisela Bock and Pat Thane, *Maternity and Gender Policies: Women and the Rise of the European Welfare States, 1880–1950s* (New York: Routledge, 1991); and Mary Ruggie, *The State and Working Women: A Comparative Study of Britain and Sweden* (Princeton, N.J.: Princeton University Press, 1984). The likely predominance of social feminists in developing and implementing any American family policy would have given such a policy a protectionist character with egalitarian elements. There was no prospect of enacting social welfare policies in the late 1940s that had explicit and strong egalitarian aims with regard to gender relations. There were many reasons for this, including a lack of significant political forces in favor of such aims. For a recent argument in favor of using egalitarian criteria to evaluate the effects of social welfare policies on gender relations, see Ann Shola Orloff, "Gender and the Social Rights of Citizenship: The Comparative Analysis of Gender Relations and Welfare States," *American Sociological Review* 58 (June 1993): 303–28.

policy could have been proposed in terms consistent with the progressive liberalism of the Democratic regime and the social feminist views of its most prominent women leaders.

Family policy initiatives might have lessened the conflicts among Democratic forces that probably would have arisen from reform proposals about gender relations. A broad-based family policy might have provided a basis for further political debate and policies regarding women's interests in building families, entering or remaining in paid employment, and engaging in public social and political activities. A progressive liberal family policy might have withstood the antistatist critique made by conservative Republicans and Democrats of new reform efforts. It is even possible that a postwar family policy might have provided a basis for reducing divisions between social feminists and equal rights feminists, as the attainment of national policies rooted in social feminist views might have gradually reduced the political opposition of social feminists to making equal rights claims. Here the wartime economic mobilization of women provided further grounds for reducing tensions. That mobilization placed many women in the position of making claims for equal treatment and pay; this was a potential bridge toward equal rights feminism.[34]

Given a significant social feminist current, a massive wartime mobilization of women, and widespread claims about the virtues of family, a family policy was a plausible Democratic approach. But no serious Democratic response was made to the postwar choices that women faced, leaving the field open for conservative calls for women to concern themselves entirely with domestic life. This result was partly due to a relative decline in the political capacities of nonstate Democratic forces, in the party and elsewhere. Who would have done the extensive work of movement- and coalition-building necessary to get the attention of Democratic leaders and to pursue an active social feminist reform policy? Nonstate Democratic forces had neither the interest nor the capacity to do so, while feminists were divided and weak as a political force.

Democratic leaders in and close to the administration were not interested in opening a new front of political conflict about gender and family. If one thinks about how such conflict would have taken place, it is easy to see how reasons could be found to justify this lack of interest

---

34. It took several more decades for a major reduction of these tensions to occur. Both currents persisted in the 1960s and 1970s but within a clearer framework of common commitments. On the egalitarian dimension of women's wartime labor mobilization, see Gabin, *Feminism in the Labor Movement*, 157–60.

(if reasons were even necessary). If, for example, the Democratic leadership had urged labor unions not to initiate or collude in postwar efforts to deprive women of wartime jobs they wanted to keep, there would have been fierce battles with both unions and employers.[35] To settle those battles on favorable terms would have required not just side-deals in the conversion process. It would have meant rethinking government labor market policies to encourage the entry of women into better-paying fields and positions. And it would have required many unions to consider basic questions about their gender composition. Even leaving aside Truman's own disinclination, it is not hard to see why Democratic leaders had little interest in such efforts.

The unimpressive effort to spur consumer activism did not yield enduring consumer groups. Nor did it address the complex of issues about gender, family, and work raised by Democratic policies in the 1930s and in the war experience. These issues were left unattended by Democratic leaders while anti-Democratic forces extolled the virtues of conventional family life.

Racial politics in the 1940s

If Democrats tended to avoid political and social questions about gender and family relations, with race relations this option was closed by the end of World War II. From then on, the Democratic order encountered racial issues as a central challenge. These issues repeatedly divided Democratic political forces – related debates are still underway and link arguments about the political meaning of equality with views of how to understand race in American life.

The starting point for analyzing Democratic racial politics is a double reality. The Roosevelt and Truman administrations were the least racist since Reconstruction, and the Democratic order was less racist than any of its predecessors. Yet Democratic practices fell well short of even modest Democratic statements about racial equality, much less the firmer pronouncements of the late 1940s.

---

35. This is not to suggest that Democratic leaders would have fought vigorously for such aims had the political costs looked smaller. Accounts of labor politics after World War II provide little basis for such a conclusion. The massive inflow of women into wartime production – 200,000 in automobile production – was followed by their exit amid huge layoffs. The key moment was employers' refusal to rehire women after the initial postwar layoffs, accompanied by a lack of union or government pressure to do otherwise. See Gabin, *Feminism in the Labor Movement*, 57–113.

The emergence of a civil rights movement

The modern civil rights movement entered its most active and successful phase after the Supreme Court decisions and antisegregation campaigns of the mid-1950s. Yet fifteen to twenty years of significant activity preceded those developments. Civil rights forces were on the scene in the late 1930s, and a mass movement took shape during World War II.[36] This early appearance of civil rights forces helps explain how the movement became so large and sophisticated in the early 1960s and why many blacks then believed they had already been very patient about gaining civil rights.

In the 1930s measures directed against the specific problems faced by blacks, as distinct from the hardships blacks shared with other groups, were not enacted. Yet administration policies were not often overtly racist. Given the encouragement of civil rights efforts by several prominent administration figures, notably Eleanor Roosevelt, the Democratic approach meant a partial turn away from past segregationist federal policies.[37]

During and after World War II a developing civil rights movement demanded that the democratic principles for which that war was fought be applied to American racial practices. These claims, backed up by mobilization efforts, influenced federal employment policies and race relations in the armed forces. The incorporation of blacks in the war effort required extensive cooperation across racial groups and yielded new experiences of relative racial equality.

Tensions arose between emerging civil rights forces and the Democratic order about formulating and enforcing administration directives against racial discrimination. One dramatic episode was a march on Washington organized by A. Philip Randolph and other civil rights leaders, which was canceled only when Roosevelt established the Fair

---

36. See Richard Dalfiume, *Desegregation of the U.S. Armed Forces: Fighting on Two Fronts, 1939–1953* (Columbia: University of Missouri Press, 1969); Herbert Garfinkel, *When Negroes March: The March on Washington Movement in the Organizational Politics for FEPC* (New York: Atheneum, 1969); Thomas A. Krueger, *And Promises to Keep: The Southern Conference for Human Welfare, 1938–1948* (Nashville, Tenn.: Vanderbilt University Press, 1967); and Daniel Kryder, "The American State and the Management of Race Conflict in the Workplace and in the Army, 1941–45," *Polity* 26, no. 4 (Summer 1994): 601–34.

37. On the Roosevelt administration and "race liberalism" – the view that blacks should be included in the general reform measures taken by the New Deal and would thereby improve their economic and social position – see John B. Kirby, *Black Americans in the Roosevelt Era: Liberalism and Race* (Knoxville: University of Tennessee Press, 1980).

Employment Practices Commission. Roosevelt's executive order regarding fair employment on June 25, 1941, raised expectations of legal and social equity and demonstrated the possibility of influencing the Democratic order through mass pressure.[38] (It also weakened the position of the Communist left among blacks, as the CP criticized civil rights leaders for jeopardizing wartime unity.)[39]

After the war civil rights forces tried to increase political and legal pressures for racial change.[40] Nationally there was deep division – less about defining the proper pace of civil rights reform than about whether it should be pursued at all. Truman was willing to make an effort, and he sometimes spoke firmly on behalf of civil rights. Democratic leaders sponsored commissions, supported bills, and issued executive orders that went beyond any measures proposed by Roosevelt. In 1947 pro–civil rights views had advanced far enough for the President's Committee on Civil Rights to propose:

> To strengthen the right to equality of opportunity, the President's Committee recommends:
>
> 1. In general: The elimination of segregation, based on race, color, creed, or national origin, from American life. The separate but equal doctrine has failed in three important respects. First, it is inconsistent with the fundamental equalitarianism of the American way of life in that it marks groups with the brand of inferior status. Secondly, where it has been followed, the results have been separate and unequal facilities for minority peoples. Finally, it has kept people apart despite incontrovertible evidence that an environment favorable to civil rights is fostered whenever groups are permitted to live and work together. There is no adequate defense of segregation.[41]

38. See John Patrick Diggins, *The Proud Decades: America in War and Peace, 1941–1960* (New York: W. W. Norton, 1988), 26–31; Louis Ruchames, *Race, Jobs, and Politics: The Story of FEPC* (New York; Columbia University Press, 1953); and Richard Polenberg, *War and Society: The United States, 1941–1945* (Philadelphia: Lippincott, 1972). The wartime experience of Chicanos in the West, especially in mining, is discussed by Clete Daniel in *Chicano Workers and the Politics of Fairness: The FEPC in the Southwest, 1941–1945* (Austin: University of Texas Press, 1991).

39. John Morton Blum provides a useful summary of events in *V Was for Victory – Politics and American Culture during World War II* (New York: Harcourt Brace Jovanovich, 1976), 188.

40. The postwar situation is outlined in Harvard Sitkoff, *The Struggle for Black Equality, 1954–1980* (New York: Hill and Wang, 1980), 11–23. The main exception to this strategic course was the antisegregation campaign of CORE, discussed in August Meier and Elliot Rudwick, *CORE: A Study in the Civil Rights Movement, 1942–1968* (New York: Oxford University Press, 1973).

41. President's Committee on Civil Rights, *To Secure These Rights, The Report of the President's Committee on Civil Rights* (Washington, D.C.: U.S. Government Printing Office, 1947).

The report advocated antidiscrimination measures in education, employment, housing, and health.

Truman supported a progressive liberal civil rights plank in the 1948 Democratic platform that was much stronger than any in Roosevelt's campaigns, though he preferred a milder statement in the hope of muting Southern opposition.[42] Serious arguments took place at the 1948 Democratic National Convention as slates of delegates selected on the basis of racist rules were challenged. The debates (centered in the Credentials Committee) strikingly resemble the famous conflicts of 1964. The Southern delegations claimed to follow customary practices and to be long-established as the real Democratic Party. They also rejected the authority of the national Democratic Party over its constituent state parties. The opposition to these delegations argued that racially restrictive practices were illegal and charged that the political forces responsible were not reliably committed to national Democratic programs or Truman's campaign. These issues were brought to the floor of the convention, where the majority report of the Credentials Committee favored the segregationist delegations. It was approved by voice vote, with much opposition, in a turbulent scene.[43]

In 1949 Truman submitted a general civil rights bill, an antilynching bill, an anti–poll tax bill, and a fair employment bill, and none of them passed. If policy results did not go much beyond what had happened during World War II, public debate grew on racism, segregation, and civil rights.[44] In conjunction with civil rights groups, the Democratic order opened a new national political space for arguments about racial discrimination. These shifts were regarded by Southern conservatives as a dire threat, and a vigorous countermobilization against federal racial liberalism rapidly appeared. At a conference early in 1948, Southern

---

42. Senator Hubert Humphrey of Minnesota played a key role in guiding the process toward a conclusion that racial conservatives deemed unacceptable. Clark Clifford later claimed to have been more worried about political expediency than Truman was. Andrew Biemiller Oral History Interview, Truman Library; Clark Clifford Oral History Interview, Truman Library, 260–1.

43. *Democracy at Work – The Official Report of the Democratic National Convention* (Philadelphia: Local Democratic Political Committee of Pennsylvania, 1948), 102–10.

44. Berman says that Truman combined strong antiracist statements with very modest actions. This reasonable description downplays the significance of the shifts in public argument about race that were under way. William Berman, *The Politics of Civil Rights in the Truman Administration*, (Columbus: Ohio State University Press, 1970), 67, 77, 157–8. On Southern antagonism to administration initiatives, see Robert A. Garson, *The Democratic Party and the Politics of Sectionalism, 1941–48* (Baton Rouge: Louisiana State University Press, 1974), 229–41.

governors meeting with Senator McGrath, then head of the Democratic National Committee, strongly criticized Truman's civil rights policies. Strom Thurmond, Governor of South Carolina, began the meeting:

> Do you, as Chairman of the Democratic National Committee, deny that the proposed anti-poll tax law, the proposed anti-lynching law, the proposed FEPC [Fair Employment Practices Commission] law, and Federal laws dealing with the separation of races, and each of them, would be unconstitutional invasions of the field of government belonging to the states under the Bill of Rights in the Constitution of the United States?[45]

Democrats and civil rights

There was no prospect that emergent civil rights forces would ally with the conservative opposition to the Democratic order. Policy declarations by the national Democratic leadership and the policy efforts of the administration made the Democratic order an unavoidable reference point. This also meant rejecting the Henry Wallace campaign, though left political currents had gained strength among blacks. The themes of this rejection were put clearly by William Hastie, Governor of the Virgin Islands:

> We are not misled by the civil rights position now stated by this new party and its special effort to woo the Negro vote. We remember well and bitterly that the followers of the Communist Party line scuttled an equally aggressive civil rights program overnight in 1941 when Germany attacked Russia. They did not hesitate then to urge us to forget about civil rights in America and concentrate entirely upon their primary objective of aiding Russia. . . . We can and will win the civil rights fight under President Truman's leadership. Nothing but bitter disillusionment and a reactionary Republican administration could result from following the Wallace will-o'-the wisp.[46]

Yet relations between civil rights forces and the Democratic order were difficult. The civil rights movement was ambivalent – the Democratic order was the framework in which civil rights efforts were possible, but it was often an unyielding terrain on which to battle for changes in racial politics. This complexity was due in large part to Democratic fears that even very modest reform efforts in racial politics might cause great political damage.

45. Transcript, Conference of Southern Governors with Senator J. Howard McGrath, Chairman of the Democratic National Committee, February 23, 1948, Publicity Division, DNC File, Papers of John H. Redding, Truman Library.
46. William H. Hastie, Press Release, Democratic National Committee, October 13, 1948, White House File – Political, Papers of Philleo Nash, Truman Library.

The appropriate analogy is with the initial experience of the labor movement in relation to the Democratic order, and the differences are striking. While the labor movement helped found the Democratic order, the modern civil rights movement took active mass forms only after the Democratic order had been constructed. And while expressions of Democratic support for civil rights were unprecedented, there was no achievement equivalent to the Wagner Act for the civil rights movement in the 1930s and 1940s.

Administration ties with civil rights organizations in 1947–9 were far less substantial than those that the unions had forged in the 1930s. While there were few members of either the labor movement or the civil rights movement in Congress, leading administration positions, or high party offices, there were far more representatives and close allies of labor than of the civil rights movement in middle- and lower-level positions.[47] Compared with the labor movement, there were few places where blacks could establish real power in or even close relations with the Democratic Party. This was out of the question in the South; outside the South, blacks had few real political options. There was no question of blacks dominating urban Democratic organizations.

Debate about the role of the labor movement in the Democratic order took a substantial labor presence for granted. With the civil rights movement, little was taken for granted. In the 1940s civil rights forces employed core themes of the Democratic order to make their case for racial change, and the principled merit of the case was evident. Yet serious reform of race relations entailed grave political dangers. Democratic conservatives who were willing to cooperate with the political order (especially from border states and the less conservative parts of the South) might become ardent opponents. And racial conservatives already opposed to the Democratic order might be spurred to high levels of mobilization. Democratic leaders from the mid-1940s on faced the problem of conforming to their own declared principles by responding credibly to the proposals of civil rights forces. How could the Democratic leadership act responsibly on civil rights without intensifying bitter divisions and weakening the political order?

47. Hastie recalls that while prominent civil rights leaders had some access to the administration, their organizations had little influence as such. He also makes an interesting point about the effects of the Cold War on racial politics: Because Truman had less need of Southern support than did Roosevelt for his international policy, he was freer to antagonize Southern Democrats with progressive racial policies. William H. Hastie Oral History Interview, Truman Library, 1/5/72.

A stronger Democratic civil rights policy?

Was a stronger advocacy of civil rights feasible and potentially successful? What might it have gained? In the late 1940s a full national attack on all legal and customary segregation would not have been politically workable (much less an attack on informal major practices of racial discrimination). But there may have been an opportunity for a more serious campaign against Southern segregation than the administration contemplated.

Democratic caution was often explained – and justified – as necessary to limit Southern defections.[48] Yet the intensity of conflicting positions on civil rights made even caution a risky choice, as major confrontations were certain. While significant support existed in the South for national Democratic policies outside the field of racial politics, major Southern defections from the Democratic order were taking place in 1946–7, prompted by apprehension about the Democratic racial course. The presidential candidacy of South Carolina's Strom Thurmond in 1948 demonstrated what Southern unhappiness with racial change might mean.[49]

A more aggressive civil rights policy focused on Southern segregation would certainly have generated fierce opposition. Would it have been worth the cost? To answer this question, it is important to gauge the costs of the cautious Democratic policy. One cost was to limit the potential for the civil rights movement to identify actively with the Democratic order and for the regime to incorporate that movement as it had done with labor a decade earlier. The Democratic treatment of civil rights issues in making administrative and legislative choices was guarded and hesitant. Unprecedented reform initiatives were combined with dubious compromises. The uncertain commitment of Democratic leaders encouraged civil rights forces to support the Democratic order from a distance even when these forces relied on its initiatives to open public debate and propose racial change. (This distance was fine with the many Democratic leaders who were not eager to be identified

---

48. "Transcript of Conference of Southern Governors with Senator J. Howard McGrath," February 23, 1948, "Publicity Division, 2/13/48–4/20/48" folder, DNC File, Redding Papers, Truman Library.

49. On Southern politics in the 1940s see Numan V. Bartley and Hugh D. Graham, *Southern Politics and the Second Reconstruction* (Baltimore, Md.: Johns Hopkins University Press, 1975), 24–50; Alexander Heard, *A Two-Party South?* (Chapel Hill: University of North Carolina Press, 1952); and V. O. Key, Jr., *Southern Politics in State and Nation* (New York: Alfred A. Knopf, 1949).

with civil rights and unexcited about blacks occupying important positions.)

A more aggressive civil rights course might have encouraged an earlier expansion of mass civil rights activism in closer relation with the regular political forms of the Democratic order. Here Democratic caution had the unintended effect of helping create a dilemma that plagued civil rights action from the late 1940s to at least the mid-1960s. Civil rights forces faced a difficult choice between litigation and mass civil disobedience and other forms of unconventional political mobilization. A focus on either was risky and open to criticism – for narrow legalism or impatient disruptiveness. This difficult choice was in large part created by the political exclusion of blacks from the main conventional forms of Democratic power – in the state, the party, and, to a slightly lesser extent, the labor movement. This exclusion affected precisely the forms of political action that could have been more easily combined either with legal efforts or mass mobilizations – electoral campaigns, lobbying, local and national fights about agency performance, and so on. Democratic leaders had no appetite for the fierce intra-Democratic battles that would have been needed to open up normal political options for emergent black political forces.[50]

Further, caution in civil rights did little or nothing to weaken the position of Southern conservatives in the House and Senate. The national Democratic course avoided any sustained efforts to undermine these forces. In the 1930s many Southern Democrats were willing to support New Deal legislation so long as it did not make a frontal attack on Southern racism and paternalism in politics, agriculture, and industry. The national underdevelopment of social welfare provision and low levels of unionization provided wide room for maneuver within those limits – thus legislation that enabled strong industrial unions to gain recognition did not compel or guarantee unionization in hostile Southern communities.

In the late 1940s Southern political elites were not opposed to welfar-

---

50. In the North a logic of electoral competition should have led to a far more rapid and extensive inclusion of blacks than took place. Mechanisms of racial exclusion undermined this logic, in both urban and state politics. A good combination of works for understanding the racial dynamic is Steven P. Erie, *Rainbow's End: Irish-Americans and the Dilemmas of Urban Machine Politics, 1840–1985* (Berkeley: University of California Press, 1988); and Dianne M. Pinderhughes, *Race and Ethnicity in Chicago Politics – A Reexamination of Pluralist Theory* (Urbana: University of Illinois Press, 1987). Erie's account focuses on Irish-Americans, and Pinderhughes focuses on blacks – who would have seen their political status greatly improved if they had been facing the problems encountered by Irish-Americans.

ist settlements between strong unions in the North and Midwest and large firms. Yet there were few other major national reform initiatives that would not jeopardize distinctive Southern arrangements. Large increases in unionization, minimum wage levels, or social welfare provision would certainly have done so. Ongoing socioeconomic changes jeopardized segregation in the South and further isolated that region by making obsolete the equivalents of segregation in other parts of the country.[51] After core Democratic reforms were in place, Southern conservatives became a growing impediment to further reform on many fronts.

It is hard to imagine the Truman administration waging all-out political war on Southern segregation. Not doing so made sense from the perspective of those concerned with maintaining the Democratic order, who already had enough fights on their hands. Yet the policy of the Truman administration gave rise to a dynamic that caused trouble for the Democratic order from the late 1940s until its demise. The pro–civil rights position was strong enough to encourage the action of civil rights forces and ensure that they regarded the Democratic order as the basis of their actions. But that position was ambivalent and calculated in ways that made civil rights forces cautious about the Democratic leadership and uncertain about the depth of their commitment. Thus relations between civil rights forces and the progressive liberal leadership were tense. At the same time, the regime's recognition of the legitimacy of the claims of civil rights forces threatened its adversaries without greatly weakening them, spurring a determined response.

Perhaps there was no better means of combining Democratic principles with practical judgment than the cautious support for civil rights of the late 1940s. Policies aimed at dismantling explicit legal forms of racial segregation in the South would have led to great political turbulence. Yet they were compatible with Truman's commitments and those of the main Democratic institutions to ending formal and legal modes of racial discrimination. There were two moments when such policies might have been implemented through administration directives and legislation. One moment was 1943–5, when stringent measures might have been justified in terms of wartime requirements. The other moment was after the 1948 election, when Truman's victory might have been translated into a more aggressive and successful effort to achieve some of the civil rights policies

---

51. Urbanization, industrial growth during and after the war, and the expansion of government employment opened positions to blacks and spurred movement away from southern rural areas. Doug McAdam, *Political Process and the Development of Black Insurgency, 1930–70* (Chicago: University of Chicago Press, 1992), 65–116.

that were proposed and other policies focused on weakening Southern segregation.

The obvious rejoinder is that Southern resistance in alliance with the national conservative opposition would simply have stopped such efforts, both in Congress and in state and local governments. Thus it is necessary to expand the range of speculation, to imagine a sustained political campaign by the leaders of the Democratic order on behalf of an adventurous course of racial reform. Given such a campaign, Democratic successes in 1944 and 1948 might have created a situation in which clearly drawn pro–civil rights measures could have been put into effect as presidential directives or passed as bills. (The first method was employed in 1948 to continue desegregating the armed forces.)

What might have resulted from an aggressive major campaign against Southern segregation? First, it might have won valuable racial reforms compatible with core Democratic commitments. Second, this course might have preempted part of the massive Southern resistance to desegregation that occurred over the next decade and a half.[52] Legal changes might have been enforced firmly in ways that took them off the immediate political agenda and narrowed the basis for the countermobilization of Southern opposition to desegregation that began soon after the end of World War II.

Third, campaigns against Southern segregation might have weakened the power of Southern conservatives to block Democratic reforms in other areas. This would not have happened mainly by turning such conservatives out of office, as one can presume the Southern electorate would have rallied around defenders of segregation in response to federal attacks. But more forceful federal action might have compelled major Southern compromises, rather than only spurring greater resistance. It might even have been possible to weaken links between Southern racial conservatives and Republican and Democratic racial moderates in ways that reduced the political strength of the former.

For an energetic antidiscrimination course to have been possible, civil rights legislation and administration directives would have had to focus sharply on Southern segregation. There would have been far too many opponents for a sweeping national antidiscrimination program to have been pursued. But a partial reform of race relations, aimed at undermining legal segregation in the South, might have resulted. Such a reform might have had a further positive effect on the political order, one that in the late 1940s could not be foreseen. Strong action against Southern

52. See Numan V. Bartley, *The Rise of Massive Resistance: Race and Politics in the South during the 1950s* (Baton Rouge: Louisiana State University Press, 1969).

segregation might have helped separate out the main elements of racial subordination by highlighting the most explicit and legalized forms of unequal treatment. This separation might have enabled efforts at racial reform to move along the multiple dimensions of racial inequality in the United States over several decades – first in the 1940s by targeting the most dramatic forms of legal segregation in the South, then in the next two decades taking on other types of legal and customary segregation throughout the country, and then addressing the deep inequities remaining after the removal of formal racial inequalities.

It might have been possible to single out egregious forms of Southern racial discrimination for immediate attention, and then move toward the application of basic liberal principles of citizenship to blacks. Thus the result of an earlier aggressive reform policy might have been the development of several distinct pro–civil rights coalitions over the course of the Democratic order. The eventual benefit to the Democratic order might have been considerable: Racial politics could have been rendered less explosive over time by a sequence of reform measures in which not all problems were on the table at the same time.

Democratic caution about civil rights in the 1940s contributed to a daunting situation in the early 1960s, when multiple demands about changing race relations were bound closely together – demands to end Southern segregation, to eliminate legal forms of racial discrimination everywhere, to remove less formalized but entrenched discriminatory practices throughout the country, and to reform the social and economic conditions to which blacks were subject.[53]

It is easy to think of obstacles to the antidiscrimination course I have outlined, but they do not include Democratic commitments. Strong opposition to legal segregation required the consistent application of principles that helped define the Democratic order: state intervention for reform purposes, opposition to formal racial discrimination, and encouragement of new interest organization. Vigorous opposition to Southern segregation was recommended in the more aggressive practices of the Fair Employment Practices Commission during World War II, in the 1947 report on civil rights, and in the Democratic civil rights platform in 1948.

To answer the question about a more aggressive civil rights policy posed earlier: It might have been feasible to undertake such a policy,

---

53. These issues can be distinguished in terms of different modes of equality: of legal status, opportunity, and conditions or resources. For a discussion of racial politics in the 1960s that relies on these distinctions, see David Plotke, *Democratic Breakup* (Cambridge University Press, forthcoming).

targeting Southern segregation. And that policy would have had some chance of success, without being overwhelmed by Southern resistance or undermining the entire Democratic order. An aggressive antisegregation policy might have had positive effects for the Democratic order, perhaps outweighing the costs of an even greater Southern resistance than the one that occurred in the late 1940s. This course would have been risky, and it is easy to see how progressive liberals who wanted both to advance a broad reform agenda and to undermine segregation might have judged it politically unwise. While no choice was without major problems, the caution of Democratic civil rights initiatives eventually turned out to be a major source of trouble.

The counterfactual course I have sketched was not likely. Yet such speculation is based on the most plausible further move to the left available to the Democratic order in the late 1940s. It is on firmer ground than the arguments of critics of the domestic policies of the Truman administration who regret the failure of American politics to take a social democratic turn after World War Two.[54] The latter argument expresses reasonable views of how public policies and modes of political participation might have been improved in the 1950s and 1960s. Yet it has little basis in realistic judgments about what was possible in the 1940s. The construction of a large, durable social democratic current in national politics would have required radical discursive shifts even in the labor movement. Social democracy was only one labor perspective, along with revised AFL voluntarism, progressive liberal reformism, Catholic social unionism, and Popular Front Communism. For such a current to dominate the Democratic order would have required basic thematic shifts and organizational changes in the party and state as well as other movements and interest groups.

After World War II Western European social democracy was uncertain about whether to advocate a systemic replacement of capitalism by socialism as its strategic framework, though significant currents in mass social democratic and socialist parties retained that aim. Yet such parties advanced policies very different from those of the Democratic order. Social democrats usually proposed significant state ownership of firms. They usually proposed extensive public provision of health care and family support. And most social democratic parties still advocated a

---

54. See Ira Katznelson, "Was the Great Society a Lost Opportunity?," and Nelson Lichtenstein, "From Corporatism to Collective Bargaining,"; in Steve Fraser and Gary Gerstle, *The Rise and Fall of the New Deal Order, 1930–1980* (Princeton, N.J.: Princeton University Press, 1989).

major redistribution of economic resources. These differences indicate the sweeping political changes required to turn Democratic progressive liberalism into a social democratic project.[55]

To imagine vigorous national policies against Southern segregation from the end of World War II through the remainder of the decade does not presume such fundamental political changes. Yet if speculation about a different Democratic racial politics engages actual strategic choices in 1944–9, it points to a political course that only a small minority of Democratic forces supported.

Thematic continuities

In 1947–9 the Democratic order continued to express a reformist progressive liberalism.[56] The reform legacy of the New Deal was not betrayed by the Truman administration in the late 1940s. From his twenty-one point program in September 1945 through his presidential campaign and 1949, Truman argued for extending and deepening the New Deal, including new reform efforts in housing, health, and civil rights.[57]

Yet several thematic shifts did take place. Populist motifs were relatively more prominent than laborist elements among the regime's democratic themes. Economic themes emphasized the prospects and virtues of growth more than was typical in the 1930s. And the anti-Communism of the Democratic order was expressed more vigorously and prominently than in the preceding decade. The meaning of the first shift was ambiguously conservative, since Democratic populism could express a variety of political meanings. The other two shifts more clearly marked a conservative reworking of Democratic commitments. The emphasis on growth could at times displace rather than complement other progressive

55. On postwar social democracy see Gosta Esping-Andersen, *Politics against Markets: The Social Democratic Road to Power* (Princeton, N.J.: Princeton University Press, 1985).
56. At the time, some progressive liberals and many to their left criticized Truman for allegedly betraying New Deal progressive reformism. Ironically, these claims were less accurate than the equally polemical attacks by conservatives who claimed that New Deal liberalism had survived Roosevelt to dominate and distort national political life. Many conservatives perceived basic continuities between Truman and Roosevelt; this view was developed by conservative commentators and theorists in the 1950s. See George H. Nash, *The Conservative Intellectual Movement in America – Since 1945* (New York: Basic Books, 1976).
57. A good selection of Truman's main statements on domestic reform appears in Barton J. Bernstein and Allen J. Matusow, ed., *The Truman Administration: A Documentary History* (New York: Harper & Row, 1966), 86–157.

liberal social and economic themes. And the Cold War could combine with domestic anti-Communism to diminish the space for arguments in favor of new reform. Yet core Democratic themes were continuous with those of the previous decade, and neither growth nor anti-Communism became the exclusive and defining obsession that critics of Democratic policies have charged.

Truman's speeches and public statements stressed democratic and populist themes more in 1947–8 than before or after.[58] He claimed to defend citizens against threatening forces:

> The object of this 80th Congress, it seemed to me, was to take the bargaining power away from labor and give it back to the special interests. . . . You know, that Congress had some of the most terrific lobbies that have ever been in Washington in the history of the country. They had the real estate lobby, the one that turned the rent control program loose, and they had the speculators lobby, and they had the National Association of Manufacturers lobby, whose interest is not the public interest.[59]

The attack on special interests was part of a populist critique of privileged economic groups. Truman's own history and sometimes rocky relations with the unions made it unsurprising that his left themes would be mainly populist. Democratic leaders addressed "the people" both as individuals and as members of salient groups. New groups entered prevalent depictions of a wide popular Democratic bloc – blacks, a notion of the "middle classes" that included new groups of salaried employees, and consumers joined labor, the poor, professionals, farmers, and (occasionally) youth.

In the late 1940s there were innumerable positive references to working people as a core Democratic group. But any notion of a class party, however broadly conceived, was absent or explicitly rejected. Instead, the Democratic order was defended as a popular and democratic project. And the Republican Party was charged with being a class party on the

---

58. Truman's major public statements resulted from a collective decision making and writing process in which Clark Clifford, George Elsey, Samuel Rosenman, and Charles Murphy were crucial. The development of major speeches and statements is discussed in the oral history interviews of George Elsey and Charles Murphy at the Truman Library, including a ninety-page memo by Charles Murphy on the production of major administration speeches and party platforms. Charles Murphy, "1948 Speech Preparation Memo, Presidential Campaign," Papers of Charles Murphy, Confidential File, Truman Library. See also 1948 Presidential Campaign, Speech File folder, Papers of George M. Elsey, Truman Library.

59. Truman, "Rear Platform Remarks – Rock Island, Illinois, September 18, 1948," *Public Papers* 1948, 292–3.

grounds that it was tied to narrow social groups and its policies fostered class division.[60]

The meaning of growth

The postwar Democratic emphasis on growth is best understood as part of a continual effort to balance commitments to reform and stability. In the late 1940s – after two decades of Depression, conflict, and war – progressive liberals identified economic and political stability with Democratic reformism. Democratic leaders argued that their political order was responsible for stability and prosperity, as when Truman asked:

> Did the Republican leaders care what happened to you in the Depression? Did the Republican administration provide the jobs you needed? Did they save your homes or protect your bank deposits? They either didn't care what happened to you or they didn't know what to do about it. They just sat and waited for prosperity to come from around the corner.

> The Democrats took action. Prosperity couldn't get around the corner until it had some help. . . . It took a government that was willing to try new ideas. It took a government that put human rights above property rights. You got that kind of government when you elected Franklin Roosevelt. . . . The Democratic Party has always been the party of progress and liberalism, the party that puts human rights first.[61]

In the 1930s the progressive liberal leadership stressed the urgency of change. Amidst social breakdown, stability had to be created; radical reforms were legitimate means of achieving social order. By the late 1940s such arguments for reform could not be easily made. There more often seemed to be a choice between reform and stability. Yet Democratic discourse continued to link stability not with order per se but with social and economic development – the latter would protect and consolidate prior reforms and facilitate new ones. Democratic practices were defended as fair means of ensuring stability – which now also referred to a new international situation. As Truman said,

> Our immediate task is to remove the last remnants of the barriers which stand between millions of our citizens and their birthright. There is no justifiable reason for discrimination because of ancestry, or religion, or

60. This formulation appears in the work of the Clifford group. "Strictly Confidential" Memorandum 9/15/48, Campaign Material folder, Political File, Papers of Clark Clifford, Truman Library.
61. Truman, "Remarks," Jersey City, October 7, 1948, *Public Papers of the Presidents of the United States – Harry S. Truman, 1948* (Washington, D.C.: Government Printing Office, 1964).

race, or color. . . . The support of desperate populations of battle-ravaged countries must be won for the free way of life. . . . They may surrender to the false security offered so temptingly by totalitarian regimes unless we can prove the superiority of democracy. . . .

For these compelling reasons, we can no longer afford the luxury of a leisurely attack upon prejudice and discrimination. There is much that State and local governments can do in providing positive safeguards for civil rights. But we cannot, any longer, await the growth of a will to action in the slowest State or the most backward community. Our National Government must show the way.[62]

The leadership of the Democratic order always posed its ability to reach economic objectives as a major element of claims to national leadership. In the 1930s the main Democratic economic aims were economic stability and minimal social security. Even a return to pre-Depression levels of economic activity was regarded as a real accomplishment, and significant growth beyond those levels was an aspiration. After the war the first economic aim was to avoid a deep new downturn, which was widely feared. When no such decline occurred, this was hailed as a Democratic achievement. When the war-inspired recovery put growth within reach as an enduring peacetime process, it was highly attractive to progressive liberals. Democrats claimed credit for economic and social security and prosperity, as in their 1948 platform:

Ours is the party which rebuilt a shattered economy, rescued our banking system, revived our agriculture, reinvigorated our industry, gave labor strength and security, and led the American people to the broadest prosperity in our history.[63]

Growth was regarded as legitimate and desirable from the outset, even when many took the Depression as evidence of deep and perhaps permanent tendencies toward stagnation. Postwar progressive liberals advocated growth as a means of achieving prosperity, which was conceived both as increasing gross national product and enhancing social security. Growth was a major economic and social commitment, not an aim that precluded all others.[64]

62. Truman, "Address Before the National Association for the Advancement of Colored People," June 29, 1947, Washington, in Truman, *Public Papers of the Presidents of the United States – Harry S. Truman, 1947* (Washington, D.C.: Government Printing Office, 1961).

63. "Democratic Party Platform of 1948," in Donald Bruce Johnson, ed., *National Party Platforms*, vol. 1, *1840–1956* (Urbana: University of Illinois Press, 1978), 430.

64. For a major statement on these matters, see Truman's 1949 state of the union message, *Public Papers of the Presidents of the United States: Harry S. Truman, 1949* (Washington, D.C.: Government Printing Office, 1964), 1–7. See also Craufurd D.

No radical break was involved in striving for growth and praising its virtues, as progressive liberal leaders saw growth as conducive to broad reformist aims. This view may not have been correct, but it was not naive. While growth can reduce pressures for redistributive reforms in favor of an all-round expansion of benefits, it can also have reformist effects by providing room for political and social experimentation and lessening the bitterness of economic conflict. In the postwar context economic stagnation would have undermined reform efforts by strengthening the position of the least reformist sections of the Democratic order and enhancing the prospects of its conservative opponents.

Critics of the politics of postwar growth are partly right to note the diminished emphasis on redistributive measures in the late 1940s. Yet even in the 1930s redistribution was not proposed as the main intrinsic aim – the purpose of economic and social policy was to achieve prosperity and reduce forms of impoverishment that made it impossible for those suffering from it to function as responsible citizens. In Depression conditions, with limited social welfare provision, those aims required measures with significant redistributive effects.

Neither the progressive liberal leadership nor major elements of the Democratic bloc planned to continue redistributing resources until general equality was achieved. When postwar economic prospects brightened, Democratic leaders thought growth could yield general prosperity and also alleviate hardship by allowing modest redistributive efforts, which that same growth would make politically more feasible.[65] This course was rightly perceived as very different from more individualistic Republican conceptions of prosperity. Democratic leaders presumed extensive government action, well beyond what Republican views allowed, and saw that action as helping to create balanced prosperity rather than tending to the problems at the margins of market-based growth.

Although the Democratic order might be criticized for not being a left-populist or social democratic project of sustained redistribution, there was little betrayal involved, as extensive government planning and radically egalitarian outcomes were not the aim. Some in and close to the leadership of the Democratic order hoped to give significantly more weight to left-progressive and social democratic themes after World War II. But there is little sign that this course was possible, given the modesty of social democratic impulses in and around the Democratic order and

Goodwin, "Attitudes toward Industry in the Truman Administration: The Macroeconomic Origins of Microeconomic Policy," in Michael J. Lacey, ed., *The Truman Presidency* (Cambridge University Press, 1990), 89–127.

65. Hamby, *Beyond the New Deal,* 298–300.

the strength of conservative forces opposed even to further progressive liberal initiatives. A major expansion of redistributive themes in the discourse of the Democratic order was also made more difficult by wartime expansion and postwar growth. Both tendencies redrew lines between the working class and the poor that had been blurred by the economic collapse of the 1930s and made it harder to argue plausibly that the two groups faced a common dire fate.[66]

In the late 1940s the main themes of the Democratic order predominated, regarding moderate social reform, economic improvement, and equitable political bargaining. Where these conceptions were not wholly accepted, they provided the framework for political debate. "Liberal" and "conservative" views contended *within* the new order as claims that the reform process needed rapid extension or that consolidation was preferable. Since Democratic themes appeared to be political common sense, broad adherence to progressive liberal principles could coexist with conservative stances on particular issues or with a self-description as moderate.

After the mid-1930s progressive liberal discourse expanded to include new elements, rather than reiterating a closed doctrine. The themes advanced by new movements and interest groups were partially incorporated into the main formulations, and the arguments of critics were also taken into account. Roosevelt and the Democratic leadership in the mid-1930s provided a model for future Democratic efforts. He claimed to be left of center – yet moderately to the left of center and committed to flexibility in applying progressive liberal principles. This presentation understated the extent to which the political spectrum had been redrawn, while helping to legitimate that new spectrum by presenting Democratic policies as responsibly near its center. Truman also presented himself as (slightly) to the left of center, now referring clearly to the center of the political spectrum defined by the Democratic order.

---

66. The Democratic approach to welfare provision contained only limited redistributive elements: "By the 1940s, America had acquired a unique, unsatisfactory, semiwelfare state. The New Deal had expanded vastly the role of the federal government and altered its relation to the states. States spent much more for welfare, which they administered more professionally. Government had assumed a degree of responsibility for economic security unprecedented in the nation's history. Still, the new structure had been erected partly on an old foundation. . . . It modified but did not erase archaic distinctions between the worthy and unworthy or the ablebodied and impotent poor; it created walls between social insurance and public assistance that preserved class distinctions and reinforced the stigma attached to relief or welfare; in no way did it redistribute income or interfere with welfare's role in the regulation of the labor market and the preservation of social order." Michael Katz, *In the Shadow of the Poorhouse – A Social History of Welfare in America* (New York: Basic Books, 1986), 247.

When in 1947–8 he moved to the left, he made his greatest contribution to sustaining the Democratic order.

It was not automatic or easy for the Democratic reinterpretation of American liberalism to become and remain dominant. That result had to be won through political argument and conflict, as it was in the late 1940s. Democratic forces attacked political groups and currents to their right who proposed perspectives that were fiercely antistatist and opposed altogether to the New Deal, clearly racist, or vehemently anti-union. These attacks drew a line to the right of the Democratic order that could mark the limits of legitimate criticism – once that line was drawn, Democratic efforts sought to place conservative critics on its illegitimate side and thus repeatedly sought to divide the opposition between "responsible" and irresponsible critics.

Criticism from Truman's right took several forms. A fundamentalist opposition to the New Deal (from Republicans and some conservative Democrats) rejected most government economic and social regulation. Antifederal criticism often took on a racial character, as in Thurmond's presidential campaign and other campaigns for state and national office in the South.[67] Moderate critics and the most conservative adherents of the new regime argued that core New Deal measures had been and remained worthwhile, but they viewed further reform as unnecessary and often undesirable.

By the late 1940s the presence of a political order suffused by Democratic common sense had created a mainly centrist dynamic among opponents. The hope of political effectiveness encouraged fundamentalist conservative opponents of the Democratic order to formulate their arguments in terms similar to those of more moderate critics. Pure and simple antiunionism was rearticulated as criticism of unfair practices by powerful unions, while virulent racism took shape as concern for communal and individual rights against federal intrusion. As with Taft-Hartley, the drift toward the Democratic center by previously adamant opponents of the regime enhanced their political effectiveness – but at great cost, as basic opposition to the Democratic order from the right moved toward the margins of American political life. Even when antagonists of the regime inflicted political defeats on the Truman administration, they were constrained to represent those outcomes as reasonable ways of tempering modern Democratic realities.

67. Bartley and Graham, *Southern Politics and Second Reconstruction,* 50–3; Everett Carll Ladd with Charles D. Hadley, *Transformations of the American Party System: Political Coalitions from the New Deal to the 1970s* (New York: W. W. Norton, 1975), 135–7; and Jack Bass and Walter DeVries, *The Transformation of Southern Politics: Social Change and Political Consequence since 1945* (New York: Basic Books, 1976), 5–6.

10

Democratic anti-Communism and the Cold War

Present Soviet policy can be roughly described as a policy of kicking at doors. If the doors fly open, the USSR moves in. But, if the doors are locked, the USSR does not break down the door because it does not want to get involved in a fight with the householder or its friends. The policy of the Truman Doctrine is a policy of locking doors against Soviet aggression.

— Arthur Schlesinger, Jr., 1949 [1]

Long and passionate controversies surround the origins of the Cold War, its effects on American politics, and the meaning of domestic political campaigns against Communism. This chapter assesses the Democratic order in relation to the international setting of the late 1940s. Old debates are not made irrelevant by the end of the Cold War but rather reignited, combined with new questions when the premise of a strong and enduring Soviet Union no longer exists. The meaning of the events this chapter discusses is still in part being established by contemporary political conflicts whose result is uncertain. Durable orthodoxies have been destabilized by the surprising course of events in Eastern Europe and the countries of the former Soviet Union. This disruption opens space for new arguments about what happened and what it meant for politics in the United States.

I emphasize the central role of political antagonisms in generating the Cold War and spurring a fierce campaign in the United States against a politically weak Communist movement. The previous chapter concluded by noting that Democratic leaders sought to draw and enforce a political boundary on the right. They sought to distinguish legitimate from illegitimate opposition to Democratic policies and used that boundary to weaken both types of opposition. A similar process, in more dramatic forms, occurred to the left of the Democratic order. In analyzing rela-

---

1. Arthur Schlesinger, Jr., *The Vital Center*, (Boston: Houghton Mifflin, 1949), 224.

tions among the Cold War, the Democratic order, and anti-Communism in the United States, I focus on domestic dynamics.[2]

Did the Democratic order shape the Cold War?

World War II helped consolidate the Democratic order, and Democratic progressive liberalism shaped the aims and conduct of American participation. The success of the war enhanced the political legitimacy of the Democratic leadership. Relations between international and domestic politics became more complex when wartime antifascist alignments were replaced by U.S.-Soviet conflict. I aim to answer two questions: How did the Democratic order shape the Cold War? How did the Cold War affect the Democratic order?

After World War II the Democratic leadership pursued internationalist policies regarding American political involvement and the shape of new international economic institutions. Democratic progressive liberals thought it was feasible and desirable to achieve an ordered world in which interstate relations were organized fairly; this meant suspicion of nondemocratic regimes and of colonial domination.[3] Progressive liberals

2. One might instead try to explain domestic outcomes in terms of international configurations; the likely referent would be the experience of nations in World War II. Yet there was no simple relation between the war's results and domestic political shifts. Some winners moved to the left (Britain); some moved to the right without destroying a prior regime (the United States).

3. I use the term "suspicion" to avoid implying that the Democratic leadership sought vigorously to undermine colonial relationships. Regarding postwar American foreign policy, I rely mainly on these works: John Lewis Gaddis, *Strategies of Containment – A Critical Appraisal of Postwar American National Security Policy* (New York: Oxford University Press, 1982); Alonzo L. Hamby, *Beyond the New Deal: Harry S. Truman and American Liberalism* (New York: Columbia University Press, 1973); Gabriel Kolko, *The Politics of War: The World and United States Foreign Policy, 1943–1945* (New York: Random House, 1968); Joyce Kolko and Gabriel Kolko, *The Limits of Power: The World and United States Foreign Policy, 1945–1954* (New York: Harper & Row, 1972); John Patrick Diggins, *The Proud Decades: America in War and Peace, 1941–1960* (New York: W. W. Norton, 1988); Melvyn P. Leffler, *A Preponderance of Power – National Security, the Truman Administration, and the Cold War* (Stanford, Calif.: Stanford University Press, 1991); David Mayers, *George Kennan and the Dilemmas of U.S. Foreign Policy* (New York: Oxford University Press, 1988); Wilson D. Miscamble, *George Kennan and the Making of American Foreign Policy, 1947–1950* (Princeton, N.J.: Princeton University Press, 1992); Arthur M. Schlesinger, *The Cycles of American History* (Boston: Houghton Mifflin, 1986); Jack Snyder, *Myths of Empire: Domestic Politics and International Ambition* (Ithaca, N.Y.: Cornell University Press, 1991); and Barton J. Bernstein, ed., *Politics and Policies of the Truman Administration* (Chicago: Quadrangle Books, 1972), especially Barton J. Bernstein, "American Foreign Policy and the Origins of the Cold War," 15–77.

did not fully accept the dichotomy between the national interest and political values that has been central to most realist conceptions of international politics. Their view was that American national security would be enhanced in a world composed of more rather than less democratic regimes, with fewer forms of colonial and semicolonial domination. Thus states that were more democratic were expected to be politically and militarily less dangerous to the United States.[4]

Postwar progressive liberalism was deeply influenced by political and military failures to confront the fascist regimes early and strongly enough. The experience of an antifascist war and revelations of Nazi atrocities greatly increased skepticism about whether authoritarian regimes could be nonexpansionist.[5] Progressive liberals proposed that American policies encourage open regimes – "open" meant respect for citizens' political rights and relatively unconstrained participation in the international economy. The core Democratic image was of liberal societies that would not be a military threat to the United States or one another.[6] Sustaining liberal market regimes was proposed as a way to make a dangerous postwar world less hazardous. This aim was attractive for domestic forces beyond the core support of the Democratic order. Postwar progressive liberals claimed to recognize the dangers of international entanglements, but they considered the dangers of isolation to be greater.[7] On this ground the Democratic argument could defeat doctrinaire attacks. It could also withstand more sophisticated critiques

---

4. A similar claim is common in studies of international relations; countries with liberal democratic political systems are not likely to go to war against each other.

5. Those who hoped that the wartime alliances would persist and that the United States, Britain, and the Soviet Union could continue to work together were confronted with a problem: Did anything make the Soviet Union basically different from Nazi Germany from a liberal and democratic perspective? For progressive liberals there was often a degree of ambivalence as their answers became increasingly negative in 1945–6. Hamby, *Beyond the New Deal*, 87–119.

6. Support for open markets by Democratic leaders is sometimes taken as evidence that American policy was dominated by internationalist business groups. These groups definitely preferred open markets, and had influence with the administration. Yet if the preference for open markets depended only on the perceived self-interest of business, American policies would have been less dynamic and ambitious, because of enduring public opposition to American international involvement and suspicion of business elites.

7. The continuity between World War II and the Cold War was affirmed in Democratic publicity. Strong claims were made that Republican isolationism rendered that party a less reliable opponent of international Communism than the Democratic Party. Pamphlet, "Who Voted to Strengthen the Free World?" Democratic National Committee, Folder K, Political File, President's Secretary's File, Harry S. Truman Library.

Table 10.1. *Explaining the Cold War*

	Reactive Soviet policy	Aggressive Soviet policy
Reactive U.S. policy		Democratic Cold War liberalism (Schlesinger)
Aggressive U.S. policy	American revisionism (Williams)	Democratic containment (the present work)

that recommended limiting rather than eliminating the international role of the United States.[8]

How does one assess Democratic responsibility for the emergence of the Cold War? For years, answers to this question were sharply divided between two alternatives depicted in Table 10.1.[9] In the conventional view, the Cold War was a defensive response by the United States and its allies to aggressive Soviet actions and to the threat to liberal societies posed by Soviet power and Communist doctrine. In the revisionist view, American policy was largely to blame for turning a conventional balance-of-power situation into a frighteningly dangerous conflict, especially by making anti-Communism into a political crusade. Many proponents of the latter view go on to argue that economic motives generated American policies and the resulting international tensions.

8. Republicans inclined toward isolationist views were in a difficult situation, trying to balance fierce anti-Communism in domestic politics with impulses to restrict American international commitments. World War II by no means eliminated isolationist currents from American political life, but it destroyed much of their popular support and left the most doctrinaire proponents of isolationism with far less influence than in the early and mid-1930s. Conservatives such as Robert Taft increasingly put their criticism of American foreign policy in terms of a reluctance to pay the anticipated costs of expansive policies, rather than opposing internationalism per se. Conservative critics of Democratic international policies provided no clear criteria by which American commitments could be limited. This left them uneasily poised between acting as a loyal opposition to Democratic (or bipartisan) policies and making a sharp move toward neo-isolationist positions. See David Green, *The Language of Politics in America: Shaping Political Consciousness from McKinley to Reagan* (Ithaca, N.Y.: Cornell University Press, 1987), 171–201; and John B. Judis, *Grand Illusion: Critics and Champions of the American Century* (New York: Farrar, Straus, and Giroux, 1992).

9. Arthur J. Schlesinger uses these terms: "The Open Door school argues that the American drive for empire caused the Cold War. The geopolitical school argues that the Cold War caused the American drive for empire." Political conflict – differing judgments

Table 10.2. *Analyzing American foreign policy*

	Reactive U.S. policy	Aggressive U.S. policy
U.S. political aims	Democratic Cold War liberalism	Democratic containment
U.S. economic aims		American revisionism

With the end of the Cold War and of the Soviet Union, this history will be debated anew, probably for many years.[10] In my view, both American and Soviet policies were assertive and often aggressive. Democratic progressive liberals played a major role in shaping the severe political and ideological conflicts that defined U.S.-Soviet relations. Democratic policies, motivated by political commitments to contain Communism, sustain open economies, and encourage liberal polities, were an active response to the ways that Soviet power expanded during and after World War II. Democratic leaders perceived the conflict with the Soviet Union as continuous with the battle against fascist regimes. The Cold War was regarded as having an antiauthoritarian political content, a view shared by many progressive liberals who had initially hoped for amicable relations with the Soviet Union.[11] Political antagonisms formed the core of the Cold War – rather than either economic or strategic concerns. Table 10.2 links views of the character of American

about how to organize large modern societies – gets little recognition in either case. Schlesinger, *Cycles of American History*, 163.

10. A number of efforts have been made to mediate between defenses of American policies and the most stringent critiques of them. Among works that state such aims are Gaddis, *Strategies of Containment;* and Leffler, *Preponderance of Power.* The first is, on balance, favorable in its assessment of American policy. A work about the 1940s that remains interesting, written outside the framework of American arguments, is Fernando Claudin, *The Communist Movement from Comintern to Cominform* (New York: Monthly Review Press, 1975).

11. Those involved in formulating Democratic policies emphasized political opposition to Soviet expansion as their primary consideration. Clark Clifford is emphatic on this point in his oral history interview at the Truman Library (Washington, D.C., March 23, April 13, April 19, May 10, July 26, 1971; March 16, 1972; and February 14, 1973) 370–8. For an interesting critique of revisionist arguments see Geoffrey S. Smith, "Harry, We Hardly Know You: Revisionism, Politics, and Diplomacy, 1945–54 – A Review Essay," *American Political Science Review* 70, no. 2 (June 1976): 560–82.

foreign policy with views of the goals of that policy – my view is that political aims were central.

The choice of containment

For decades the Cold War was defined by the American policy of containment. The most famous formulation of this policy was George Kennan's in 1947 – his efforts crystallized tendencies well underway rather than inventing a new course.[12] In varying forms, the policy of containing Soviet power was taken up by successive American administrations. Kennan's key argument was made precisely where he broke with a purely realist account of international politics. He claimed that the Soviet Union was not simply another great power. Instead, Kennan and other proponents of containment considered the Soviet Union to be an expansionist power driven by political and ideological commitments as well as by more conventional security concerns. These political pressures (some of them pre-Soviet in origin) encouraged a more expansionist and dangerous Soviet foreign policy than would be expected from balance-of-power thinking by leaders of a less ideologically ambitious Russian state.

From these judgments it was a short step to claim that Soviet power was expansionist in ways that jeopardized both American national security and liberal values. Kennan was somewhat more reflective in taking this step than were many Democratic leaders in 1947–9, and he rarely relied on lurid images of Soviet and Communist rule. But there was no basic distortion of his argument in the course of its implementation by the Democratic order.

Containment fit well with Democratic internationalism. Progressive liberals saw containing Soviet power as central to American global political responsibility. Thus anti-Soviet containment was regarded as consistent with Democratic principles. The domestic political success of the Democratic order combined with compelling formulations of the containment doctrine to reframe the American debate. Thus Democratic leaders sought to find the right mix of military and political elements in

12. Kennan played a major role in the movement away from the wartime alliance with the Soviet Union. His two most influential statements regarding containment were his long telegram of February 1946 and his anonymous article in *Foreign Affairs* in July 1947. Both statements insisted that the Soviet Union was a real threat to the United States, as the result of great power and Russian nationalist as well as Communist motives. He argued for a broad political and strategic opposition to the Soviet Union, not only a military response. See Mayers, *George Kennan and US Foreign Policy,* 95–126.

policies toward the Soviet Union. And they debated whether American responses should be local (i.e., within the same setting as the Soviet action in question) or global (raising the costs of Soviet action by attacking any appropriate Soviet interest).

Kennan later criticized other interpretations of containment, including the assertive and militarized version propounded in the final years of the Truman administration, notably in the crucial memorandum written for the National Security Council, NSC68. There was no basic change in Democratic strategy from 1947–8 to 1951–2.[13] Consider the much greater variation between containment and other possible American positions toward the Soviet Union. One, the policy of the Henry Wallace campaign in 1948, proposed to establish friendly coexistence with the Soviet Union on the basis of a recognition of its new power and a generous interpretation of Soviet security needs. The other policy, which could be termed "hostile disengagement," was supported by isolationist currents in and around the Republican Party. Its proponents argued for making clear the depth of American antagonism toward Soviet power, while trying to limit direct confrontations in Europe and elsewhere. The practical aim was to focus on defending American territory.[14]

The latter position was unstable because it offered no response to Soviet expansion consistent with the deeply anti-Communist views of its proponents. They wanted to avoid American entanglement in European affairs, but they could not deny that the outcome of political battles there was of vital concern to the United States. Their hostility to Soviet power was, if anything, greater than that of the Democratic leadership. In all likelihood the combination of intense anti-Communism and isolationism that predominated in conservative Republican circles soon after World War II would have resulted in an even more dangerous Cold War policy than containment. It would have been apt to lead to military action as a dramatic response to a particularly threatening Soviet action. Elements of that danger are visible in the Eisenhower-Dulles interpretation of containment, which after 1952 meant a less active engagement with Soviet power and more reliance on threats of military force to deter Soviet expansion.[15]

13. On the shift from Kennan's version of containment to the more aggressive version proposed by NSC 68, see Gaddis, *Strategies of Containment*, 83–120. NSC 68 itself was first published in the *Naval War College Review* 27 (May–June 1975): 51–108.
14. On Republican views and the isolationist currents within them, see Gaddis, *Strategies of Containment*, 119–40.
15. Eisenhower occupied a position relatively close to Truman in postwar arguments about America's international role. He opposed isolationist currents in Republican politics. He judged Soviet policies harshly, but did not believe that the Soviet Union

In political argument in the late 1940s and early 1950s, the containment position predominated. It offered at least as good an account of Soviet actions as competing positions could provide. This perspective was flexible enough to accommodate a range of views about how containment ought to be pursued, most of which were compatible with the views of the Democratic order's leadership about the international role of the United States.[16] Containment meant a sustained, broad engagement with Soviet power and allied Communist forces. The Soviet Union was regarded as posing a special political danger. Its leadership was considered to be untrustworthy, and it was regarded as seriously expansionist. Here Kennan's account of the Soviet Union was influential among progressive liberals because it portrayed that nation as dangerous without hyperbolic claims about Soviet and Communist messianism. The basic image of the Soviet Union as a strong but insecure power driven by political motives to endanger liberal regimes came to be widely accepted throughout the Democratic order in 1947–9.

Gauging Soviet aims

If the Cold War originated partly in Democratic conceptions of how to deal with Soviet power, much depends on how one assesses Democratic judgments about the Soviet Union. Did the Soviet leadership believe it desirable to expand Soviet power? If so, what means were regarded as appropriate? In sum, was the Soviet Union expansionist after World War II? The answer is a qualified yes.

Hyperbole about Soviet messianism aside, the Soviet leadership thought it highly desirable to increase Soviet power.[17] They believed the

soon after World War II intended to initiate a new war of conquest, and he communicated this view to Truman. See Stephen Ambrose, *Eisenhower: Soldier, General of the Army, President-Elect, 1890–1952*, vol. 1 (New York: Simon and Schuster, 1983), 449.

16. Gaddis periodizes American policy in this way: Kennan's version of containment, from 1947–9; NSC 68 from 1950 through 1953; the Eisenhower/Dulles "new look" policy to 1961; and flexible response, from 1961 to 1969. This periodization is reasonable, but in each phase perspectives similar to the dominant interpretation of the other three phases also existed. Gaddis, *Strategies of Containment*, 1–3.

17. Partly out of conviction and partly to win popular support and overwhelm bastions of isolationist sentiment, Democratic leaders in 1947–9 often depicted Stalin and the Soviet leadership as plotting to take over the world. In campaigns for the Marshall Plan and the Truman Doctrine such charges flourished. Republican leaders competed to inflate the currency of anti-Soviet attacks. The public record in 1947–9 is replete with melodramatic accounts of what Soviet power was about and provides ample material for revisionist critiques of Democratic themes.

most secure basis for doing so was the emergence of allied states with similar political and economic systems. Their understanding of the post-war world – organized around Leninist theories of imperialism – led them to think this expansion would occur mainly via domestic develop-ments, as decaying capitalist states would be the site of efforts at social transformation. But they thought it was legitimate to use Soviet military and political power to provide support for friendly regimes. Melvyn Leffler outlines an American and Democratic view of the situation in Europe that, while different in tone from much early Cold War rhetoric, is congruent with Soviet leaders' own view of their prospects:

> U.S. officials in the spring of 1947 saw themselves faced with an unprece-dented crisis. No one feared Soviet military aggression. But the long-term balance of power seemed imperiled by the exchange crisis in Europe, immi-nent economic disarray, the prospective proliferation of autarkical arrange-ments, and the anticipated capacity of European Communist parties to capitalize on these circumstances. If the United States did not respond, the Soviets would reap the advantages.[18]

The perceptions of these policy makers were mainly right. Soviet leaders sought a selective expansion of Soviet and Communist power. They believed that the decay of imperialism would allow this expansion to occur mainly by political means, but this view did not rule out military support to friendly new regimes.[19]

The Soviet Union was not the conspiratorial association often depicted in Democratic Cold War discourses. But it was more energetic and ambitious than the cautious and introverted power depicted in revision-ist accounts of the Cold War. A Soviet policy of selective expansion had several dimensions. Near Soviet borders, expansion responded to secu-rity concerns. Where the country in question was economically more

18. Leffler, *Preponderance of Power*, 163.
19. These judgments rely not only on the works cited earlier in this chapter but on a selection from the vast literature on the Soviet Union and the early Cold War. To gauge Soviet aims, the international relations literature needs to be supplemented by the literature on the international communist movement. During the Cold War there was a division of labor between analysts of international relations and students of Communism; this division was buttressed by the predominance of realist conceptions of international relations for which political ideology is of little interest. The revision-ist critique aimed to focus attention on the dangers of American foreign policy. Its proponents rarely took Soviet politics seriously as Communist politics. The unfortu-nate result was that revisionist critiques of American policy produced almost nothing of interest regarding the character of the Soviet regime. Skepticism about Soviet ideology is warranted on many levels. But in the long arguments about the origins of the Cold War, revisionist skepticism tended to decay into a cynicism that dismissed political aims as serious motives.

advanced than the Soviet Union, expansion was expected to be economically beneficial.

Moreover, increasing the number of Soviet-type states was regarded as a desirable political objective. In the late 1940s Soviet leaders either took their Communist ideology seriously or were constrained to act as though they did – in either case they sought and welcomed the formation of Communist and pro-Communist regimes. Soviet leaders were sensitive to risk and aware of the limitations of their position. Yet they regarded their own state and its network of alliances as ascending forces, and they sought to advance this process. They had substantive political objectives that they took seriously.[20]

A conventional great power might simply increase its allies and clients with little regard for the internal character of their societies. For strategic and political reasons, the Soviet leadership strongly preferred that its allies and clients be Communist states. Other alliances were made when this option did not exist.[21] After World War II, given a choice between a regime like the one that emerged in Finland and the one that emerged in Hungary, the Soviet leadership chose the one analogous to Hungary when it was possible to do so without running great risks.

Argument about postwar Soviet objectives was vigorous in and around the Democratic order. Large parts of the non-Communist left initially hoped that coexistence could be achieved on the basis of recognizing a Soviet sphere of political and military influence. Here events in Czechoslovakia had a powerful meaning for political argument in the United States, well beyond the strategic importance of that country. The Communist coup in Czechoslovakia in 1948 – at the least supported by

20. The logic of political conflict in the West during the Cold War led critics of containment to understate the extent of postwar Soviet expansionism. This tendency appears in different forms in Gabriel Kolko, *The Politics of War;* Joyce Kolko and Gabriel Kolko, *The Limits of Power;* Ronald Steel, *Pax Americana* (New York: Penguin, 1977); and the political writings of E. P. Thompson about the Cold War, especially *Beyond the Cold War: A New Approach to the Arms Race and Nuclear Annihilation* (New York: Pantheon, 1982).

21. As with American policy after World War II, it is not possible to deduce Soviet policy from thin realist premises. Postwar Soviet choices were derived partly from the leadership's political commitments to Communism and the forms of Marxist theory with which those commitments were linked. Soviet Marxism contained two elements that provided a strong push toward confrontational policies: a view of capitalism as in a crisis-ridden phase that would make its leaders more adventurist and aggressive; and a reductionist account of politics such that differences between democratic and authoritarian capitalism were downplayed. Both points were taken seriously. After World War II, when argument occurred in the Soviet leadership about the likelihood of new economic crises and imperialist aggression by the West, positions that stressed the likelihood of both tended to prevail.

the Soviet leadership – dashed remaining progressive liberal hopes of nonantagonistic relations with the Soviet Union.[22] Czech events vividly demonstrated the basically hostile attitude of the Soviet leadership and its allies toward liberal regimes. It was plausible that a durable Finnish-type outcome could have occurred in Czechoslovakia. And it was difficult for Democrats to accept that a liberal Czech regime posed a strategic threat to the Soviet Union. But Soviet leaders clearly regarded such a regime as a potential source of trouble.

The Czech experience showed that the Soviet Union would help destroy liberal institutions to establish a Communist regime in a nonhostile country when such action was feasible. Soviet political discourse emphasized the importance of creating favorable contexts for Communist advances, mainly through political struggle in capitalist countries. In the Soviet understanding, events in Czechoslovakia were a means of defending prior and ongoing Communist advances, not of overt aggression. The main Soviet postwar political conceptions recommended a purposeful political advance toward forming pro-Soviet regimes, accompanied by warnings of the dangers of "adventurism." While the use of force had a political role in Soviet views, the latter were not a doctrine of conspiracy or of insurrectionary efforts to seize power in Western countries.[23]

Soviet discourse was neither secret nor unavailable to American analysts. Democratic leaders could form overall judgments of Soviet aims based on a combination of diplomatic interaction, observation of Soviet policies, and (very modest) familiarity with Soviet Marxism. Their conclusion was not that tanks were about to roll toward Paris, though this was often the flavor of anti-Soviet argument in Congress and by the administration. The conclusion was that Soviet policy aimed to take every reasonable opportunity to create Soviet-type regimes.

Statements of Democratic policy paid insufficient attention to Soviet security concerns and were not much concerned with the effects of assertive American policies on Soviet perceptions. But revisionist accounts in the 1970s and 1980s focused too much on these aspects of American policies, and never provided a persuasive account of Soviet aims.[24] The early postwar Democratic view, despite the florid ways in

22. On the Czech events and their effects on American politics, see Hamby, *Beyond the New Deal*, 220–1, 230–1; and Leffler, *Preponderance of Power*, 203–7.

23. This is evident in Claudin's account of postwar European Communism, which regrets that these parties were not more actively revolutionary. Claudin, *Communist Movement from Comintern to Cominform*, vol. 2, *The Zenith of Stalinism*, 474–9, 590–7.

24. In the four decades after World War II, political debate about the Cold War tended to dichotomize conceptions of Soviet policy between purely realist notions of the Soviet

which it was presented, was more accurate than the main contending views – militant anti-Communist conceptions of the Soviet Union as a vast conspiracy, neo-isolationist views of the Soviet Union as merely a great power anxious about its borders, and Popular Front or Communist views of that country as a wholesome progressive force occasionally given to clumsy inattention to Western sensibilities. The basic Soviet stance was one of selective (not messianic) expansion both on political and strategic grounds.

The early Cold War policy of the Democratic order soon went beyond posing the objective of containment. That policy led to expectations and then commitments which constrained Democratic leaders. Containment made the United States and its allies vulnerable to requests for protection from corrupt and authoritarian regimes whose leaders claimed to be holding the line against Soviet expansion. In the 1940s progressive liberals believed in making alliances where necessary to gain crucial foreign policy aims, as during World War II. But the Democratic containment policy never provided clear guidelines that could distinguish necessary from unprincipled alliances. Given a global commitment to confronting Soviet power, the result was to build into containment the likelihood of extending alliances to include dubious and expensive partners. The Cold War soon acquired features that were not legitimate by the Democratic standards that could justify a basic policy of containment.

The Democratic order played a major role in the origins of the Cold War. Given Democratic commitments and the character of the Soviet Union and its leadership, confrontation was probable. The Democratic

Union as another big power trying to ensure its security and melodramatic accounts of a messianic state committed to expansion regardless of cost or risk. Most revisionist critics of American policy were not enthusiastic about the Soviet Union per se, although in the late 1960s anti-imperialist views led some analysts to regard Soviet policy sympathetically to whatever extent it had the effect of reducing American power, notably in the Third World. Yet the most interesting revisionist accounts rarely attempt to theorize Soviet aims and policy beyond rejecting the most extreme notions of Soviet messianism and conspiracy. Thus William Appleman Williams's work contained little analysis of the Soviet Union or Soviet foreign policy while offering analogies as silly as the following: "As with Spain in 1897, therefore, so with Russia in 1945; each was held responsible for American wealth and welfare." See William Appleman Williams, *The Contours of American History* (Chicago, Ill.: Quadrangle, 1966), 474. This inattention to Soviet policy has continued to be prevalent among critics of American foreign policy. In an interesting critical review of Melvyn Leffler's *A Preponderance of Power*, Cumings stresses the need for self-conscious theoretical analysis of the Cold War. Yet he says almost nothing about Soviet policies or Communist theories of imperialism in the first two decades after World War II. See Bruce Cumings, " 'Revising Revisionism,' or, The Poverty of Theory in Diplomatic History," *Diplomatic History*, November–December 1993, 539–69.

leadership devised and then implemented a distinctive anti-Soviet policy of containment. It did so actively, out of political opposition to Communist doctrine and strategic apprehension about Soviet power. Democratic policies were continuous with the internationalist orientation that guided the Democratic conduct of World War II, not a preemptive reaction to Republican anti-Communism in the United States.[25]

The domestic effects of the Cold War

Given the substantial Democratic role in shaping the Cold War, what were the latter's effects on the Democratic order? The Cold War reinforced core elements of the Democratic order while encouraging a conservative turn within it. The reinforcing effects of the Cold War were mainly of the same type as those caused by World War II, though more modest. Given a Democratic government as the director of the initial Cold War effort, pressures toward national unity tended to reinforce Democratic practices and institutions. The Democratic containment policy was advocated as continuous with the antifascist effort of World

25. Some have argued that the Cold War was mainly about preserving markets for American business. Clearly a containment policy was compatible with most views of the interests of American business, but that congruence does not demonstrate a primary causal role either for business elites as political actors or for economic motives in defining Democratic policies. American policy makers preferred open markets to closed economies as part of an overall preference for liberal regimes, which they also preferred on political and national security grounds. The primacy of economic elements in defining American foreign policy in these years could be defended in two ways. It could be claimed that these elements furnished the primary self-conscious aim of American policy makers; or it could be claimed that economic forces determined American policies by structuring the set of feasible choices for those policy makers. The first approach runs into trouble in the postwar years because it fails to provide a plausible interpretation of the explicit articulation of political, economic, and security concerns by policy makers. The latter did not say that the aim of open markets *defined* their preferences. The second approach is partly true in the way that economic determinism is usually partly true: Systemic pressures encouraged policy makers to prefer policies that would enhance the economic prospects of American capitalism. But these pressures cannot be presumed to be sufficient to select one from among a number of feasible courses.

American policies in the Cold War have also been attributed to log-rolling arrangements between Democratic internationalists concerned about Europe and Republicans concerned about Asia. This explanation understates the role of political arguments in favor of containment. These arguments had gained sufficient strength to structure foreign policy debate by 1947–8, to the point that recalcitrant political forces were rarely in a position to bargain on basic principles. There were differences of emphasis between those whose main concerns were focused on Europe and on Asia, but containment defined a framework for negotiating them. For the log-rolling argument see Snyder, *Myths of Empire*.

War II and thus deserving of broad support. Yet the Cold War limited new reform efforts. The near-equivalent of wartime pressures toward unity narrowed the possibilities of reform in areas where no clear prior consensus had been formed. The Cold War provided a large supply of ammunition for conservatives to attack domestic reform efforts as Communist-inspired and therefore illegitimate. Thus racial conservatives attacked racial reform projects on the grounds that Communists favored and were sometimes involved in them. Doubtless racial conservatives would have found other symbols and threats with which to oppose racial reform. Yet antireform forces in racial politics benefited when they could link their cause to the dangers posed by U.S.-Soviet conflict.[26]

How one assesses responsibility for such effects turns on assigning responsibility for the Cold War. If the Cold War was the result of American aggressiveness alone, then its domestic consequences should be regarded as the results of the choices of the Democratic leadership. If the Soviet regime is assigned significant responsibility for the Cold War, then conservative domestic pressures appear to be unintended results of both Democratic and Soviet policies. The second view is more accurate.

Democratic anti-Communism in the United States

The issues surrounding the Democratic anti-Communist campaign in the late 1940s remain knotted and controversial. With the end of the Cold War, they no longer refer to a conflict in which the United States is engaged. Perhaps the end of the Cold War will help reframe longstanding arguments in a fruitful way. Here the question is whether and how Democratic anti-Communism influenced the Democratic order. I first give a brief answer; then, to fill it out, I review the history of relations between the Democratic order and Communist and Popular Frontist currents in the 1930s and 1940s, to see why conflict erupted in such a fierce way after World War II. Communists and Popular Frontists were bitterly disappointed and often stunned by what happened in the late 1940s, and understanding why helps clarify the political core of the Democratic order.

---

26. Charges that reform currents in racial politics were linked with Communism were effective in encouraging a mobilization of segregationist forces in the South in the late 1940s and strengthened their ties with antiunion forces. On anti-Communism in the South, see Numan V. Bartley, *The Rise of Massive Resistance: Race and Politics in the South during the 1950s,* (Baton Rouge: Louisiana State University Press, 1969); and Barbara S. Griffith, *The Crisis of American Labor: Operation Dixie and the Defeat of the CIO* (Philadelphia: Temple University Press, 1988), 118–61.

What did Democratic anti-Communism mean?

What was the meaning of the anti-Communist upsurge for the Democratic order? What caused it to take place?

The postwar anti-Communist surge meant a shift toward more conservative options within the Democratic order. It occurred because conditions that allowed partial convergences between the Democratic Party and the Communist Party ended after World War II. There had been a significant association of Popular Front Communism with elements of the New Deal (as in the NLRB). These links were exaggerated and rendered in frightening colors by opponents of the Democratic order (and some of its more conservative adherents). Anti-Communism drew on and heightened fears about national insecurity; the result was to strengthen the hand of those who rejected new social and political experiments. Moreover, marginalizing the Communist Party had some conservative effects, because that party had helped to build the new industrial unions and open up national political argument about racial discrimination.

The Communist Party was a major force on the American left from the Depression until the late 1940s; the campaign against it meant a conservative turn. But that shift did not transform the Democratic order. Democratic leaders always claimed their policies would ensure popular rejection of systemic alternatives on the right or left. Anti-Communism partly defined the Democratic order through clear and adamant opposition to visions of a "Soviet America" in which economic and political power would be centralized and fused. There was no Democratic enthusiasm for an authoritarian closure of political argument and organization.

A Soviet America – a state-socialist regime dominated by a single party – was the core vision of the Communist Party in the 1930s and 1940s.[27] In 1935 Earl Browder, the Communist leader most identified with Popular Front views, declared aims wholly unacceptable to Democratic progressive liberalism:

> The question is, then, given the American working class in undisputed power, what would be the possible and probable course of the development of the economic and social life of the country?

27. This conception predominates both in Popular Front works such as Earl Browder, *The People's Front in the United States* (New York: International Publishers, 1938), and in William Z. Foster's *History of the Communist Party of the United States* (New York: International Publishers, 1952). My claims about the official party program and the long-term perspectives of the party's main leadership are not equivalent to the idea that all members of the organization were enthusiastic Stalinists. But people who could not endorse some version of the dominant conception were likely to leave soon.

The new government would immediately take over and operate all the banks, railroads, water and air transports, mines and all major trustified industries. Minor industries, municipal public utilities and the distributive occupations would be reorganized as functions of local government or as cooperatives or, in some instances, as auxiliaries of major industries. Large-scale agriculture would be taken over and operated by the government, while the mass of small farms would be encouraged to combine into voluntary cooperatives for large-scale production with state aid.[28]

Granting the distance between Democratic progressive liberalism and Communism, a question remains: Did the campaign against Communist influence cause a rupture with New Deal reformism? The least persuasive view among those who would answer yes considers that anti-Communism was deliberately used as a means of moving politics to the right through attacking a political party that, though small, was nonetheless a powerful force for reform. In this view the success of the anti-Communist campaign itself marked a sharp break in national politics.[29] The claim that Democratic anti-Communism was a calculated means of blocking reform relies on a wrong premise – that Democratic leaders aimed to stop reform and betray the New Deal. It was conservative opponents of the Democratic order who tried to stigmatize the regime as Communist-influenced and undermine it. Thus when conservative forces in Congress from the late 1930s onward attacked the NLRB as full of Communists, they sought to weaken the Wagner Act and undermine the Democratic state.[30]

More plausibly, it has been argued that a break with New Deal reformism was the unintended result of Democratic anti-Communism. The latter grew rapidly after the war, partly out of fear that failing to draw a clear line between the Democratic order and Popular Frontism would mean electoral disaster. In this view, while Democratic anti-

28. Browder's quote is from "What Is Communism? A Glimpse of Soviet America," *New Masses* 16 (July 9, 1935), reprinted in Richard Polenberg, ed., *Radicalism and Reform in the New Deal*, (Reading, Mass.: Addison-Wesley, 1972), 117–18. On Democratic opposition to communist goals and to communist forms of organization and politics, see William E. Leuchtenburg, *Franklin D. Roosevelt and the New Deal, 1932–1940* (New York: Harper & Row, 1963), 281–3.
29. This view appears in sympathetic accounts of the Wallace campaign and in Popular Frontist analyses of events in the late 1940s. See Richard M. Freeland, *The Truman Doctrine and the Origins of McCarthyism* (New York: Alfred A. Knopf, 1972); and Allen Yarnell, *Democrats and Progressives: The 1948 Presidential Election as a Test of Postwar Liberalism* (Berkeley: University of California Press, 1974).
30. On anti-Communism in conservative attacks on the NLRA, see James A. Gross, *The Reshaping of the National Labor Relations Board – National Labor Policy in Transition, 1937–1947* (Albany: State University of New York Press, 1981), 3–11, 215–32, 251.

Communism may have been partly a tactic to protect the Democratic order from assaults by conservatives, the result was a political rupture. This view is more realistic than the first, but it also errs in claiming a fundamental shift in national politics.

In the late 1940s Democratic leaders sought to stigmatize the Communist Party and eliminate its political influence. Democrats attacked Communist practice and doctrine: antidemocratic long-term goals, undemocratic modes of political leadership and decision making, a strong tendency to form quasi-clandestine and manipulative organizations, and uncritical political support of the Soviet Union.[31]

Progressive liberals stressed that the New Deal was serious about reforming and preserving a liberal market society in the United States. Criticism of business and calls for a strong regulatory role for the state never meant enthusiasm for a state-party nexus along Soviet lines. Truman believed he was true to the founding commitments of the regime when he attacked Popular Frontism as pseudo-liberalism corrupted by the Communist Party.

The political substance of the anti-Communist campaign was compatible with basic Democratic commitments. Democratic progressive liberals opposed long-term Communist goals and affirmed their commitment to a regulated market society. They opposed the party's adherence to the shifting positions of the Soviet Union. This allegiance was recognized in the 1930s, but it did not preoccupy leaders of the emerging political order because of the modest political role of the Communist Party and the limited power of the Soviet Union.[32]

Was Democratic anti-Communism justified?

This account of progressive liberal views does not justify Democratic actions. Democratic policies, not McCarthyism, established a loyalty

31. Democratic anti-Communism was articulated in these terms in 1949 in Schlesinger's *Vital Center*, 127–9. The clandestine side of Communist organization was a major target of Schlesinger's critique. It also provided a fat target for populist attacks on the Communist Party, because it made it easy to depict that party as a secret foreign-inspired association.

32. Some Democratic leaders argued that their brand of anti-Communism was superior to Republican anti-Communism: it was more attentive to the social and economic problems that could provide bases for Communist appeals, and more respectful of political liberties, while no less implacably opposed to Communist principles and strategies. The claim that Democrats were better anti-Communists than were Republicans was sincere, not just a strategic maneuver to deflect Republican attacks. It was frequently made in Democratic campaign efforts in 1947–9. Such claims appear often in Internal Security folder, Correspondence of the Chairman, Papers of J. Howard McGrath, Democratic National Committee Records, Truman Library.

program in federal employment, expelled Communists from positions of influence throughout the Democratic order, and sought to isolate or destroy unions with Communist or pro-Communist leaders.[33] Many anti-Communist policies cannot be justified on grounds of deep political disagreement: legal restrictions on the party per se, prohibition of Communist Party membership for federal employment, refusal of legal recognition to trade unions with Communist leaders, and efforts to require nonstate public organizations (not only trade unions) to exclude Communists.

Ruling out such measures would have left open numerous avenues for anti-Communist political efforts: criticizing the doctrines of the Communist Party and its allies, trying to defeat candidates for public office who had Popular Front ties, and campaigning to defeat Popular Front leaders in trade unions and other associations. Democratic leaders and progressive liberal intellectuals in principle recognized a distinction between political opposition to Communism and efforts at legal and political suppression of Communist ideas and organizations. In practice they often overlooked this distinction. Thus, when Arthur Schlesinger wrote a qualified defense of Democratic policies that entailed inquiries about the loyalty of federal employees, he framed the problem in terms guaranteed to produce abuses:

> There can be no serious question that the USSR, through the MGB, the American Communist Party and the Communist front organizations, has commissioned agents to penetrate the "sensitive" branches of the Government, such as the State Department, the Department of National Defense and the Atomic Energy Commission. The conspiratorial character of the Party insures that some of the most dangerous agents will have no Party cards or even overt Party associations. What is the Government to do?[34]

33. Anti-Communist efforts spread widely from a concern with the loyalty of government officials to unions, universities, and cultural institutions. In addition to the works cited previously by Hamby, Healey, May, and Richmond, see Paul Buhle, *Marxism in the United States: Remapping the History of the American Left* (New York: Verso, 1987); David Caute, *The Great Fear: The Anti-Communist Purge under Truman and Eisenhower* (New York: Simon and Schuster, 1978); Ellen Schrecker, *No Ivory Tower: McCarthyism and the Universities* (New York: Oxford University Press, 1986); and Athan Theoharis, "The Rhetoric of Politics: Foreign Policy, Internal Security, and Domestic Politics in the Truman Era, 1945–1950" and "The Escalation of the Loyalty Program," both in Bernstein, *Politics and Policies of Truman*, 196–241, 242–68.

34. Schlesinger, *Vital Center*, 213. More recently, David McCullough's biography of Truman compiles the main second thoughts by Democratic leaders about these policies, emphasizing that Truman, Clifford, and others acted mainly to preempt stronger and more illiberal forms of Republican anti-Communism and that top administration figures did not believe there was a loyalty problem in federal employment. This line of defense entails an inaccurate account of what Democratic leaders actually thought at

If the Communist Party per se is defined as a Soviet conspiracy, it follows that a responsible American leader would be justified in using almost any measures to uproot it. Many progressive liberals – including members of the Supreme Court – argued on similar grounds that legal attacks on the Communist Party were on balance legitimate. That party deserved special treatment because it was a distinctively dangerous group with destructive and illegal aims.[35]

Were they right? The answer is no. But in a field mined with the results of four decades of bitter argument, any answer needs elaboration. Legal restriction and political suppression of the Communist Party could be justified in two ways – by features of that organization or by emergency conditions.

Was the CPUSA an organization whose central features made its restriction legitimate? The American Communist Party was a radical response to social conditions in the United States *and* a political organization subservient to the Communist Party of the Soviet Union.[36] To grasp its character, it is necessary to distinguish between these two features. And it is crucial to make a further distinction between the Communist Party's *political support* for the Soviet Union – however fawning and uncritical – and *conspiratorial actions* aimed at enhancing that country's military strength.

Given Democratic commitments, and a background of liberal and democratic norms, only conspiracies with illegal aims should have been the object of legal action. Neither advocacy of radical domestic policies nor political support for the Soviet regime warranted such attention (as distinct from stringent political criticism). Even showing that individual Communists were involved in illegal pro-Soviet acts would not justify destroying the Communist Party as an organization unless it could be shown that such acts were a central and continual feature of party

the time. It is also an unflattering form of justification. It depicts Democratic leaders as manipulative and cynical with regard to basic political liberties, in permitting loyalty programs and related efforts that they believed to be unnecessary rather than standing up to Republican attacks. Democratic political leaders were eager to preempt Republican efforts, but they believed that a national threat merited stringent measures. They were more wrong than cynical. See David McCullough, *Truman* (New York: Simon and Schuster, 1992), 550–3.

35. For an important statement of liberal anti-Communism, see U.S. Supreme Court Decision on Constitutionality of 9(h) of the Labor-Management Relations Act of 1947, October Term, 1949, majority opinion by Chief Justice Vinson, separate (mainly concurring) opinion by Justice Jackson.

36. For a similar formulation about the Communist Party, see Bert Cochran, *Labor and Communism: The Conflict That Shaped American Unions* (Princeton, N.J.: Princeton University Press, 1977), 3–5.

activity. By these criteria – which proposals to abridge liberties of association and expression need to meet – Democratic anti-Communism was on weak ground, and many of its legal and administrative actions could not be justified.

Harvey Klehr and his coauthors seem to make a more negative assessment of the Communist Party, partly on the basis of documents from recently opened archives in Russia:

> As the documents in this volume show, however, the belief that the American Communist movement assisted Soviet intelligence and placed loyalty to the Soviet Union ahead of loyalty to the United States was well founded. American communism was certainly a radical political movement – a heretical dissent from the American tradition. But the Communist Party of the United States of America was also a conspiracy financed by a hostile foreign power that recruited members for clandestine work, developed an elaborate underground apparatus, and used that apparatus to collaborate with espionage services of that power.[37]

This formulation combines charges of different types, all of them politically damaging. But the claim that would make the Communist Party a legitimate object of legal action is not made clearly as such. I extract the following: "The Communist Party was a conspiracy to collaborate with espionage services of [the Soviet Union]." If Klehr and his coauthors had wished to make this strong claim about the nature of the Communist Party they presumably would have done so. I conclude that their evidence does not sustain a claim beyond the one made earlier: The Communist Party was not only a radical political organization, but a staunch supporter of the Soviet Union, and some of its members engaged in clandestine activities to provide such support.[38]

---

37. Harvey Klehr, John Earl Haynes, and Fridrikh Igorevich Firsov, *The Secret World of American Communism* (New Haven, Conn.: Yale University Press, 1995), 326.

38. Soon after the passage cited earlier, Klehr and his coauthors evaluate the anti-Communist campaign in the United States in this way: "Although many innocent people were harassed, the secret world of the CPUSA made such excesses possible. Without excusing these excesses, historians need now to take into account the CPUSA's covert activities and collaboration with Soviet intelligence." Klehr et al., *The Secret World of American Communism*, 326–7. This formulation is evasive because it does not even suggest what it would mean to take into account such activities in the context of the overall aims and activities of the Communist Party and its members. Thus the authors seem unwilling to claim in a straightforward way that the scale of illegal activity by Communists warranted treating the organization per se as a conspiracy to commit espionage. No one knows precisely what will be revealed or disproven in further ex-Soviet archival materials. What is clear is that the financial and political dependence of the American Communist Party on the Soviet Union was extensive, and this relationship was clear at the least to top party leaders.

In the anti-Communist campaign there was also a lack of judgment about the scale of any conceivable Communist threat. The Communist Party was never important as an independent electoral force. It could never legitimately claim to represent mass political forces insofar as it posed state-socialist objectives. Nor was there any danger of its taking over a revolutionary movement – in these decades there were few episodes and no sustained periods in large cities or regions when majorities in mass movements saw their actions as part of a strategy aimed at a revolutionary political break.[39] The Communist Party did not control any major American institution – in the labor movement its power never enabled it to dominate the CIO. It had numerous members and allies among intellectuals and artists, and it gained a degree of influence in an emergent civil rights movement. If one adds up its activities, they did not even approach making the Communist Party a genuine political threat to liberty or national security in the United States.

In the late 1940s the CPUSA advanced radical proposals in furious rhetorical style. It made plans to operate clandestinely in the face of what it regarded as an incipient American authoritarianism. But its severe misreading of American politics could not credibly be viewed as preparation for an insurrection (with what following?).

The main features of the Communist Party did not justify legal restriction or political repression. It was not primarily a conspiracy or a cover for Soviet espionage, although it engaged in clandestine activities and some of its members sought to provide whatever aid they could to the Soviet regime. The Democratic anti-Communist campaign ignored cru-

---

39. What did "revolutionary" mean at this time? The proper standard is not whether or not insurrectionary activity was contemplated. Rather it is willingness to support political parties and other organizations that declared their aim to be replacing capitalism with socialism and intended to use a wide range of means to gain that end. By this standard, Communist Parties and parts of some Socialist Parties in western Europe could claim significant popular support for revolutionary aims, though never majority support. In the United States the extensive popular protest in the 1930s and 1940s was militant and often politically radical, but not revolutionary. Sympathetic analysts of popular protest sometimes blur this crucial point. They downplay the role of political commitments in favor of depicting popular protest in terms of its capacity for disrupting prevailing political alliances; or they suggest that the absence of revolutionary commitment is not important, since such views take full shape only in moments of crisis when organized revolutionaries can take advantage of the opportunities presented. For an account of the first type, see Frances Fox Piven and Richard Cloward, *Poor People's Movements: Why They Succeed and How They Fail* (New York: Vintage, 1979); for the second, see Michael Goldfield, "Worker Insurgency, Radical Organization, and New Deal Labor Legislation," *American Political Science Review* 83, no. 4 (December 1989): 1257–82.

cial distinctions – between political associations and conspiracies, and between radical views and illegal practices – in seeking to marginalize American Communism. Republican anti-Communism, notably including McCarthyism, took such extravagant forms that the Democratic role in the late 1940s was partly overshadowed. Conservative excesses even allowed later Democratic claims that their anti-Communist campaign had been preemptive and politically unavoidable to gain more credence than they deserved. The Democratic campaign against the Communist Party and Popular Frontism in 1947–9 helped prepare the way for McCarthyism, even if most Democratic liberals rejected McCarthy.

The other possible way to justify legal restrictions would be to show that dire emergency conditions existed. In such circumstances legal but subversive and disruptive practices might warrant restriction. This is a hard case to make in general, and the postwar American situation did not allow making it well. Political conditions were not so precarious that state-sponsored attacks on a modest, unpopular political force were necessary for national security. The United States was not in danger of military attack. The growing intensity of Soviet–American conflict did not warrant restricting political liberties. Nor could external political challenges combine with internal disorder to produce a dire threat – partly due to the building of the Democratic regime, political and social order was much greater than in the 1930s.

The gap between Democratic discourse and the actual scale of American Communism in the late 1940s led to murky and inconsistent efforts at justification. On the one hand, proponents of Democratic anti-Communism stressed the rigor of Truman's loyalty program in searching for Communists in the federal government. On the other hand, they stressed the modest results of this search – and went on to claim that Republican warnings of Communist power were inflated. Here is a Democratic National Committee statement in 1948:

Q: *Is the Government full of Communists?*
A: No. Results of the President's loyalty program show that there are virtually no Communist spies or sympathizers in the government. *Under that program the government is required to discharge all employees as to whose loyalty there is even a reasonable doubt.* It is not necessary to prove that they are Communists. Practically all Federal employees – 2,255,642 of them – have been checked by the FBI for loyalty. This check is made against all the information in the files of the FBI. Much of this information is without foundation or is the result of malicious gossip. Nevertheless, if any information is found in these files against any government employee, a full investigation is ordered. The FBI has ordered 6,773 such investigations.

Final action has now been taken in 1,092 of these cases. *Out of this total 59 cases were decided unfavorably to the employee.*[40]

This statement vividly shows the erasure of distinctions between Communism as an objectionable political doctrine or organization and pro-Soviet Communism as a security threat. It also reveals that a vast intrusion into the lives of federal employees produced no serious results beyond the damage done to those who were investigated.

Although Democratic anti-Communism had many unjustifiable elements, it did not much damage the regime. As no basic break with Democratic policies occurred, anti-Communism cannot be claimed to have caused one. Did Democratic leaders have a reasonable choice? Could the regime have survived conservative attack if they had refused most anti-Communist legal action and avoided the hyperbole about conspiracy in favor of a political campaign against the CPUSA? Yes, given the strength of Democratic forces and the weakness of the Communist Party. A full defeat of Popular Frontism could readily have been achieved through political means such as those deployed against the Wallace campaign in 1948.

The Democratic break with Popular Frontism

My account poses a problem. If Democratic anti-Communism was always there in principle, what accounts for the prominence and vigor of anti-Communism after World War II? The Democratic shift to unqualified antagonism was due to changes in the political context and to strategic failures of the Communist Party.

To sustain this answer requires looking at relations between the Democratic order and the Communist Party from the mid-1930s on. I first explore the domestic side of this dynamic and then return to international pressures.[41] In domestic politics, special conditions muted conflicts between progressive liberal and Communist views in 1936–7 (and then during World War II). The economic and social crises, the underde-

---

40. Emphasis added. Democratic National Committee Research Division, Fact Sheet No. 11, *Communism and Loyalty,* 1948 (n.d.), Records of the Democratic National Committee, Truman Library. The loyalty program was initiated by Truman's Executive Order 9835, on March 21, 1947.

41. Within the large and growing literature on Communist Party activities in the 1930s and 1940s, I have relied on works from varied political and analytical perspectives, including works by Buhle, Draper, Howe and Coser, Isserman, Klehr, Naison, Richmond, and others. In addition, the Communist press is a good source of information on Communist views and to some extent practices.

velopment of American social welfare policy, and the militant antireform choices of employers all opened space for convergence if not real alliances. Thus the extreme domination of management in pre-NLRA industrial relations created a wide zone of potential reform where progressive liberal and Communist views could join to encourage unionization. In social welfare provision, the modest level of existing programs allowed a degree of programmatic agreement on building a partial welfare state. Business opposition to Democratic reformism supplied progressive liberal and Popular Front discourses with similar negative images of selfish elites unconcerned about national wellbeing.

In the 1930s and the 1940s, the tactical flexibility of some state and city Communist Party branches allowed local cooperation to be built between Popular Frontists and progressive liberals. Communists participated extensively in these decades' mass reform movements. Party members – in trade unions, among the unemployed, in urban and rural protests about rents and services – sought to build organizations and attain reform objectives without stressing the goal of state socialism.[42]

Convergence between the Democratic order and Popular Frontism was further encouraged by the political turbulence of the 1930s, as the line between deep reforms and incipient fundamental changes was not always evident. Nor was it always easy to distinguish between illegality as a last resort aimed at forcing employers or local elites to yield to reform demands, and illegality as an imagined means of building a revolutionary movement.

In the early 1940s the Democratic order organized an international war against fascist regimes. Even after the Hitler-Stalin pact, Popular Frontism was partially rebuilt on the basis of a new convergence between Democratic liberals and Communists regarding the main aims of the war.[43] The experience of domestic and international Popular Fronts led many – not only Communists – to imagine that a lasting alliance had been built. When fragile working relations burst apart into political

42. For works sympathetic to the Popular Front direction of the party, see Dorothy Ray Healey and Maurice Isserman, *Dorothy Healey Remembers a Life in the American Communist Party* (New York: Oxford University Press, 1990) (reissued as *California Red – A Life in the American Communist Party* [Champaign: University of Illinois Press, 1993]); and Alexander Richmond, *A Long View from the Left: Memoirs of an American Revolutionary* (Boston: Houghton Mifflin, 1973). For a critical account of the Popular Front that stresses the late and opportunistic manner in which the Communist leadership came to recognize Roosevelt's administration as the leadership of a genuine popular front, see Harvey Klehr, *The Heyday of American Communism: The Depression Decade* (New York: Basic Books, 1984), 186–206.

43. Maurice Isserman, *Which Side Were You On? – The American Communist Party during the Second World War* (Middletown, Conn.: Wesleyan University Press, 1982).

combat soon after World War II, the rapid change caught more than a few proponents of the Popular Front by surprise.

After World War II the conditions favorable to a convergence between Democratic and Popular Front efforts were gone. As key Democratic reform battles had been won, there was much less need for the cadres that the Communist Party had provided. By 1947–9 successful New Deal reform also made it relatively easy to distinguish between progressives who wanted to consolidate and extend reforms and those who saw reform as a modest step toward state control of the economy and political rule by a militant unified party. However deeply committed to Popular Front strategies and discourse sections of the Communist Party became, however committed many organizers were to their local projects, party aims focused on creating a Soviet-style state socialism. It made no sense to think this aim could be achieved in the United States, but the Communist Party and most Communists took it seriously in the 1940s. Thus basic political differences were highlighted, and any association with Communists was purely a political liability for progressive liberal initiatives and the Democratic order.

Democratic arguments about Popular Frontism did not lead to a real split in the Democratic order. Instead, a large majority rejected a small minority and the political isolation of the CPUSA was increased and brightly illustrated.[44] The great majority of Democratic progressive liberals supported Truman against Wallace, often citing Communist influence in the Wallace campaign:

> The Progressive Party does not repudiate Communism, as Franklin Roosevelt did. It represents, on the contrary, the most serious attempt in the history of our nation by a totalitarian group to capture and destroy American liberalism.[45]

---

44. It is easy to overstate the extent of the split by focusing attention on controversies among intellectuals and the labor movement after World War II. Even in these precincts, pro-Democratic forces won every major conflict. See Steven M. Gillon, *Politics and Vision: The ADA and American Liberalism, 1947–1985* (New York: Oxford University Press, 1987), 33–65.

45. Harold Ickes, "An Appeal to the Liberals in America"; this statement was a draft of an ADA statement that Ickes sent to Oscar Chapman. Letter, Ickes to Chapman, October 14, 1948, "1948 Campaign, H-O" folder, Papers of Oscar Chapman, Truman Library. Americans for Democratic Action played a significant political role in identifying the Wallace campaign with the Communist Party. One frequent argument was that the Soviet Union wanted Wallace to run to weaken Truman in favor of a right-wing candidate whose policies would lead to political polarization. The Communist analysis of political developments gave some credence to this charge. In this view, right-wing tendencies among economic and political elites were so strong and liberals like Truman were so ineffectual in responding to them that it made little difference

International sources of domestic conflict

The international developments that led to the emergence of the Cold War strongly reinforced the logic of domestic politics in isolating the Communist Party in 1947–9. In the mid-1930s the Soviet Union urgently sought allies in opposing the Nazi regime. This need, along with the evident failures of the ultraradical phase of international Communist politics in the late 1920s and early 1930s, led most Communist Parties to try to form broad alliances in their own countries. The aim was to stop fascist and far-right governments from taking power. At that time, American Communists' ties to the Soviet Union probably tempered their most fiercely sectarian tendencies. In labor relations, the opposition of the Communist Party to versions of the NLRA in 1934 and 1935 was more than a local application of the ultra radicalism of the international Communist movement in the early 1930s. It was congruent with radical syndicalist and antistatist currents in American labor politics, such as in the International Workers of the World (IWW), which the CPUSA inherited and amplified in the 1920s and early 1930s. The international Communist turn toward a Popular Front strategy preceded and helped to define the shift of American Communists toward a broader labor politics.

In 1939–41 the Communist Party's defense of the Nazi-Soviet pact caused a sharp decline in its political standing. But the wartime alliance between the Soviet Union and the United States allowed the party at least to regain membership.[46] When postwar relations deteriorated between the United States and the Soviet Union, the Communist Party's already limited prospects rapidly declined. By the late 1940s crucial changes had taken place in relations among the American Communist Party, the Soviet Union, and the Democratic order. The international view of the American Communist Party was always closer to the outlook of the Soviet leadership than to dominant Democratic views. But that was not a crippling problem when international affairs were not central in domestic politics (as in most of the 1930s) or when the United States and Soviet Union were allied in World War II. As the Cold War took shape, a Communist Party allied with the Soviet Union was an unambiguous liability if linked in any way to the Democratic order.

---

whether he or a Republican were elected president. Thus, an independent candidacy was reasonable, because its potential negative results in aiding a Republican candidate were of declining importance amid the overall shift to the right.

46. On the wartime role of the Communist Party, see Isserman, *Which Side Were You On?*; and Harvey Klehr and John Earl Haynes, *The American Communist Movement – Storming Heaven Itself* (New York: Twayne Publishers, 1992), 93–101.

Would a less ardently pro-Soviet American Communist Party have been less vulnerable to political attack? The intensity of conflict between the United States and the Soviet Union in the Cold War suggests otherwise, though it is not inconceivable. A much greater autonomy from the Soviet Union than was shown even by the Italian Communist Party would have been necessary to reduce significantly the attacks on the American Communist Party. Yet efforts at such autonomy would certainly have resulted in that party breaking up. The Soviet Union would not have tolerated a unified and independent Communist Party in the United States and would have used its power and prestige to prevent it, by forcing a full split in the party if other means failed. In reality the American Communist Party in the mid-to-late 1940s never diverged from the Soviet Communist Party.[47]

The Communist misunderstanding of progressive liberalism

In 1947–9 domestic and international developments made the Communist Party highly vulnerable by removing the prior bases of its alignment with the Democratic order. The ferocious attack that ensued was aided by the party's maladroitness.

In the 1930s and 1940s the Communist Party survived and sometimes flourished when its strategy meant immersing party activists in major reform projects – industrial unions, civil rights, antifascism – rather than opposing Democratic reforms or calling for a Soviet America. After World War II the Communist Party soon moved from zealous and uncritical support for administration war efforts to a reckless attack on many of its Popular Front allies and the main forces of the Democratic order. This turn started with the campaign against Earl Browder, the party's Popular Front leader, who was compelled to resign his position in 1945.

Communists in 1947–9 treated any equivocal action by leading Democrats as revealing a calculated betrayal of the past decade's reformism. They risked the destruction of remaining Popular Front alliances in deciding to throw their political resources into the campaign to elect Henry Wallace president in 1948. Denouncing former associates and excoriating centrist Democrats and moderate Republicans as fascists, the

47. After the dismissal of Earl Browder, there was no significant episode in which CPUSA policies entailed criticism of the foreign or domestic policies of the Soviet Union. Nor is there any indication that the Communist Party pursued any major policies in the United States that diverged from the general course proposed by the Soviet leadership of the international Communist movement.

Communist Party lost whatever chance it might have had to survive the early Cold War as a political force of modest size and importance.

The Democratic attack on the Popular Front after World War II led to angry claims of betrayal by Popular Front leaders and activists. The frequency and apparent sincerity of statements of surprise about these alleged betrayals show a double naivete among supporters of People's Front policies. At one level, protestations about the terrible things done to the CPUSA and allied groups show that the party was better at making brutal political attacks than at responding to them. When they had the power to encourage illiberal policies toward their political enemies, as with the treatment of Trotskyists in World War II, Communist and Popular Front groups were glad to do so. Nothing suggests they would have become more interested in fair principles of political competition if their power had increased.

Communist and Popular Front claims of betrayal also reveal a deep misunderstanding of Democratic liberalism. The failure to recognize the depth of Democratic opposition to Popular Front practices suggests that many Popular Frontists were basically unable to grasp the fact that progressive liberalism was a distinctive political view. They seem to have imagined Democratic liberals as "undeveloped" reformers who would have supported the full Popular Front program if they had been more sophisticated or consistent. In this conception, reformist liberals lacked a coherent political agenda; yet even with their limitations, they provided suitable partners for the People's Front. Here was a failure to understand that the Democratic order aimed to create an enduring dynamic between economic and social development and democratic reform. The CPUSA was unable to recognize this as a plausible political project.

Disbelief in the possibility of a progressive liberal model led Communists and Popular Frontists not to take Democratic discourse seriously. They strongly held the view that the problems of capitalism were beyond the reach of any reformist program, a position long articulated by the international Communist movement in its critique of social democracy.[48] Given this belief, advocates of a reformist project must either be well-intentioned and naive advocates of social improvement, or cynical

---

48. The Communist view of reformism relied heavily on the Leninist critique of non-Communist socialist currents in Europe. Despite its harshness, this critique was internal in the sense that it referred to a shared socialist critique of capitalism on both moral and efficiency grounds. Both the harshness and the socialist referents of the Communist critique of reformism made it ineffective in the United States, where the real competition was not with social democracy but with a progressive liberalism that was strongly committed to market institutions.

opponents of real change. In this conception one can see the basis for the oscillation between paternalistic friendliness and vindictive antagonism in Communist stances toward progressive liberals. There was no space for considering the latter as proponents of a credible view of how to organize social and political life.

Reforming capitalism – in a broad and active way – was precisely what Democratic progressive liberals had in mind. They did not simply hope for a better tomorrow, looking for guidance on what that might be. Democratic political leaders and intellectuals aimed to reshape the society that had produced the Great Depression. They believed it was feasible to achieve a more dynamic and open society within the framework of liberal and market institutions. Progressive liberals wanted to reform authoritarian labor relations, avoid economic collapses through government economic policy, reduce extreme poverty and provide minimal social security, and encourage the political entry of new groups. These aims were articulated clearly and debated at length.

In the 1930s and 1940s large parts of the Democratic political bloc had a considerable understanding of what it meant to engage in a sustained reform process. New Deal leaders claimed they intended to prevent revolution and they were serious, even if references to revolution were partly meant to scare opponents and cautious supporters into accepting their proposals. Thus, as with the sit-down strikes in the 1930s, Democratic leaders could distinguish between illegality aimed at overcoming obdurate opposition to reform and violence with revolutionary objectives. There was no space in the Democratic order for Communist ideology per se, though there was ample room for individuals and groups in or close to the Communist Party (or other socialist organizations) who were willing to fight arduous battles to win major reforms.

Which Popular Front?

Conflicts in and around the Communist Party after World War II showed that organization's inability to engage politically or theoretically with progressive liberal perspectives. These conflicts first centered on what to make of the Popular Front, when the American version of a brief international debate erupted. Was the Popular Front a strategy aimed at building up alliances that could be used to defend the Soviet Union and prepare the way for a movement for socialism? Or did it mark a real change in Communist conceptions of politics, in which Popular Front reforms might yield an open-ended process of democratization without necessarily having a fixed destination in a Soviet-type regime?[49]

Popular Front efforts were considered as techniques to be used by a determined Communist leadership in charting a course toward state socialism. Alliances not governed by such a conception were unacceptable. This stance combined tactical flexibility with doctrinal rigidity.

An alternative Communist position was not articulated clearly in the United States, before or after Earl Browder's removal. The main idea was to offer a more flexible version of the Popular Front, with a wider range of allies and tactics and some degree of openness to the substantive proposals of other political forces. There was no coherent "Browderism" basically opposed to the stance of the Communist International. Browder and his allies were largely willing to accept the doctrinal and political leadership of Soviet Communists. And the American Communist Party by the mid-1940s was not capable of much political reflection or dialogue.

Yet limited and fragmented discussion of these matters did occur from the late 1930s through the war. The result was clear. Those who suggested a more flexible course were charged with proposing to eliminate the leading role of the Communist Party in favor of eclectic reform coalitions. An open conception of the Popular Front jeopardized the central political role of Communism as a long-term goal, replacing it with a view in which there was no authority behind the broad fronts that were to be built.[50]

Such charges overstated the aims of those Communists who took Popular Front discourses about political openness too seriously. Some of the latter may have envisioned a permanent restructuring of organization and policies on the Communist left, though even in World War II their number could not have been large. Such a reorientation was suggested in some of the energetic and successful efforts to implement Popular Front strategies at state and local levels in the 1930s. But the limits of

49. Two developments that could be cited to show the presence of "liquidationist" tendencies were (1) the replacement of the Popular Front by an even broader notion of a Democratic Front in 1937–9, in which the central role of the party and of Communist political doctrine were significantly diminished; and (2) Browder's brief replacement of the Communist Party with a Communist Political Association in 1944. See Klehr, *Heyday of American Communism*, 207–22; and Robert Starobin, *American Communism in Crisis, 1943–1957* (Berkeley: University of California Press, 1972), 51–70, 177–8.

50. Starobin, *American Communism in Crisis*, 71–106. The crucial document in this controversy was a commentary by French Communist leader Jacques Duclos, translated in *The Daily Worker* (5/24/45).

official Communist policy were taut, and no sustained political articulation of these local efforts occurred in national debates about Communist strategy. The orthodox choice was affirmed in postwar attacks on "Browderism" and took institutional form as the reconstitution of the Communist Party (as distinct from Browder's short-lived Communist Political Association). Communist statements affirmed state socialism:

> We Communists are dedicated to the proposition that the great American dream of life, liberty, and pursuit of happiness will be realized only under socialism, a society in which the means of production will be collectively owned and operated under a government led by the working class.[51]

This statement, from the Communist platform in 1948, was made in a text in which Communists also urged support of Henry Wallace's Progressive Party campaign. Anyone vaguely familiar with the socialist left in the late 1940s knew that when Communists referred to a "government led by the working class," they meant a government of the Communist Party. This meant that political alliances were considered purely as instruments, rather than as joint ventures, much less as forms of cooperation that might entail learning and change on all sides.

The semi-debate in the international Communist movement was brief. In the American case, there was no room for flexibility with respect to the new international line articulated by the leaders of the main Communist parties. This was not only because of the preferences of American Communist Party leaders. Even had there been a strong desire by currents in the Communist Party to begin from Browder's Popular Front strategy and elaborate it in a decidedly non-Leninist way, there was no space for doing so. The high profile of the American Communist Party in international Communist politics, owing to the centrality of U.S.-Soviet relations, made such diversity unfeasible. And the domestic weakness of the CPUSA meant that dissident currents could not find solid institutional bases for a durable, if largely tacit, opposition to national Communist policies.

Contemporary arguments

The preceding account of the Communist Party's contribution to its own political destruction has tried to explain how the Democratic order persisted while attacking forces on its left with which there had been phases of convergence. Several controversies about Communist politics, while adjacent to my concerns, have interest for understanding how the

---

51. "Communist Party Platform of 1948," in Donald Bruce Johnson, ed., *National Party Platforms,* vol. 1, *1840–1956* (Urbana: University of Illinois Press, 1978), 429–30.

Democratic order's main themes developed over time. In the 1980s and 1990s vigorous debate has occurred about how to evaluate the Communist experience in the 1930s and 1940s. To what extent should such an assessment derive from an overall judgment of the party's perspectives and strategies, and to what extent should it be based on more local judgments about what occurred in cities, industries, and even in the lives of individual Communists?

Parts of this debate replay controversies in political and social history about where to locate crucial political meanings – in national conflicts and large political organizations, or in local battles and contests about organizing social and economic practices. While few in these debates strongly defend the official political aims of the Communist Party, there is an affinity between the aspects of the Communist experience that analysts emphasize and their overall judgment of it. Those more favorable in their view of the Communist experience tend to adopt a localist and individualist approach; critics focus on national Communist Party political and organizational life.

Proponents of the latter view usually get the better of these arguments because they can so easily show that oral histories and social histories about individual Communists and local organizing efforts downplay or neglect the broader political picture. But the arguments continue, in part because the two sides are trying to make different kinds of points and have difficulty reflecting on problems with their own positions.

As a political project, the Communist Party's efforts in the 1930s and 1940s can be assessed on three main dimensions: the validity of its political goals, the character of its typical forms of organization and argument, and the effectiveness of its strategies in gaining support and achieving more immediate political objectives. Critics of the Communist Party have little problem in winning debates centered on the first and second elements: Communist leaders and many members were serious about eventually creating a Soviet America and were undemocratic and illiberal in their aims, starting with the party organization itself. Critics are generally right when they charge that social historians of American Communism evade the political issues raised by these commitments. But the critics neglect the third dimension of Communist efforts, notably the Popular Front strategy, or disparage that strategy as kitschy and politically cynical.

Communist politics was a bleak disaster in its vision of a Soviet America. It was a crude and sometimes sordid failure in its attempt to apply Leninism in an advanced market country. Yet in its Popular Front phases, it was the most successful strategic effort by radical left currents in the United States in the three-quarters of a century after World War I.

When the Communist Party employed Popular Front strategies, even in mechanical and instrumental forms, they recruited large numbers of people and played a significant role in major reform battles about labor and racial relations. They were able partially to overcome the massive liabilities imposed by their long-term views and undemocratic forms of organization. The Popular Front strategy directed Communists toward immersion in ongoing conflicts, urged (tactical) willingness to take up demands as they emerged from popular movements, focused on immediate issues rather than long-term doctrinal goals, and sometimes practiced local tactical flexibility.

When Communists took up a strategy that placed them amidst ongoing conflicts and at times led to practices and views that threatened to liquidate the leading and privileged role of the party, they had considerable political success. They had more success taking this route than non-Communist socialists (social democrats and Trotskyists) were able to achieve via their own strategies in the same decades. The latter currents often adopted a more doctrinaire stance toward political conflicts (though in the service of more democratic doctrines), and more often than the Communist Party they sought to make explicit and direct connections between ongoing reform efforts (e.g., for unionization) and long-term (and very unpopular) socialist goals.[52] Debates about American Communism in the 1930s and 1940s detonate old arguments in the international socialist movement. Some of the most acute critics of the Communist experience have been linked by political views and personal histories to the non-Communist socialist left of the 1930s and 1940s. They are clear about how unbearable they find the romanticization of individual Communists when such accounts displace political judgments. But there is an issue about which they are less reflective – the Communist Party, an undemocratic party with undemocratic aims,

---

52. For the social democratic left, notably the Socialist Party, this course meant political isolation as a distinct current, gaining tiny votes in electoral conflicts that it never influenced. The more radical socialist currents that rejected Communist Popular Front-ism counterposed to it variants of earlier Communist Party notions of a United Front. This was a very abstract formulation in the United States in the 1930s and 1940s, because there did not exist the cognates of European socialist and social democratic parties and labor federations that were the intended partners of a United Front restricted to "working-class" organizations. "United Front" formulations were sometimes deployed by William Z. Foster and other Communist leaders in the late 1940s in justifying their rejection of "Browderism." This discourse always signified a sectarian turn, because no actual united front on a mass scale could be generated, leaving Communist leaders to portray small Popular Front and pro-Communist groupings as mass working-class forces while attacking the actual political and economic organizations of the labor and other movements.

gained far more members and played a larger positive role in unionization and racial change than its more democratic socialist competitors.

The CPUSA had no ability to bring nearer the regime it envisaged in
the United States, a Communist political order. But within the boundaries of a deep political marginality, it achieved a number of strategic
successes in the 1930s and 1940s.

In debates about Communism (which will continue long after the
Cold War) critics of the Communist Party should more fully recognize
the strategic successes of that organization. To do so is also to recognize
the overall failure of the CPUSA. Its main achievements occurred when
Popular Front strategies began to put in question the identity and orientation of the party as such. Yet the "liquidationist" course implicit in
the most flexible renditions of Populist Frontism was never the actual
Communist strategy. Such a course was blocked by the most basic
political and organizational commitments of the party.

Critics of the Communist Party reasonably become exasperated with
such claims as the following, by Robin D. G. Kelley: "But because
neither Joe Stalin, Earl Browder, nor William Z. Foster spoke directly to
them or to their daily problems, Alabama Communists developed strategies and tactics in response to local circumstances that, in most cases,
had nothing to do with international crises." Kelley's account of Communism in Alabama provides no significant evidence of political autonomy from the national direction of the Communist Party.[53] But taking
more seriously the relative successes of American Communism would
allow a fuller and ultimately more critical engagement with such localist
and social history studies. The latter's accounts of relations among
Communist political views, strategies, and personal commitments are
usually vague. This is often because no real discussion of political views
is offered, which means inattention to much of what distinguished Communists from socialists, radical democrats, or progressive liberals.

Communist political views were taken seriously by most members of
the Communist Party, and they had mainly negative effects both politi-

53. Robin D. G. Kelley, *Hammer and Hoe: Alabama Communists during the Great
Depression* (Chapel Hill: University of North Carolina Press, 1990), xiv. Kelley's
book powerfully shows the extent of political repression that faced challengers of
industrial despotism and segregation in Alabama in the 1930s. Given how small and
fragile the Communist Party was in most of Alabama – with fewer than five hundred
members in 1936–7 – it would seem important first to ascertain the reasons for this
marginality and to evaluate various strategies in terms of their capacity to overcome it
and perhaps even influence the overall shape of politics in the state. Kelley seems
relatively uninterested in these questions, and mainly evaluates Communist strategies
in terms of their capacity to encourage and sustain a radical subculture among
African-American workers.

cally and personally. It was precisely the vagueness and evasiveness and the public downplaying of explicitly Communist formulations in the Popular Front phases of the 1930s and 1940s that allowed major strategic results to be achieved. Here there were two important positive reference points. One was the substantial practical role of Communists in building unions. The other was their significant contribution to raising the issue of racial injustice in American political and social life. These reference points showed that individual Communists could become effective and even heroic (rather than brutal, sectarian, or rapid ex-Communists) when the political strategy of their party allowed this possibility. The Popular Front strategy made it possible for state and local Communist organizations and individual Communists to make a democratic contribution.

Yet at the same time that the Communist Party aided several major reform struggles, it separated tens of thousands of activists from the prospect of playing a significant long-term role in American politics. Even in the mid-1930s, Communists usually could not hope to gain public office or be appointed to prominent public positions. Nor could they assume leading positions in nongovernmental public associations without fear of compromising the effectiveness of those organizations. Attention to the local and individual stories of dedication and courage that social historians have provided thus leads to a different conclusion than the ones they recommend: What is striking is the amount of political loss as talented and determined people tried to maneuver within the constraints of Communist doctrine. There is a good deal of political sadness in the Communist experience, as people whose initial aims were often mainly democratic made choices that enduringly placed them on the margins of American political life.

This chapter's account of the success and marginality of the Communist Party may shed light on an issue that arises in the historiography of that party and also concerns national party politics in the 1930s and 1940s. The size of the Communist Party is not in much dispute – its peak was 100,000 members, with large fluctuations and high turnover. There is less agreement on what that figure meant – was it small or substantial? The reason for this uncertainty is political – whether 100,000 members defines a large or a small political organization is a function of that group's relation to other political forces. If a group of that size operates like a sect, cut off from other political currents, hostile or indifferent toward them, it is of no significance in a country as large as the United States.

If such a group has a highly active membership and is not isolated, then it is not small. If it has ongoing political relations with other forces, and can form real alliances and sustain them, it can be significant. When commentators take 80,000 or 100,000 members to signify a small group they may be confusing the size of the electorate of the two major parties with the number of committed activists. Compared with the first figure, the CPUSA was miniscule – not with the second.

In 1940 the population of the United States was roughly 130 million. To gauge the weight of the Communist Party, recall its very uneven distribution. Imagine that in half the country there were no members of the party, and divide the rest into units of 150,000. If a party membership of 80,000 were dispersed in these imaginary cities, each would have about 180 party members. This is a tiny figure compared with the number of Democratic or Republican voters. But it is not very different from the number of precinct captains one might find in a reasonably healthy party organization in a city of that size.

In the 1930s and 1940s the Democratic Party was rarely a mass party, but a network of activists and elite figures linked to a large body of voters. The virtual impossibility of fixing a meaningful number to its core networks – no one kept records, and had they been inclined, it was not clear what to record – allows the membership of the Communist Party to seem both large and small. If 180 Communists in a small city operate as a political sect, they can have meetings, sell each other literature, and form a subculture, and political life will not be affected. If they can escape this isolation, they make up a substantial force. The Communist Party's aims and strategy usually defined its membership as a very small political force, but this was not for lack of numbers.

At moments in and around Popular Frontism there emerged a political style that provided a local basis for convergence with Democratic progressive liberalism. This style was a pragmatic radicalism, marked by flexibility, adaptability, and eagerness for practical political engagement. It was always subject to being overridden by the exigencies of national Communist policies (and thus by the strategic understanding of the Soviet leadership). But in new state agencies and the organizations created by emerging political and social forces, there could be partial cooperation among Democratic progressive liberals and Popular Front Communists. Both were committed to a democratic and redistributive reform agenda, for different reasons. Communists who prided themselves on their realism and ability to unmask ideological deception were far less clearsighted about what was actually going on than the progressive liberals whose positions they could not really even understand.

The success of the Democratic campaigns

In this chapter I have tried to untangle relations between the changed international political setting after World War II – notably the emergence of the Cold War – and the Democratic order. The complexity of these relations makes it worthwhile to restate my argument.

The Democratic order shaped a national consensus in favor of fighting a long Cold War against the Soviet Union and its allies. Democratic progressive liberals ensured that this political and military effort would be conducted not only in the name of strategic concerns but on liberal and democratic grounds. The result was broad agreement for a containment policy directed against the Soviet Union, while further strengthening Democratic commitments as modern American common sense.

When the Democratic leadership organized American involvement in the Cold War, it drew both on the war against fascism and on core progressive liberal themes. That involvement helped produce a volatile, dangerous conflict with an expansionist Soviet regime. In domestic politics, the main effect of the Soviet-American conflict was further to consolidate the Democratic order, while augmenting conservative tendencies within it.

After World War II the Democratic leadership sought to demolish the Communist Party, to push it entirely outside of the Democratic order and deny it any public political legitimacy. This political aim, which could be defended on progressive liberal grounds, was achieved in significant part through illiberal laws and regulations. The Communist Party assisted in its own demise – through its allegiance to the Soviet Union, lack of serious thought about the Democratic order's political and social projects, and increasingly sectarian approach to American political life in the late 1940s. By the time full-blown McCarthyism arrived on the scene, the Communist Party had been destroyed as any sort of significant political force. Relations between the Democratic order and Popular Front Communism show the strength and durability of the left boundary of the regime. They also show that this boundary had to be clarified and enforced, rather than simply being announced.

Progressive liberals did not have to sacrifice their principles to oppose Communist influence, though they initiated or tolerated procedures they could not reasonably defend. Some conservative Republicans and Democrats wanted to use anti-Communism to destroy the Democratic order, but they failed. These critics of the Democratic order often cited the convergence of progressive liberalism and Popular Frontism at several points in the 1930s and during World War II to demonstrate the extent of political and moral decay. They misunderstood how fragile any cooperation between the Democratic order and Popular Frontism really was. But they were right about one thing that surprised and angered them almost as much as alleged Communist influence: A Democratic regime had persisted.

11

From Truman to Kennedy: the reach and limits of Democratic power

In 1947–9 the Democratic order was maintained in the face of serious challenges. Taft-Hartley, the Cold War and domestic anti-Communism, and sustained economic growth did not mean a basic political rupture. A Democratic regime persisted primarily due to the strength of the political forces built in the 1930s: The Democratic bloc was institutionalized, while Democratic discourses defined political common sense. This surprised many who expected Democratic power to perish with Roosevelt and who presumed Truman would be forced out of office in 1948.

What would a real break have looked like? In labor relations, a decisive anti-Democratic turn would have expanded Taft-Hartley to include additional severe provisions and led to other laws enabling employers to undermine independent unions and block new unionization. Charges of Democratic statism would have stigmatized the social welfare provision of the Democratic state, rolling back some of the New Deal and altogether ruling out new reforms. Liberal Keynesian policies would have been rejected in favor of reliance on market forces. Such policies were favored by significant currents in American politics. They did not occur because Democratic forces – in the state, party, and movements – had the capacity to prevent them. In 1947–9, each point of the core Democratic triangle – the state, interest groups, and the party – made a positive contribution to sustaining the Democratic order, while the primacy of the state and the presidency increased.

Anti-Democratic forces won significant victories. But to pass Taft-Hartley, block a qualitative expansion of unions, and limit Fair Deal reforms, opponents had to accept the main elements of the Democratic order. The ironic result of their efforts was to help secure the basic achievements of the Democratic order even as they sought to change it. And the conservative assault encouraged the Truman administration to move to the left in 1947–8, as it defended the Democratic order and urged new reforms in employment, civil rights, and health.

The deep changes in American politics in the 1930s and 1940s are best understood in terms of the construction and maintenance of a distinctive political order. In this process, political factors were crucial in shaping political outcomes. This emphasis on political orders and on political factors as causally important provides a way to assess contending forces in terms of their capacity to help build a regime or pose a plausible alternative. This chapter remains empirically in the 1930s and 1940s, apart from a brief discussion of the Eisenhower administrations. But its main arguments spill over those decades, toward the end of the Democratic order several decades later, and even further toward the present. I consider several emergent problems in 1947–9 and review the analytical framework proposed in Chapter 2.

A progressive liberal regime

In the 1930s and 1940s a Democratic bloc with a dynamic progressive liberal leadership built a new political order. The process of building it was disruptive and creative, cutting across institutions and creating new ones. The regime that resulted was only one among the possible outcomes of those decades' battles. The most likely alternatives to the Democratic order were moderately or sharply to its right. One can imagine several new regimes in the wide political area lying between the positions of Roosevelt and of Al Smith or Herbert Hoover in 1936. Most of them would have altogether marginalized the political forces that thrived on the left of the Democratic order and outside it. The Democratic order was stamped by its continual need to fight against political forces to its right: Hoover and Taft Republicans, more moderate Republicans, Smith Democrats, and sections of the Democratic Party in the South.

Democratic political capacities were expressed through the practices of parts of the Democratic Party, new mass political forces, and an expanding state. Progressive liberal political views were central in constituting the Democratic order and providing a framework for its normal times. The founding phase of the Democratic order was full of intense ideological debate; the outcomes were imbedded in the regime, even when its normal politics appeared to be nonideological. The Democratic order began as a sharp break with Republican antistatism – and persisted well beyond the years examined in this book in highly charged confrontations with opposing forces. These battles served to restate the core aims of the regime, with respect to adversaries on both the left (Popular Front Communism and elements of the new movements of the 1960s) and the right (McCarthyism, Southern resistance to desegregation, and Barry Goldwater).

Democratic successes in presidential elections from 1932 through 1948 were typically won by center-left efforts that united the electorate against opponents of progressive liberal reform – in social policy, labor relations, economic regulation, and eventually in racial politics. In the imagery of a political spectrum, these efforts had a dual location. They were moderately to the left of center among Democratic positions and distinctly to the left of center in terms of the entire range of significant national political positions. Democratic arguments about policies and principles made it possible to impose and sustain discontinuities at several points in the political spectrum. Thus Democratic efforts helped cut off Communist and militant populist brands of leftism, as well as unreconstructed Hooverite conservatism, from the political mainstream.

Far from being nonideological, Democratic campaigns strongly attacked opponents on both flanks by portraying their own positions as the proper combination of democratizing and modernizing policies. From its inception in the 1930s, the regime's leaders articulated a strong commitment to progressive liberal reform regarding economic and social regulation and the expansion of political participation. To consider this effort as purely interest-based coalition-building is wrong, whether the judgment is negative (as in disparaging accounts of interest-group liberalism) or positive (as with critics of party reform in the late 1960s and early 1970s).[1] Democratic progressive liberalism was a powerful political vision that sought to link democratic and modernizing aims. Democratic routines – in agencies, programs, party activities, unions, and interest organizations – derived much of their meaning from the regime's basic political commitments.

Emergent problems – relying on the state

Alongside the success of the Democratic order, there were emergent problems. These were bound up with a statist dynamic already visible at the end of the 1940s. Here I examine three areas where difficulties

---

1. See, respectively, Theodore J. Lowi, *The End of Liberalism: The Second Republic of the United States,* second edition (New York: W. W. Norton, 1979); and Austin Ranney, *Curing the Mischiefs of Faction: Party Reform in America* (Berkeley: University of California Press, 1975).

emerged from the logic of Democratic success: "statization" of the party, demobilization of the Democratic electoral base, and failure to achieve new reforms.

In 1947–9 the Democratic Party increasingly relied on the national state to supply political leadership and legitimacy for the political order as a whole. Dependence on the state was dangerous for the Democratic order because declining party capacities could not readily be replaced. The state had few means of organizing and mobilizing Democratic adherents.

When party organizations of all types declined, so did important activities such as efforts to organize party supporters at the local level in an ongoing way or attempts to mobilize Democratic voters at elections. Although the CIO's Political Action Committee was important in 1944 and again in the 1948 campaign, it was not a means of creating an enduring new quasi-party in more than a small number of places.[2] As for the fragmentary mass party forms of the prior decade, the labor movement devoted little energy to them, and other pro-Democratic movements and groups were not in a position to construct analogous political forms based on their own concerns and constituencies. Moreover, demographic shifts during and after the war expanded the proportion of the population beyond the immediate reach of existing Democratic organizations. These shifts had two interlocking dimensions: within metropolitan areas, movement from urban to suburban areas; and at the national level, movement away from the East and Midwest.

Turning to the state made good political sense for party leaders. It made sense strategically, because expanding state capacities provided a large and generally reliable source of political support without the risks of party-based mobilization efforts. It made sense normatively because the new Democratic state was so closely identified with the progressive liberal aims to which large parts of the Democratic Party and allied organizations were committed. Thus routine politics within the Democratic order often meant trying to protect and develop the regime through relying on the assistance and encouragement that could be provided by state agencies and their progressive liberal leaders. The ensuing dependence reduced Democratic Party capacities to sustain the

---

2. In a study completed prior to the 1948 election, William Riker estimated that in the mid-1940s what he termed CIO "machines" dominated about twenty-five congressional districts. He claimed that in roughly another seventy-five districts the CIO had considerable power in the Democratic Party, but without dominating it. William H. Riker, "The CIO in Politics 1936–1946," (Ph.D. dissertation, Harvard University, 1948), 345.

political order. By the late 1940s these issues were discussed in the Democratic order in terms of lethargic overconfidence resulting from so many electoral victories.

If this dynamic undermined the modest efforts to construct new party forms in the 1930s, it did not destroy a golden past. Before 1932 the party was excluded from national power, so the state's growth did not transfer power and resources away from a party that had been vital and energetic before being corrupted by national success.

Does it make sense to say that the decline of organized Democratic Party forms encouraged a statist course for the party? Weren't urban machines "statist" in the first place? The statism that was now growing had a different character than conventional patterns in which private forces – including parties – colonize the state. Even in the least stringent conception of what is required for a political organization to count as a machine, the point of the term is to describe the capacity of nonstate forces to control government through creating organizations that depend on access to state resources. Political machines put public institutions and practices at the service of private interests.

In the merging of party and state in the 1930s and 1940s, however, newer organizations and surviving machines tended to become clients of the national state. Federal policies and programs provided resources for these organizations, including a new political legitimacy they could claim as local representatives of the new order. Even where new organizations arose and seemed to resemble older ones, they relied on state initiatives.[3] No major Democratic force had both a compelling need and the ability to change the situation. Beyond organizing and mobilizing electoral support in presidential years, the national Democratic Party had little capacity for political initiative. Leading progressive liberals such as Clark Clifford recognized the weakness of the party and concluded that it was crucial to strengthen links between the presidency and interest groups.

Other (less powerful) liberals made organizational proposals. The report to the American Political Science Association, *Toward a More Responsible Two-Party System,* urged "responsible" party government

---

3. Even analysts who emphasize the adaptive capacities of machines in the 1930s recognize the destructive effects of the war and postwar conditions on the machines. Erie cites the movement of parts of the white population to suburbs, the changing shape of middle-class demands so that machines could do less to meet them, and the influx of new minority populations not incorporated within the machines as factors that weakened old machines and made it difficult to build new ones in the 1940s. Steven Erie, *Rainbow's End: Irish-Americans and the Dilemmas of Urban Machine Politics, 1840–1985* (Berkeley: University of California Press, 1988), 145, 181.

based on more active parties with coherent programs, powerful leaderships, and more accountable elected representatives:

> The existence of a national program, drafted at frequent intervals by a party convention both broadly representative and enjoying prestige, should make a great difference. It would prompt those who identify themselves as Republicans or Democrats to think in terms of support of that program, rather than in terms of personalities, patronage and local matters.[4]

The authors of the APSA report were mainly Democrats concerned about the fate of the New Deal who saw party reform as both an intrinsic good that would strengthen representative institutions and as a means of preserving the New Deal and extending its perspectives. Their recommendations were made in view of the failure of new Democratic reforms to be passed after 1948 and the weight of a conservative Southern Democratic caucus in Congress. Yet little of the party reform they recommended was likely in 1947–9, at a moment when the reform party in the United States was divided and its progressive liberal sections were increasingly oriented toward the national state.[5] Whatever slight chance for a "European" turn in the shape and operation of national parties had existed in the founding years of the Democratic order was gone.

Demobilization

Tendencies toward demobilization meant that the party and the labor movement had difficulty sustaining their efforts of the 1930s or innovating. By demobilization I mean a declining ability to turn political support into actions that immediately benefit the political order, including voting. Leaders of the Democratic order recognized a decline in political participation, which occurred across groups and regions. Many people who had engaged actively in politics in the 1930s were reducing their commitments and were not being replaced. Local party units were hav-

---

4. *Toward a More Responsible Two-Party System,* a report of The Committee on Political Parties, American Political Science Association (New York: Rinehart and Company, 1950), 10. The report proposed plausible democratic reforms alongside vague and grand objectives, with little sense of how the two might be connected. Without a cabinet system or proportional representation in congressional elections, the main proposals would have been unlikely to produce the desired effects.
5. The central proposal was to establish a Party Council of about fifty members, made up of representatives from the National Committee, national and state elected officials, recognized party groups, and cabinet officials. The council would develop and coordinate party policies. Proponents argued that integrative and nationalizing tendencies in American social and economic life required a more national politics – again, a progressive liberal project was conceived as both national and democratic (as against southern localism). *Toward a More Responsible Two-Party System,* 33, 43.

ing trouble finding people to do their work. In 1948 Democratic leaders and activists worried that only part of the declining participation that had weakened the 1944 campaign could be attributed to wartime constraints.[6]

The decline in political participation was due partly to postwar desires for stability after years of turbulence.[7] Demobilization was also encouraged by a statist Democratic course that provided few resources for developing local organizations. Beyond voting, it was not clear what the practical meaning of supporting the political order could be for most individuals. Democratic calls to rally the troops did not recognize that prior successes and institutional change made it difficult to define the forms and aims of political participation. The victories of the prior decade seemed to have achieved basic goals, now making extensive and demanding forms of participation much less important.

These factors probably discouraged political activism. They may also have influenced voting rates, which to the dismay of Democratic leaders were falling. The decline of voting from the late nineteenth century through the 1920s was interrupted in the 1930s. Voting rates then declined again, to 55.9 percent in 1944 and 53.0 percent in 1948. The latter figure was the lowest in the Democratic period, well below the average voting rate of 60 percent in presidential elections from 1932 through 1964.[8] In 1948 voting rates fell more sharply among supporters of the political order than among its opponents.[9] In contrast to the phase

---

6. Some complaining about a lack of Democratic volunteers might be discounted as a strategy for extracting resources. Yet the volume and intensity of such complaining suggests that at least a good portion of it was sincere. As usual, no one kept detailed records about any form of participation. But the complaints and apprehension were widespread.

7. The point is not that the end of the war created a conservative longing for various pasts. Blacks were not eager to return to patriarchal southern settings they had left; women were ambivalent, not wholly enthusiastic, about reducing their participation in the labor market. Rather, the exertions of political and social struggle of the 1930s and the sacrifices and dangers of the war made new offers of political mobilization less attractive. See John Patrick Diggins, *The Proud Decades: America in War and Peace, 1941–1960* (New York: W. W. Norton, 1988), 26–8; and Elaine Tyler May, "Cold War – Warm Hearth: Politics and the Family in Postwar America," in Steve Fraser and Gary Gerstle, eds., *The Rise and Fall of the New Deal Order, 1930–1980* (Princeton, N.J.: Princeton University Press, 1989), 153–81.

8. Bureau of the Census, *Historical Statistics of the United States – Colonial Times to 1970,* Y27–78, "Voter Participation in Presidential Elections, by State: 1824 to 1968" (Washington, D.C.: Government Printing Office, 1975), 1071–2.

9. Limited survey research does not provide extensive evidence on this point, but it was believed by participants in that year's campaign and by analysts of the election. The fact that nonvoters were more Democratic than voters in their orientation supports this

of regime formation, working-class and broad popular support now seemed partly in tension rather than joint aspects of building a new order. In normal politics (as distinct from regime politics), relations among political forces linked to class divisions often take on a zero-sum character – there seems to be a necessary trade-off between support from two sides of any major social line of demarcation. One example of how this dynamic was recognized by political actors was the reluctance of the CIO to run its own officers as candidates for public office, due to fear that such initiatives would provoke opposition not only from Republicans but from Democrats critical of the CIO.[10]

Further demobilizing tendencies emerged as the unintended result of the use of new media, including television. Studies in the 1940s and 1950s argued that the effects of radio, television, and mass-circulation papers and periodicals were not great and that most such effects were filtered through networks of personal influence.[11] While these media were not instruments of a looming totalitarian regime in the United States, they did spur tendencies toward demobilization and a statist centralization of politics.

Using the new media was desirable for Democratic leaders and supporters, given a reasonable concern for short-term political effectiveness. But problems arose in learning how to use them. For example, an attempt was made in 1948 to conduct thousands of simultaneous precinct meetings, at which participants would listen to a national broadcast. Calls would then be placed to the national speakers; after the show, further discussions of the proceedings would be held at the local meetings. This format was rapidly abandoned because of its complexity and because consultants advised party leaders that it was dull and poorly produced.[12] The shows do seem to have been dull. Perhaps the format was unworkable, an expensive way to reach a narrow audience of already committed Democrats. Yet what is striking is the brevity of this effort and the absence of serious experimentation with new media.[13]

interpretation. Angus Campbell and Robert Kahn, *The People Elect a President* (Ann Arbor: Survey Research Center, Institute for Social Research, University of Michigan, 1952), 38.

10. Riker, "CIO in Politics," 316.
11. See Paul Lazarsfeld et al., *The People's Choice* (New York: Columbia University Press, 1948); and Elihu Katz and Paul Lazarsfeld, *Personal Influence* (New York: Free Press, 1955).
12. These efforts are described in "Radio Show, 9/2/47" folder and "Radio Show, 10/2/47" folder, DNC Records, Harry S. Truman Library.
13. I can think of no reason that anyone might have had for disguising or suppressing evidence about creative Democratic media efforts. I found no examples of serious inquiry into how to employ the new media in the records of the Democratic Party and

The media were used as a cheap new way to reach an audience, with little apparent thought for even medium-term consequences and little consideration of potential uses of the media for political communication and deliberation. In Democratic practice, the increased use of media simply meant replacing expensive organizational efforts with cheaper media-based education and recruitment. Whether different ways of using the new media might have been efficient while encouraging new forms of participation among Democratic supporters is hard to know – the question was not really considered.

To portray the statist involution of the party and the demobilization of Democratic supporters as the main features of politics in 1947–9 would be wrong. Truman was elected, and the efforts of the Democratic Party and the labor movement were vital to that outcome. Yet these tendencies were definitely present. Old machines were further eroded; new organizations came more and more to rely on the national state; the quasi-independent labor and populist parties of the previous decade were mostly gone; and the sporadic efforts to build local mass party forms had dissipated. Because the Democratic order was much broader than the Democratic Party, these changes and more could occur without the regime collapsing. Yet such changes threatened to limit the forms of political support available to the Democratic order.

Programmatic stagnation

A third area of problems was the failure to achieve nearly as much in the way of major reforms as had been won in the 1930s.[14] Except for housing, and in a different way, veterans' programs, there were no successful reform initiatives in 1947–9 on a scale comparable to those

its leaders or in Truman's political records. Nor are significant cases discussed in the campaign accounts of Robert Donovan, Alonzo Hamby, Merle Miller, Cabell Phillips, and John Redding cited previously. There are, however, numerous accounts of radio shows that sound at best uninspired and at worst painfully maladroit, such as "Youth Chooses Democracy," CBS Radio 6/5/48, 4/20–7/1/48 folder, Papers of John H. Redding, Truman Library.

14. An interesting document from 1952 tabulated a seven-year record of legislative action based on recommendations drawn from Truman's 21-point program of September 6, 1945. To summarize: Truman proposed a substantial reform agenda; on the most ambitious points, such as full employment and civil rights, his administration had little success; he had more success in distributing new benefits to specific groups (e.g., veterans). "Appendix B, Final Report, Legislative Record of the President," 8/8/52 File Truman – Legislative Recommendations of the President, Records of the Democratic National Committee, Truman Library.

of the New Deal.[15] The lack of new reform was a major potential source of trouble; reform initiatives helped the Democratic order to recruit and organize new constituencies.

For a major national reform to take place, two elements had to be present: strong support from the progressive liberal leadership and mobilized mass political forces fighting for that reform and/or a Democratic electoral victory. These two factors did not guarantee reform, but without them it was unlikely, partly because opposition from the business community and conservative political forces could so often be presumed.

In 1947–9 the failure of most efforts to extend the New Deal was due to the interplay of diminished popular mobilization, political conflicts that limited progressive liberal capacities, and substantive programmatic difficulties. Democratic problems in each area were partly the unintended results of the victories of the previous decade. Mobilization was hampered by a mismatch between the administration's areas of programmatic interest and the possibilities for activism.

Sustained popular involvement could not be produced on demand but depended on prior political experiences, substantive commitments, and organizational resources. When progressive liberals in the Truman period aimed to extend the New Deal into areas not addressed in the 1930s, relevant constituencies were often neither well organized nor clearly defined. One major area where progressive liberal leaders and popular Democratic forces did not converge was health care. Proposals for national health insurance and expanded public provision of health care, beginning in 1945, were supported by a significant part of the Democratic leadership. But no major popular mobilization occurred on this issue, while intense opposition from professional associations helped block reform.[16]

Divisions in the Democratic order and a more flexible opposition

15. Democratic policies strongly encouraged the growth (most of which was suburban) in postwar housing starts for single-family units. Even the extent of Democratic accomplishments in housing can be debated. For a critical view of Democratic housing efforts, see John H. Mollenkopf, *The Contested City* (Princeton, N.J.: Princeton University Press, 1983), 74–80. See also Kenneth Jackson, *Crabgrass Frontier: The Suburbanization of the United States* (New York: Oxford University Press, 1985).

16. In November 1945, Truman sent his "Special Message to the Congress Recommending a Comprehensive Health Program." He failed to make progress before or after 1948 on this program, which included national health insurance, hospital construction, and medical research – all with a major federal role. *Public Papers of the Presidents of the United States – Harry S. Truman, 1945* (Washington, D.C.: Government Printing Office, 1961), 475–6.

weakened Democratic capacities to initiate and implement reform efforts. Both limits were linked to the prior decade's successes. Divisions within the Democratic political order appeared insofar as many progressive liberals in the administration and Congress wanted to enact new reforms but met considerable resistance from others in the administration and from congressional Democrats. The Democratic majority in Congress after 1948 was not a majority for opening wide new fronts on behalf of major reforms, but for maintaining and reshaping the New Deal. There was tension between those for whom the Democratic order should be defined as a permanent effort to formulate and achieve major new reforms while securing old ones, and others who thought the need for major reform had been diminished by the accomplishments of the prior decade.

In the late 1940s moderate critics of the Democratic order and diehard opponents could work together effectively, both on measures such as Taft-Hartley and in blocking new reform efforts. Earlier Democratic reforms had been greatly aided by the unusual political weakness of their opponents, owing to popular skepticism about conservative proposals in the mid-1930s and the shaky economic position of many firms and industries. The failure of the intransigent conservative front against the New Deal in 1935–7 led to the splintering and weakening of the most irreconcilable forms of opposition. A grudging acceptance of the Democratic order by parts of previously hostile elites took place in the next decade, an acceptance that for many always depended on there being no feasible way of destroying it. The new aim was to reach a reasonable balance, as proponents of Taft-Hartley claimed with regard to labor relations. This stance provided a good basis on which anti-Democratic forces could deflect reform projects.

The demobilization of Democratic support and the strength of a partially integrated opposition narrowed the space for reform. Within the space available, the Democratic order was not programmatically effective – again, partly due to prior Democratic successes. The reform agenda in the 1930s relied on several prior decades of political debate and on extensive state-level policy experimentation. After World War II progressive liberals did not have a set of developed and popular reform proposals.[17]

17. While progressive liberals expressed their disappointment with the legislative results, they seem to have been disinclined to examine the limits of their own proposals. This lack of reflection was true both of the left-progressive initiatives of the National Resources Planning Board during the war and of the legislative efforts by Democratic leaders in 1948–9. See Alan Brinkley, *The End of Reform: New Deal Liberalism in Recession and War* (New York: Alfred A. Knopf, 1995); and Alonzo L. Hamby,

Critics of the Democratic order in the 1940s tend to blame the lack of major new reforms on a conservative thematic shift. Thus Alan Brinkley claims in *The End of Reform* that as of 1945:

> The critique of modern capitalism that had been so important in the early 1930s (and, indeed, for several decades before that) was largely gone, or at least so attenuated as to be of little more than rhetorical significance. In its place was a set of liberal ideas essentially reconciled to the existing structure of the economy and committed to using the state to compensate for capitalism's inevitable flaws. . . .[18]

This account is misleading insofar as it refers to the main policies of the Democratic order. In the 1930s there was much criticism of the American economy and its leaders, but the basic Democratic commitment to liberal market institutions was very strong. Democratic leaders aimed to regulate the economy and reform some of its practices, and the new economic structure was in large part their achievement. Their acceptance of that structure was not a betrayal of anticapitalist commitments: As Democratic political leaders repeated endlessly against attacks from the right in the 1930s, they had no such commitments.

Brinkley's formulation has a second characteristic problem in suggesting a Democratic betrayal of a left-progressive or social democratic promise in the 1940s. Not only was there little such promise; the preoccupation with disappointment and betrayal diverts attention from the thematic problems of all sections of the Democratic order. The desire to initiate new reform projects had not disappeared. But progressive liberals had very few actual proposals that were compelling and plausible. There was no "end of reform," as a regime committed to sustaining recent reforms and undertaking new ones was still in place. But there was great theoretical and practical difficulty in defining a new course.

What new reform agenda could retain support from the main constituencies of the Democratic order while attracting new forces and muting anti-Democratic efforts? How could the next group of progressive liberal reforms be defined in appealing and practical forms? It is easy to cite measures in social welfare provision and economic regulation undertaken in other countries that might have been attempted, from family policy to more active labor market policies. But it would have required a major work of creative adaptation to devise viable cognate policies for the United States.

The actual programs proposed were mainly of two kinds. Some

Beyond the New Deal: Harry S. Truman and American Liberalism (New York: Columbia University Press, 1973), 311–51.

18. Brinkley, *The End of Reform*, 6.

sought to implement a Democratic commitment to employment and growth, as in the Employment Act of 1946. Others tried to extend progressive liberal reform to new spheres, as in medical care or housing. In the first case the onset of postwar growth made it hard to claim that extensive direct government action was essential to sustain employment. In the second case the proposals were attractive in principle for core Democratic supporters but did not motivate any burst of activism. Housing reform stands out as a partial success – there were energetic new initiatives, from veterans' programs through the 1949 Housing Act. Public support made political mobilization appear likely if no major expansion of housing were undertaken. And business elites were not wholly opposed to Democratic housing policies: They supported programs that aided the market in single-family dwellings, while resisting public housing as "socialism."

The lack of major new reforms was not only a problem from the standpoint of progressive liberal principles. It was a potential problem for sustaining the political order. In the 1930s reform had created and maintained support both among those most directly affected and among those who viewed reform as a sign of the Democratic order's modern and public-spirited character. When in the late 1940s few major reforms took place, the benefits to the regime of a new reform dynamic were not available.

From Truman through Eisenhower

While the statist direction of the Democratic Party, tendencies toward demobilization, and blocked reform caused trouble in 1947–9, their main negative meanings were potential. The strength of the regime was such that no Democratic collapse followed Stevenson's defeat in 1952. Dwight Eisenhower was a conservative caretaker for the Democratic order.

Truman's decision not to seek reelection in 1952 opened the way for Eisenhower, who had been sought as a presidential candidate by both parties. The key struggle was for the Republican nomination in 1952. Had it gone to Robert Taft or someone of similar views, a Republican campaign to destroy the Democratic order might have ensued, with failure the likely result. Though Eisenhower had to accommodate the Republican right to gain the nomination, his election victories and his administrations were those of a mainly loyal Republican opposition.[19]

---

19. See Hamby, *Beyond the New Deal*, 481–502; and Stephen E. Ambrose, *Eisenhower: Soldier, General of the Army, President-Elect, 1890–1952*, vol. 1 (New York: Simon and Schuster, 1983), 459, 515, 540–70.

In 1952 Eisenhower followed his defeat of Taft for the presidential nomination with a centrist course that accepted most of the New Deal and sought to isolate the far right. Had he waged an explicitly anti-Democratic campaign on basic issues, the election would have been closer. Seemingly above partisan divisions, Eisenhower gained the votes of working-class and lower-middle-class Democrats who did not fear that voting for a national patriotic hero would jeopardize New Deal reforms.[20]

Eisenhower and his advisers distinguished themselves from unreconciled opponents of the New Deal by affirming a broad state responsibility for economic and social regulation and not trying to repeal major parts of the New Deal.[21] This lack of interest in breaking up the regime produced conflict with forces that questioned the Democratic order: Taft Republicans in the late 1940s and early 1950s, Southern opposition to civil rights, and the volatile anti-Communism of Senator Joseph McCarthy.[22]

Eisenhower's administration sought to limit the growth of state activities and expenditures, but the New Deal policies and new state agencies of the 1930s and 1940s were not dismantled. State agencies often remained strongly Democratic through the 1950s, as Democratic personnel stayed in civil service positions and the Democratic purposes of the agencies were encoded in law and imbedded in routine practices. Genuine opponents of the Democratic order in the Republican Party, among

20. This view of Eisenhower's victory appears in Angus Campbell, Gerald Gurin, and Warren Miller, *The Voter Decides* (Evanston, Ill.: Row, Peterson and Co., 1954), 65, 175. Heinz Eulau argued that in 1952 and 1956 two broad class coalitions were electorally present, with many voters voting against their perceived class interests in favor of Eisenhower. His identification of a modest significant relationship between class and party resembles Alford's. Heinz Eulau, *Class and Party in the Eisenhower Years* (New York: Free Press, 1962).

21. Robert Griffith stresses the conservatism of Eisenhower's administrations. Yet his account makes clear that this conservatism meant an effort to administer existing political relations in ways that would minimize conflict and restrain the growth of the state. Robert Griffith, "Dwight D. Eisenhower and the Corporate Commonwealth," *American Historical Review* (February 1982): 87–122. See also David Green, *The Language of Politics in America: Shaping Political Consciousness from McKinley to Reagan* (Ithaca, N.Y.: Cornell University Press, 1987), 200–40.

22. Eisenhower had no problem with assaults on Communism. Yet when McCarthy began to challenge the loyalty of the government and army, Eisenhower helped bring McCarthy's career to a close. In the 1952 campaign, Eisenhower avoided criticizing McCarthy, partly to show his willingness to cooperate with the Taft forces in the Republican Party. Ambrose, *Eisenhower*, vol. 1, 543, 566. On the army-McCarthy hearings and the reluctance of the Eisenhower administration to confront McCarthy, see Robert Griffith, *The Politics of Fear: Joseph R. McCarthy and the Senate* (Lexington: University Press of Kentucky, 1970), 243–69.

Southern Democrats, and on the far right were frustrated by the lack of any deep change in the character of the still-Democratic state.

If Eisenhower had tried to break the back of the regime, he would have faced great resistance from Democratic forces in federal agencies, Congress, the judiciary, and interest groups, as well as from public opinion.[23] While the Democratic Party's organization was not powerful, the ensemble of Democratic forces was strong enough to discourage or repel challenges to the premises of the regime (e.g., a repeal of Social Security, legislation to destroy the NLRA, or a refusal of any economic regulation).

The endurance of the Democratic order meant continued reform pressures in the 1950s, notably in civil rights. Political forces advocating reform had a number of avenues along which to proceed, including the courts and Congress.[24] Even the federal executive was a source of partial support if the issues were defined as preserving order by tempering the actions of diehard opponents of reform. Precisely this framing took place in civil rights. Eisenhower was very reluctant to enforce antisegregation decisions by the Supreme Court. Yet given sufficiently high levels of political conflict about racial reform, as in Arkansas regarding school integration, he was willing to enforce a moderate interpretation of federal court decisions against an increasingly radical opposition.[25]

Eisenhower sponsored no prolabor legislation, but widespread fears that Taft-Hartley would initiate waves of antilabor laws were not realized. The main labor legislation, the Landrum-Griffin Act (Labor-Management Reporting and Disclosure Act of 1959), came after several years of congressional hearings about corruption in the labor movement. It called for greater regulation of internal union life and underlined some

---

23. Republicans had a majority in both the House and Senate only in 1953–4. Bureau of the Census, *Historical Statistics of the United States – Colonial Times to 1970*, Series Y 204–210, "Political Party Affiliations in Congress and the Presidency: 1789 to 1970," 1083.

24. Democratic power shifted toward Congress after 1952, given the Republican presidency. An organized congressional expression of Democratic progressive liberalism took shape late in the decade. The Democratic Study Group in Congress described itself as "the first real effort in modern Congressional history by progressive Democratic Members to function as a unit on a broad range of issues." Pamphlet, "Democratic Study Group," 9/63, Democratic Study Group folder, Records of the Democratic National Committee, Johnson Library. There are many accounts of legal efforts to gain civil rights reform after World War II. For a recent version of this story, see Mark Tushnet, *Making Civil Rights Law: Thurgood Marshall and the Supreme Court, 1936–1961* (New York: Oxford University Press, 1994).

25. See Harvard Sitkoff, *The Struggle for Black Equality, 1954–1980* (New York: Hill and Wang, 1980), 23–60.

of Taft-Hartley's restraints, but it was not comparable to that measure in its scope or severity.[26]

The Eisenhower administrations inhabited a regime they had not created and did not aim to destroy. This awkward location meant there was little prospect of building an enduring Republican majority or even of generating powerful anti-Democratic themes. Though economic growth continued and the Cold War did not become an actual military conflict, these accomplishments and Eisenhower's personal prestige did not translate into support for the Republicans. Nixon could not benefit from Eisenhower to the extent that Truman could benefit from being Roosevelt's successor. John F. Kennedy's narrow victory in 1960 showed that Democratic capacities remained considerable – winning the presidency did not require creating a new set of popular ties and institutional commitments. Kennedy could not plausibly depict Richard Nixon in 1960 as committed to destroying the Democratic order. But he did claim that new modernization and reform were the order of the day. In foreign policy Kennedy argued that Eisenhower's version of containment was not assertive enough in political conflicts with the Soviet Union and in developing and applying new military technologies.[27]

Kennedy won in 1960 as a Democratic loyalist, without much specifying the content of the new phase of reform that he proposed. The domestic focus of the early Kennedy administration was on modernization, augmenting prosperity, and government reorganization, rather than on democratic initiatives.[28] The new administration recognized the

26. The seven titles of the Landrum-Griffin Act (of September 14, 1959) provided a "bill of rights" for members of labor organizations, required extensive reports from labor organizations on financial and organizational matters, and regulated union elections. Such measures entailed further regulation of union affairs by the federal government, without placing any equivalent demands upon employers. The campaign for the act had negative effects on the political standing of the labor movement by widely broadcasting a strong impression of corrupt and antidemocratic procedures within trade unions. See Robert F. Koretz, ed., *Statutory History of the United States: Labor Organization* (New York: Chelsea House, 1970), 682–792.

27. Kennedy stressed the need for a more systematic and integrated approach to foreign policy. See John Lewis Gaddis, *Strategies of Containment – A Critical Appraisal of Postwar American National Security Policy* (New York: Oxford University Press, 1982), 198–201.

28. See Bruce Miroff, *Pragmatic Illusions: The Presidential Politics of John F. Kennedy* (New York: McKay, 1976); Richard Neustadt *Presidential Power: The Politics of Leadership from FDR to Carter* (New York: Wiley, 1980), 150–5; Thomas C. Reeves, *A Question of Character: A Life of John F. Kennedy* (New York: Free Press, 1991); Arthur M. Schlesinger, Jr., *A Thousand Days: John F. Kennedy in the White House* (Boston: Houghton Mifflin, 1965); and Garry Wills, *The Kennedy Imprisonment: A Meditation on Power* (Boston: Little, Brown, 1982).

narrowness of its victory and first interpreted this as warranting caution about aggressive reform efforts in domestic politics. Progressive liberals often criticized the Kennedy administration, while Americans for Democratic Action assailed the caution of the Democratic leadership in Congress as a major barrier to legislative accomplishments in 1963.[29] In 1962 and 1963 reform efforts were presented as extensions of prior Democratic commitments, and the administration had sufficient resources to begin. This turn was partly due to a highly mobilized civil rights movement that gained national attention and forced confrontations on terms unfavorable to segregationists in the South.[30] New official attention to poverty underlined the administration's links with the New Deal legacy of state-based reform. Yet poverty was now regarded as a special misery for discrete subgroups of an increasingly affluent population, rather than a general affliction. The title of Michael Harrington's book, *The Other America: Poverty in the United States,* signals the distance traveled from the 1930s, when poverty engulfed entire social groups and threatened much of the country.[31]

The grim course of events enhanced reform prospects in the short term, as Kennedy's assassination was interpreted as not only the brutal end of an individual life but as a violation of a Democratic national

29. And Democrats were divided: The average "Liberal Quotient" of Democratic Senators from southern states was 25 percent, compared with 79 percent for Democratic Senators from outside the South. "First Session of Congress Indifferent," Press Release, Americans for Democratic Action, December 29, 1963, ADA Rates the 88th Congress folder, Records of the Democratic National Committee, Lyndon B. Johnson Library.

30. Among the many studies of the civil rights movement and the passage of civil rights legislation in the 1960s, see Carl M. Brauer, *John F. Kennedy and the Second Reconstruction* (New York: Columbia University Press, 1977); Clayborne Carson, *In Struggle: SNCC and the Black Awakening of the 1960s* (Cambridge, Mass.: Harvard University Press, 1981); David J. Garrow, *Bearing the Cross: Martin Luther King, Jr., and the Southern Christian Leadership Conference* (New York: Vintage, 1988); Hugh Davis Graham, *The Civil Rights Era: Origins and Development of National Policy* (New York: Oxford University Press, 1990); Steven Lawson, *Black Politics: Voting Rights in the South, 1944–1969* (New York: Alfred A. Knopf, 1976); Doug McAdam, *Political Process and the Development of Black Insurgency, 1930–1970* (Chicago, Ill.: University of Chicago Press, 1982); and Manning Marable, *Race, Reform and Rebellion: The Second Reconstruction in Black America* (Jackson: University Press of Mississippi, 1984).

31. Harrington highlighted zones of poverty that were not getting the attention they merited in political and policy argument. This shift in focus reflected a real decline in poverty and a perception that it endangered limited groups and rflectedgions. See Michael Harrington, *The Other America: Poverty in the United States* (New York: Macmillan, 1962); and Michael Harrington, *Fragments of the Century: A Social Autobiography* (New York: E. P. Dutton, 1973), 171–4.

commitment to a new course of reform. Thus remembering and honoring Kennedy meant pursuing his reform efforts, even supporting measures more ambitious than those his administration had supported. The full story of the Kennedy administration's contribution to a new and dramatic reform phase – which mainly occurred after his death – lies beyond the scope of this book. Here it is enough to underline that no basic political breaks occurred when Eisenhower replaced Truman or when Kennedy defeated Nixon. The ironic course of the Democratic order in the 1960s saw great triumphs followed by a rapid demise.

The Democratic order and the logic of political orders

How should my initial claims about the course of the Democratic order be assessed? In Chapter 2 I proposed:

1. The Democratic order originated in the 1930s through an active political process of building new institutions and discourses (phase one). There were serious economic, social, and political crises in the United States; building the Democratic order entailed their resolution. The initial leadership for the political order came from sections of a previously existing political force. Yet the new order required a political construction of new political subjects, beyond mobilizing existing forces. The political order was defined by new relations among the state, the dominant party, and social and political movements, as well as new relations between political and socioeconomic processes.

2. Major institutional and discursive continuities marked the four decades of the Democratic political order. These continuities registered the capacities of the party, state, and movements to recruit, organize, mobilize, and educate political support for the Democratic order (phases two and three).

3. Political tensions emerged within the political order, and sustaining its dynamism proved difficult. The Democratic order was founded not only through energetic new mobilizations and a transformation of the Democratic Party but through an expanding state. Over time, the party and other Democratic forces increasingly relied on the resources of the national state, tending to merge into it, while the new state was identified with the party. This reduced the capacity of Democratic political forces to organize and mobilize. In the face of an emergent party-state apparatus, the space available at the top for further new political forces was limited, yet the political order continued to stimulate their formation (phase three).

4. Major problems for the Democratic political order developed in relation to socioeconomic processes. Growth reshaped socioeconomic relations in ways that strained the Democratic order by weakening social groups important to it and eroding Democratic political networks. Growth also yielded new socioeconomic groups which were not sources of Democratic support – partly because of obstacles posed by the Democratic order's reliance on the state (phase three).

Table 11.1. *Supporting the Democratic order*

	State		Party		Movements	
	Mid 1930s	Late 1940s	Mid 1930s	Late 1940s	Mid 1930s	Late 1940s
Recruitment	4	3	3	2	4	2
Organization	2	2	3	2	3	2
Mobilization	3	2	3	2	4	3
Education	4	3	3	2	3	2

4 -- Substantial capacity to provide political support.
3 -- Moderate capacity to provide political support.
2 -- Limited capacity to provide political support.

5. The Democratic order ended (in the late 1960s and early 1970s) owing to political failure to cope with statism and socioeconomic change. These tendencies arose from Democratic efforts to sustain the political order and spur growth – over time they eroded support for the Democratic order, weakened its political capacities, and opened it to attack. In the resulting conflicts the Democratic order was destroyed. The appearance of new political forces did not doom the Democratic political order, but failure to integrate them was very damaging. The ensuing dynamic polarized opponents of the new political groups against the Democratic order. This new opposition, in conjunction with elements of the conventional opposition, defeated the leading forces of the Democratic order (phase four).

As this book has focused on the construction and maintenance of the Democratic order, most of what can be concluded regards the first two claims. But that restriction is not so narrow – what is at stake is how to conceive major episodes of change in American politics and how to understand ensuing phases of relative stability. In both respects, the first and second claims accurately identify the core features of the Democratic order and of its development in the 1930s and 1940s. The first claim, about building a political order, captures the central processes in 1935–7, when new political forces redefined the framework for political action. The second asserts that the Democratic order persisted via durable forms of providing political support. In 1947–9 Democratic forces in the state, party, and movements had the capacity to sustain the regime. Table 11.1 uses numbers to represent the main lines of my argument about how the Democratic order was built and supported in the 1930s and 1940s.

The account proposed in Chapter 2 accurately depicts the main dynamics that shaped the origins and early development of the Democratic order. The latter began with dramatic discursive and institutional shifts, as a new political bloc created a new framework for normal politics. The creation of the Democratic order was a political project. It cannot be understood in mainly economic terms, either as a direct function of the Depression or as the result of interest-seeking by economic coalitions. Nor does it make sense to consider the Democratic order as due to state elites' efforts to create order, when building a new type of state was itself a core part of the Democratic project. While a realignment approach remains descriptively useful, its themes do not come close to grasping the dynamic and powerful political action required to give potential electoral change an enduring political meaning.

The third claim states that significant political strains emerged from an internal dynamic. Such strains can be glimpsed in 1947–9, and statism was an emerging problem for the Democratic order – a strong further claim is unwarranted here. Similarly, one can observe potential socioeconomic strains linked to Democratic accomplishments, as postindustrial change signaled an eventual weakening of pro-Democratic social groups. I proposed that both types of strains would be present relatively late in the course of the Democratic order – they were already visible in 1947–9. But their causal importance was not evident in these years. My claims about the remaining two decades of Democratic dominance assert that the increasing concentration of power in the state hollowed out the regime and reduced the ability of nonstate agents to supply political support, crucially with the Democratic Party and labor movement. Postindustrial development undermined political networks that had been central to the Democratic order. These claims remain to be demonstrated, though they gain a degree of plausibility from the accuracy of the first and second claims. While the interaction of statism and postindustrial growth eventually undermined the Democratic order, this interaction aided the new regime in the 1940s, when it appeared as a source of political strength on behalf of Democratic principles and welfare-enhancing socioeconomic modernization. The preceding chapters do not show that the demise of the Democratic order in 1968–72 was caused mainly by statism and postindustrial change, though I believe this to be true and argue the case elsewhere.[32]

Chapter 2 also argued that Democratic political commitments were crucial in defining the international role of the United States. I proposed that Democratic internationalism initially strengthened the regime through its success in World War II, while eventually leading to an

32. See David Plotke, *Democratic Breakup* (Cambridge University Press, forthcoming).

overexpansion of commitments that became dangerous. At the end of the 1940s it is mainly Democratic successes that are visible. Yet once Democratic internationalism and opposition to the Soviet Union were in place as deep political commitments, they had significant unintended effects on the Democratic order, from the conservative turn encouraged by Cold War policies to the major role of the Vietnam debacle in dismantling Democratic power.

The formation and development of the Democratic order also confirm parts of the approach to political orders proposed in Chapter 2 and recommend that model as a framework for analyzing political orders. The model distinguishes four phases: (1) building a political order, (2) consolidation and maintenance, (3) maintenance and emergent conflict, and (4) decline and demise. While the preceding account of the Democratic order mainly confirms claims about the first two phases, the analytical phases and the empirical sequence do not entirely correspond. At the start there is a good fit between the regime-building posited for phase one and processes at work in the formation of the Democratic order. And that good fit is a strong argument for a regime perspective in analyzing change in American politics. Yet rather than phase two (i.e., 1947–9) exemplifying only signs of healthy development, with a third phase (i.e., 1963–5) manifesting mainly strains and trouble, both periods were mixed. Regime maintenance dominated in each case; strains were also present at both times, though they were far more serious in the later years. The Democratic order was much more successful in its policy accomplishments in 1963–5 than in 1947–9; the model suggests that declining achievements would be apt to accompany increasing strains.

This variation between what the model suggests and the actual course of the Democratic order indicates that judgments about the strength of a regime can best be made by distinguishing two questions: What is the balance between forces tending to sustain and undermine a political order? What are the prospects for that order to generate major substantive achievements? The answer to the second question is limited by the answer to the first (e.g., a regime months away from its final ending is unlikely to achieve major victories), but those limits are relatively broad.

The two subperiods of the Democratic order examined in this book were of different lengths. The first phase was shorter than the second, which extended for years in both directions from 1947–9. This variance derives from differences between two modes of political conflict, one at the outset and end of a political order, the other between those moments. The first mode – of regime politics – is more intense and turbulent, mobilizes mass forces more powerfully, and demands more time and resources. It tends to be of shorter duration than a phase of normal politics, partly because there are great obstacles to the indefinite maintenance of high levels of collective action.

The basic relation between the conflicts of phases one and four and those of phases two and three is that conflicts over the character of the regime frame routine politics. The distinction between normal and regime politics is analytically significant for the stakes and forms of political conflict. For normal times, accounts of pluralist bargaining, the placement of forces on a linear political spectrum, and the limited extent of citizen involvement in politics can provide accurate descriptions. Yet generalizing from these phenomena to global analyses of politics is dubious, because the normal times of political orders are only part of the story. Such normal times are established through prior phases of sharp political conflict with different forms and rhythms. The founding battles build a framework for routine bargaining and define the boundaries and main issues of the political spectrum.[33]

The model recognizes normal political times without naturalizing them as politics per se. But both that model and my initial claims about the Democratic order may understate the conflictual, dynamic side of maintaining political orders. Moments of bracing conflict such as the 1948 election occur during a political order, for several reasons. Forces opposed to the political order continue to exist after its formation, even if they are greatly weakened. In conjunction with dissatisfied adherents of the political order, they can challenge newly conventional practices. Moreover, the practices and basic commitments of the regime need to be reshaped over time, and these changes can produce conflict.

Enduring political orders are achieved with the active participation of large groups of people, in dialogue with many more. The Democratic order in the 1930s and 1940s was created and sustained through political processes with substantial thematic and dialogic elements. Establishing a political order means a redeployment of force, as with labor relations in the 1930s. But if changes in the organization of force were not framed by sustained dialogues and agreements, they would be jeopardized by great political instability. For a political bloc to form requires dialogue with prospective adherents of the regime and with adversaries.[34] Many of the latter have to be persuaded to compromise; some may

---

33. Thus, the distinction between regime and normal politics also contrasts a politics of identity with a politics of bargaining. Regime politics is about defining political identities that are salient in many settings, and about persuading people that such political identities are reasonable frameworks for making political and social choices.

34. In William Riker's very different view, political dialogue and deliberation have little weight: "The fundamental dynamic of political life is [the] restless search for the issues and alternatives around which a new winning coalition can coalesce." Thus,

even need to be shown that the proposed arrangements are preferable to the uncertain prospects of extraconstitutional action.

This book has analyzed the formation and maintenance of one political order. One case cannot wholly validate the general approach proposed in Chapter 2. But the dynamics at work in building and sustaining the Democratic order appear widely in advanced market societies: Amidst diverse crises that weaken a regime, new political forces arise. They resolve ongoing crises while proposing a new model of development and arguing for a new political common sense. Winning these battles means expanding the capacities of new political forces and institutionalizing their achievements.

The preceding analysis also shows that political commitments are central to regime maintenance, that they define and guide the pursuit of self-interest. Many social scientists (and political cynics) are fond of stressing the advantages of self-interest as against forms of action in which actors claim to be inspired by principle (the bad results of good intentions). Yet my account of the Democratic order suggests that there are many times when it makes sense to reverse such arguments. In building a political order, narrowly self-interested action would often make it harder even to achieve the goals defined by narrow interests, given the familiar problems of cooperation among self-interested individuals.

When political actors who wanted to sustain the Democratic order and achieve its goals in the 1940s made proregime choices amid resource and time constraints, their choices often yielded reliance on the state. But choices taken without much regard for regime commitments are likely to be even more corrosive, because they can directly weaken the political framework of the regime. When the fusion of political commitment and self-interest that arises in the initial phases of a political order begins to decay, narrowly self-interested action by regime supporters has corrosive effects. This is part of the story of the labor movement in the 1950s and 1960s, of Democratic ambivalence about black political participation in the 1940s, and of the later acquiescence of Democratic leaders in a Vietnam policy that a number of them doubted.

disequilibrium is a basic political condition, while the rise of issues that sustain it is an almost random process. If disequilibrium means any condition short of perfect harmony among individuals, Riker's vague claim would be right. Yet there are substantial phases of difficult yet durable stability when settlements persist; at the national level, these are political orders. William H. Riker, *Liberalism against Populism: A Confrontation Between the Theory of Democracy and the Theory of Social Choice* (Prospect Heights, Ill.: Waveland Press, 1982), 209.

12

Was the Democratic order democratic?

The previous chapter returned to the main arguments about the course of political orders and the shape of the Democratic order presented in Chapter 2. This chapter considers the political meaning of that regime: In what sense was the Democratic order democratic? Its proponents claimed that label, but were they entitled to do so? I will assess the overall effects of the Democratic order, its relation to other imaginable regimes (notably social democratic regimes), and the character of Democratic political leadership.

The Democratic order and American political development

What were the political effects of the Democratic order? Its practical accomplishments included ending the Depression and winning World War II, both on democratic terms. A central feature of the Democratic order was its distinctive and powerful fusion of democratic and modernizing themes. Leaders of the Democratic order made persuasive arguments for a democratic expansion of interest-group organizations and political participation, as well as for government action to spur social and economic development. Their arguments succeeded, and their policies had broad effects that were mainly congruent with stated aims. That the Democratic order eventually ended means failure only if one wrongly imagines that regimes can be permanent in advanced market societies.

In the regime politics at the beginning of the Democratic order, fierce conflicts arose as competing forces tried to define the practical meaning of liberal, democratic, and progressive conceptions. Those who built the Democratic order linked new programmatic and policy aims with enduring democratic and progressive themes. As these themes were elaborated in the 1930s and 1940s, especially as regards the labor movement, new social and political forces entered American politics. This was a major democratic achievement.

Along with expanding political participation, the Democratic order focused political life on a presidential/state center. Nonstate political forms declined over time with respect to the national state; this decline stemmed from choices made by Democratic actors in trying to sustain the policies and institutions of Democratic progressive liberalism. The statist trajectory went beyond what was intended by many Democratic progressives. With respect to democratic values, the dangers of this presidential and statist tendency are substantial and the virtues are mainly instrumental, having to do with whatever ends it helps to attain.

Criticism of the statist dynamic of the Democratic order is legitimate. Yet it is simplistic to project the antistatist climate of the 1980s or 1990s backward to reject state intervention or criticize the reliance of movements on support from the executive and the courts. Such critiques are too often based on the wrong premise that in the 1930s and 1940s there were other routes toward reform that might have been reasonably successful without generating equally serious long-term problems. The Democratic leadership and the state with which it was increasingly intertwined over time were central for democratic reform. Without state actions, the changes in labor and social policies achieved in the 1930s and 1940s would not have happened. State power was crucial in protecting the ability of industrial unions to organize and survive.

Antistatist proponents of reform have offered counterimages of how reform might better have taken place: through movements that might have shifted public opinion over time and eventually overwhelmed opponents through electoral means, or through increasingly militant local conflicts that might finally have defeated antiunion groups in mounting displays of power. Yet without state support in programs, policies, and law, reform efforts would have withered because they would not have been able to defeat adversaries who were willing to use economic coercion, political force, and violence (authorized by local authorities or organized privately).

Despite the depth of antistatism in American politics, most state actions retained normative force, thereby enhancing the legitimacy and strength of democratic movements that received government support. The national state – first the executive and parts of Congress, later the courts – also encouraged participation in democratic movements. State control over force, though never complete, reduced the risks of participation by individuals. Strikers and other social and political activists in 1935–7 knew that the stance of the federal government reduced the chances of their being killed, badly injured, or imprisoned (though such outcomes remained possible).

In sum, the Democratic state as it emerged via the building of a new

Democratic order was essential to attaining democratic reforms. These reforms redefined the range of legitimate agents in American politics and encouraged the later mobilization of other groups during and after the Democratic order, notably the civil rights and feminist movements. From a democratic perspective, the history of the Democratic order provides no grounds for drawing a simple antistatist moral, even though its central dynamic reveals the eventually corrosive results of relying on the state for political support.

The Democratic order also asserted an extensive role for government in shaping economic development. This meant defending the ability of government to regulate social life more fairly and efficiently than markets or communal forms alone could manage.[1] The expansion of public activity protected a wide array of social groups from the hardships of unregulated markets. Through investment in human capital and infrastructure as well as Keynesian fiscal policies, public efforts improved economic performance. Democratic reforms were insufficient, both regarding persistent inequalities of political power and participation and regarding vulnerability to economic and social hardship. Yet given the prior American situation and the alternatives, Democratic reforms were a major democratic advance.

The appropriate contrast is with the preceding Republican order and the main Republican alternatives to the Democratic order in the 1930s and 1940s. The dominant Republican views doubted the compatibility of liberal forms of modernization with democratic political openings. Thus the Republican order was born amidst fights against populism and the militant labor politics of the late nineteenth century, and it continued to define itself against popular radicalism in the first decade of this century and the 1920s. Republican forces in the 1930s and 1940s denounced all the Democratic reforms that expanded state intervention as corrupt, clientelistic, and illiberal.

In Republican themes for most of the first half of the twentieth century, growth, modernization, and administrative efficiency were usually counterposed to democratic and popular impulses toward expanded political participation and wider state regulation. The Democratic order denied these dichotomies. Its leaders and activists claimed that expanding political democracy and encouraging modernization are compatible, and even mutually necessary. Leaders of the subsequent Republican order from Nixon through Bush affirmed market-based order as a

---

1. Over the course of the Democratic order, such commitments were embedded in law, administrative agencies, and judicial practices, to the point that mainstream currents in the subsequent Republican order did not seek to overturn them altogether.

way to sustain growth and protect liberal principles. They emphasized that efforts at democratization tend to undermine social and economic development and to weaken liberal political forms.

A sometimes fashionable skepticism declares there to be no principled differences in American national politics and asserts that presidential politics is only about interest-based competition among powerful groups. This view wrongly minimizes the deep and longstanding political conflicts about how to sustain democracy, create order, and encourage social and economic development. If the enduring categories of American liberalism can encompass a wide range of positions, this flexibility is partly due to the Democratic order's aggressive reworking and articulation of democratic themes. Where the terms of a democratized liberalism are inadequate, as has often seemed true in racial politics, the reason is less often that some obviously appropriate concepts have been excluded than that such concepts remained to be developed.

The complexity of the Democratic order lies in its simultaneous achievement of major democratic reforms and its statist trajectory. These two elements were inseparable, both institutionally and in the commitments and self-understanding of prominent Democratic political actors. Reliance on the state resulted in tendencies toward political stagnation even a decade after the regime had been built. It eventually encouraged a ferociously antistatist popular opposition, along with a growing concentration of executive power. The Democratic experience suggests that those concerned with building and maintaining a political order face a basic problem. To deny or ignore the need to concentrate power in the state would make it virtually impossible to build a political order. To reject the state would also make governance difficult, even were a political order somehow to be built. Yet the more realistic course – to rely on the state to achieve major political aims – tends to diminish nonstate political capacities, yielding a logic of decay from which it is hard to exit. Democratic leaders had no answer to these dilemmas in the 1940s – indeed, they rarely even recognized them, given their reasonable political and strategic preferences for relying on a Democratic state.

Despite the potential for conflict between statism and democracy, the balance sheet of the Democratic order in the 1930s and 1940s is clear: The main effects of expanding political participation, broadening legitimate forms of interest-group organization, and increasing state activity aimed at alleviating severe hardship and softening the blows of market failures were highly democratic.

Critics of the Democratic order claimed it was tyrannical, as in its illiberal willingness to use the state to regulate economic activity and thereby limit property rights. Such critics failed to persuade citizens and voters that Democratic policies meant a basic threat to liberal commitments to representative government, liberties, and market relations.

Democratic arguments were mainly not claims about the need for emergency measures. Instead, Democratic discourses linked interpretations of liberal principles with analyses of political and economic tendencies in such a way as to propose a durable new framework. This framework was proposed as valid beyond the Great Depression, as a durable response to emergent conditions. Even when critics of the Democratic order cited real problems with the new interpretations of liberalism, they could make only very modest political gains. The basic rejoinder was powerful: No modern interpretation of liberalism is without tensions and risks, and the practical dangers to liberal institutions and practices posed by the radical antistatism and formalism of opponents of the Democratic order were clearly very large. Nothing guarantees that political losers deserve their fate, but those who attacked the Democratic order as tyranny were substantially responsible for their defeat.

The Democratic order and social democracy

The main alternatives to the Democratic order were regimes well to its right.[2] These routes were closed off in arduous political battles with Hooverite and later Taft Republicans, conservative Democrats, and allied business and civic associations. Rejecting these alternatives occurred via constitutional and democratic procedures, as their candidates were defeated by convincing margins in a series of presidential elections. With regard to democratic norms, the likely effects of such alternatives, had any of them managed to gain national power, would have been mainly negative. In the Depression and then after World War II, the deep

---

2. I have underlined the strength of the conservative opposition to the Democratic order in the 1930s and 1940s, especially as compared with the weakness of political forces aiming to establish a different regime well to the left of the new political order. In the historiography of American labor relations, it appears that this issue is often combined with the issue of structural determination. The result is that scholars such as David Brody are led to claim that the New Deal model was fully determined by structural forces, when their real aim seems to be resisting the idea that Democratic labor relations amounted to a conservative resolution of conflicts that could have had much more radical outcomes. As with the political order in general, other labor relations outcomes were possible, and most of them were more conservative and less favorable to labor than the one that occurred. See David Brody, "Workplace Contractualism in Comparative Perspective," in Nelson Lichtenstein and Howell John Harris, eds., *Industrial Democracy in America – The Ambiguous Promise* (Cambridge University Press, 1993), 176–205.

hostility of these forces toward state economic regulation, social welfare provision, and independent unions would not have produced democratic results. At least through Reagan, most Republican political forces implicitly conceded the democratic inadequacies of their predecessors in the 1930s and 1940s by claiming to accept the core of the New Deal while rejecting only its excesses and the distortions of the Great Society.

In the 1930s and 1940s the likelihood of a social democratic outcome was much smaller than that of more conservative results (and smaller than the chance of an unstable populist turn). Yet strong claims have been made that stress the proximity of the Democratic order to a social democratic course. For some, the Democratic order was almost equivalent to social democracy. For others, the evolution of the new political order in the late 1940s betrayed a serious earlier promise. In both cases – whether stressing its accomplishments or its failures, the Democratic order is defined by its relation to an imagined social democratic regime.

Analytical clarity is hard to attain in this area, given varying conceptions of social democracy. In one view, social democracy designates the vision, programs, and policies of political parties and allied organizations – notably trade unions – that referred to themselves as socialist, social democratic, or laborist. The leading international centers of social democracy were in Western Europe after World War I.

Another definition of social democracy is very general: Here, "social democratic" refers to every democratic political force in advanced market countries interested in market regulation and social welfare provision. This definition includes a wide range of political projects and distinguishes them from libertarianism, traditional conservatism, and many strands of Christian democracy. But it merely relocates debates about the differences among social liberal, progressive, populist, socialist, Communist, and other forces, recasting them as arguments about variants of a single social democratic approach. There is little analytical gain in this broad definition, which tends to obscure the deep conflicts that have occurred among these varied political currents.

If we use the more specific definition of social democracy (which stays closer to how political forces defined themselves), several points follow. First, from World War I to 1950 no party in the United States designating itself as socialist or social democratic received more than 5 percent of the national presidential vote in two successive elections.[3] Second,

---

3. I use this low standard to look not for potentially winning social democratic forces but for plausibly durable and significant groupings. Inability to clear this threshold can be taken as a good measure of marginality as an autonomous political force, even if the tendency in question could gain some influence within a major party.

virtually every current present in socialist and social democratic parties in Western Europe appeared in one form or another in the United States, either as small independent political organizations or as modest tendencies linked to the Democratic Party.

These realities compel a choice. We can compare socialist traditions across countries or compare the largest popular and democratic parties in different countries, but we cannot do both at the same time with any set that includes the United States. The second comparison is clearly the right one if the aim is to understand distinctive features of American political orders. Yet even with this choice, the comparison between the Democratic Party and European social democracy is complicated by the major changes in the political meaning of "social democracy" over the course of the twentieth century. In the late nineteenth and early twentieth centuries, most socialist parties proclaimed revolutionary aims while being divided about means. European socialist parties firmly advocated basic changes that would greatly reduce the social and economic role of market institutions, if not eliminate them altogether. After World War I and the Russian Revolution, socialist parties generally retained a commitment to an eventual abolition of capitalism while affirming liberal norms and parliamentary institutions. This commitment was gradually modified; by the end of the 1950s, many but not all socialist and labor parties accepted in principle the basic forms of liberal market societies. They declared their intention of pressing for political and social reforms that would expand egalitarian and democratic values and strengthen the position of unions and the working class.

The political distance between the Democratic Party and most European socialist parties, on a wide range of fundamental matters, was very large in the first five decades of this century. That distance diminished every decade thereafter. By the 1980s and 1990s some of the remaining differences could be regarded as a legacy of different political traditions rather than as deep ongoing differences. But it is misleading to project this convergence back half a century to treat the Democratic order as a social democratic project.

Differences between the Democratic order and social democratic forces in the 1930s and 1940s existed along several dimensions: political visions, immediate and medium-term programs, party forms, the role of the labor movement, and practical achievements. First, the eventual aim of most socialist and social democratic parties was to create a new type of society, minimally characterized by social and/or state ownership of primary economic resources. This aim was understood to mean eliminating or radically limiting capitalist class and property relations, though not necessarily abolishing market forms. The aim was to transform capitalist societies regarding both distributive shares and the relative power of different social and political groups.[4] Although social democratic and socialist parties in Europe advocated replacing capitalism with another model, that model was not always clear by the 1930s. Sometimes it was a variant of state socialism, with relatively open political forms; sometimes the aim was to forge a robust middle way between Communism and unfettered Hooverite capitalism. But social democratic aims in the 1930s went well beyond a measured reform of market institutions such as that conducted by the Democratic order.

Perhaps these anticapitalist positions in the 1930s were a legacy of the socialist movement of the earlier decades of the twentieth century, and few took them seriously. The political record of the late 1940s suggests a less cynical view: Social democratic parties gradually and hesitantly modified their radical commitments. The Swedish Social Democrats produced a "Post-War Program" in 1944 which advocated changing the

> economic organisation of bourgeois society so that the right of determination over production is placed in the hands of the entire people, the majority is liberated from dependence upon a few owners of capital, and the social order based on economic classes is replaced by a community of citizens cooperating on the basis of freedom and equality.[5]

In 1945 the British Labor Party announced:

> The Labour Party is a Socialist Party, and proud of it. Its ultimate purpose at home is the establishment of the Socialist Commonwealth of Great Britain – free, democratic, efficient, progressive, public-spirited, its material resources organised in the service of the British people.[6]

4. Two factors may help explain why analysts of American political development have often understated the depth of change that most European social democrats advocated well into the twentieth century. First, the American socialist – as distinct from communist – tradition was organizationally weak and not impressive in its accomplishments as an independent force after World War I, though many socialists played significant public political roles in the 1920s and later. Second, the Communist and Popular Front critique of social democracy as not serious about real change had political effects well beyond the ranks of adherents to Popular Front Communism. Whatever the cause, American analysts have often blurred the distinction between revolutionary means and radical aims that was constitutive of post-World War I European social democracy, often suggesting that the disinterest of the latter forces in revolution meant that their differences with American progressive liberals were more rhetorical than substantive.

5. The Swedish "Post-War Program" is quoted in Malcolm B. Hamilton, *Democratic Socialism in Britain and Sweden* (New York: St. Martin's Press, 1989), 180.

6. "Let Us Face the Future," Labour Party Statement of Policy, April 1945, in Frank Bealey, ed., *The Social and Political Thought of the British Labour Party* (London: Weidenfeld and Nicolson, 1970), 164.

Social democratic and labor parties still expressed strongly anticapitalist aims in the late 1940s.

The opposition of Democratic progressive liberals to a socialist form of economic life was clear in the mid-1930s and thereafter. The writings of New Deal intellectuals from the early years of Roosevelt's first administration are full of calls for planning. But these statements rarely contemplate and almost never advocate government ownership and control of economic resources. By the mid-1930s full-planning themes were at most secondary and often absent altogether from Democratic discourse. The goal of progressive liberals was a dynamic and equitable market society, not a socialist regime.[7]

Second, the programs of socialist parties and governments were considered in terms not only of their ability to address immediate problems but in terms of their contribution to basic social change. Short- and medium-term political choices were often justified as representing the future in the present (socializing an industry or expanding social provision) or as improving the long-term prospects of socialist forces.

Democratic progressive liberals were by no means nonideological. In seeking to achieve a more democratic and dynamic market society, they saw major reforms as part of a process aimed at repairing the severe problems created by pre-Depression market and political forms. New reform commitments were undertaken with vigor, and it was presumed that further efforts would be necessary in the future. Yet these reforms were not measured against an image of a radical change of social system.

Third, socialist and social democratic parties in Europe in the 1930s and 1940s retained significant if declining mass party forms, sometimes continuous with those of the late nineteenth and early twentieth centuries. Their organizations usually included direct means of recruiting individuals as party members. Members were then organized to carry out party activities, whose overall course was set by a party leadership chosen at national meetings. While caution is needed in assessing socialist party leaders' claims about the vibrancy and scope of their parties' mass forms, the distance between social democratic parties in Britain or Sweden and the Democratic Party was large. In the latter, mass party forms were never predominant, and in most states and cities they were

---

7. Many social democrats doubted that this Democratic goal was attainable if democratic and egalitarian norms were taken seriously. The political success of the Democratic order in the 1930s and 1940s played a significant role in encouraging European social democratic parties to abandon any notion of a change of social system in the 1950s. Democratic reforms were often taken to show that the limits of what could be achieved within the framework of market institutions and liberal politics were less taut than social democrats had believed.

absent. Where they existed they were new and usually fragile, based on the mass mobilizations of the 1930s. Machine-like party organizations, which remained significant in a number of states, were not active membership organizations.

Fourth, the labor movement had a special role in virtually every social democratic party in Western Europe. Sometimes this role was constitutional, providing labor unions with a privileged position in selecting party officials and nominating party candidates for public office. The special role of the labor movement was often explicit in party programs, which identified that movement as a core element of the party. In the United States the labor movement had no such privileged role in the Democratic Party. Labor was a crucial pro-Democratic interest group, but its needs and aims were much less central to the Democratic order than were those of labor movements in Western Europe to social democratic parties there.

Finally, the distance between social democratic and progressive liberal conceptions was substantial with regard to policy outcomes. When social democratic parties had or shared governmental power, they sought to achieve significant elements of radical reform programs that were understood as part of a process that might lead toward socialism. Industries were nationalized; economic planning was installed; and social welfare programs were expanded, as in labor market, health-care, and family policies.

The social democratic parties had different short-term agendas and were always constrained by opposition forces. Consequently, it is possible to downplay differences between the Democratic order and European social democracy by searching through European cases to find areas of overlap – in some countries labor relations remained unregulated; in others few industries were nationalized; comprehensive family policies were not always adopted. This is a confusing procedure because it abstracts from coherent political projects in an arbitrary way. When social democratic governments had a good opportunity to introduce significant portions of their positive program, as in Britain or Sweden after World War II, they put measures into effect that were linked with their long-term visions and well to the left of what Democratic leaders enacted or desired.

These comparisons indicate the inadequacy of a generic use of "social democratic" to include all left-of-center governments and parties in Europe and the United States in the 1930s and 1940s. The distinctive features of the Democratic order were progressive liberal – emphasizing both terms. Its similarities with social democratic and socialist parties and governments do not warrant using a single category for both unless the aim is simply to distinguish them from authoritarian regimes and from conservative governments opposed to market regulation.

Assessing Democratic liberalism

What is at stake in recognizing the distance between the Democratic order and Western European social democracy in the 1930s and 1940s? There are implications for assessing the normative meaning of accounts of American exceptionalism, for deciding how to judge Democratic strategic choices, and for weighing the relative political merits of progressive liberalism and social democracy in the United States.

First, on American exceptionalism. To underline the key features of the Democratic order in positive terms – as an ambitious progressive liberal conception – means seeing distinctions among liberal conceptions as normatively and analytically significant. Most formulations of American exceptionalism in effect claim that only a narrow range of meanings is possible within a liberal framework. This compression limits understanding, whether the depiction of the Democratic order and other reform projects as "nonsocialist reformism" is meant to convey approval or criticism.

Positive terms are clearer, and they improve our understanding of what the Democratic order actually was. The Democratic order, for example, was the American regime most favorable to labor organization and the political efforts of labor-based groups. And if we recognize that American radicalism even in the 1930s was more democratic and populist than socialist, that recognition helps explain how Democratic discourse encouraged a broad popular mobilization.

The "nonsocialist" character of the Democratic order does not provide much support for Hartzian positions that take American liberalism to be fixed and certain. The Democratic order was not guaranteed by liberal commitments. It had to be created against bitter opposition, as a controversial interpretation of what liberalism ought to mean in modern American political practice. Key elements of Democratic discourse – the emphases on (popular) group organization, state intervention, and democratization – had been rejected by the preceding American regime and were affirmed only through difficult battles.

Yet there is little in the story of the Democratic order in the 1930s and 1940s to warrant overstating diversity in American political life by presenting liberalism as only one among a number of traditions. There has never been a moment when American politics was purely, happily, and smoothly liberal. But the capacity of national regimes to sustain liberal commitments while reinterpreting them was dramatically illustrated by the Democratic order, which was a successful project of national political integration. The leaders of the Democratic order showed it was possible to link democratic and modernizing commitments in building a durable American regime – and that deep conflict and thematic change can accompany widely shared liberal commitments.

To assess Democratic strategic choices in the 1930s and 1940s, it is useful to recognize the large distance between the regime's progressive liberalism and social democratic conceptions in those decades. Appreciating this distance makes clear that a social democratic course could not readily have been taken by the Democratic leadership. That leadership – and most of the Democratic bloc – had deep differences with social democratic perspectives that it did not wish to give up. And had something dramatic happened to cause a sweeping change of view, the obstacles to moving from a progressive liberal to a social democratic course would have been very great. Thus claims of either undue caution or betrayal are flawed judgments based on misleading premises – Democratic leaders were not cautious social democrats, but bold progressive liberals. Their lack of interest in pursuing social democratic options cannot be understood as a betrayal of principles they did not share.

Democratic abilities were developed and employed in blocking the real political alternatives, which were posed from the right. It was unlikely that an unreconstructed Hooverite Republicanism would gain popular approval in the mid-1930s or later. The challenge was to prevent a consolidation of a broad opposition that included die-hard critics of the New Deal along with centrist Republicans and conservative Democrats who opposed the more ambitious progressive liberal reforms or the steady growth of the Democratic state. In strategic terms the main choices of the progressive liberal leadership were effective. Given the mainly democratic effects of the Democratic order, most of those choices should also be judged as reasonable by democratic standards. Where criticism is due – as with the Democratic order's caution in racial politics after World War II and its failure even to consider reform initiatives in gender politics in those years – such criticism refers to actual Democratic aims and principles. It does not rely on criteria that progressive liberal political forces did not share, as is required if one criticizes the Truman administration for failing to install full-scale economic planning aimed at guaranteeing full employment.

A further question about social democracy remains. What if there had been a real chance of a social democratic turn – say, in the direction of the British Labour Party – rather than that course being at most interestingly counterfactual?

This course would have been marked by such shifts as an expanded and more formal role for labor in the Democratic Party, along with numerous labor officials and activists running for office and receiving public appointments; much stronger efforts to sustain high employment; government planning of major sections of the economy; sharply expanded government social welfare provision; and significantly more progressive tax policies.

Leaving aside the implausibility of such a course in the United States, would it have been better on democratic grounds? The answer is a qualified yes. Such a course would most likely have included egalitarian and participatory effects exceeding those of the Democratic order, and for those reasons it can be preferred. But its statist dynamic would have been stronger earlier than that of the Democratic order, with negative long-term results. Moreover, to establish and sustain the centrality of labor politics in a country as diverse as the United States would have been a mixed development in democratic terms. By expanding the labor movement and strengthening unions, a social democratic regime might have drawn wider sections of the population into politics. Similarly, increased social welfare provision might have had democratic results for the most disadvantaged groups. Yet it is not clear that the many democratic themes and proposals of American movement and interest group politics (such as those regarding ethnicity, gender, race, and region) would have flourished in a social democratic political order. Nor is it clear that a laborist regime would have been able to address the problems that these movements made into political issues.

Judged by democratic criteria, the balance sheet of an imaginary social democracy looks mainly positive in the 1930s and 1940s. That is partly because the most serious potential problems with this course might be expected to arise later – as political stagnation, economic inefficiency, and cultural and social narrowness. Thus while a social democratic turn would have had democratic benefits, these benefits do not appear so overwhelming as to make progressive liberal views indefensible in democratic terms.

Democratic political leadership, force, and democracy

Judged in terms of its effects in expanding participation, regulation, and social welfare provision, the Democratic order was a democratic course. Judged in terms of the likely alternatives – a very implausible social democracy that would have been somewhat more democratic, or a reconstructed Republican opposition that was far more likely and far less democratic – the Democratic order also deserves a positive assessment.

Another important issue in gauging the democratic claims of the Democratic order has to do with democratic processes. If democracy were considered only as minimal rules prescribing open elections with relatively free political competition, this book could end with the previous section. By this standard there was nothing undemocratic in the emergence and development of the Democratic order. But for fuller notions of democracy, my account of the Democratic order has disturbing elements.

Was forming the Democratic order democratic? Was the rapid and massive accumulation of political power by the Democratic order compatible with democratic commitments? Was the extensive redeployment of force implied in new forms of industrial relations and economic regulation legitimate? Did the marginalization of political opponents tend to become political suppression?

My answer to these questions is that building the Democratic order was a democratic project. But this answer is not obviously true. To justify it requires paying attention to the forceful and disruptive side of regime politics in American political development.

Building and maintaining the Democratic order centered on the construction of a Democratic political bloc and on the ambitious and bold efforts of its progressive liberal leadership. These efforts make up an unfamiliar story within the conventions of studies of American political development. When major changes in American politics are evaluated, the most common questions are about electoral change, presidential leadership, and constitutional reinterpretation. I will not repeat the discussion of realignment theories from Chapter 1, save to underline that they greatly downplay the role of active political leadership. This makes them insensitive even to posing questions about the normative character of the political initiatives that are registered in realignment.

As for presidential leadership, the term is unavoidably misleading as regards modern regime changes. Roosevelt figures prominently in all efforts to understand when presidents succeed in making their agenda the national political agenda. Yet from at least the point of the multi-authored Commonwealth Club speech in 1932, "Roosevelt" designated both a strikingly adept political leader and an emerging Democratic leadership. The problem was not that Roosevelt had advisers; in democratic terms, a candidate or elected official is entitled to have them.

Conservatives grasped that something unusual was going on. Their uproar about Roosevelt's early advisers – with its anti-intellectual and nativist themes – was not effective. Nonetheless, the organizers of this failed attempt to arouse the nation were onto something: American politics was being reshaped by a progressive liberal leadership that was not elected as such. Instead, it was assembled across governmental and other institutions, and its members took strong action based on shared political conceptions. Conservative critics decried this process, even naming it a conspiracy. This charge had little effect, because conspiracy and corruption were the wrong categories with which to understand what was happening.

In building a regime, Democratic leadership was not only presidential – it was also exercised by the progressive liberal leaders of a new political bloc. These leaders reshaped political forms and redefined political discourses. The formation of a political order created a newly powerful executive, not only as an expanded office of the presidency but also as a complex political agent composed of many individuals, including – but not limited to – Roosevelt.

Part of what presidents do, as Stephen Skowronek and Harvey Mansfield have argued in different ways, is push the limits of legitimate political action as they redefine what presidents are able to do.[8] In regime politics presidents push these limits as part of forming a broad new political leadership and a wide political bloc, neither of which is reducible to the efforts or preferences of the president. The elected president is part of a thick network of individuals with shared political commitments. Regime-building spills across institutions, reshaping political practices at many levels. When leadership is powerful yet hard even to name in conventional terms, democratic questions arise: Who is making all these (surprising) decisions? What authorizes the president to take such strong action? Who has allowed state employees to become political agents? To answer these questions by repeating that the president was fairly elected is not adequate, because the actions in question less often cause an argument about legality than about legitimacy. What is going on exceeds the conventional limits of presidential power, and the regime that is being built goes beyond the president's electoral program.

As for constitutional reinterpretation, there was plenty of that in the 1930s, and rethinking continued in the next decade. But placing that process at the center of political change runs into problems that no analyst of constitutionalism in the United States has overcome. These problems are about linking law and politics. If reinterpreting the Constitution is considered as mainly a response to political pressure – say, to Roosevelt's attempts to influence the Supreme Court – one might just as

8. Stephen Skowronek, *The Politics Presidents Make: Leadership from John Adams to George Bush* (Cambridge, Mass.: Harvard University Press, 1993); and Harvey C. Mansfield, Jr., *Taming the Prince: The Ambivalence of Modern Executive Power* (Baltimore, Md.: Johns Hopkins University Press, 1989).

well speak of that pressure as the cause of any major judicial change. And law would lack any special role. Yet if law is conceived as a mainly autonomous practice with regard to politics, with jurists cognizant of political events but not forced to adhere to their course, then it is necessary to spell out a clear logic of judicial change. Such a logic would have to be strong and determinate enough to explain why the NLRA could be found constitutional in 1937, when all signs are that a similar measure would have been rejected ten or five years earlier.

Most accounts of political development as constitutional reinterpretation founder in this area. What seems to get lost is a sense of regime change as forceful and dynamic political activity, in which bitter rivals compete and some suffer disastrous defeats. The prevalent image instead is one of common striving to reach a new level of interpretive agreement: History appears as reflection on the meaning of the Constitution. Such a history exists, but it cannot be equated with an overall political history full of discontinuities and forceful exclusions.

Presidential leadership and constitutional change are crucial elements of building a political order, but not its defining moments. The key points in building a political order are about developing a new political leadership, forming a new political bloc, and waging arduous political battles against adherents of the old political order. A similar point holds for efforts to sustain the Democratic order – thus I am using a metaphor and condensing claims about networks of political relations in referring to Truman as an agent of Democratic renewal in 1947–9.

Here problems arise in reconciling political realities and democratic commitments. In the presidential and constitutional stories, there is room for turmoil. But the main agents are defined from the start as legitimate – elected presidents, properly constituted courts – and so are most of their actions. It only takes a moment's reflection on events in the 1930s to note the seriousness of arguments about legitimacy in a real regime change. The conservative opposition to the Democratic order sharply attacked Roosevelt, his top advisers, and the whole New Deal project. Who elected Tugwell? Who voted for a radical expansion of social provision and a basic redefinition of the government's role in labor relations? Who authorized the employees of ambitious new government agencies to act as Democratic agents? Who justified emergency welfare measures becoming new sites of Democratic patronage and propaganda?

One might fairly respond that 1936 was a national referendum on the new Democratic order. Even so, what progressive liberals extolled as an experimental and open stance could be seen in a different light by political opponents: There was much that was adventurous and not clearly authorized about the deep changes of the 1930s. A political leadership formed across institutions, accumulated great power, reconfigured and expanded the state, and redefined political common sense. Popular support was won for these moves, but it would be wrong to depict this support as having been well established before the changes were well underway.

What opponents of the emerging political order might have said more often and clearly was that the Democratic project was illegitimate because it was the work of a progressive liberal leadership that had not been elected as such. The new leaders lacked a clear public location and were not responsible. Thus while Roosevelt defeated Hoover, that did not authorize Tugwell, Perkins, Wagner, and the CIO leaders to reshape American political institutions and practices.

There were additional grounds for questioning the regime's legitimacy. One was its alleged exclusion of opponents. The losers in regime changes are not always able to distinguish between severe defeat and suppression. The political message sent to Herbert Hoover and Al Smith in 1935–7 was not only that their programs were rejected. They were ruled out as serious contenders for national power, both as individuals and as proponents of overall political positions. Some viewed this course of events as unfair treatment of their views.

Once again, critics of the new political order had no case in narrowly procedural terms – no one stopped them from complaining loudly about the New Deal in whatever forms they chose. Was the Democratic order nonetheless oppressive in its aspiration to create a new political common sense that would virtually define Hoover's positions as irrelevant and erroneous? This question is not answered by noting that Republican leaders engaged in and endorsed political exclusion and even suppression on a number of occasions in the post-1896 Republican order.

If democracy really means unconstrained conversation aiming toward consensus, then any hegemonic efforts by Democratic leaders appear as unwarranted exclusions. Yet when procedures remain open and real political competition persists, such dialogue is only part of a democratic process. Another part is the formation of substantive political ends and the struggle to achieve them. As part of this effort, competing forces strive to attain what might be called a democratic hegemony, in which their opponents are repeatedly defeated in public argument to the point that they are no longer taken seriously if they persist in raising the same objections to the new course. Such a political project entails real exclusions, even when they do not involve any explicit breach of liberal procedures. Anti-New Deal Republicans and the most conservative Democrats were not suppressed in the 1930s – they were repeatedly defeated and pushed to the margins of political life. They often found it easier to question the legitimacy of this outcome than to explain its political logic. To put it bluntly, they were fairly (and not permanently) excluded.

Another objection to Democratic regime-building concerns the use of force. When regime politics occurs, force is also present. It often rises to the surface of political life, rather than being imbedded within legal and political discourses as a potential means of settling disputes.

Even when legal procedures are followed, force is evident in the transition from old to new interpretations of procedures and of basic principles. In the 1930s a dramatic increase in government economic regulation was often perceived as a forceful breakup of practices long justified with reference to the common law and substantive due process. This perception had merit in the sense that the emerging Democratic state was redefining property rights and enforcing new understandings. At the same time, conventional uses of force in industrial relations – injunctions against labor backed up by police, employers' use of private violence, and so forth – were disrupted.

Both with regulation and government support for unions, the presence of force in major phases of political change was brought sharply into focus by its use in dramatic new ways. Legal and forceful acts against those who block the new regime are hard to locate in democratic terms. This was a source of the uproar over Democratic toleration of illegal workplace actions in the mid-1930s, beyond the self-serving complaints of employers. The message to employers – one that enraged them – was that they could no longer use force to bar unions from their enterprises. The image of the sit-down strikes was so powerful not only because of the militancy of the workers but because these strikes stated unmistakably the Democratic order's dramatic redeployment of force. This shift greatly reduced the vulnerability of union organizers and activists. The progressive liberal leadership in effect allowed labor to use force to compel employers to respect New Deal policies.

There is a further problem with regime-building, in the tension between creating a new political order and constitutional commitments. Antistatism in American politics often finds strength or at least solace in the separation of powers, so that constructing an overarching political center is difficult. But building a political order combines power across branches of the government, and across the divide between state and nonstate organizations (parties, unions, civic associations). As a new political bloc takes shape across institutions, it often creates links that are questionable. New state agencies are politicized and emerging political forces can become quasi-clients. Rules and informal commitments are not only reinterpreted – they are sometimes violated or avoided in practice.

One might respond to these worries by asserting that so long as there are further elections, no basic normative problems arise. Unwanted regime-building efforts can be blocked. But this response is inadequate in light of the political capacities that those engaged in regime-building can develop. Thus anti-Roosevelt Democrats and Republicans complained not only about losing but also about being overwhelmed. Their complaints are unappealing, as their preferred political course would have been disastrous. But their sense of being overwhelmed by an emerging regime that was legal but whose course was not clearly authorized was more than the whining of bad losers.

Here is the basic problem: Democratic politics requires commitment to democratic principles, not just instrumental adherence to rules. But actual democratic polities undergo phases of deep and disruptive change in which those seeking to build political orders push up against and sometimes go beyond procedural limits. Can regime change occur in a manner consistent with democratic commitments?

In a model of democracy defined only by dialogue and deliberation, an overall change of political course might *follow* full discussion of national alternatives and sustained reflection by citizens on their preferences. Yet in regime politics, an emerging political bloc may gain wide support for a general course as it is already underway. Its leaders take dramatic steps, pushing against legal limits to get something accomplished. Thus few people voted for the Democratic order before its construction was far advanced, although something like the new regime was a plausible inference from Roosevelt's campaign in 1932. Once established, the Democratic order was ratified when national elections put it in question, as in 1948. Such ratifications had plebiscitary elements. These elements were not large enough to be problematic by minimalist standards of democracy as open electoral competition. But they are troubling with regard to democratic norms of full and informed debate before major decisions.

Given these tensions, is it possible to conceive of a regime politics that is more than minimally democratic? One requirement for such a politics is to recognize that phases of disorder and severe conflict are deeply rooted in basic features of modern democratic politics, rather than being unfortunate episodes that are readily avoidable through good judgment. Democratic polities undergo and probably require phases of disruptive change. I will not repeat the arguments of Chapter 2 about why political orders exist at all. Given that they do exist, strong forces make it difficult to change them easily, ranging from the self-interest of regime leaders to the wide variation in the extent to which citizens concentrate their attention on politics. Phases of dramatic conflict and change limit the extent to which political orders decay into corrupt regimes that restrict entry and block innovation. The main modern alternatives to an imperfect and potentially dangerous regime politics are worse – an authoritarian closure of political options by an enduring regime, or an unraveling of political and social relations spiraling downward toward bleak end points.

Recognizing that major disorder and political breaks are likely in contemporary democratic polities removes grounds for saying that anything goes on such occasions so long as the aim is an eventually legitimate political order. *Regime politics is part of modern democratic politics, not a pure emergency that warrants whatever leaders decide to be necessary.*

How can a regime politics be both democratic and effective – pushing at legal and conventional limits without demolishing them, responding to crises and disorder with more democratic forms of political integration? Several criteria can be used in preferring some choices to others in such phases – and thereby enhance the prospects of a democratic mode of regime politics. First, more democratic forces can be identified in terms of what sort of political order they propose to build. Is it plausible that such a regime could exist, and, if so, would it be democratic? Do these forces show some awareness of what might happen if their proposals did not work out perfectly in practice? Second, political forces can be measured by whether the accumulation of power they aim for is apt to be enduringly extraconstitutional or "only" unconventional and disruptive of the practices of the prior regime. Third, proponents of new political orders can be interrogated as to whether they imagine building the final regime – or a sturdy but impermanent way of reaching valued results. Any longings for political immortality give strong reasons to doubt statements of democratic aims or of loyalty to constitutional forms.

All three criteria are involved in assessing a regime-building project such as the Democratic order – its main features indicate a positive conclusion, though not without qualifications. Democratic progressive liberals built a new political order with mainly democratic aims. Their forceful and sometimes quasi-legal efforts did not either strive for or yield a regime of permanent extralegal measures. And while some Democratic liberals imagined that the flexible and expansive regime they had built was the last modern American regime, many others did not. In any case, they were never close to making this happen. The Democratic order that dominated the 1930s and 1940s ended dramatically two decades later.

The experience of the Democratic political order does not show how smoothly democracy operates. It does show the amount of conflict and the extent of forceful disruption required for political renewal. In this chapter I have assessed the process of building the Democratic order by three criteria – the character of its effects, its relation to plausible alternatives, and the nature of its leadership. Building the Democratic order had mainly democratic effects. These are highlighted by comparisons with the renovated Republican regimes that were proposed as its most serious competition. With Democratic leadership, things are more complex. There was little overt law-breaking, but progressive liberals made a turbulent and rapid change of political direction, turning a popular rejection of the Republican order into a distinctive new political framework. They sought to marginalize opponents who could not be persuaded to accept the new political order. By the standards of a deliberative democratic politics straining toward broad agreement, the creation of the Democratic order looks rough but not illegitimate.

Regime politics is a basic element of modern American political development. The problem is how to limit its dangers, not how to imagine its disappearance. In these terms, building the Democratic order was a vigorous and adventurous effort that at times came near the limits of democratic action. It is reasonable to approve of the basic course taken by Democratic progressive liberals, considering it as a creative and, on balance, democratic form of regime politics.

Democratic political leadership can include taking bold and surprising initiatives prior to the conclusion of public deliberation, and inflicting severe and destructive defeats on unyielding adversaries. These choices are imposed by the logic of deep political conflicts about basic issues. To recognize these features of political leadership is not to consider them as costless, much less as happy displays of strength. Whatever successes result from creating and sustaining a regime should be regarded as impermanent and subject to challenge. Progressive liberal leaders were not as reflective or self-critical as these formulations recommend, especially when the Democratic order was in place. It is fair to conclude that the Democratic order was democratic – in its main effects, against the real alternatives, and even in its formation. But it surely did not provide the last word about how to fashion a democratic regime politics.

Index